The Historical Atlas of North American Railroads

A CARTOGRAPHICA BOOK

THIS BOOK IS PUBLISHED BY:
CHARTWELL BOOKS, INC.
A DIVISION OF BOOK SALES, INC.
276 FIFTH AVENUE, SUITE 206
NEW YORK, NEW YORK 10001, USA

ISBN-13: 978-0-7858-2781-8
ISBN-10: 0-7858-2781-1

QUMNRMINI

THIS BOOK IS PRODUCED BY
CARTOGRAPHICA PRESS
6 BLUNDELL STREET
LONDON N7 9BH

PUBLISHER: SARAH BLOXHAM
MANAGING EDITOR: JULIE BROOKE
PROJECT EDITOR: SAMANTHA WARRINGTON
ASSISTANT EDITOR: JO MORLEY
DESIGNER: ANDREW EASTON AT UMMAGUMMACREATIVE
PRODUCTION MANAGER: ROHANA YUSOF

CARTOGRAPHY:
MALCOLM SWANSTON
JEANNE RADFORD
JONATHAN YOUNG
ALEXANDER SWANSTON

PRINTED IN SINGAPORE BY
STAR STANDARD INDUSTRIES PTE LTD.

THE
HISTORICAL ATLAS
OF
NORTH
AMERICAN
RAILROADS

JOHN WESTWOOD
AND
IAN WOOD

CHARTWELL
BOOKS, INC.

CONTENTS

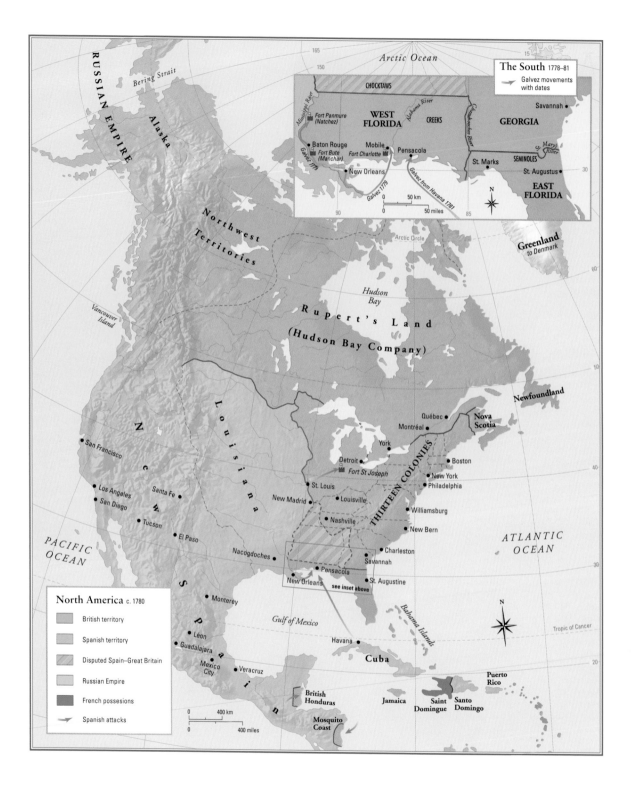

RUSSIAN EMPIRE

Bering Strait

Alaska

Arctic Ocean

Northwest Territories

Vancouver Island

Hudson Bay

Rupert's Land
(Hudson Bay Company)

Arctic Circle

Greenland
to Denmark

Newfoundland

Québec
Montréal
Nova Scotia

York

Detroit
Fort St Joseph

Boston
New York
Philadelphia

San Francisco

Los Angeles
San Diego

Santa Fe

Tucson

El Paso

St. Louis

New Madrid
Louisville

Nashville

Williamsburg

New Bern

THIRTEEN COLONIES

Charleston
Savannah

PACIFIC OCEAN

Nacogdoches

Pensacola
New Orleans
St. Augustine
see inset above

ATLANTIC OCEAN

Monterey

Gulf of Mexico

Havana

Cuba

Bahama Islands

Tropic of Cancer

Léon
Guadalajara
Mexico City
Veracruz

British Honduras

Jamaica

Saint Domingue

Santo Domingo

Puerto Rico

Mosquito Coast

L o u i s i a n a

N e w   S p a i n

North America c. 1780

- British territory
- Spanish territory
- Disputed Spain–Great Britain
- Russian Empire
- French possesions
- Spanish attacks

0   400 km
0   400 miles

The South 1778–81

→ Galvez movements with dates

CHOCKTAWS

WEST FLORIDA

CREEKS

GEORGIA

Savannah

Mississippi River

Alabama River

Chattahoochee River

St. Marys River

Fort Panmure (Natchez)

Baton Rouge
Fort Bute (Manchac)

Mobile
Fort Charlotte

Pensacola

Galvez 1779

New Orleans

Galvez 1779

Galvez from Havana 1781

St. Marks

SEMINOLES

St. Augustus

EAST FLORIDA

0   50 km
0   50 miles

N

MAP LIST

INTRODUCTION

"LET THE COUNTRY BUT MAKE THE RAILWAYS, AND
THE RAILWAYS WILL MAKE THE COUNTRY."

Across wide rivers, over the rolling Great Plains, and through jagged mountain ranges, the "tea-kettle" locomotives of the early railroads opened up the lands of the United States, helping to build a mighty nation.

These words referred to the first public railroad. It may have been built in Britain, but it is difficult to think of any country that would benefit more from its railroads than the United States of America. The 50 years after the end of the Civil War in 1865 saw a nationwide transformation made possible by the arrival of railroads. Before this, America's economic growth was limited to the slow pace of canals and other water transport for freight, and to horses and coaches for passengers and mail. The coming of faster, more reliable transport was one of the most important factors that helped to create a modern industrialized nation.

It was the canal companies who laid the first tracks, while early passenger trains had stagecoach-type bodies on railroad wheels, with locomotives imported from Britain. However, it soon became clear that British construction methods were too expensive and too unsuited to the needs of a vast, rapidly developing country. The all-American railroads that followed were laid cheaply and quickly, while locomotives were manufactured locally to suit specific, local requirements. Railroads spread rapidly, opening up a host of new opportunities for the development of abundant natural resources.

Many more tracks, both great and small, were laid and carried passengers and freight to previously undeveloped territories. Locomotives developed along well-defined lines, increasing in size and power while retaining the characteristics of earlier years—simplicity, reliability, and ease of maintenance. As the railroad system developed, passenger amenities improved and safety features, such as continuous automatic brakes, were introduced and perfected.

By the early part of the 20th century, the railroad network had reached its maximum length, bringing a large part of the country within easy reach of a station. Locomotives had grown in size, weight, and sophistication, allowing increased train speeds and train weights—particularly for freight. Locomotive-builders were not only able to satisfy the needs of the United States, but were also healthy exporters.

Technology was keeping pace. The abundant coal in the eastern part of the United States, lumber, and the large natural deposits of oil had all been staple fuels for steam locomotives, but the mighty steam locomotive had reached its zenith. The increasing reliability of oil-fueled diesel engines, and their ability to run vast distances without attention, soon saw their rapid introduction—even to the detriment of electrified lines, which had been installed where traffic density made it viable. Meanwhile, other forms of transport were developing rapidly, particularly air travel, which became economic when it offered faster journeys between large population centers.

The availability of the automobile had already reduced the pressure on commuting, with modern roads being built at a fast pace. Rail travel became less popular until the war in Europe and the Far East found railroads hard-pressed to keep up with the nation's new mobility. It was a temporary respite. Post World War II, many formerly profitable railroads had to reduce their operation, shed some traffic, and combine with others to survive. The light construction of the original lines cost the companies dearly later, as practically every main line had to be expensively rebuilt. Yet America's railroads, and the industry that supported them, had served the country well. Today's railroads still have their place and, in fact, environmental pressures may yet see a move toward a new form of modern train travel.

CSX Transportation is one of the two Class I railroads in the United States that serve most of the East Coast. Formed in 1986, and owned by the CSX Corporation, it is the product of mergers of some of the oldest railroad companies in the United States, including the Baltimore & Ohio, the Chesapeake & Ohio, and the Seaboard Air Line.

Amtrak was created in the early 1970s to relieve the nation's railroads of the responsibility of running loss-making passenger services. It operates services throughout the country.

OPENING THE TRADE ROUTES

FOR EARLY PIONEERS VENTURING ALONG RIVERS OR OVERLAND TRAILS, JOURNEYS COULD BE MEASURED IN DAYS OR EVEN WEEKS. BUT HIGHWAY AND CANAL CONSTRUCTION BEGAN TO MAKE TRAVEL CHEAPER AND EASIER.

By 1800, the spreading frontiers of the United States were a long way from the Eastern Seaboard, in terms of both distance and journey time. The cities of the East were the main markets for the abundant agricultural produce and raw materials that lay inland, but transporting the goods to them was a considerable problem. To understand the vital role that the railroads eventually played in opening up the movement of people and goods, it is instructive to appreciate how they were transported before the arrival of the "iron horse."

For anything heavier than a man could physically carry or haul, the first American settlers employed draft animals—mules, oxen, and horses. The small farm carts used for local transport were an important part of any rural economy. Around 1720, the distinctive Conestoga wagon first appeared, taking its name from the region where it was introduced by German settlers. A heavy freight carrier with broad wheels and hauled by as many as eight draft animals, a Conestoga wagon was much larger than the "covered wagons" used by later settlers on the Oregon Trail to the new territories in the West. Long and rugged enough to carry a load of around eight tons (7.2 tonnes), the Conestogas often formed part of lengthy wagon trains. These slow-moving columns provided a vital link in the economies of the Thirteen Colonies and, after the American Revolution, were used to open up routes for inland commerce with Ohio.

At this time there were few long-distance paved roads in the country. The first, the Lancaster Pike, built privately from 1792–5, ran for some 60 miles (97 km) between Lancaster and Philadelphia in Pennsylvania. The National Road, otherwise known as the Cumberland Road, was a government construction begun in 1811, which provided an important overland route between the Potomac and the Ohio rivers. It was gradually extended to 620 miles (998 km), finally linking Baltimore, Maryland, to

A heavy Conestoga wagon of the type used for bulk overland transportation from the 18th century onward. The other main means of transporting heavy cargo was by riverboat or barge.

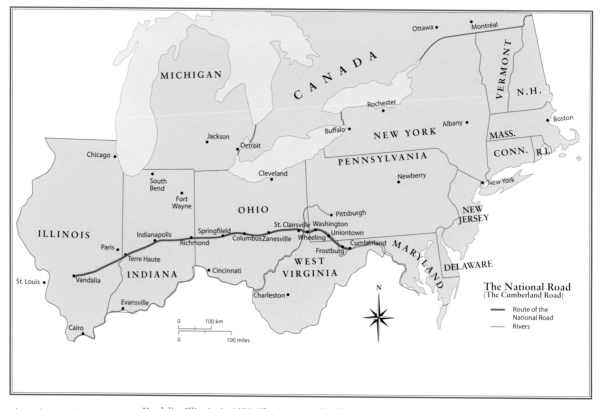

A grand undertaking at the time, the National Road for a decade or two was of prime importance in the development of Ohio and Indiana. After the railroads it lost much of its significance.

Vandalia, Illinois, in 1839. The intention had been for a National Road to go all the way through to the Missouri and Mississippi rivers, but funds ran out. The most heavily traveled route led southwest through the Great Appalachian Valley, stretching some 700 miles (1,127 km) from Canada to Alabama, which had been an important part of north-south communications since the first Native Americans settled in the area. The Great Wagon Road ran from Philadelphia, Pennsylavania, to Augusta, Georgia. The route went inland through the Pennsylvanian settlements of Lancaster and York, crossing the Blue Ridge Mountains to Cumberland Valley, over the Potomac, and down the Shenandoah Valley to Roanoke, Virginia. From there, a section also called the Carolina Road led past Winston-Salem, Salisbury, and Charlotte, North Carolina, to Augusta, Georgia.

A branch at Roanoke led on to Tennessee and Kentucky, taking the Wilderness Road along the trail blazed through the Cumberland Gap by Daniel Boone in 1775. Despite the constant danger of attack by tribes of Native Americans, a flood of pioneers had established numerous frontier settlements, and the route became an important drover's way over which hogs and cattle were driven to market in the East. In the 1790s, the Governor of Kentucky commissioned a road to be laid on what had previously been a steep, rocky trail that was only passable on foot or horseback.

Wagon trains were slow, covering only around 15 miles (24 km) a day, and were relatively expensive. Much of the earliest bulk transportation network in the country relied on the navigation of natural waterways, especially the great rivers that ran through the center of the continent—the Mississippi, the

Missouri, and, first of all, the Ohio. The westward flow of the Ohio River meant that it was the most convenient route to take from western Pennsylvania. Upon reaching the junction of the Ohio and the Mississippi rivers, pioneers would travel north on the Mississippi to St. Louis, Missouri, from where they could continue up the Mississippi and join the Missouri, or alternatively follow a land route to the West.

Most traders would head south on the Mississippi. The mountain ranges to the east and west ensured that the great river's only outlet to the oceans was where the Mississippi led to the port of New Orleans, Louisiana. From there, traders were able to take larger boats beyond the mouth of the river, on to the Gulf of Mexico, and to other ports in the Americas and Europe. This was an important route for the export of goods from the center of the continent, since the overland route east over the Appalachian Mountains

The Cumberland Gap in the Blue Ridge Mountains. The old Wilderness Road ran through here on its way to Tennessee and Kentucky, following a route pioneered by Daniel Boone.

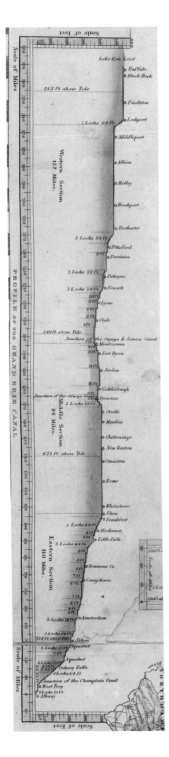

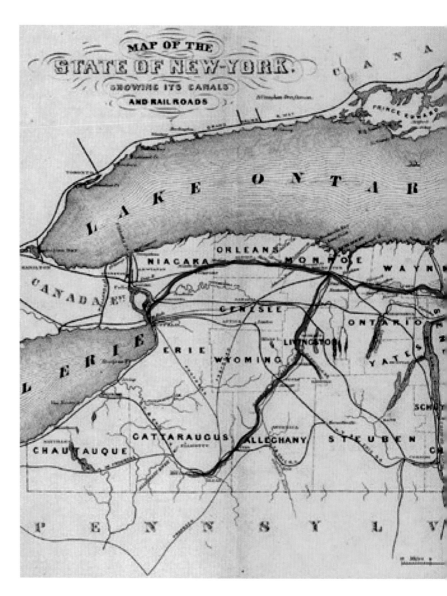

was extremely difficult and dangerous. One of the main reasons for the Louisiana Purchase of territory from France in 1803 was the need of the settlers in the Ohio Valley to ensure secure access to New Orleans.

Two natural waterways running into the Atlantic, the Hudson and the Potomac, both offered routes by which the wealth of the interior could flow to the sea. It should be mentioned that waterfalls and treacherous rapids formed barriers to the free movement of water transport, and neither river linked up with the great rivers in the center of the continent. Solutions to these problems were proposed by George Washington, whose experience as a surveyor led to

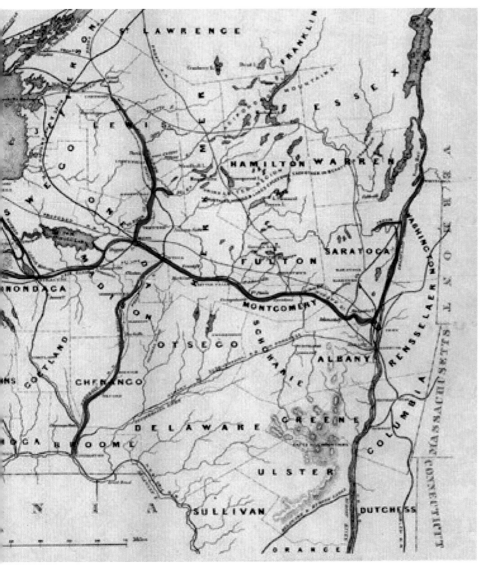

The 363-mile course of the Erie Canal, running westward from Albany. This survey map of 1858 shows later feeder canals branching out to the side of the main watercourse.

him favoring the Potomac River through his home state of Virginia. He championed the construction of a canal system to bypass the falls, together with the use of steamboats to accelerate upstream navigation, and sank a lot of his own money into the venture until his death in 1799. Thomas Jefferson also favored developing the Potomac, pointing out that the Hudson froze over in winter and that its outlet at New York City was farther from the traffic that flowed along the Ohio and Mississippi rivers than the Potomac's outlet at Alexandria, Virginia. He also thought that the number of locks required for lifting boats up and down over the 600 ft (183 m) rise that lay between Albany on the Hudson and Lake Erie made it impossibly uneconomic.

Opposite page: This elevation shows the scale of the project. A complex network of locks was needed to handle the drop of 600ft (183m) between Albany and Lake Erie.

The North River Steamboat (sometimes known as the Clermont) of Robert Fulton, a pioneer of steam power. From 1807, this began a successful, regular passenger service on the Hudson River between New York City and Albany. It was the first commercial steamboat service in the world. Steamboats began operations along the length of the Mississippi five years later, slashing journey times from four months to a little over a month. This was gradually reduced to well under a week.

In spite of the merits of Washington's and Jefferson's case—which ensured that the Potomac route was eventually developed—it was the opening of the Erie Canal in 1819, and its completion in 1825, that ensured the future of the Hudson and New York as the primary shipping route. The Erie Canal, and the other feeder canals that soon followed to link it to the lumber forests and coal mines, would have a profound effect on the development of the eastern cities and of the railroad network. Canal traffic boosted the importance and wealth of New York City and State, and increased the markets for the farmers of the Midwest. It encouraged the western migration of immigrants and made boom towns out of such places as Syracuse, Rochester, and Schenectady, New York, which lay along the route. It also took trade from other eastern ports such as Philadelphia, Pennsylvania, and Baltimore, Maryland.

The natural result was that many of the early railroads linked the canal towns, therefore providing passengers with a faster alternative to the leisurely water traffic. Canal traffic was limited to around walking pace, partly due to the speed of draft animals, and partly because anything faster created a wash that risked eroding the clay bottom, undercutting the banks, and causing the channel to silt up.

The building of railroads on other routes was encouraged by the cities and towns that had lost trade to the Erie Canal and now wanted to be able to offer a transport network of their own.

Building the Erie Canal had another benefit for any railroad entrepreneur. At 363 miles (584 km) long and with 83 locks, its construction had shown that Jefferson had been wrong about the logistics. By cutting transport costs between the Eastern Seaboard and the wilderness of the western interior to around five percent of what they had been, the development of the Erie Canal also made economic sense. The plan had been for it to carry 1.5 million tons (1.36 million tonnes) of freight a year, but this figure was immediately exceeded.

A great deal was discovered during the construction, on which the first civil engineers in the country were forced to learn their trade the hard way. Since all the work was carried out by manual laborers, the first 15-mile (24 km) stretch took two years to build, at that rate it would take half a century to finish the job. When solutions were found to the main problems of clearing the trees and shifting the dirt with stump-pullers being designed and built, and mule carts being supplied to haul away the spoil, the rate of progress increased enormously and more workers were brought in.

To follow the planned route, the designers had to construct embankments and carve or blast cuttings through solid rock. They had to build an enormous aqueduct and cross the swamps of Montezuma Marsh, which proved to be one of the most difficult sections, with many workers succumbing to the swamp fevers carried by the mosquitoes. The cut would finally be completed in winter when the insects were dormant, but the ground was frozen hard. Similar problems were to face anyone attempting to build a railroad over any significant distance.

Keelboats (background) and flatboats (foreground) were the early solution to transporting cargo on the inland waterways. These craft were pictured on the Ohio River near Pittsburgh in the late 18th century. Moving a laden keelboat upriver was hard and slow work.

First railroads, 1700-1830

There were railroads in north America long before there were steam engines to run on them

Waggonways similar to this one were used for centuries as a means of reducing friction and guiding loaded cars. The first railroads in the USA were probably of this type, or the even simpler "gravity road," down which wagons rolled under their own weight.

The origin of the railroad as a means of transporting goods and minerals using vehicles with flanged wheels can be traced back to mining in the Ruhr coalfields of medieval Germany, when wooden rails were used. Toward the end of the 17th century, bulky carts were made with four "rowlets" fitting the rails, suggesting a type of flanged wheel, which made movement so easy that one horse could draw four or five bulky carts laden with coal. The author Daniel Defoe wrote of coal being loaded "into a great machine called a Waggon," and run on an artificial road called a "waggonway."

The development of railroads as a "public" means of transportation took place in Great Britain in the 18th century, when a coalition of colliery owners linked their mines by waggonways, in some cases using a double track so that loaded and empty "trains" would not interfere with one another. Because the railroads ran from inland regions to the banks of navigable rivers, their routes were arranged on a falling grade so it would be easier for a horse to pull a loaded wagon. It was thought necessary to keep a load horizontal when descending a grade, so the leading wheels of the wagon were of larger diameter than the trailing ones. On some wagons, the leading wheels were spoked, while the trailing ones were solid wood. Flanges 1 in (2.5 cm) or 1.5 in (4 cm) deep were fixed to the inner faces of the wheels to provide a guide. Wagons had a primitive lever brake acting upon the rear pair of wheels; on tracks running down to the rivers, there was usually one horse to a wagon, and trains of wagons were not run.

On some stretches of early colliery waggonways, the loaded vehicles would run by relying on gravity, when the horseman would transfer from front to rear, hitch a ride on the wagon, and control the speed with the handbrake while the horse trotted behind. Later, where horses pulled a train of three or more wagons, a "dandy car" was provided for the horse to ride in during the downhill gravity run.

The Incline on the Granite Railway, photographed in 1934, after modernization that included adding metal guide channels and motorized cable operation.

In America and Canada, by the time the Erie Canal opened, a number of short railroads had already been built. The earliest of these were temporary trackways along which men or draft animals could haul loaded wagons, or gravity railroads. The earliest recorded "gravity road" in North America was built in 1764. It was constructed at the Niagara portage in Lewiston, New York, for military purposes by Captain John Montressor, a British engineer and cartographer.

The earliest record of a trackway intended to be a permanent commercial carrier is of the Leiper Railroad connecting Ridley Creek to Crum Creek in Pennsylvania. Thomas Leiper was a wealthy tobacconist and friend of Thomas Jefferson, who owned a stone quarry near Chester. Leiper had already made successful experiments with a short length of track before he built his line in 1810, which linked his quarry with the nearest waterway. The route was laid out by the engineer John Thomson and the mapmaker Reading Howell. The railroad closed 19 years later and was replaced by the Leiper Canal until the railroad was reopened in 1852, eventually becoming the Crum Creek Branch of the Baltimore & Philadelphia Railroad. Several similar wooden railroads were built in the next decade. However, a charter granted to the New Jersey Railroad Company in 1815 for an ambitious plan to link the Delaware rivee near Trenton to the Raritan river near New Brunswick came to nothing because it failed to attract investors.

Thomas Leiper built the first commercial trackway between Ridley Creek and Crum Creek in Pennsylvania. He used it to move stone from his quarry to the nearest navigable waterway.

The Leiper Railroad may claim to be the first commercial railroad in the United States, but the first to evolve into a common carrier without an intervening closure was the Granite Railway at Quincy, Massachusetts. Construction began in April 1826 and it went into operation in October that year. In 1871,

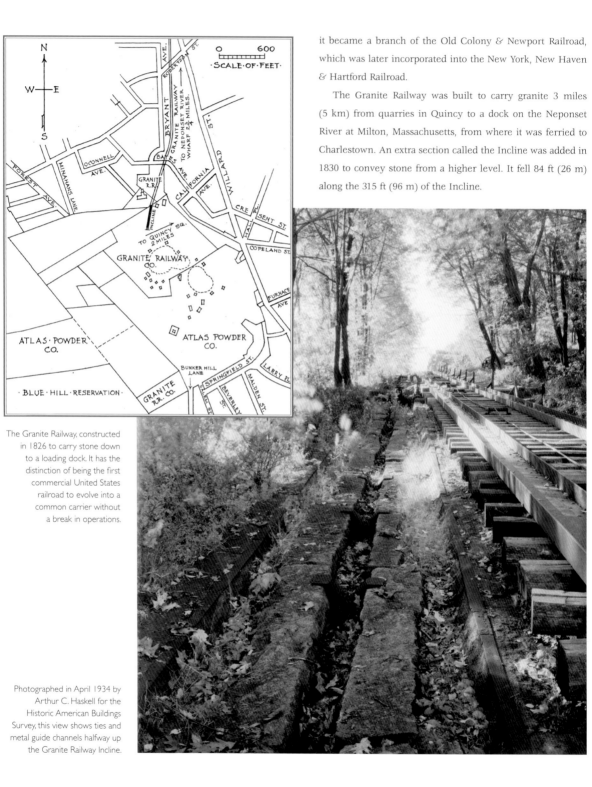

it became a branch of the Old Colony & Newport Railroad, which was later incorporated into the New York, New Haven & Hartford Railroad.

The Granite Railway was built to carry granite 3 miles (5 km) from quarries in Quincy to a dock on the Neponset River at Milton, Massachusetts, from where it was ferried to Charlestown. An extra section called the Incline was added in 1830 to convey stone from a higher level. It fell 84 ft (26 m) along the 315 ft (96 m) of the Incline.

The Granite Railway, constructed in 1826 to carry stone down to a loading dock. It has the distinction of being the first commercial United States railroad to evolve into a common carrier without a break in operations.

Photographed in April 1934 by Arthur C. Haskell for the Historic American Buildings Survey, this view shows ties and metal guide channels halfway up the Granite Railway Incline.

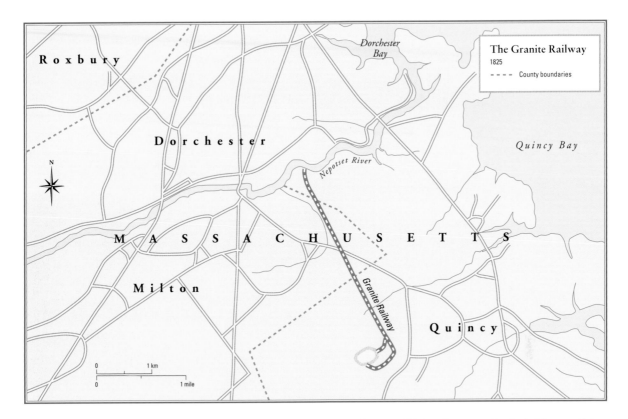

The president of the Granite Railway Company was businessman and state politician Thomas Handasyd Perkins, who organized its finances and its charter. The railroad's designer and architect, Gridley Bryant, modeled it on similar systems in use in Britain, but incorporated ideas of his own. Trains of three wagons were drawn by teams of horses and were equipped with 6 ft (1.8 m) diameter wheels that ran on wooden rails faced with iron and laid 5 ft (1.5 m) apart. Bryant's innovations included railroad switches or frogs, and a turntable, which he never patented.

As well as being the first commercial railroad to go into continuous operation in America, the Granite Railway also made history as the site of the first fatal railroad accident in the United States when, on July 25, 1832, passengers taking a tour of the Incline were thrown off after a cable broke, resulting in one fatality and causing severe injuries to three other visitors.

The railroad operated as Bryant had designed it for almost 50 years. After it became part of the Old Colony & Newport Railroad, wagons were drawn directly to Boston, bypassing the dock. In the early 20th century, the Incline was given metal guide channels and converted to motorized cable haulage. After the branch closed in 1973, the Incline and the Granite Railway itself were added to the National Register of Historic Places—and artifacts from the original structure, including the switch frog displayed at the Chicago World's Fair in 1893, are on display at the site.

The early railroads and canals were built to haul freight, not to carry people. For most of the population, personal transport outside of towns still meant walking or riding on a horse or cart.

The Granite Railway provided a more efficient means of moving stone from the quarry to the dock on the Neponset River. After 50 years in use, stone began to be hauled directly to Boston and the road closed.

Above: One of Gridley Bryant's historic switch frogs, with a plate recording the date of its exhibition at the World's Fair. Above right: Drawing showing the working details of a frog.

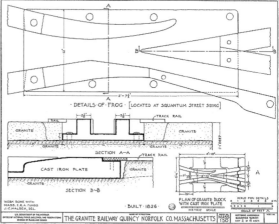

The horsedrawn buggy was not introduced until the middle of the century, and in the early 1800s even the stagecoach, icon of the "old West" had not yet appeared. Stagecoaches or mail coaches had existed since the middle of the 18th century in Europe, but in the United States the Butterfield Overland Stage service was not inaugurated until the late 1850s.

By 1830, the nation was ready for the railroad. The building of the Erie Canal and the Granite Railway showed that driving tracks overland would pose no insurmountable difficulty, while the abundance of passengers and freight promised rich rewards to entrepreneurs. All that was needed was the steam-engine technology already developed in Britain.

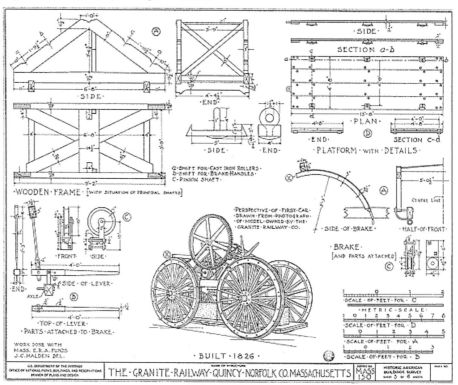

An engineering drawing showing the details of the first car used on the Granite Railway.

A replica of the first granite car used on the Granite Railway. Quarried stone was loaded onto the wooden platform slung beneath the car; the platform could be raised and lowered by means of a hand winch on top of the car.

The remains of a braking device lying abandoned by the track at the top of the Incline.

ORIGINS OF THE STREETCAR

EARLY IN THE 19TH CENTURY, INCREASING INDUSTRIALIZATION AND POPULATION GROWTH LED TO A NEED FOR IMPROVED PUBLIC TRANSPORTATION IN THE CITIES OF NORTH AMERICA. THIS NEED WAS MET FIRST BY HORSE-DRAWN VEHICLES, THE FORERUNNERS OF THE MODERN-DAY STREETCAR.

The horse-drawn streetcar was descended from the street omnibus or coach. The first horse-drawn streetcars resembled steel-wheeled stagecoaches running on iron straps or tracks that were fastened to wooden strips or stone blocks fixed to the street surface. The early horsecars built by the John Stephenson Car Company of New York City in the 1830s and 1840s had the driver sitting on top overlooking the team of horses. The passengers crouched below, handing their fares up through a trap door in the ceiling, and those travelers who were slow to pay could expect to hear the driver's whip rapping sharply on the roof. The horsecar's iron wheels were smaller than the spoked, wooden wheels of the typical carriage, because smooth iron rails had less rolling resistance than the unpaved or cobblestoned streets of the day, but the lower bodies of these first horsecars still had the inswept curve built into most carriages for wheel clearance. In fact, many early streetcar bodies retained this same "ogee" body section, which allowed wagons and carts to pass by on crowded streets. The cabin above swelled outward to provide hip room.

The earliest incantation of the horsecar was little more than a wooden box mounted on wheels, which ran along wooden strips or stones set in the surface of the street.

Later horsecars began to resemble their glamorous steam-powered cousins and they became, in effect, miniature railroad cars, with straight-sided cabins and clerestory roof designs. The driver descended to a platform in front of the passengers, from where he drove the horses or mules in a standing position, and a conductor joined the team to collect the fares. Wheels shrank to railcar proportions. These design trends were not

incompatible and features were freely mixed. The overriding consideration was that the horsecars should be as light as possible, and their evolution culminated in a combination of the carriage-maker's elegance and the mechanical directness of the railcar.

A late example of a horsecar in New York. Such vehicles resembled scaled-down railroad cars, with end platforms and clerestory roofs.

With the example of the steam locomotive before them, companies operating horsecars came to realize that draft animals were really not the perfect power source for urban transportation. They were, after all, living in the industrial age and drawing closer to the unimaginable wonders of the 20th century. A modern city had little use for thousands of manure-producing animals, which could work for only four hours a day and consumed grain by the bushel basket whether they were working or not. The realization that this system was not only archaic but also fragile was emphasized by a calamity in 1872. In that year began the "great epizootic," a virulent and lethal flu-like disease that killed thousands of horses throughout Canada and the United States, and halted horsecar services in many cities for weeks. Almost 20,000 horses sickened in New York City alone, and the death rate in Philadelphia, Pennsylvania, approached 200 a day. Desperate cities tried oxen as replacements, and some even used teams of men to pull the cars, but with little success.

Although the disease had run its course by 1873, the lesson was plain: find a mechanical substitute for horsepower. So began a decade-long search for a powered alternative to horse transport. After fruitless experiments with steam, compressed air, naphtha, and even methane gas, the electric streetcar was developed. In the process, city workers gained tremendous freedom to travel unprecedented distances for a nominal fare. A ring of "streetcar suburbs" grew up around most cities, and in the United States, only the greater freedom granted by the automobile and the motor bus could turn people away from the rail-bound electric streetcar, or trolley.

RAIL TRACK DEVELOPMENTS

PROPONENTS OF THE EARLY AMERICAN RAILROADS TURNED TO BRITAIN FOR ITS ADVANCED TECHNOLOGY. DURING THE LATE 1820S, SEVERAL DELEGATIONS OF UNITED STATES ENGINEERS VISITED THE PIONEER BRITISH LINES, AND OFTEN PLACED ORDERS WITH MANUFACTURERS FOR ROLLING STOCK.

The Delaware & Hudson line brought back some Stephenson locomotives to try out in 1829 at Honesdale, Pennsylvania, where the Delaware and Hudson Canal Company had a tramway to bring down coal from the mountains to the terminal of the canal. Its wooden track, however, which was laid on wooden trestles after the fashion of some British tramways, proved too frail for the locomotives, which then had to be discarded. John Bloomfield Jervis, an engineer who had worked on the Erie Canal, and then the Delaware & Hudson and Mohawk & Hudson railroads, was among those who were very aware that iron rails, necessarily imported from Britain at that time, were too expensive

for American circumstances. It seemed far more sensible to exploit that rich local resource, lumber. The result was the bar rail, which used iron for the running surface only. This type was later known as the strap rail, a term that wrongly suggested that the metal surface was just a thin belt. In fact, it was a genuine bar 1 in (2.5 cm) thick and 2 in (5 cm) wide. This was fixed to a strip of hardwood, usually maple or walnut, which in turn rested on the wooden rails, which were 12 in (30 cm) deep and perhaps 8 in (20 cm) wide.

Various methods were used to anchor rails; the Baltimore & Ohio Railroad opted for stone blocks, but when the supply was interrupted temporarily, it switched to wooden ties, which proved much more resilient.

The bars were attached by spikes located in countersunk holes. Ideally, this construction, with its crossways ties, should have rested on an embankment, but some railroads found it cheaper to lay supporting trestles instead or to sink piles. On the New York & Erie line, the trestle idea came to a bad end when it caught fire. The Mohawk & Hudson Railroad half buried the underlying frame, while the Baltimore & Ohio Railroad, which always liked to be different, thought stone blocks would be the best support. But a strike in the local quarry cut off supplies of blocks, and the Baltimore & Ohio turned temporarily to wooden crossties instead; to its surprise, it found they were better than stone blocks, thanks to their resilience.

This kind of rail was used for several decades, even though, as trains became heavier and faster, it became a handicap. However, in the early years, the main problem was not the rail, but the curves. Lines laid along city streets, as they often were, frequently turned corners and, as demolishing buildings was out of the question, could only negotiate those corners by using very sharp curves. Jervis chose the flexible 4-2-0 wheel arrangement for his locomotives for that reason, and the type became almost a standard layout before being superseded by the 4-4-0 when it was patented in 1836, by which time most sharp curves had been bypassed.

An example of strap rail. Thick steel straps, or bars, were attached to a strip of hardwood with metal spikes. This assembly was fixed to wooden rails or crossties of a thicker section.

One problem with the strap rail was that the spike holes were weakened by rot, loosening the bar. Lateral pressure from wheel flanges tended to push the rails apart, and some roads widened the gauge by 0.5 in (12 mm) or sometimes more, for easement; wheels were wide enough to allow this. After some years, a few railroads replaced the bars with iron bridge rails, as used on the Great Western Railway of England. This had a bridge-form cross-section and was quite successful; bridge rails appear to have been the first iron rails to be produced in America.

The American press, even at that early stage eager to campaign against the railroads, agitated for the abolition of the strap rail. It pointed out the perils of what it called "snakeheads," when dislodged iron bars might be forced through the floors of moving trains and cause horrific injuries. Such occurrences seem to have been far rarer than the journalists claimed, but because of the need to use heavier locomotives, and the increasing maintenance cost of this type of rail, it ceased to be laid around mid-century. In the South especially, however, where capital was short, it remained in use into the 1860s.

The long-term replacement for strap rail had existed in the United States since 1831, when the president of the Camden & Amboy Railroad, Colonel Robert L. Stevens, visited the North of England and ordered 500 15-ft (4.6-m) iron rails of the so-called flanged T-rail cross-section (later known as flatbottom rail). This married the bullhead design used in Britain (which had a railhead that bulged to give a broader running surface) to a base consisting of a horizontal flange that could be spiked directly to the crossties rather than laid, as in Britain, in a chair that itself was bolted or spiked to the tie. This kind of rail became the world's standard type; even the British railways moved from bullhead to flatbottom in the 1950s. Long before then metallurgy had produced the steel rail, far more resilient and less likely to fracture than iron rails, although the chemistry of steel and the techniques of rail rolling would continue to be researched until to the present day. Rail weight would grow from the 36 lb/yd (17.8 kg/m) of the Camden & Amboy to 140 lb/yd (69 kg/m) by the mid-20th century.

Cross-section of flatbottomed rail. The top was bulbous to provide a running surface for train wheels, while the base was wider, allowing the rail to be spiked directly to the ties.

Harnessing the Power of Steam, 1800-34

The invention of the steam locomotive changed the face of the world and put the finishing touch to the developments of the industrial revolution.

It was the indirect and highly competitive association of two men, both ingenious mechanical engineers, which first blazed the trail. In 1765, James Watt, mathematical instrument maker at Glasgow University, Scotland, had to repair an instructional model of a Newcomen Cornish beam engine, and he hit upon the idea of using a separate condenser as a means for effecting great economy in the use of steam. His innovation created such interest that eventually he went into partnership with Matthew Boulton, an industrialist in the West Midlands of England. The firm of Boulton and Watt prospered in the building of stationary steam engines, but it was when they began to receive orders for pumping engines in the Cornish tin mines in the Southwest of England that the practice developed by Watt had its first and only influence on the future of rail transport. One of the young men who saw the Watt engines installed in Cornwall was Richard Trevithick, and while Watt was timorous and self-effacing, albeit a superb mechanic, Trevithick was bold and confident to the point of rashness. While Watt used steam at comparatively low pressure, Trevithick at once began to build engines using much higher pressure, and instead of condensing the steam after use, he exhausted it into the atmosphere; his first engine was nicknamed "Capt. Dick's Puffer."

From stationary engines used in the Cornish tin mines, Trevithick turned to rail traction, but not before he had experimented with a locomotive on the roads in Cornwall, to the alarm of the populace. In 1803, such a demonstration in London led to the "road carriage" getting out of control and tearing down the railings outside a private house. He became associated with industrial activities in South Wales, and then there came the famous wager that led to the building of the first steam railroad locomotive. The bet, between two prominent ironmasters, challenged Trevithick's "tram wagon" as it was called, to haul a load of 10 tons (9 tonnes) over the 9¾ miles (15.6 km) from Pen-y-Darren to Abercynon

Built by English father and son George and Robert Stephenson, the Rocket embodied all the basic features of successful steam locomotive design.

Richard Trevithick, from Cornwall in the Southwest of England, was the first in the world to build a steam railroad locomotive. His design would inspire many other engineers.

Basin on the Glamorganshire Canal. That Trevithick won the bet for his sponsor is a matter of history, and now interest centers on the design of the locomotive. It had but one cylinder and, to carry the drive over dead center, there was an enormous flywheel. The piston, through the conventional crank/connecting-rod mechanism, rotated a small pinion wheel, which drove a large gearwheel. This engaged with gears mounted on the same axles as the road wheels of the locomotive. It was a triumph, but it had shortcomings.

Although Trevithick himself took very little part in the development of his locomotive after this first experiment, those who followed profited by its failures. It frequently broke down, and its relatively great weight compared with horse-drawn wagons broke many rails. Matthew Murray of Leeds, in the North of England, for example, suggested having two cylinders working cranks at right angles to each other. This eliminated the "dead center" position and dispensed with the huge flywheel. This suggestion was incorporated into Blenkinsop's locomotives that were put to work on the Middleton Colliery railway near Leeds, in 1812. Since it was thought that the contact between a smooth rail and a smooth wheel tire would not provide a good enough grip to enable a locomotive to haul a heavy load, in 1811 Blenkinsop had taken out a patent for a toothed rail laid to one side of the running rail, in which a gear mounted on the axle of the locomotive worked as a pinion in a rack. Locomotives of this type, hauling trains of coal cars, did achieve a certain degree of reliability, though progress was slow and the geared arrangement expensive. One of the Blenkinsop engines was purchased by Blackett for trial at Wylam Colliery, Northumberland, and the outcome was that the toothed-rail arrangement was considered unnecessary. By the time this engine was at work, a man named George Stephenson was beginning to come into the picture.

In 1814, with the financial backing of his employer, Lord Ravensworth, Stephenson built his first locomotive for the Killingworth Colliery. It had many shortcomings, and the second Killingworth locomotive, in which Isaac Dodds was the joint patentee with Stephenson, was a vast improvement. The noise of the exhaust, about which many complaints were made, was practically silenced by turning the exhaust steam into the chimney, where it performed a second function, that of sharpening the draft of the fire and increasing the rate of steam production. Then the complicated gear drive was superseded by connecting the crosshead directly to the driving wheels through the connecting rod. In this locomotive in 1815, Stephenson and Dodds together had reached nearly all the fundamental points of the orthodox, classic steam locomotive: two cylinders, simple direct drive, exhaust turned from cylinders into chimney to increase draft on the fire. In the second Killingworth locomotive, the partners had incorporated a synthesis of all the best features of the

Trevithick's steam locomotive had a massive flywheel to carry the cranks over dead center. Drive was passed to both axles through a large gear wheel.

pioneer work of Trevithick, Blenkinsop, Matthew Murray, and Blackett, and the way was now clear to introduce steam locomotive power on the projected Stockton and Darlington Railway.

The celebrated Locomotion, engine No. 1 of the first public railway in the world, incorporated all the best features of the Killingworth Colliery locomotives, but its working conditions on what was virtually a main line were, by comparison, much more severe. The Locomotion was found to be incapable of steaming continuously for any length of time, and stops had to be made to raise steam. In the meantime, George Stephenson was away and engaged with the surveys and estimates for the Liverpool and Manchester Railway and had left his faithful assistant Timothy Hackworth in charge of the Stockton and Darlington, and to that painstaking and able man fell the task of making the pioneer locomotives reliable work units. In 1827, he built the Royal George locomotive at Shildon Works. It was much larger than any of the previous engines built by Stephenson, and had six coupled wheels. Hackworth increased the steaming capacity by arranging the flue from the firebox to the chimney in the form of a U, instead of a single large pipe, and so presented an increased area of flue tube in contact with the water. Hackworth was also the inventor of the blast pipe, a narrowing cone, through the nozzle of which the exhaust steam passes at high velocity and creates an intense draft on the fire. The Royal George steamed very freely, but it was a curious thing to look at. Because of the return flue, the firedoor was at the chimney end of the boiler, and the fireman rode on a separate tender propelled in front of the engine, while the engineer was at the rear end, where there was a second tender carrying the water supply tank. The greatly improved performance of the Royal George was in many ways a turningpoint in railway history, because until then,

Top: The Stephensons' Rocket came out on top at the Rainhill trials to find the best type of locomotive for England's Liverpool and Manchester Railway. *Above*: Robert Stephenson, son of George, was one of the most noted pioneers of steam locomotive design.

Another competitor in the Rainhill trials was the Sans Pareil locomotive built by Timothy Hackworth. Although it performed well, poorly made components let it down.

in the later 1820s, there were many who felt that locomotives could not be made sufficiently reliable, and that cable traction would be the only preferable alternative.

The directors of the Liverpool and Manchester Railway, construction of which was nearing completion, decided to stage a competition, called the Rainhill trials, for the best type of locomotive to work the line. Although Hackworth had done so much to pull the Stockton and Darlington Railway around from failure, George Stephenson and his son, Robert, felt that his Royal George type of locomotive was rather clumsy and slow, and in entering a locomotive for the competition they introduced some further novel features, particularly in the boiler. To promote rapid evaporation by increasing the surfaces in contact with the water, the flue from the firebox to the chimney was split up so that instead of passing through one large tube, the hot combustion gases passed through a nest of much smaller ones. This feature was suggested not by a fellow engineer, but by the secretary of the company, Henry Booth. As the first of its kind, it gave much trouble in the construction stage, because there was great difficulty in fitting the tubes to the boiler ends without leakage occurring. Robert Stephenson persevered and eventually turned out a first-class job. The engine was the famous Rocket, which steamed very freely.

Hackworth also entered the competition, and at his own expense built a four-wheeled engine, the Sans Pareil, which had the return-flue type of boiler. But the conditions of the competition staged at Rainhill did not require such a massive engine as the Royal George, and the Sans Pareil had only one tender, propelled in front while the engineer stood on a small platform jutting out at the rear. Hackworth's engine was sound enough in concept but he was rather let down by some of the suppliers of parts. One of the cylinders was badly cast and burst at one point, then the feed pump supplying water to the boiler failed, and that, of course, put an end to the engine's participation.

The third competitor, the Novelty of Braithwaite and Ericsson, made some spectacular runs, but broke down frequently, and eventually the Rocket of George and Robert Stephenson was the only one of the three to stay the course. Not only did it win the competition and ensure that the Rocket became the first standard engine type on the Liverpool and Manchester Railway, it also became a world prototype. It incorporated all those basic design features that were perpetuated for more than 100 years in locomotives of increasing size all over the world, culminating in the gigantic "Big Boys" of America's Union Pacific Railroad, which were built in 1941.

When it came to day-to-day working on the Liverpool and Manchester Railway, however, the Rocket type did not prove entirely satisfactory. Robert Stephenson overcame the trouble of jerky and rough riding by introducing the Planet type in 1830, which had the cylinders between the frames situated beneath the smokebox. All the machinery became largely concealed, but while this produced a much

To improve on some of the deficiencies of the Rocket, Robert Stephenson developed the Planet. This had its cylinders mounted between the frames, which provided a much smoother ride.

smoother-riding engine, another type of problem was introduced—that of a driving axle that had to incorporate two cranks between the frames. The problems were, however, of manufacture rather than of principle, and locomotives with inside cylinders became very popular in Britain. The Planet type followed the Rocket type in having only a single pair of driving wheels, though situated at the rear instead of at the leading end of the locomotive. A single pair of driving wheels was favored for passenger trains because it allowed a greater freedom in running, but the four-wheel coupled type, as in the Locomotion and the Sans Pareil, was more suitable for freight trains, because it provided greater adhesion in hauling a heavy load. Locomotives of this latter type were among the first exported from Great Britain to North America. They were, however, not to have any lasting influence on the continent. In the United States, the first-ever railroad, the Baltimore & Ohio, initially relied upon horsepower from its inception in 1827, but by 1830 New York industrialist and inventor Peter Cooper had made a large investment in Baltimore & Ohio land, and in his determination to see the railway succeed, set to work to produce a steam locomotive.

COMING OF THE IRON HORSE

THE FIRST COMMERCIAL RAILROADS WERE LAID DOWN IN BRITAIN
IN THE EARLY 1820S, BUT THEIR POTENTIAL DID NOT ESCAPE THE
NOTICE OF UNITED STATES. VARIOUS ENVOYS WERE SENT TO STUDY
THE PIONEER BRITISH LINES AND THEIR REPORTS INFLUENCED THE
PLANNING AND CONSTRUCTION OF RAILROADS IN AMERICA.

To prove the ability of his
new steam locomotive, Tom
Thumb, Peter Cooper organized
a race against a horse, each
pulling a carload of people.
Sadly, mechanical failure let the
horse win, but Cooper had
demonstrated the potential
of his machine.

In 1825 William Strickland made a study for the Pennsylvania Society for the "Promotion of Internal Improvement." Others sent to study pioneer British lines in the latter part of the decade were Horatio Allen of the Delaware & Hudson Canal Company, and George W. Whistler, Jonathan Knight, and Ross Winans for the Baltimore & Ohio Railroad. Horatio Allen and Ross Winans both attended the Rainhill trials near Liverpool, England, in 1829 when, on October 26, George Stephenson's Rocket was awarded first prize. The reports compiled by these men were to exert a strong influence on those responsible for the planning and construction of the early United States railroads.

February 28, 1827 is one of the most important dates in the history of railroads in the United States: It was the day on which the State of Maryland granted a charter to the promoters of what was to become the Baltimore & Ohio Railroad. The aim was to reach the Ohio River and funnel commerce into Baltimore. The original route, which was surveyed with the help of the United States Army, included the splendid Carrollton Viaduct.

Some historians hold that the Granite Railway in Quincy, Massachusetts, a horse-worked, iron-faced wooden track, which received its charter on April 3, 1826, and opened later the same year, was the first railroad in the United States. Be that as it may, the Baltimore & Ohio Railroad was the very first common carrier, and also the first to offer scheduled freight and passenger services to the general public.

August 28, 1830 was another red-letter day. Peter Cooper, an industrialist and inventor, had constructed a small experimental steam-driven locomotive at his Canton Iron Works in Baltimore. Working with scrap iron and borrowed wheels, and using gun barrels for boiler tubes, he built America's first homemade

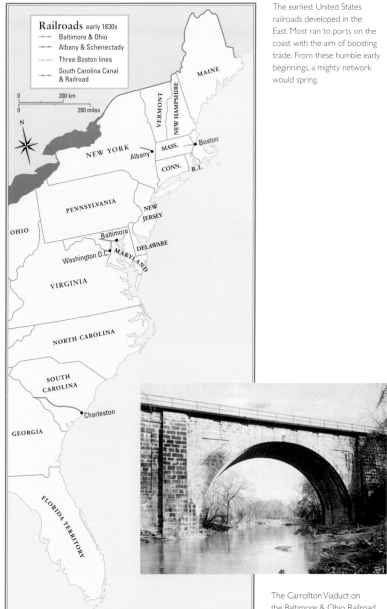

Railroads early 1830s
- - - Baltimore & Ohio
- - - Albany & Schenectady
——— Three Boston lines
——— South Carolina Canal & Railroad

0 ___ 200 km
0 ___ 200 miles

The earliest United States railroads developed in the East. Most ran to ports on the coast with the aim of boosting trade. From these humble early beginnings, a mighty network would spring.

The Carrollton Viaduct on the Baltimore & Ohio Railroad. Charles Carroll laid the first foundation stone for this bridge on July 4, 1828. The 92-year-old—the sole surviving signatory of America's Declaration of Independence—lived to see the railroad completed as far as Point of Rocks, 73 miles (117 km) southwest of Baltimore.

Cooper's Tom Thumb was the first steam locomotive built in the United States. He had assembled it from a variety of materials, including gun barrels, which he used as boiler tubes.

railroad steam locomotive, the Tom Thumb. The first part of the Baltimore & Ohio Railroad had a 14-mile (23-km) stretch of double-track, iron-faced wood road between Baltimore and Ellicott's Mills worked by horses. Cooper staged a race between Tom Thumb, drawing a carload of directors, and a horse-drawn car. The draft for the boiler of his little steam locomotive was provided by a belt-driven fan, and in the course of the race, the belt would not stay in place, and so steam pressure was lost. On this occasion, the horse won, but the contest certainly served to convince many people of the potential practicability of steam as a power source.

Cooper's locomotive had a vertical boiler with the stack extending directly from the boiler end, and although it had many defects arising from the primitive methods used in its construction, it paved the way to success. It was followed by locomotives of the same general type, built by the firm of Davis and Gartner. The Atlantic, made by the same partners in 1832, was the first of the so-called grasshopper type, again with a vertical boiler, and the cylinders acting through large rocking shafts mounted on the top of the boiler.

Peter Cooper was an industrialist and inventor who was determined that the Baltimore & Ohio Railroad should succeed. That determination led him to design and build his own steam locomotive.

Motive power was at first imported from Britain, with the firm of Foster, Rastrick & Company of Stourbridge, England, building the first steam locomotive, the Stourbridge Lion, which cost $2,914, for the order of Horatio Allen of the Delaware & Hudson Canal Company. This was delivered in August 1829 for use on a coal line that was being built over the 11 miles (18 km) from Carbondale to Honesdale, Pennsylvania. Even at 7 tons (6.3 tonnes), it was too heavy for the lightly laid wood and iron road, and in particular was deemed unsuitable for a wooden trestle over Lackawaxen Creek. Although Allen himself drove over the trestle and back at 10 mph (16 km/h), many people thought it too dangerous.

Improvements were made to the track and the Stourbridge Lion was given a second try, but its unsprung weight led to derailments, and it was laid aside at Honesdale. In 1849, its boiler and cylinders were removed for use in a foundry in Carbondale. Many years later, the owners shipped the parts to the Smithsonian Institution in Washington, D.C. A full-size, working replica of the Stourbridge Lion is now on permanent display at Honesdale.

On October 9, 1829, the Delaware & Hudson inclines and levels were opened, but these were worked by cable and gravity. January 15, 1831 saw the inauguration of 6 miles (10 km) of track out of Charleston, South Carolina: the first railroad in the United States to provide a regular service for passengers, and freight hauled by steam. In 1833, the line was extended to Hamburg, just across the Savannah River, to make a total length of 136 miles (219 km), the longest railroad in the world at that time. Its role as a public railroad and common carrier is notable, as up to then most lines had been built for specific purposes, such as coal, lumber or freight transportation, and were used almost exclusively by their owners.

While Peter Cooper's Tom Thumb was going through its teething troubles on the Baltimore & Ohio Railroad, the Charleston & Hamburg Railroad (later to become the South Carolina Railroad Company) received the first operational locomotive to have been built in America, at West Point Foundry of New York City. The Best Friend of Charleston, a much larger engine of the vertical-boiler type, was put to work in December 1830, and goes down in history as the first locomotive to operate a regularly scheduled passenger run in the United States. It was, unfortunately, destroyed by a boiler explosion on June 17, 1831, after the fireman, irritated by the noise of escaping steam, had foolishly held the safety valve down!

The Delaware & Hudson Canal Company imported an English locomotive, the Stourbridge Lion, to work a coal line between Carbondale and Honesdale, Pennsylvania. This photo shows a coal train on the line in later days.

Horatio Allen drives the Stourbridge Lion over the trestle at Lackawaxen Creek to prove it capable of taking the locomotive's weight.

THE BOOM BEGINS, 1830-37

THE 1830S SAW A RAPID EXPANSION IN RAILROAD BUILDING IN THE UNITED STATES, CONCENTRATED MOSTLY IN THE STATES TO THE EAST OF THE MISSISSIPPI AND MISSOURI RIVERS.

The first train to run in New York State was hauled by the locomotive De Witt Clinton, in August 1831. It reached a speed of 15 mph (24 km/h), hauling a train of passenger cars modeled on the stagecoach.

During this first boom, such railroads as the Baltimore & Susquehanna (built 1828–32), Camden & Amboy (built 1830–1), Boston & Providence, Philadelphia & Reading, Newcastle & Frenchtown (1831), Paterson & Hudson River, Morris & Essex, Mohawk & Hudson, Saratoga & Schenectady, Western of Massachusetts, South Carolina, and others soon became familiar names. The Baltimore & Ohio opened to Frederick, Maryland, 60 miles (97 km) west of Baltimore, on December 12, 1831. The Elizabethtown & Somerville Railroad was incorporated the same year and later it formed part of the Central Railroad of New Jersey. The Main Line of Public Works, a canal built by the Commonwealth of Pennsylvania, was chartered to build a line from Philadelphia westward to Columbia on the Susquehanna River. This later became part of the Pennsylvania Railroad.

One of the earliest railroads owed its existence to the Erie Canal. This had been profitable from its inception, unlike the Main Line in Pennsylvania or the Chesapeake & Ohio Canal in Maryland. However, the Erie Canal merged with the Mohawk River in Schenectady, beginning a widening route with several locks downriver to the Hudson & Albany. By water, the 40-mile (64-km) route took more than a day—so rather than stay with the barges, passengers would disembark to take the 17-mile (27-km) land route by

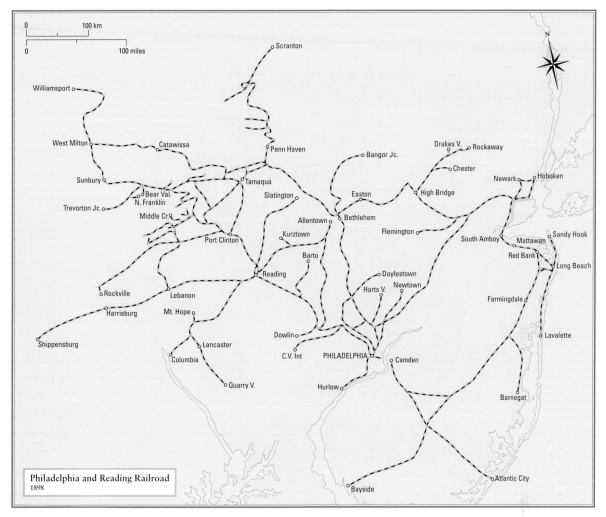

Philadelphia and Reading Railroad
1898

coach, passable in a quarter of the time and at half the expense. Seeing the potential for an expanded land transportation system between Schenectady and Albany, George Featherstonhaugh (pronounced Fanshaw) of Duanesburgh, New York, ran a newspaper notice on December 28, 1825 announcing the formation of the Mohawk & Hudson Railroad Company, which was chartered in 1826. The road's original right of way from the historic marker northwest to Schenectady was opened for service on August 9, 1831.

Another notable American locomotive of early days, more in the contemporary British style, was the De Witt Clinton of 1831, which began work between Albany and Schenectady. This was an 0-4-0 type with a horizontal boiler and a stack at the leading end after the style of the Locomotion on the Stockton & Darlington Railway. While American manufacturers were making their first attempts at locomotive building, the Stephenson inside-cylinder, 0-4-0 type, developed on the Liverpool & Manchester, had a limited phase of popularity, and in 1831 the firm of Robert Stephenson & Company of Newcastle supplied some locomotives, including the John Bull, to the United States' Camden & Amboy Railroad.

The pioneering Philadelphia & Reading Railroad, built originally to link Philadelphia with Reading and nearby anthracite mines, developed into the extensive Reading Railroad, much of which flourished to become part of Conrail in 1976.

This excerpt from the 1833 South Carolina transportation map shows the 136 miles (219 km) route of the railroad from Charleston to Hamburg, which was built and operated by the South Carolina Canal & Railroad Company. The railroad was, at the time, the longest in the world.

The DeWitt Clinton locomotive, named after the governor of New York State mainly responsible for the Erie Canal, made its first run on the 17 miles (27 km) of the Mohawk & Hudson Rail Road on July 2, 1831 before going on show at the New York World's Fair later that year. It was the first steam locomotive to operate in the state and only the second to be built in the United States—also by West Point Foundry.

May 1831 also saw an important technical advance with the introduction of iron rails, which were an improvement on lumber with iron straps. The first flanged T-rail, imported from Britain, was laid in Pennsylvania for the Camden & Amboy Railroad. However, such rails were made of cast iron, which broke easily and could only be laid in short lengths, so that they soon became uneven. At this time, there was no general agreement on rail gauges. In April 1832, the 6-ft (1.83-m) gauge New York & Erie Railroad was chartered. Many other railroads were chartered the same year, such as the Portsmouth & Roanoke Railroad, which later formed part of the Seaboard Air Line Railroad.

In 1833, the New York & Harlem Railroad opened, the Paterson & Hudson River Railroad was chartered between Paterson, New Jersey, and Jersey City, and also chartered was the Paterson & Ramapo Railroad north to Suffern, just across the New York line. The South Carolina Canal & Railroad Company at this time had the world's longest line in service. The Philadelphia & Reading Railroad was chartered, and the Central Railroad & Canal Company of Georgia was organized. Also that year, the Petersburg Railroad opened between Petersburg, Virginia, and Roanoke River opposite Weldon, North Carolina.

The following year, 1834, the Philadelphia & Columbia Railroad opened 81 miles (130 km) of line in Pennsylvania. This was the first state-owned track. During this boom period, the Cayuga & Susquehanna Railroad was completed between Owego and Ithaca, New York State, and later renamed the Lackawanna & Western Railroad.

In 1835, Senator Chase of Ohio introduced a bill to Congress to provide for a survey of four possible routes for a coast-to-coast railroad. Much interest, research, and speculation was raised, but no positive action was taken. Elsewhere, however, ground was broken for the New York & Erie Railroad near Deposit on November 7; the Morris & Essex Railroad was chartered to run from Morristown, New Jersey, to New York; the Boston & Lowell Railroad opened on June 24, followed by the Boston & Worcester

Baltimore &
Ohio Railroad 1830

From its early, humble beginnings, the Baltimore & Ohio Railroad eventually spread throughout the Northeast.

Railroad on July 4. By this time, the Baltimore & Ohio Railroad had reached Washington, D.C. from Relay, Maryland.

The first combined steam railroad and steamboat service came into effect on the route from Boston, Massachusetts to New York City. The journey took 16 hours, but this was eventually reduced to 14 hours.

The Andover & Wilding Railroad opened in August 1836, the Elizabethport to Elizabeth, New Jersey, opened with horse traction, and the Louisa Railroad was chartered to run from Taylorsville (Doswell) westward to points in Louisa County, Virginia. The completion of the Erie Canal had shown the potential for unlocking the vast natural resources of the interior, and for 12 years from 1825, the building of canals and railroads captured a large part of American public attention, occupying endless debates in Congress and state legislatures, and provoking speeches from governors and presidents. In 1831, President Andrew Jackson spoke with pride at the high wages earned by laborers constructing these works, which he said were "extending with unprecedented rapidity." There was much debate about the constitutional power of the government to promote such projects on a federal level, because the work was on such a vast and accelerating scale. Railroads had proved themselves successful, and there was a seemingly exponential growth in planned projects. In 1830, only 23 miles (37 km) had been constructed but by the following year, this figure had increased to 94 miles (151 km), and by 1836, the total construction had risen to 1,273 miles (2,049 km).

Technical improvements, 1830-40

THE 1830S SAW IMPORTS OF BRITISH LOCOMOTIVES, BUT DEVELOPMENT OF THE NORTH AMERICAN RAILROAD INDUSTRY WAS AIDED BY A DUTY ON IMPORTED IRON PRODUCTS AND THE DESIRE TO "BUY AT HOME."

The Camden & Amboy Railroad in Pennsylvania imported the locomotive John Bull from England. Of the Planet type, the locomotive was built by Robert Stephenson and supplied as a kit of parts. During its long life it went through numerous adaptations and modifications.

At the same time that it was laying the United States' first imported flanged T-rail from Britain, the Camden & Amboy Railroad also imported a locomotive. John Bull, a four-coupled-wheel "Planet" type was shipped over as a kit of parts from Robert Stephenson & Company, England. Isaac Dripps, who added his own modifications, including the earliest cowcatcher, assembled it. This historic engine is now at the Smithsonian Institution, Washington, D.C.

Although British builders were willing to work to United States' specifications, British locomotives were designed for well-aligned tracks and they were soon found unsuitable for the lightly laid American railroads. Now a fast-growing nation, the United States quickly launched its own locomotive manufacturing facilities. Britain had by now established the basic fundamentals of locomotive design that were to remain to the end of the steam era, but from the late 19th century on, many of the major technological advances in steam locomotion were well established in the United States, decades before they were introduced in Britain. Despite the very poor quality of some of the products of the emerging builders, 1841 would see the import of the last British locomotive—the Gem of the Philadelphia & Reading Railroad. By this time, there were about 120 imported steam locomotives, but these accounted for only about 25 percent of those in service in the United States.

What would become one of the most famous builders of steam locomotives in the world began in 1831, when Matthias Baldwin of Philadelphia established his works. Baldwin's first experimental locomotive was built that year. Unusually, it burned coal, which was widely available in the area rather than wood, a more common fuel. Baldwin's first commercial locomotive was made in 1832 and was called Old Ironsides. A 2-2-0 design, it was built to the order of the Philadelphia, Germantown & Norristown Railroad, which tried to renege on the last $500 payment. The Baldwin Locomotive Works would go on to build more than 1,500 engines by the time its founder died in 1866.

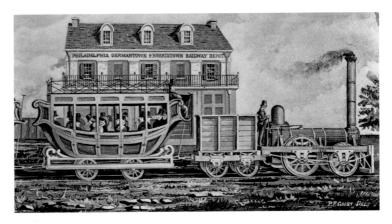

Built by Baldwin Locomotive Works, Old Ironsides was the company's first commercial locomotive, supplied to the Philadelphia, Germantown & Norristown Railroad. This illustration, by P. F. Goist and Frederick Gutekunst, marks the first run of a train in Pennsylvania, on November 23, 1832.

This was a fertile period for experimentation. The first "leading truck" incorporated in a locomotive, to make a 4-2-0 layout, was designed by John B. Jervis of West Point Foundry. Known as Locomotive Experiment, the prototype was supplied to the Mohawk & Hudson Railroad. Later known as Brother Jonathan, it was claimed to have reached a speed of 80 mph (129 km/h).

In 1833, iron-bar frames were introduced into the United States with the delivery of the 0-4-0 Liverpool, designed by the British engineer Edward Bury. Until this time, frames had been made of reinforced lumber, but within two years iron frames were in general use. The last locomotives to use wooden frames were built by Baldwin in 1839. The first 4-4-0 type locomotive was developed by Henry R. Campbell of the Philadelphia, Germantown & Norristown Railroad, and built by James Brook of Philadelphia. Campbell was granted a patent on February 5, and the eight-wheeler was later to become a classic design, known as the "American" type. However, that same year, Isaac Dripps produced a strange 8-coupled-wheel machine, the Monster, for the Camden & Amboy Railroad, combining both rod and gear coupling of wheels. In 1834, Imlay built a new passenger car, "Victory," for the Philadelphia & Columbia Railroad. This was an innovation, as it ran on two four-wheel trucks. Although it was not quite the world's first (one had been built for the St. Étienne-Lyon railroad in France), it was the first car of its type built in America. In 1836, the Cumberland Valley Railroad introduced "bunk" cars, enabling passengers to lie down, even though journeys were short. In 1840, two distinct types of passenger cars were introduced: those costing higher fares were called "Best Cars", while the more common type were just "Accommodation Cars."

The first locomotive to have a leading truck was the work of West Point Foundry. It was supplied to the Mohawk & Hudson Railroad, where it was known as Brother Jonathan.

SAFETY ON THE TRACKS

WITH THE GROWTH OF RAILROADS—AND THE NUMEROUS ACCIDENTS THAT OCCURRED—SAFETY MEASURES HAD BEGUN TO BE CONSIDERED DURING THE 1830S.

Above: Charles Babbage was an English mathematician and mechanical engineer. He designed the first cowcatcher, subsequently a common feature of United States locomotives.

Right: The headlight was an important train safety feature; this type comprises a square case containing an oil lamp in front of a parabolic reflector.

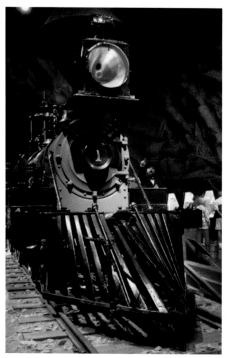

A steam locomotive hurtling down a railroad track was not only a danger to anyone—or anything—that should happen to get in its way, but also was susceptible to damage or even derailment should a collision occur. In 1833 the first pilot wheels, or "cowcatcher," were fitted to John Bull by the Camden & Amboy Railroad. The pilot was mounted at the front of a locomotive to deflect obstacles from the track. It was invented by the English mathematician and mechanical engineer Charles Babbage in the 19th century, when he was working for the Liverpool & Manchester Railway. Pilots were not used on European locomotives, since their railroad systems were generally fenced off, while the North American tracks were not.

The pilot deflected an obstacle hit at speed, pushing it upward and sideways out of the way; it had a blunt wedge shape and shallow V appearance in plan. The earliest pilots consisted of bars mounted on a frame; later types were of smoother sheetmetal. Cowcatchers were adopted by many other railroads, and became used universally from about 1855. A well-made cowcatcher could throw a buffalo weighing 2,000 lb (907 kg) some 30 ft (9 m).

Many locomotives were fitted with a bell and a steam whistle to warn of their approach. The whistle was also used to signal the train crew when the engineer wanted to apply the train's brakes.

The following year, a grade-crossing accident on the Boston & Worcester Railroad prompted a demand for all locomotives to carry warning bells. The State of Massachusetts enacted a law requiring warning bells for locomotives and other states followed. By 1839, bells had become commonplace on locomotives. Made of brass, they weighed between 60 and 215 lb (27 and 98 kg), were operated by a cord from the engineer's cab, and could be heard from a quarter of a mile (0.4 km) away.

Other safety systems were also employed: semaphores were used to control trains between Newcastle and Frenchtown, Pennsylvania, while, in 1836, there was the first reported use in the United States of a locomotive steam whistle. The whistle comprised a thin, circular bell, closed at the top and sharp at the lower edge; steam was vented from a narrow, circular orifice directly beneath the edge of the bell and entered the interior, setting up vibrations inside. The more rapid the vibrations, the higher the tone of the whistle. Tone was influenced by the size of the bell and the pressure of the steam: the larger the bell, the lower the tone; the higher the steam pressure, the higher the tone. To avoid the shrill noise of a common whistle, chime whistles were used so tones harmonized to give an agreeable chord.

John Bull was fitted with Babbage's first cowcatcher, also known as pilot wheels. The wedge-shaped device could throw obstacles clear of the locomotive's path.

Locomotive headlights were introduced in 1840. Nighttime operation could be hazardous over twisting single tracks, and a lookout had to be kept for broken rails, misaligned switches, damaged trestles, and animals on the track. At first, a square case fitted ahead of the stack housed an oil lamp. Later, a parabolic reflector incorporating a central wick gave a beam for 1,000 yd (914 m).

AFTER THE PANIC OF 1837

THE SPECULATIVE BOOM IN RAILROAD BUILDING LED TO RAMPANT INFLATION, UNDERPINNED BY PAPER MONEY ISSUED BY NUMEROUS LOCAL BANKS. THE BUBBLE FINALLY BURST IN 1837— THE RESULT OF A DISASTER THAT HAD BEFALLEN NEW YORK CITY.

Fires raged through New York City in December, 1835, consuming the Stock Exchange and most buildings on the southeast tip of Manhattan and around Wall Street. The disaster wiped out the fortunes of many Erie Railroad shareholders, delaying construction work. A great financial and

A contemporary illustration of the conflagration that destroyed the commercial heart of New York in 1835. Many Erie Railroad investors suffered as a result, which delayed construction of the railroad.

RUPERT'S LAND
To Hudson's Bay Company 1670
CANADA
WASHINGTON
Oregon Country
OREGON
IDAHO
MONTANA
NORTH DAKOTA
MINNESOTA
SOUTH DAKOTA
Iowa Territory 1838
WISCONSIN
Wisconsin Territory 1836
MICHIGAN
1837
WYOMING
Unorganized Territory
NEBRASKA
IOWA
NEVADA
UTAH
COLORADO
KANSAS
CALIFORNIA
ILLINOIS
INDIANA
OHIO
PENNSYLVANIA
NEW YORK
MAINE
VT.
N.H.
MASS.
CONN.
R.I.
NEW JERSEY
DELAWARE
MD.
D.C.
WEST VIRGINIA
VIRGINIA
MISSOURI
KENTUCKY
TENNESSEE
NORTH CAROLINA
SOUTH CAROLINA
ARIZONA
NEW MEXICO
OKLAHOMA
ARKANSAS 1836
Disputed Area
MISSISSIPPI
ALABAMA
GEORGIA
REPUBLIC OF TEXAS
TEXAS
LOUISIANA
Florida Territory
FLORIDA
1840

United States Territorial Growth
1775–1970
Union States
US Claims
US Territories
Unorganized Territories
Claimed Areas
Canadian Territories

By 1840 the United States comprised the Union States in the East with territories in Florida, Winsconsin and Iowa. A central unorganized territory existed, while Texas was an independent republic, with Mexico a foreign area and New Mexico disputed. In the north west Oregon was an area claimed by the United States As the railroads spread, this picture changed radically as boundaries were disputed and changed.

commercial crisis began in March 1837 and reached its height in May, with what became known as the Panic of 1837—one of the worst economic disasters in history. The banks stopped payment in gold and silver, and many closed their doors forever.

Despite the financial problems of 1837, the railroads continued to grow apace. At the beginning of the 1840s, there were more than 345 locomotives running along the tracks of the United States. In 1837, the Northern Cross Railroad was chartered to connect Quincy, Illinois to a point on the Indiana state line; later it was renamed the Wabash Railroad. Also during this year, the Baltimore & Ohio Railroad opened a branch to Washington, D.C. from Relay (Washington Junction). The line included a stone viaduct across the Potomac River at Harper's Ferry, West Virginia. Connection with the Winchester & Potomac Railroad constituted the first junction of two railroads in the United States.

In 1838, the Grand Trunk Western Railroad opened the first section of a line from Detroit, Michigan, to Chicago, Illinois, the Richmond & Petersburg Railroad was connected to the Petersburg Railroad, and the construction of the Erie Railroad was restarted.

Two years later, in 1840, the New York Central & Hudson River Railroad opened from New York to the state capital, Albany, and the Wilmington & Raleigh Railroad opened 161 miles (259 km) of line from Wilmington to Weldon, North Carolina. There were some 2,800 miles (4,506 km) of railroads in the United States. The greatest mileage, 754 miles (1,213 km) was in Pennsylvania. The majority of railroads were built to what would become the standard gauge of 4 ft 8½ in (1.4 m); others varied between 3 ft (0.9

The financial panic of 1837 brought many families to destitution, as depicted in this contemporary illustration, in which a beleaguered father, unemployed and penniless, finds himself under pressure from his starving family and the rent collectors at his door.

m) and 5 ft (1.53 m), while the Erie Railroad adopted 6 ft (1,83 m). In 1841, the first train ran on the New York & Erie Railroad. And while the construction costs of the low trestle bridges it required drove the company into bankruptcy soon after opening, construction of the new railroad continued regardless.

After the financial panic, the depression that lasted until 1843 dealt the fledgling railroad industry a hard blow. It resulted in near-failure for locomotive builder Matthias Baldwin, but owing to leniency on the part of his creditors and his decision to take on several partners, he was able to weather the storm and recovered in six years. Baldwin's plant in Philadelphia, Pennsylvania, went on to become the largest locomotive factory in the world. However, many other locomotive builders went under, among them George and Charles Sellers, and the Cardington plant, which had produced the locomotives *America* and *Sampson* for the Philadelphia & Columbus Railroad. That same year, the Champlain & Connecticut River Railroad was incorporated to build between Bellows Falls and Burlington, Vermont, as part of a route from Boston, Massachusetts to Ogdensburg, New York. The Central Railroad of Georgia reached Macon from Savannah in October 1843, and its expansion continued in 1846 when it opened 171 miles (275 km) from Augusta to Atlanta. Also that year, the Nashville, Chattanooga & St. Louis Railroad was incorporated. The Old Colony Railroad opened between Boston and Plymouth,

The John Molson is a replica of a locomotive built in 1849 by Kinmonds, Hutton, & Steel of Dundee, Scotland, which ran on Canada's Champlain & St. Lawrence Railroad.

Massachusetts, and consolidated with the Fall River Railroad. This was the earliest constituent of what became the New York, New Haven & Hudson River Railroad.

In 1846, an early example of trade-in was acceptance by Baldwin of his first locomotive, Old Ironsides, as part payment on a new locomotive. The construction of the Atlantic & St. Lawrence Railroad commenced, and the following year, the Alton & Sangamon Railroad was chartered to run from Springfield, Illinois to Alton, 20 miles (32 km) north of St. Louis, Missouri. The Atlanta & La Grange (Atlanta & West Point) Railroad was chartered; the Galena & Chicago Union Railroad was under construction. The New Albany & Salem Railroad was organized to build from New Albany, Indiana, on the north bank of the Ohio River, opposite Louisville, Kentucky, to the shore of Lake Michigan.

Also in 1847, the Milwaukee & Waukesha Railroad was chartered, as was the Rock Island & La Salle

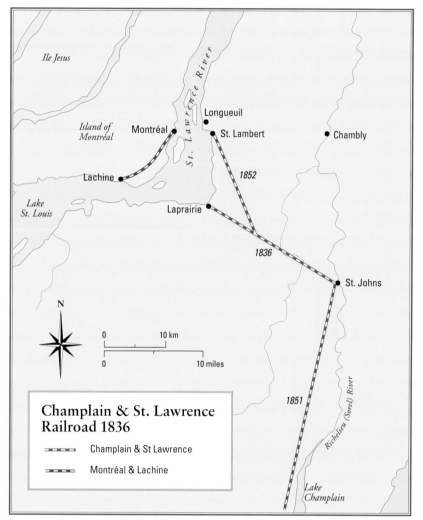

Railroad, which was to build between Rock Island, Illinois, and La Salle, connecting with the Illinois & Michigan Canal; later, it was renamed the Chicago & Rock Island Railroad. The New York & Erie Railroad had reached Port Jervis, New York, on the Delaware River, 74 miles (119 km) from Piermont by December 31. In October 1848, the Galena & Chicago Union Railroad opened its tracks between Chicago and Maywood, Illinois, a forerunner of the Chicago & North Western Railroad. At the end of the 1840s, the Evansville & Eastern Illinois Railroad was chartered to build north from Evansville, Indiana, and the Ligget's Gap Railroad combined with other lines in eastern Pennsylvania to form a corporate structure of the future Lackawanna & Western Railroad. The Aurora Branch Railroad was built from Aurora, Illinois, to Turner Junction to connect with the new Galena & Chicago Union Railroad, with train services to Chicago chartered. Later, this railroad became the Chicago, Burlington & Quincy Railroad.

The Champlain & St. Lawrence was Canada's first railroad, forming an important part of the route from Montreal to New York, accomplished mainly by steamers on Lake Champlain and the Hudson River. It was extended to New York in 1851 and became part of the Grand Trunk Railroad in 1872.

NORTH DAKOTA

MINNESOTA

MICHIGAN

Duluth • Ashland • • Ishpeming

Oakes •

WISCONSIN

Aberdeen •

Minneapolis • • Green Bay
St. Paul

WYOMING

Pierre •

SOUTH
DAKOTA

Sheboygan

Rapid City •

Wyeville •

Madison • • Milwaukee

Wood •

Mason City •

Chadron •

Casper

Sioux City •

Evansville
Clinton • Chicago

Lander •

Des Moines •

IOWA

Omaha • • Council
• Bluffs

NEBRASKA

Peoria •

Lincoln •

ILLINOIS

Superior •

Benid •

**Chicago &
North Western**

—— Chicago, St. Paul,
Minneapolis &
Omaha
---- Trackage rights

N

| 0 | 100 km |
| 0 | 100 miles |

Chartered in 1836, the Chicago & North Western Railroad grew to have one of the largest networks in the Midwest. Its tracks spread northward from Chicago into Michigan, west into Wyoming and south into Illinois.

An artist's impression of life on the Erie canal at Lockport's flight of five locks, with a railroad bridge in the distance. Construction of the canal had provided important lessons for railroad builders and had shown the economic advantages of linking the interior of the country with the Eastern Seaboard.

Opposite: By 1840, many railroads were beginning to establish themselves in the East.

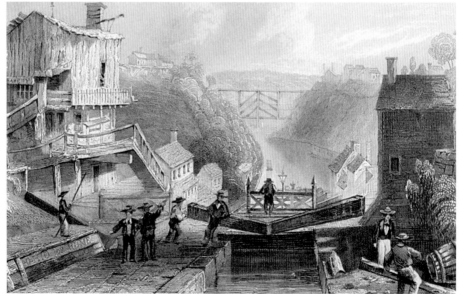

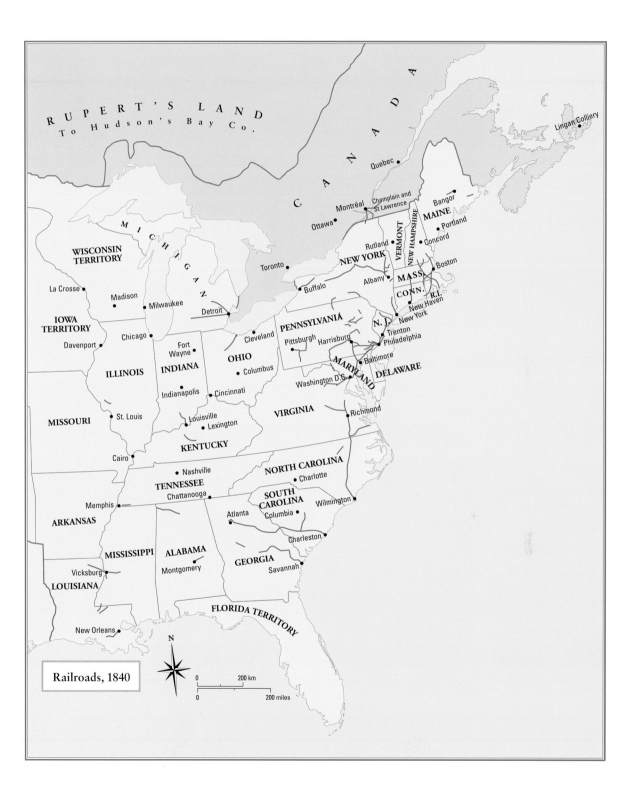

RUPERT'S LAND
To Hudson's Bay Co.

C A N A D A

Quebec

Montréal

Champlain and
St Lawrence

Bangor

Ottawa

MAINE

Portland

MICHIGAN

Rutland

Concord

NEW YORK

VERMONT

NEW HAMPSHIRE

WISCONSIN
TERRITORY

Boston

Toronto

Albany

MASS.

La Crosse

Buffalo

CONN.

R.I.

Madison

Milwaukee

New Haven

IOWA
TERRITORY

Detroit

Cleveland

PENNSYLVANIA

N. J.

New York

Davenport

Chicago

Fort
Wayne

Trenton

Philadelphia

OHIO

Pittsburgh

Harrisburg

Baltimore

ILLINOIS

INDIANA

Columbus

MARYLAND

DELAWARE

Indianapolis

Cincinnati

Washington D.C.

MISSOURI

St. Louis

Louisville

VIRGINIA

Richmond

Lexington

KENTUCKY

Cairo

Nashville

NORTH CAROLINA

Charlotte

TENNESSEE

Chattanooga

SOUTH
CAROLINA

Wilmington

Memphis

Atlanta

Columbia

ARKANSAS

Charleston

MISSISSIPPI

ALABAMA

GEORGIA

Vicksburg

Montgomery

Savannah

LOUISIANA

FLORIDA TERRITORY

New Orleans

Lingan Colliery

N

Railroads, 1840

0   200 km

0   200 miles

Abe Lincoln's whistle-stop tours, 1849 and 1861

THE HISTORY OF THE UNITED STATES ABOUNDS WITH MEMORABLE RAILROAD TRIPS, BUT THE TOURS OF PRESIDENTIAL CANDIDATES, AND THE FINAL JOURNEYS OF DECEASED PRESIDENTS, REVEAL THE IMPORTANCE OF THE RAILROADS. ONE OF THE FIRST POLITICIANS TO MAKE USE OF THE TRAIN WAS ABRAHAM LINCOLN.

Trains were the primary form of overland transportation for almost a century, becoming symbols of America's movement and progression. It was hardly surprising that political campaigners used the railroads as a means of meeting the electorate face to face. Abraham Lincoln (1809–65), a young lawyer, had worked as a railroad lobbyist and attorney in Illinois, where one of his clients was the Illinois Central Railroad, which the young lawyer defended in tax litigation. He also represented the Alton & Sangamon Railroad in 1851 in a dispute with one of its shareholders. In a landmark case he defended the Rock Island Railroad in a suit that confirmed the railroads' right to build bridges over navigable rivers. He also defended the Chicago & Alton and the Ohio & Mississippi railroads in other litigation. So great was Lincoln's reputation that the New York Central Railroad attempted to hire him—for the huge salary of $10,000—on the eve of his presidential election, which he, of course, declined.

During his election campaigning, Lincoln had traveled widely throughout the country seeking support from the electorate. In 1849, his travels had been at times slow and arduous when, traveling by stagecoach, steamboat and rail, he had journeyed from Illinois to Washington. In 1861, when president-elect, his travels during a lengthy whistle-stop tour had been more rapid because he exclusively used the railroads. After his election as President, Lincoln undertook another landmark whistle-stop tour by rail from his home in Illinois to Washington. When his train arrived in Harrisburg, Pennsylvania, the rumor of an assassination attempt was circulated and the new President left town by an alternative route.

Abraham Lincoln was President of the United States from March 4, 1861 to April 15, 1865. He was an outspoken opponent to the expansion of slavery and also a respected railroad and transportation lawyer.

Abraham Lincoln's Travels
1849 and 1861

1849 trip

— ‒ — Rail

• • • • • Stagecoach

——— Steamboat

1861 trip

— · — Rail

During his presidency, Lincoln signed into law the Pacific Railroad Act on July 1, 1862, which authorized and subsidized the Union Pacific and Central Pacific railroads, which eventually completed the first transcontinental railroad in 1869. On November 18, 1863, Lincoln and his party traveled on a special, brightly decorated, four-car, Baltimore & Ohio Railroad train from Washington, D.C. At Baltimore's Camden Station, the train was pulled through the city streets by a team of horses to Bolton Station, the depot of the North Central Railroad The train then steamed north to Hanover Junction, switched tracks to the Hanover Branch and Gettysburg lines and continued on to Gettysburg, Pennsylvania.

At the public dedication of the new National Cemetery—founded in honor of the 51,000 casualties of the three-day Battle of Gettysburg five months earlier—Lincoln delivered one of the most significant Presidential addresses of all time, marking a key point in America's history, while reinforcing the President's continuing association with railroading. The next time Abraham Lincoln would pass this way, in April 1865, he would be lying in state in his funeral train, killed by an assassin's bullet.

Hanover Junction, Gettysburg, Pennsylvania, and the arrival of President Abraham Lincoln's official train en route to Gettysburg for dedication of the National Cemetery. The man in front of the center window, wearing a stovepipe hat, is believed to be President Lincoln.

THE CLASSIC AMERICAN LOCOMOTIVE, 1840-60s

BY THE 1840S, THE 4-4-0 WHEEL CONFIGURATION WAS THE MOST WIDELY USED IN THE UNITED STATES ON WHAT WAS TO BECOME KNOWN AS THE CLASSIC "AMERICAN" EIGHT-WHEELER.

E arly locomotives burned coal or anthracite, but wood soon became widely used. Production of live embers and sparks from wood-burners proved a constant hazard and a common expense in compensation payments. Many different designs of stack with varying efficacy were used. Probably most widely employed was a design by French & Baird. It became a favorite on Southern railroads, where track-side pine forests and cotton fields made spark-containment a vital consideration.

Robert Stephenson's link-motion valve gear was first fitted to locomotives in England. While it was soon adopted in the United States, it was not accepted there as quickly as in Britain, although it was later to become standard in the American eight-wheeler.

Introduced in February 1836 with a patent taken out by Henry R. Campbell, chief engineer for the Philadelphia, Germantown & Norristown Railroad, by 1842 the 4-4-0 eight-wheeler had become the most widely used locomotive in North America. In the Whyte notation, 4-4-0 signifies that the locomotive had a two-axle truck that helped to guide it into curves and two driving axles coupled by a connecting-rod. The eight-wheeler

Constructed in 1861, the locomotive William Crooks is a classic 4-4-0, and one of the few Civil War veterans still surviving. It was the first locomotive to operate in the United States state of Minnesota, and the first placed in service on the St. Paul & Pacific Railroad, which later became part of the Great Northern Railroad. Executive J.J. Hill used the locomotive to pull his personal train, and he later saved it from being scrapped when faster, more powerful engines were being introduced.

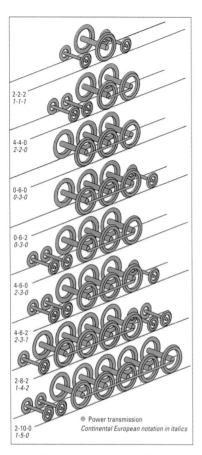

2-2-2
1-1-1

4-4-0
2-2-0

0-6-0
0-3-0

0-6-2
0-3-0

4-6-0
2-3-0

4-6-2
2-3-1

2-8-2
1-4-2

2-10-0
1-5-0

● Power transmission
Continental European notation in italics

Steam locomotive wheel notation, although perhaps a mystery to the uninitiated, in fact is a simple system. A distinction is made between driving and trailing wheels.

was a flexible locomotive, which rode uneven tracks well, was suited to all classes of service, including switching, and was simple to maintain and repair. Low in first cost and relatively powerful, it was a truly national locomotive. Campbell's prototype 4-4-0 weighed 12 short tons (11 metric tonnes), had 14-in (36.5-cm) diameter cylinders, with a 16-in (40-cm) piston stroke; its driving wheels were 54 in (1.37 m) in diameter, and it could maintain 90 lb per square inch (620 kPa) of steam pressure. It was estimated that the locomotive would be able to pull a 450-short-ton (408-metric-tonne) train at 15 mph (24 km/h) on level track, which would beat the strongest of Baldwin's 4-2-0s in tractive effort by about 63 percent.

Despite the success of Campbell's prototype, its frame and driving gear were to prove too rigid for the railroads of the day, making it prone to derailments. In 1837, the company of Eastwick & Harrison had built Hercules, a version of the 4-4-0 for the Beaver Meadow Railroad; this refinement of the type had a leading truck that was separate from the locomotive frame, meaning that it would be more suitable for the tight curves and quick grade changes of the railroads. There were a number of other designers, such as William Norris, but the name most firmly associated with the outside-cylinder 4-4-0 is that of Thomas Rogers. Campbell successfully sued other manufacturers and railroads for infringing his patent, and Matthias Baldwin settled with Campbell in 1845 by purchasing a license to build 4-4-0s.

Eugène Bourdon of Paris, France, perfected a practical steam-pressure gauge in 1849, which is still in use today. Since steam engines had become bigger and operated at higher pressures, there were numerous accidents and failures. The Bourdon pressure gauge consisted of a tube that would straighten at higher pressure, moving a gear that rotated a needle. Although highly accurate, it could be damaged by rapidly changing pressures. The gauge was introduced into the United States by Edward Ashcroft, and was readily accepted. It is still used to measure the pressure of gases and liquids today.

Although the 4-4-0 became known as the "American" type, due to the large number that were produced and used in the United States, the term would not be known until 1872, when *Railroad Gazette* published an article about the locomotive. Before this article, the type was known simply as the "Standard" or "Eight-wheeler." So successful was the type that many of the earlier 4-2-0 and 2-4-0 locomotives had been rebuilt as 4-4-0s by the middle of the 19th century. During the 1840s, the dimensions of the type increased, with a longer boiler and a connecting-rod attached to the front driving axle, larger-diameter drive wheels, and a fire grate of a larger area. In the 1850s, the wheelbase of the leading truck and the driving axles were extended, and the boiler increased in width, giving more steam power. In 1852, the "Most modern 4-4-0" was introduced in the United States. This was the New Jersey, which epitomized the type built in increasing numbers over the next three decades as the classic "American" eight-wheeler. Its chief characteristics were two outside cylinders, a spread (long) wheelbase leading truck, Stephenson link-motion, and a wagon-top boiler.

By 1855, the typical eight-wheeler had the following characteristics: 4-4-0 with 15 x 20-in (38 x 51-cm) outside cylinders, 60-in (1.5-m) wheels, 100 lb (45 kg) of steam pressure, weight 20 tons (18 tonnes),

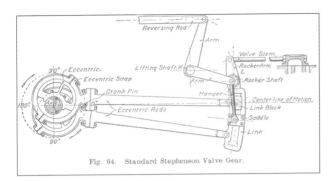

Fig. 64. Standard Stephenson Valve Gear.

and tractive effort 6,375 lb (2,892 kg). This type was represented by the General, a product of Rogers Locomotive Works, Paterson, New Jersey, which was preserved and is today exhibited in the Smithsonian Institution, Washington D.C. The General is slightly larger than other eight-wheelers, with 15 x 22-in (38 x 56-cm) outside cylinders, 60-in (1.5-m) wheels, 140 lb (64 kg) of steam pressure, weight 22 tons (19.8 tonnes), and tractive effort 9,820 lb (4,454 kg).

Robert Stephenson's link-motion valve gear was eventually adopted in the United States, becoming standard on the American eight-wheeler.

The first American coal-burning locomotive, Daniel Webster, completed trials on the Illinois Central Railroad in 1855. By this time, there were about 6,000 locomotives in the country, and most were burning wood rather than coal. Two years later, with the 1,000th locomotive built by Norris, there were about 9,000 locomotives in service.

In 1858, Levi Bissell patented a swiveling, two-wheel leading truck, known as a "pony truck." From this time, the smaller-wheeled 2-6-0 began to supersede the 4-4-0 for freight work. The 4-4-0 was not universally adopted, however. In 1847, the world's first 4-6-0, Chesapeake, was built by Norris for the Philadelphia & Reading Railroad. The ten-wheeler had small driving wheels and was intended primarily for freight work.

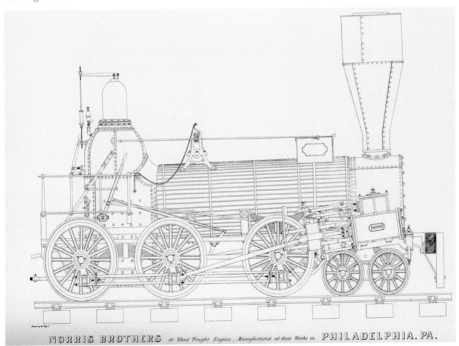

NORRIS BROTHERS 10 Wheel Freight Engine. Manufactured at their Works in PHILADELPHIA. PA.

The world's first 4-6-0 locomotive was built by Norris Brothers of Philadelphia for the Philadelphia & Reading Railroad. Named Chesapeake, it was used mainly for freight work.

THE TELEGRAPH REVOLUTION

BEFORE THE ARRIVAL OF THE TELEGRAPH, MESSENGERS HAD BEEN THE MOST RELIABLE MEANS OF COMMUNICATING OVER DISTANCE. BY THE LATE 1800S, TELEGRAPHS WERE IN WIDESPREAD USE.

Samuel Finley Breese Morse invented a telegraphic communication system using electrical pulses sent along a wire. Known as Morse Code, the system proved invaluable for sending messages quickly over long distances. It became a vital part of railroad equipment.

The telegraph greatly speeded up mankind's ability to communicate, especially over long distances, and it proved invaluable across the vast expanses of the United States. Numerous types of telegraph had been developed in England, but it was the American Samuel Finley Breese Morse (1791–1872) who invented the system that was eventually adopted in the United States.

Returning from a period of art study in England, Morse began to conceive the notion of an electric telegraph, wrongly believing this to be unique, and later acquired partners to help him in the development of the system. In 1837, two Englishmen, William Fothergill Cooke and Charles Wheatstone, had patented the "five needle" telegraph system, whereby needles were used to translate the electric signal into words, but the system had its drawbacks because the needles quickly wore out.

Morse developed a method that would become known as Morse Code—a series of dots and dashes sent by electrical impulses along a wire to a receiving point, where they were deciphered into a message. Working to perfect the system, he developed a suitable insulation for the wires consisting of hemp soaked in tar. Convinced of the telegraph's widespread potential, Morse began to demonstrate the system to businessmen during the late 1830s and also met with committees of Congress, seeking funds for a large-scale test. Many people were skeptical about Morse's assertion that messages could be sent from city to city over a wire, but he carried on. Morse patented the idea in 1840, and in 1843, his Magnetic Telegraph Company received the sum of $30,000 from Congress for the construction of the first telegraph line in the United States, which ran from Baltimore, Maryland to Washington, D.C.

The development of the railroads, and that of the telegraph, were inextricably linked from the outset when, in 1827, the Baltimore & Ohio Railroad—the country's first common carrier to be chartered—had begun constructing its line into the West. The Baltimore & Ohio 's Mount Clare Workshops had designed and built a machine that could simultaneously plow a trench and bury a lead pipe containing the telegraph wires. The discovery, however, that the wires contained in the pipes were improperly insulated meant that the entire telegraph line had to be dug up and restrung overhead on wooden poles in the usual way.

By 1844, the first inter-city electromagnet telegraph in the world was completed. On May 24, Samuel Morse sent the first test message from the Capitol building in Washington D.C. to Baltimore, Maryland. The biblical quotation, "What Hath God Wrought!" was written by Anne Ellesworth, the daughter of the Commissioner of Patents. The following day, a telegram was sent back to Morse, marking the establishment of the first commercial use of telegraph on the railroad's right-of-way.

Even so, the Baltimore & Ohio was dubious about the system's worth, and many other railroad companies simply refused to allow the electric wires to be strung along their roadbeds. By the late 1800s, however, various private companies, leasing Morse's patent, had constructed telegraph lines from Washington to as far afield as Boston, Massachusetts and Buffalo, New York.

Telegraph had been in use in Europe as a means of train dispatching since 1839, and this had resulted in a laudable record free of accidents caused by trains running into each other. In the United States, railroad companies were initially distrustful of the system. Hurried and somewhat poor-quality construction of the first telegraph lines meant that the network was not wholly dependable, and there were accidents on an almost daily basis on the railroads, which caused extensive damage to rolling stock and track, and in some cases resulted in the loss of life.

Telegraph rapidly became an intrinsic part of the railroad structure, with offices consisting of small residences built close to the track with a small board platform between to enable the efficient transmission of messages becoming standard. Colored flags mounted on a pole would signal instructions to a train: a

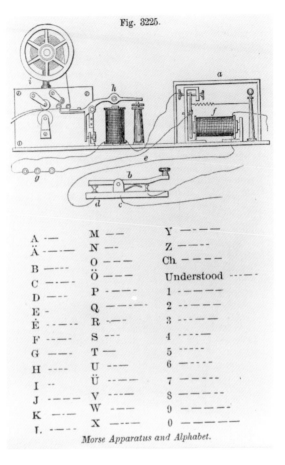

Fig. 3225.

Morse Apparatus and Alphabet.

Morse Code relied on short electrical pulses (dots) and long pulses (dashes) to pass messages. Each letter of the alphabet and numerals were given specific combinations of dots and dashes so that messages could easily be coded and deciphered. A simple key device was used to make and break the circuit to transmit the electrical pulses.

green pennant allowed the train to proceed without stopping, a red one demanded that it stop, and a white one revealed that there was another train close by in front or behind, requiring caution from the crew. Eventually, semaphore—a system of flags—was used to advise train crews of the need to stop or collect a message. Bamboo hoops were used to pass telegraph messages to trainmen, either as the train passed by or when it stopped at the station. On the operator's desk there were two sending keys and receiving relays and, as improvements were introduced, a switchboard that linked the numerous telegraph wires to leads, which enabled the operator to plug into specific circuits, such as the "dispatcher's wire."

The broader adoption of telegraph as a vital part of the railroads occurred in 1849, when Charles Minot, the superintendent of the New York & Erie Railroad, persuaded his board of directors to grant the telegraph company that was running a commercial line through Erie territory a right-of-way along the track from New York to the Great Lakes. His arrangement, later to become the standard

A written message could be passed to a moving train by means of a length of bamboo called a Train Order Hoop, which was easily retrieved by a member of the train crew inserting his outstretched arm through the loop.

practice on most railroads, would give clerks and depot managers a double duty as telegraph operators. This meant that the railroads would incur no other charges for the unlimited use of the system.

In 1850, the first transatlantic telegraph cable was laid beneath the Atlantic Ocean between London, England, and Halifax, Nova Scotia, and by 1858, direct telegraphic communication was established between the United States and Great Britain. The system worked for only one month before it failed after attempts were made to increase the speed of communication. The transatlantic link would not be re-established until after the American Civil War.

On June 16, 1860, members of Congress voted to authorize the Pacific Telegraph Act, a bill instructing the Secretary of the Treasury to subsidize the construction of a transcontinental telegraphline running from the Missouri River to the Pacific coast. The following year the Overland Telegraph Company of California, and the Pacific Telegraph Company of Nebraska, were formed. Poles were set for the Nebraska company's telegraph line westward from Julesburg, Colorado, to Salt Lake City, Utah, and the Overland Telegraph Company's line from Fort Churchill, Nevada, was begun. On October 26, 1861, the lines were joined at Salt Lake City, allowing San Francisco, California, to be in direct telegraphic contact with New York City. The line was soon upgraded with a multiwire line along the length of the transcontinental railroad's right-of-way.

A typical railroad telegraph key. The device made and broke the electrical circuit, sending pulses along the wire that were heard as short and long tones (dots and dashes).

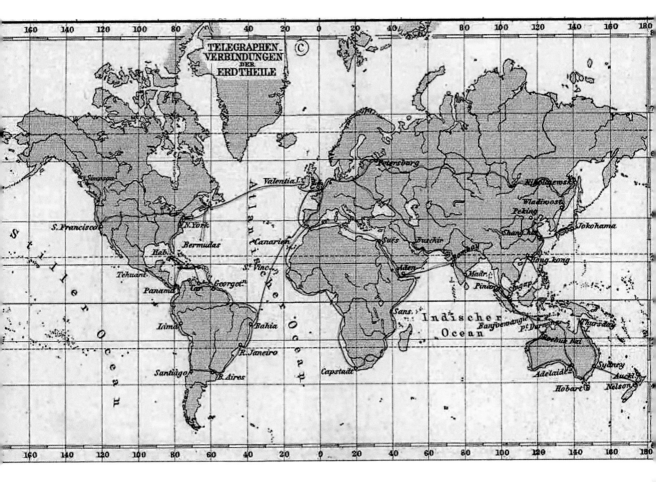

Between the 1860s and 1880s, contracts were taken out between the railroad companies and the telegraph companies. The latter would be charged with supplying the poles, wire, and telegraphic instruments required for new lines, for both their use and that of the railroads, while the railroad companies would transport all this equipment along the track at a cost of $30 per mile (1.6 km). The railroad companies' employees would be responsible for maintaining the telegraph lines. The telegraph companies would own receipts for all messages, by either party, at its offices set up along the line. It was at this time that Western Union began to dominate the network by buying up smaller telegraph businesses. By 1866, it had acquired more than 300 companies, and by the 1880s, it operated such agreements with more than four-fifths of United States railroad companies. Western Union sent 80 percent of the country's messages along its wires, which linked more than 12,000 offices. Many of the company's telegraph offices on small branch lines doubled as railroad stations, and provided commercial telegraph facilities for the general public.

The use of telegraphy began to diminish during the 1900s with the improvement of technology and other sources of communication, such as the telephone and teletype, although it remained a mainstay with the railroads for many years.

Eventually, telegraph lines were laid around the world, including across the Atlantic Ocean. These permitted rapid intercontinental communication.

RAILROAD EXPANSION, 1850S

BY 1850, THE MILEAGE OF UNITED STATES RAILROADS
EXCEEDED 9,000 MILES (14,483 KM). NEW YORK STATE LED
THIS GROWTH WITH 1,361 MILES (2,190 KM) OF TRACKS,
SOME 121 MILES (195 KM) AHEAD OF PENNSYLVANIA. THE
RAILROADS, HOWEVER, HAD NOT YET PENETRATED WEST
OF THE MISSISSIPPI RIVER.

In 1850, the Louisa Railroad reached westward to Charlottesville, Virginia, and became the Virginia Central. The Louisville & Nashville Railroad was chartered, and the Milwaukee & Waukesha became the Milwaukee & Mississippi Railroad. The Mobile & Ohio Railroad launch was aided by Congress' Land Grant Bill. The Norfolk & Petersburg Railroad was chartered to build a line connecting those two Virginia cities, and was the earliest constituent of the Norfolk & Western Railroad On April 22 the following year, the Milwaukee & Mississippi Railroad reached Waukesha, Wisconsin, a distance of some 20 miles (32 km), while the Nashville, Chattanooga & St. Louis Railroad opened its first 9 m (14 km). Ground was broken for the 5ft 6-in (1.68-m) gauge Pacific Railroad at St. Louis, Missouri on July 4, 1851. This year also saw the start of the first rail tunnel in the United States. Called the Hoosac Tunnel, it was located in the Berkshires, in Massachusetts.

By December 1852, there was a through road from Philadelphia to Pittsburgh, Pennsylvania. Construction of the first rail suspension bridge began over Niagara River, New York. The Chicago & Aurora Railroad (formerly the Aurora Branch Railroad) was authorized to build a line to Mendota, Illinois. On October 10, the first train to run between Chicago & Joliet, Illinois—the Rock Island Railroad—was hauled by a 4-4-0 locomotive. The New York & Erie Railroad leased the Paterson & Hudson River Railroad and the Paterson & Ramapo Railroad, and built a connection at Suffern, New York. The Mobile & Ohio Railroad opened its line running from Mobile to Citronelle, Alabama, a distance of 30 miles (48 km). The

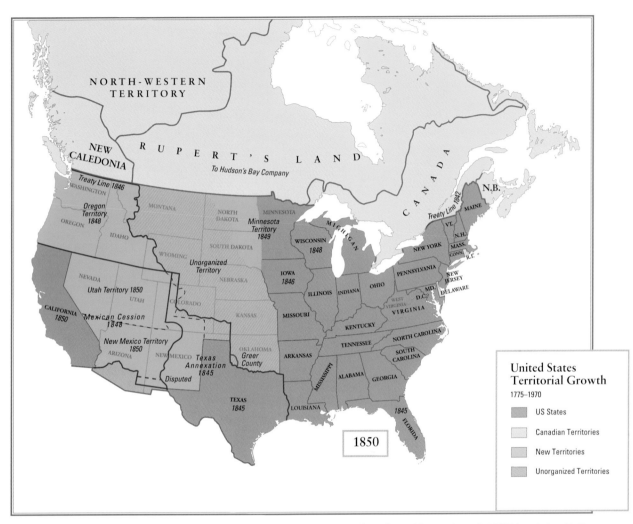

NORTH-WESTERN TERRITORY

NEW CALEDONIA

R U P E R T ' S   L A N D
To Hudson's Bay Company

C A N A D A

N.B.

Treaty Line 1846
WASHINGTON

Oregon Territory 1848

OREGON

MONTANA

IDAHO

NORTH DAKOTA

MINNESOTA

Minnesota Territory 1849

WISCONSIN 1848

MICHIGAN

Treaty Line 1842

MAINE

VT.

N.H.

NEW YORK

MASS.

CONN. R.I.

WYOMING

SOUTH DAKOTA

IOWA 1846

PENNSYLVANIA

NEW JERSEY

NEVADA

Utah Territory 1850

UTAH

Unorganized Territory

NEBRASKA

ILLINOIS INDIANA OHIO

MD.

DELAWARE

D.C.

CALIFORNIA 1850

Mexican Cession 1848

COLORADO

KANSAS

MISSOURI

WEST VIRGINIA

VIRGINIA

New Mexico Territory 1850

ARIZONA NEW MEXICO

Texas Annexation 1845

KENTUCKY

NORTH CAROLINA

OKLAHOMA

Greer County

TENNESSEE

SOUTH CAROLINA

Disputed

ARKANSAS

MISSISSIPPI ALABAMA GEORGIA

TEXAS 1845

LOUISIANA

1845

FLORIDA

1850

United States Territorial Growth
1775–1970

- US States
- Canadian Territories
- New Territories
- Unorganized Territories

New York City–Albany through-rail route was also established. When the first 4 miles (6 km) of the Pacific Railroad opened in 1852, it enabled the first train to operate west of the Mississippi River.

On January 1 the next year, the Baltimore & Ohio reached the Ohio River at Wheeling, West Virginia, 379 miles (610 km) from Baltimore, almost 25 years from commencement of the railroad. The Niagara Falls suspension bridge opened on March 8. On August 1, the Pennsylvania Railroad reached the Ohio River at Pittsburgh, Pennsylvania, and the New York Central & Hudson River Railroad opened throughout as far as Buffalo, New York. The Evansville & Eastern Illinois Railroad opened from Evansville to Vincennes, Indiana, and the Delaware, Lackawanna & Western Railroad was established. The Nashville, Chattanooga & St. Louis opened to Bridgeport, Alabama, and the Atlantic & St. Lawrence Railroad completed its tracks between Portland, Maine, and Montreal, Canada. The line was leased by the Grand Trunk Railway of Canada. By the end of this year, 13 railroads between Albany and Buffalo were consolidated as the New York Central.

By 1850, Wisconsin, Iowa, Florida, Texas, and California had been granted statehood while across the frontier Lower Canada (French) and Upper Canada had been united as the Province of Canada. Nova Scotia had its own colonial government and the vast territories to the west were the business of the Hudson's Bay Company.

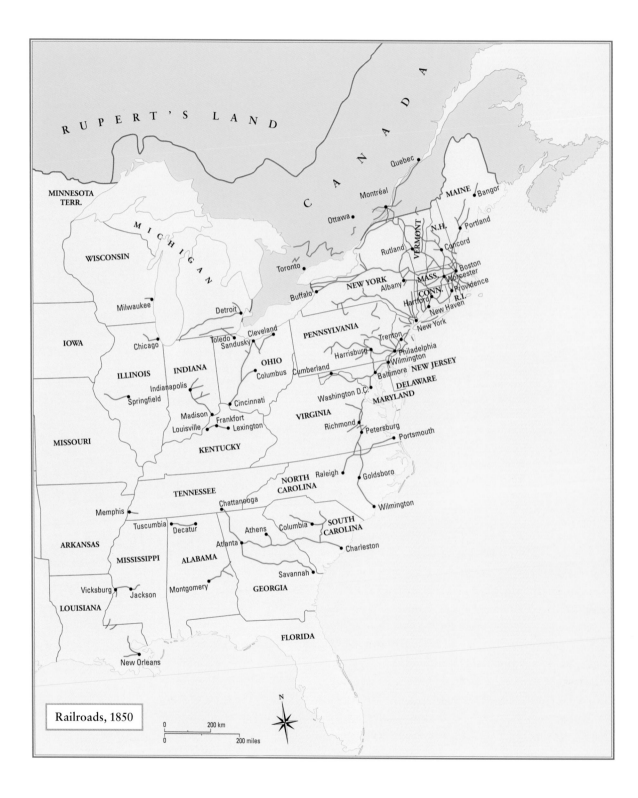

RUPERT'S LAND

CANADA

Quebec

MINNESOTA TERR.

Montréal

MAINE Bangor

MICHIGAN

Ottawa

WISCONSIN

VERMONT N.H. Portland

Rutland Concord

Toronto

Albany Boston

Buffalo NEW YORK Worcester

Milwaukee

Detroit CONN. R.I. Providence

IOWA Hartford

Cleveland New Haven

Chicago Toledo Sandusky PENNSYLVANIA New York

ILLINOIS INDIANA OHIO Columbus Harrisburg Trenton

Springfield Indianapolis Cumberland Philadelphia Wilmington

Madison Cincinnati Baltimore NEW JERSEY

MISSOURI Louisville Frankfort Washington D.C. DELAWARE

Lexington MARYLAND

KENTUCKY VIRGINIA Richmond Petersburg Portsmouth

TENNESSEE NORTH Raleigh Goldsboro
CAROLINA

Memphis Chattanooga Wilmington

Tuscumbia Decatur Athens Columbia SOUTH
CAROLINA

ARKANSAS Atlanta Charleston

MISSISSIPPI ALABAMA Savannah

Vicksburg Jackson Montgomery GEORGIA

LOUISIANA

FLORIDA

New Orleans

Railroads, 1850

N

0   200 km
0   200 miles

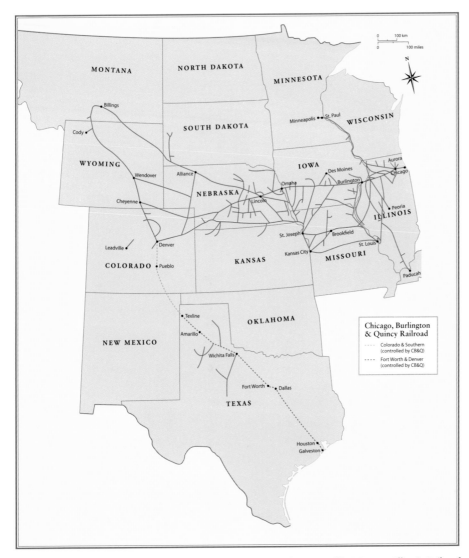

The famous Chicago, Burlington & Quincy Railroad grew out of the Galena & Chicago Union and Aurora Branch railroads.

In 1854, rails reached the Mississippi at Rock Island, Illinois, the Evansville & Eastern Illinois Railroad opened to Terre Haute, Indiana, and the Chicago & Rock Island line opened to Rock Island on February 22. Chattanooga, Tennessee was reached by the Nashville, Chattanooga & St. Louis Railroad, with a connection to Atlanta, Georgia provided by the Western & Atlantic Railroad. The Atlanta & La Grange Railroad opened with 5-ft (1.52-m) gauge.

In 1855, five years after it was begun, the Hoosac rail tunnel cut through the Berkshires in Massachusetts, and was opened to traffic. Some railroads were renamed: the Wilmington & Raleigh Railroad became the Wilmington & Weldon Railroad, and the Chicago & Aurora was renamed the Chicago, Burlington & Quincy Railroad. The Baltimore & Ohio opened from Grafton to the Ohio River at Parkersburg, West Virginia. A railroad was opened between Galesburg and the eastern bank of the

Opposite page: By 1850, previously isolated railroads were linking up to form regional networks.

Water transport played a vital role in moving passenger and freight traffic in the United States hinterland before the coming of the railroads. In the 1850s, the best route for Northwest traffic to reach the sea was north –south via the steamboats that operated on the Mississippi and Ohio rivers.

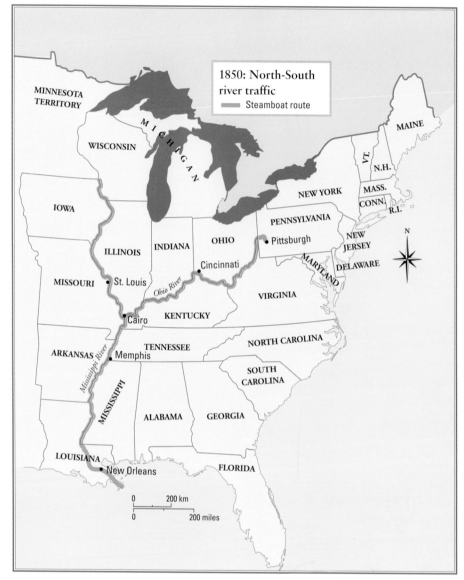

1850: North-South river traffic
━━━ Steamboat route

Mississippi, opposite Burlington in western Illinois. The Delaware & Cobb's Gap Railroad was completed (part of the Delaware, Lackawanna and Western Railroad), making an end-on connection with the Central of New Jersey at Hampton, New Jersey.

In 1856, a string of railroads, including the Chicago, Burlington & Quincy, linked Chicago with Quincy, Illinois, via Galesburg. A bridge, later known as Government Bridge, Mississippi River, was also planned, connecting the Chicago & Rock Island Railroad with the newly created Mississippi & Missouri Railroad. The Mississippi & Missouri had been proposed by Thomas C. Durant as Iowa's first railroad, and would link Davenport and Council Bluffs, Iowa.

Companies operating steam ships on the Mississippi opposed the bridge over the river, complaining that it would pose a navigation hazard and alter their trade monopoly. The bridge crossed an island that was formerly the site of Fort Armstrong, so the Department of War was also involved in the decision. Future Confederate President Jefferson Davis, Secretary of War under President Franklin Pierce, initially approved the bridge, considering that the first transcontinental railroad was going to pass through the South to Los Angeles, California. Davis eventually opposed the bridge, believing that it would result in the transcontinental railroad passing through the north. He ordered that construction be halted, but the courts would not agree and the bridge opened on April 22, 1856. Not long after, on May 6, 1856, the steamer Effie Afton hit the bridge, destroying itself and one of the spans. The bridge was rebuilt and reopened on September 8. This year saw the start of 10-year "war" between railroad and steamboat interests, during which no new bridges were built. During this time, steamboat companies sued to have the bridge dismantled. The Mississippi & Missouri Railroad and the Rock Island Railroad hired Abraham Lincoln to defend the bridge. The case was heard in the Supreme Court and was decided in the bridge's favor in 1862.

Meanwhile, the Mississippi & Missouri and Rock Island railroads had merged to become the Chicago, Rock Island & Pacific Railroad. Durant formed a new company called the Union Pacific. In 1866, the bridge was considered inadequate for the increasing loads carried by the railroad and replaced by a

The current Government Bridge—built in 1896 on the piers of the 1872 structure and 1,500 ft (457 m) from the original—is the fourth crossing of the Mississippi in this vicinity. It is a twin deck structure carrying rail and road traffic, but with two tracks to ease the rail traffic bottleneck.

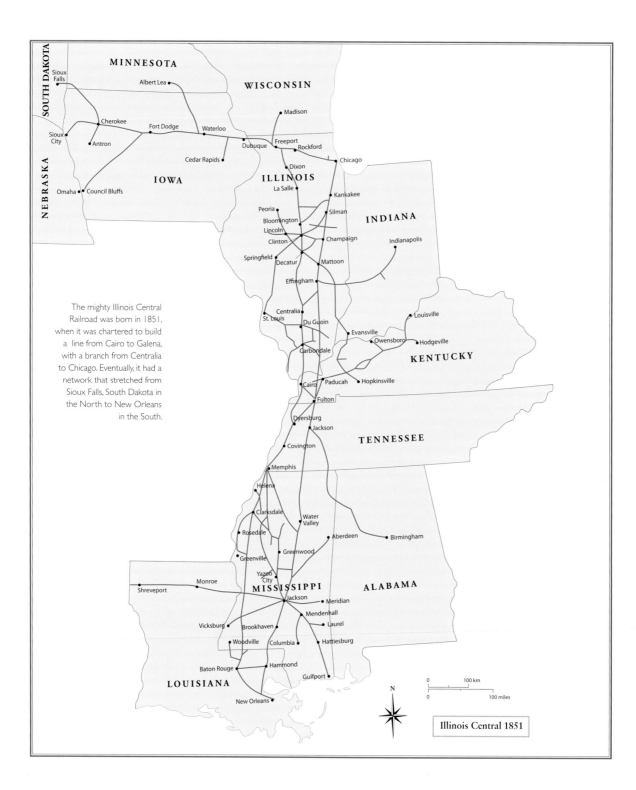

The mighty Illinois Central Railroad was born in 1851, when it was chartered to build a line from Cairo to Galena, with a branch from Centralia to Chicago. Eventually, it had a network that stretched from Sioux Falls, South Dakota in the North to New Orleans in the South.

Illinois Central 1851

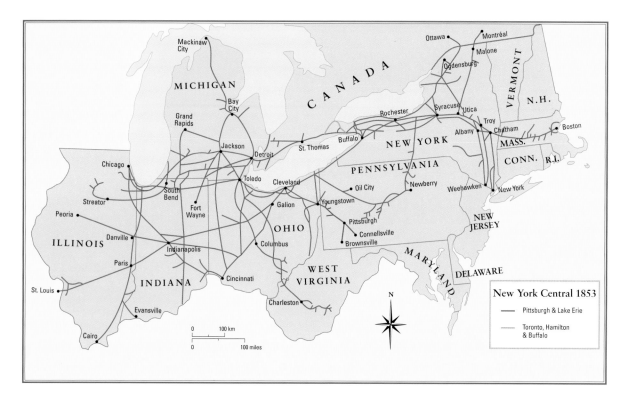

New York Central 1853
— Pittsburgh & Lake Erie
— Toronto, Hamilton & Buffalo

heavier wooden structure that reused the original piers. In 1872, at a new location on the western tip of Arsenal Island, an iron twin-deck bridge that carried a single rail line and a separate roadway replaced this structure. The original bridge was abandoned.

By the year 1857, the rail network had extended from Charleston, South Carolina, to Memphis, Tennessee, although gauges varied from 2 ft (610 mm) to 6 ft (1.83 m). The Milwaukee & Mississippi Railroad reached Prairie du Chien, the Atlanta & La Grange Railroad was re-named the Atlanta & West Point, while the New York & Erie Railroad entered receivership and reorganized as the Erie Railroad with Jay Gould as president.

A financial crisis in 1857 caused the closure of many small lines and railroad construction companies, many of which had unwisely extended credit to potential purchasers. For example, although Seth Wilmarth was under contract to build a large number of locomotives for the Erie Railroad, which had promised payment in cash, a sudden financial flurry caused the railroad to renege on the deal, and payment was offered in stocks instead. Wilmarth's creditors demanded cash. He was forced to suspend production.

Also typical was the Breeze, Kneeland & Company of New Jersey, which was forced to close by "the iniquitous conduct of certain western railroad managers who were buying engines on credit while they knew their companies were hopelessly insolvent."

During 1859 the first major railroad to abandon wood- for coal-burning locomotives was the Reading Railroad.

The famous New York Central Railroad opened its first line between Albany and Buffalo in 1853. It would go on to become one of the greatest United States railroads of the 20th century, operating in the Northeast and around the Great Lakes, where its Water Level Route ran to Chicago. As with many great railroads, it encountered financial difficulties in the 1970s and became part of the Conrail experiment. Eventually, it merged with its major rival, the Pennsylvania, to form the Penn Central.

THE PACIFIC RAILROAD SURVEYS, 1853-55

IN 1853, JEFFERSON DAVIS ORDERED SURVEYS FOR THE RAILROADS, REPORTING ON THE GEOLOGY, ZOOLOGY, BOTANY, AND PALEONTOLOGY OF THE LAND, WITH ETHNOGRAPHIC STUDIES OF THE NATIVE AMERICANS.

B y the year 1848, the United States encompassed a vast expanse of territory that stretched across the continent from the Atlantic to the Pacific oceans, but the only ways to get from one coast to the other (other than by sea) were difficult and dangerous journeys by horse or wagon, crossing mountain ranges. Gold had been discovered in California, and it became a priority to establish a faster and more convenient way to cross the continent with passengers and freight. The obvious answer was the construction of a transcontinental railroad. Various government-sponsored expeditions had already been undertaken during the early 1840s, and numerous routes put forward. No single route could be decided upon, however, since rival groups were determined that the railroad would pass through their state or town, with the promise of the economic riches that would result.

In 1853, the United States purchased from Mexico an area of 29,640 square miles (76,770 km²), a region that is now Southern Arizona and New Mexico. The purpose of the purchase had been to secure land for an envisioned southern route for a transcontinental railroad, and to compensate Mexico for lands taken by the United States. James Gadsden was sent by President Franklin Pierce to negotiate with Mexican President Antonio López de Santa Anna. The sum of $10 million was agreed upon, although only $7 million had been agreed by Congress. When the money finally arrived, $1 million had been lost. Gadsden had ulterior motives for the success of the purchase, since he was a supporter of a southern railroad and a shareholder in the railroad company that would build the line

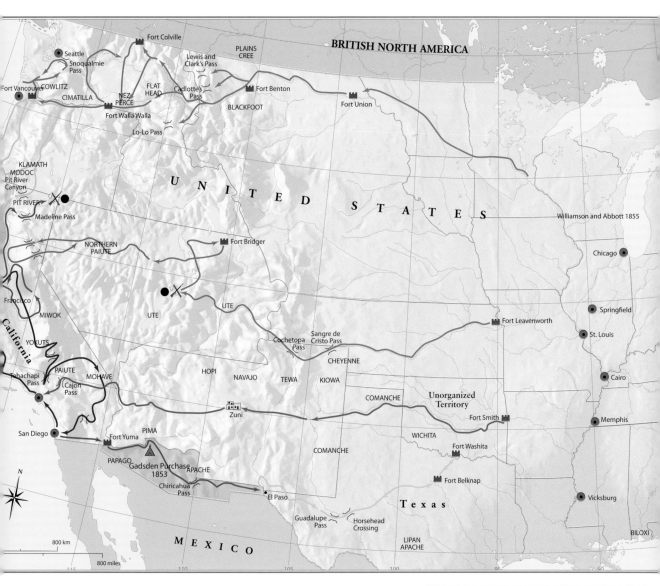

The Pacific Railroads Surveys 1853–55

US fort	Goldfields Survey 1849
Pueblo	Warner and Williamson 1849
Indian settlement	Stevens 1853
Skirmish with Indians	Gunnison and Beckwith 1853
Skirmish with deaths	Williamson and Parke 1853
Railroad's proposed commencement	Whipple 1853
Railroad's proposed destination	Parke 1854
Mountain pass	Pope 1854
Area of gold mines	Williamson and Abbott 1855

to unite Texas with California. In 1861, during the Civil War, the Confederacy created the Confederate Territory of Arizona, which included the land acquired by the Gadsden Purchase. Two years later, the Union formed its own Arizona Territory from the western half of the New Mexico Territory, which was later admitted to the Union as the State of Arizona in 1912.

A passage west that operated from 1857 until 1861 was known as the Oxbow Route, or the Butterfield Overland Mail. This stagecoach route—an early operation of American Express and Wells Fargo—transported United States mail and passengers between St.

On this page and opposite
are lithographic prints of
contemporary illustrations
produced by members of the
transcontinental railroad survey
teams, showing scenes from
their journeys.

The Canyon of Psuc-see-que
Creek, Oregon.

Negotiating a difficult incline
along the Marias River, a tributary
of the Missouri River, Montana.

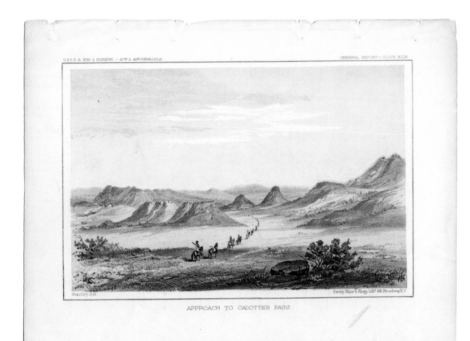

APPROACH TO CADOTTE'S PASS

The exploration party moves up the Sun River valley "in the direction of the pass between the Crown Butte and the Rattlers, prominent landmarks west of Sun River and visible at a great distance."

Having set up their own camp close to the encampment of the Assiniboine Indians, the expedition members distribrute goods to the curious members of the tribe.

DISTRIBUTION OF GOODS TO THE ASSINIBOINES.

Established in 1851, the Chicago & Rock Island Railroad became the Chicago, Rock Island & Pacific in 1866 when it acquired the Mississippi & Missouri Railroad. The road eventually spread into Colorado and New Mexico, but ran its last train in 1980, having become bankrupt.

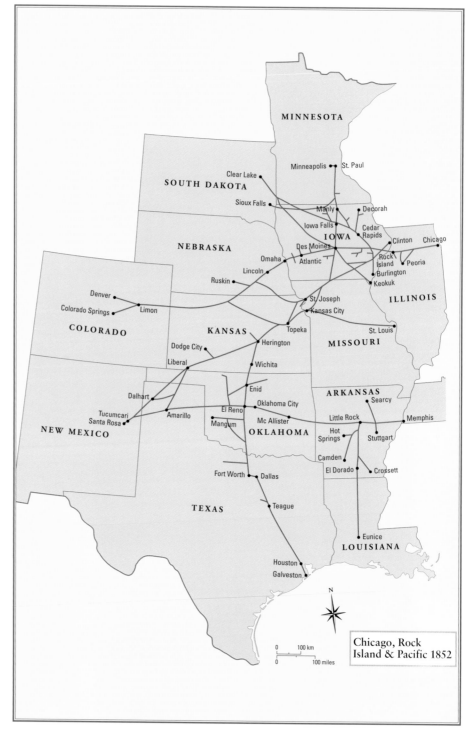

Chicago, Rock Island & Pacific 1852

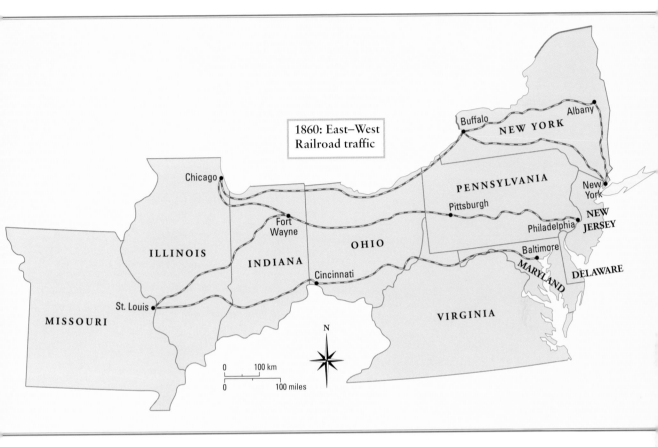

1860: East–West Railroad traffic

Louis, Missouri, and San Francisco, California, in 22 days for a one-way fare of $200. Although 600 miles (966 km) longer than central and northern routes, the Oxbow had the benefit of being free of snow that could hinder progress. At its peak, the Butterfield operation used 250 Concord stagecoaches and 1,800 head of stock (horses and mules). It had 139 relay stations and employed more than 800 people. At the outbreak of the Civil War on March 21, 1861, the final Oxbow Route was run. The Butterfield enterprise continued until 1862 under the Confederate States of America, while Wells Fargo operated stagecoach routes in the north until 1869.

The threat of Civil War prompted the formation of the Pony Express in 1860 to deliver mail at a faster pace—just 10 days—on a central-northern route that avoided the volatile southern Oxbow. On the day that the first transcontinental telegraph line was established, the Pony Express was terminated.

In 1853, Congress authorized the Secretary of War, Jefferson Davis, to commission a number of surveys, and appropriated $150,000 for the Army's Topographic Bureau to finance the project. During that year there followed four main expeditions across the West, with three supplemental surveys over the next two years.

In addition to determining the most favorable route for the transcontinental railroad, the survey teams were directed to compile reports on the general nature of the country, such as its flora and fauna, its

By 1860, thanks to the railroads, Northwest traffic could travel east–west to the Atlantic seaboard, rather than taking the long river trip to New Orleans.

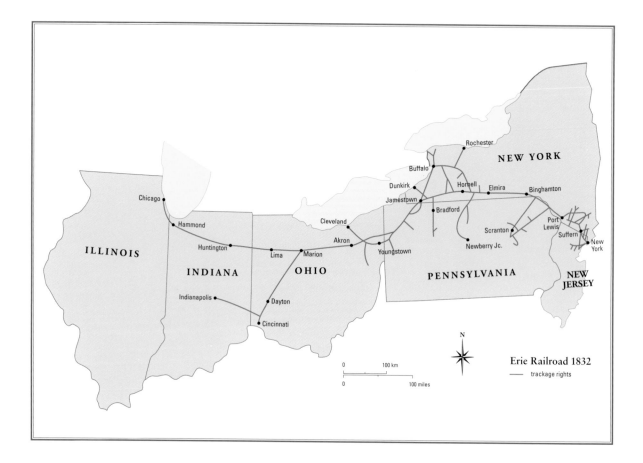

Erie Railroad 1832
— trackage rights

The Erie Railroad completed its first line, from the Hudson River to the shore of Lake Erie, in 1851. It had been conceived as a trunk line from the very outset; eventually the network extended to southern New York State and around Lake Erie to Chicago. In 1960, it merged with the Delaware, Lackawanna & Western Railroad to become the Erie Lackawanna Railroad.

geology, and climate. They were also required to compile ethnographic descriptions of the native peoples they would encounter along the way.

The Northern Pacific survey set off between the 47th and 49th parallels, from St. Paul, Minnesota, to the Puget Sound. It was led by Isaac I. Stevens who, having resigned his army commission, became governor of the Washington Territory. He was accompanied by Captain George B. McClellan and Lt. Rufus Saxton. Also attendant were the natural scientists J.G. Cooper, G. Gibbs, and George Suckley, and the artists John Mix Stanley and Gustavus Sohon. During this most comprehensive survey, photography was used for the first time west of the Mississippi.

The Central Pacific survey set off from St. Louis, Missouri, to San Francisco, California, between the 37th and 39th parallels in June 1853. The expedition was led by Lt. John W. Gunnison, assisted by Lt. Edward G. Beckwith and the artist Richard H. Kern. Other members of this survey team were George Stoneman and Lt. Governor K. Warren. The team left Westport, Kansas and traveled up the Arkansas River, arriving in the Great Basin in the fall. In a skirmish with the Ute Indians on October 26, Gunnison, Kern, and several other members of the expedition were killed. Beckwith took over command and continued the survey. He and Gunnison had considered that a route between the 38th and 39th parallels

U.S.P.R.R. EXP. & SURVEYS 35TH PARALLEL.   ITINERARY

H.B. Mollhausen.   Lith of SARONY, MAJOR & KNAPP, New York.

was unrealistic so eventually he concluded that the 41st parallel was the most practical. Although his suggestion was not considered at the time, ultimately this became the route on which the transcontinental railroad was built.

An expedition led by Lt. Ameil Weeks Whipple surveyed the route along the 35th parallel, from Little Rock, Arkansas, through Oklahoma, New Mexico, and Arizona. It then passed through the Mojave Desert to Los Angeles. Accompanying Whipple were a number of geologists, naturalists, botanists, and astronomers. In addition, the German artist Heinrich Balduin Mollhausen was recruited.

Another survey, led by Lt. Robert S. Williamson, accompanied by Lt. John Parke, traveled along the Californian coast from San Diego to Los Angeles and on to San Francisco, returning via an inland route. A further southern survey, also led by Parke in 1854, traveled between San Diego, California, and El Paso, Texas, while Pope led a team from El Paso through Texas in an easterly direction. In 1855, Lts. Williamson and Henry L. Abbot carried out a north-south survey to search for the best route for a railroad between the Sacramento Valley and the Columbia River.

The extensive results of the surveys, published in a 12-volume document by the United States War Department between 1856 and 1860, was entitled *Reports of Explorations and Surveys*, to ascertain the

Fort Smith, Arkansas, 1853-1855. Illustration from reports of explorations and surveys to ascertain the most practicable and economical route for a railroad from the Mississippi River to the Pacific Ocean. Published by the United States War Department in 1856 and 1860.

The West was cattle country, and the arrival of the railroads prompted cattlemen to drive their herds to the railheads so that they could be shipped to markets in the East. Several trails were established, running north from Texas to Colorado, Nebraska, Kansas, and Missouri. Meanwhile. the old Oregon and Mormon wagon trails were increasingly paralleled by railroads, although the Spanish Trail was still unchallenged.

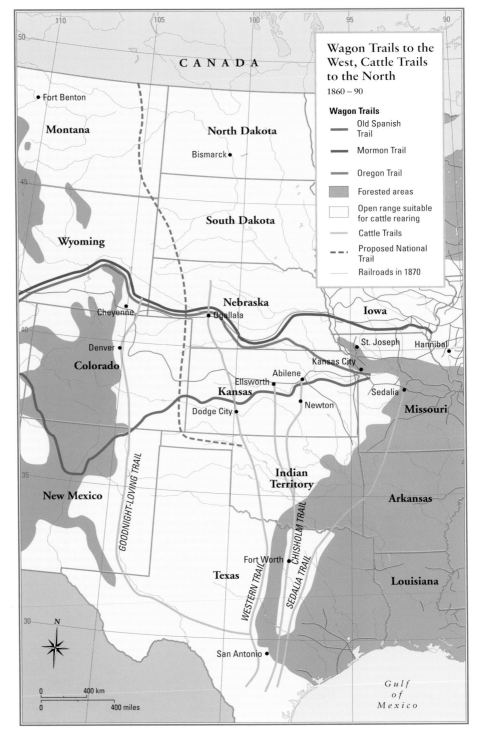

Wagon Trails to the West, Cattle Trails to the North

1860 – 90

Wagon Trails

	Old Spanish Trail
	Mormon Trail
	Oregon Trail
	Forested areas
	Open range suitable for cattle rearing
	Cattle Trails
- - -	Proposed National Trail
	Railroads in 1870

CANADA

Fort Benton

Montana

North Dakota

Bismarck

South Dakota

Wyoming

Cheyenne

Nebraska

Ogallala

Iowa

Denver

St. Joseph   Hannibal

Colorado

Kansas City

Abilene

Ellsworth   Sedalia

Kansas   Newton   Missouri

Dodge City

GOODNIGHT-LOVING TRAIL

Indian Territory

New Mexico

Arkansas

WESTERN TRAIL

CHISHOLM TRAIL

SEDALIA TRAIL

Fort Worth

Texas   Louisiana

N

San Antonio

Gulf of Mexico

0   400 km

0   400 miles

most practicable and economic route for a railroad from the Mississippi River to the Pacific Ocean. The surveys included hundreds of maps and prints, and many hand-colored illustrations of reptiles, amphibians, birds, and mammals. Each of the survey leaders believed that his route was the most advantageous for the railroad, but a final decision by Congress was not reached until after the Civil War, when the route along the 38th parallel, from Kansas City to the Pacific, was commissioned. This railroad, however, would not be completed until 1869.

The middle of the 19th century saw a major westward migration as many settlers headed west in the hope of finding a new life, lured by the promise of free land. The journey was not easy, however, and travelers faced many hardships, including a hostile indigenous population, before they reached their goal.

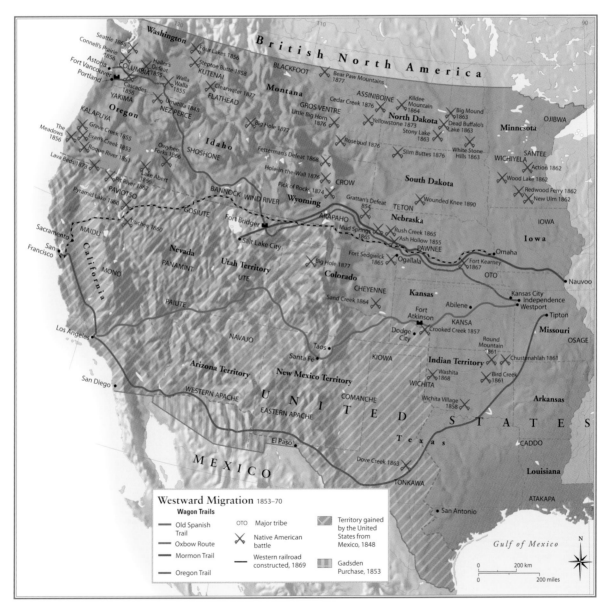

Westward Migration 1853–70

Wagon Trails

— Old Spanish Trail
— Oxbow Route
— Mormon Trail
— Oregon Trail

OTO Major tribe
✗ Native American battle
— Western railroad constructed, 1869

Territory gained by the United States from Mexico, 1848
Gadsden Purchase, 1853

0 200 km
0 200 miles

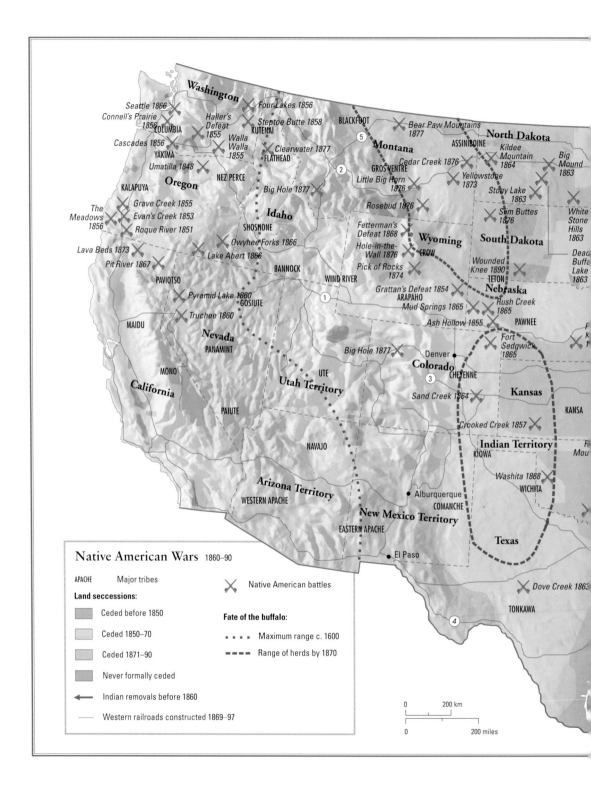

Seattle 1866
Connell's Prairie 1856
Cascades 1856
Haller's Defeat 1855
Four Lakes 1856
Steptoe Butte 1858
Walla Walla 1855
Clearwater 1877
Umatilla 1848
Grave Creek 1855
Evan's Creek 1853
Roque River 1851
The Meadows 1856
Lava Beds 1873
Pit River 1867
Big Hole 1877
Owyhee Forks 1866
Lake Abert 1866
Pyramid Lake 1860
Truchee 1860
Big Hole 1877
Bear Paw Mountains 1877
Cedar Creek 1876
Little Big Horn 1876
Rosebud 1876
Fetterman's Defeat 1868
Hole-in-the-Wall 1876
Pick of Rocks 1874
Grattan's Defeat 1854
Mud Springs 1865
Ash Hollow 1855
Kildee Mountain 1864
Big Mound 1863
Yellowstone 1873
Stony Lake 1863
Slim Buttes 1876
White Stone Hills 1863
Wounded Knee 1890
Dead Buffalo Lake 1863
Rush Creek 1865
Fort Sedgwick 1865
Denver
Sand Creek 1864
Crooked Creek 1857
Washita 1868
Alburquerque
El Paso
Dove Creek 1863

Washington
COLUMBIA
KUTENAI
YAKIMA
NEZ PERCE
KALAPUYA
Oregon
FLATHEAD
BLACKFOOT
Montana
GROS VENTRE
ASSINIBOINE
North Dakota
Idaho
SHOSHONE
Wyoming
CROW
South Dakota
TETON
Nebraska
PAWNEE
BANNOCK
WIND RIVER
ARAPAHO
PAVIOTSO
GOSIUTE
Nevada
PANAMINT
MAIDU
MONO
UTE
Utah Territory
Colorado
CHEYENNE
Kansas
KANSA
California
PAIUTE
Indian Territory
KIOWA
NAVAJO
WICHITA
Arizona Territory
WESTERN APACHE
New Mexico Territory
EASTERN APACHE
COMANCHE
Texas
TONKAWA

Native American Wars 1860–90

APACHE   Major tribes

✗ Native American battles

Land seccessions:

▨	Ceded before 1850
▨	Ceded 1850–70
▨	Ceded 1871–90
▨	Never formally ceded
←	Indian removals before 1860
—	Western railroads constructed 1869–97

Fate of the buffalo:

· · · ·   Maximum range c. 1600

– – – –   Range of herds by 1870

0   200 km

0   200 miles

The relentless westward push of the white man, aided in no small part by the railroads, had steadily constricted the range of the buffalo herds and the indigenous population, leading, inevitably, to conflict. During the second half of the 19th century, battles with Native Americans raged throughout the Midwest and West, from Texas to the Canadian border.

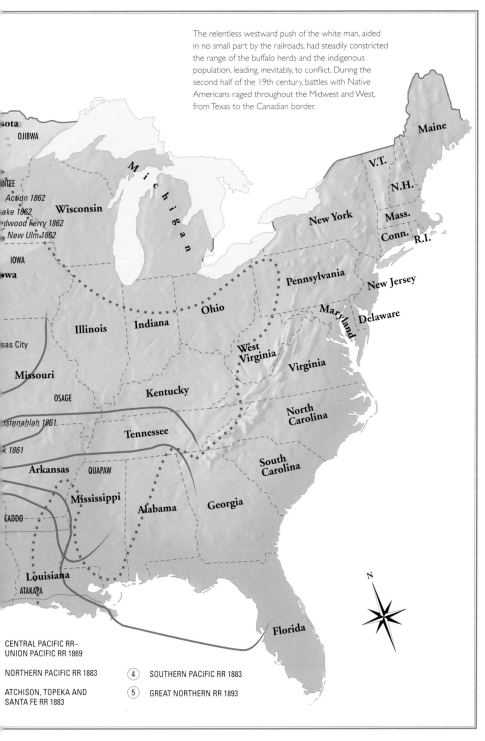

sota
OJIBWA

Maine

NTEE
Action 1862
ake 1862
dwood Ferry 1862
New Ulm 1862

V.T.

N.H.

Wisconsin

Michigan

New York

Mass.

IOWA

Conn.

R.I.

wa

Pennsylvania

New Jersey

Illinois

Indiana

Ohio

Maryland

Delaware

s City

West Virginia

Virginia

Missouri

OSAGE

Kentucky

North Carolina

stenahlah 1861

Tennessee

k 1861

Arkansas

QUAPAW

South Carolina

CADDO

Mississippi

Alabama

Georgia

Louisiana

ATAKAPA

Florida

N

CENTRAL PACIFIC RR–
UNION PACIFIC RR 1869

NORTHERN PACIFIC RR 1883

(4) SOUTHERN PACIFIC RR 1883

ATCHISON, TOPEKA AND
SANTA FE RR 1883

(5) GREAT NORTHERN RR 1893

Sitting Bull (1831–90) foresaw Custer's defeat at the Battle of Little Bighorn. He surrendered in 1881 and eventually left the reservation to join Buffalo Bill Cody's Wild West Show.

Geronimo (1829–1909), leader of the Chiricahua Apache, warred against United States for more than 25 years, surrendering in 1885. In late life he converted to the Christian religion.

George Armstrong Custer (1839–76) was a flamboyant United States cavalry commander, defeated at the Battle of Little Bighorn by Indian tribes led by Sioux chiefs Sitting Bull and Crazy Horse.

EXPANSION OF THE RAILROADS, 1860-65

BY 1860 SOME 30,635 MILES (49,302 KM) OF RAILROAD HAD BEEN COMPLETED IN THE UNITED STATES. THE GREATEST ACHIEVEMENTS WERE IN OHIO WITH 2,946 MILES (4,741 KM), ILLINOIS WITH 2,799 MILES (4,504 KM) AND PENNSYLVANIA WITH 2,598 MILES (4,181 KM). IN THE DECADE THAT FOLLOWED THERE WAS ALSO A GREAT EXPANSION OF RAILROAD BUILDING IN THE SOUTH.

At the beginning of the 1860s, the 1,000th locomotive had been built by the Norris Locomotive Works in Pennsylvania, and by that time there were about 9,000 locomotives in service in the United States. Also during this period, the modern practice of "remanufacture"—reconditioning or modernizing engines—had already been established. Another advance was the introduction of the steam injector, which replaced the somewhat unreliable boiler feed pumps. Invented by the French balloonist Henri Giffard (1825-82), who also invented the first powered airship, the steam injector had been introduced to the United States by William Sellers of Philadelphia.

The railroads continued a steady expansion, and the Morris & Essex Railroad extended from Morristown, New Jersey, to New York; the Louisville & Nashville Railroad opened between Louisville, Kentucky, and Lebanon, Tennessee, in March; it was completed westward into Nashville in May, with a new bridge over the Cumberland River and another over the Green River at Munfordville, Kentucky.

In 1861, the outbreak of the Civil War far outshadowed any financial "panic" in its effect on rolling-stock prices. For example, the price of a standard eight-wheel locomotive rose 280 percent in little over three years. Many railroads benefited considerably from inflated wartime traffic. The demands of the

United States military railroads enabled some commercial railroads to unload obsolete locomotives at a handsome profit. Other railroads, particularly in the Confederate-held states, were either halted, abandoned, or blown up. The Mobile & Ohio Railroad was completed to the port of Cairo, Illinois, on April 22; the Alton & Sangamon Railroad was extended and purchased by the St. Louis, Alton & Chicago Railroad, and the Virginia Central Railroad's westward expansion was halted by the war, despite the fact that it would have been a valuable asset to the Confederacy.

July 1, 1862 saw the signing of the Enabling Act by President Abraham Lincoln, which created the Union Pacific Railroad Company and authorized it to "lay out, construct, furnish and maintain and enjoy a continuous railroad and telegraph line, with appurtenances, from a point on the 100th meridian of longitude west from Greenwich between the south margin of the valley of the Republican river and the north margin of the valley of the Platte in the Territory of Nebraska to the western boundary of Nevada Territory." The Central Pacific, an existing California railroad company, began its line from Sacramento and built east, while Union Pacific started in the middle of the country, at the Missouri River between

By 1860, more states had been added to the Union, while little unorganized territory remained.

UNORGANIZED TERRITORY

MINNESOTA

MICHIGAN

1 week

5 days

WISCONSIN

3 days

2 days

IOWA

Chicago

Cleveland

ILLINOIS

INDIANA

OHIO

PENNSYLVANIA

NEW YORK

VERMONT

MAINE

N.H.

MASS.

Boston

CONN.

R.I.

New York

NEW JERSEY

DELAWARE

MARYLAND

NEBRASKA TERRITORY

MISSOURI

St. Louis

KENTUCKY

VIRGINIA

1 day

Norfolk

KANSAS TERRITORY

NORTH CAROLINA

UNORGANIZED TERRITORY

ARKANSAS

Nashville

TENNESSEE

SOUTH CAROLINA

MISSISSIPPI

ALABAMA

GEORGIA

TEXAS

LOUISIANA

Tallahassee

FLORIDA

N

0   200 km

0   200 miles

Speed of Travel

1860

time of travel from
New York City

Council Bluffs and Omaha, and built west. Though Lincoln did not live to see the driving of the Golden Spike—which commemorated the joining of the two sections—in 1869, the transcontinental railroad is said by many to be one of the greatest achievements of his presidency. It made it possible to travel from San Francisco to New York City in 10 days.

The year also saw the system of hand-signaling brought into use on the Hudson River Railroad; the St. Paul & Pacific Railroad ran its first train between St. Paul and Anthony (now Minneapolis), Minnesota,;and the Maine Central Railroad was incorporated. Four roads between Portland, Maine, Waterville, and Bangor, all broad gauge lines, were converted to standard gauge. The Nashville, Chattanooga & St. Louis roadway was damaged by floods in 1862.

Two years later, steel-making was revolutionized by the Bessemer process, cutting the price of steel rails by half. The process, invented by Henry Bessemer in England in 1856, was the first cheap method of making steel. It involved blowing compressed air into molten pig iron in a furnace (known as a converter). Once the excess carbon in the steel had been burnt off, other impurities in the metal formed a slag, and the furnace was emptied. Iron rails were gradually replaced, and steel rails were adopted on new projects.

In 1856, the design was perfected for the three-point suspension of the Hudson-Bissell swiveling, two-wheel leading truck for locomotives. This was also the landmark year that George Mortimer Pullman (1839–97) produced the first real sleeping car, the Pioneer, which boasted folding upper berths and extendable seat cushions for the lower berths. Further developments included the replacement of candle lighting in passenger cars with kerosene lamps. The "block" signaling system was first introduced on the New Brunswick, New Jersey and Philadelphia Railroad, on March 27.

As the Civil War progressed, on April 2, 1865 the Confederate government was evacuated by the Richmond & Danville Railroad from Richmond to Danville, Virginia. The Chicago, Burlington & Quincy Railroad had a virtual railroad monopoly in western Illinois and the southern half of Iowa. The Milwaukee & St. Paul Railroad (Milwaukee Road) was formed by an amalgamation of the Milwaukee & Prairie du Chien and the La Crosse & Milwaukee railroads. The Montgomery Railroad was shut down following an attack by Union forces a few days after General Lee's surrender.

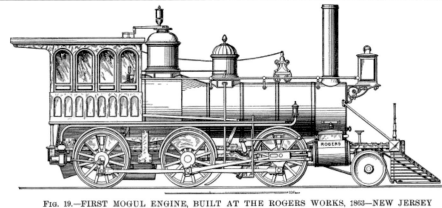

FIG. 19.—FIRST MOGUL ENGINE, BUILT AT THE ROGERS WORKS, 1863—NEW JERSEY RAILROAD AND TRANSPORTATION COMPANY.

Opposite page: By 1860, thanks to the railroads, the speed of travel from New York to many parts of the Northeast had increased considerably.

In 1863, Levi Bissell's two-wheeled, swiveling pony truck was incorporated into the first "Mogul" class locomotive, built by Rogers for the New Jersey Railroad & Transportation Company. This truck eased movement over curved track, enhancing speed and stability.

The Virginia Central Railroad was restored and was soon running again, while the Nashville, Chattanooga & St. Louis Railroad was rebuilt by the United States Government's Military Railroads Department and returned to its owners. Even as the war progressed, construction of the Union Pacific Railroad continued, reaching Kansas City, Missouri, a distance of some 279 miles (449 km).

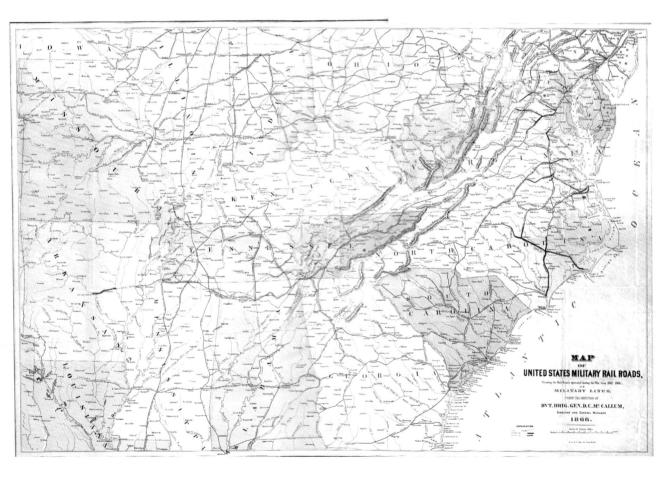

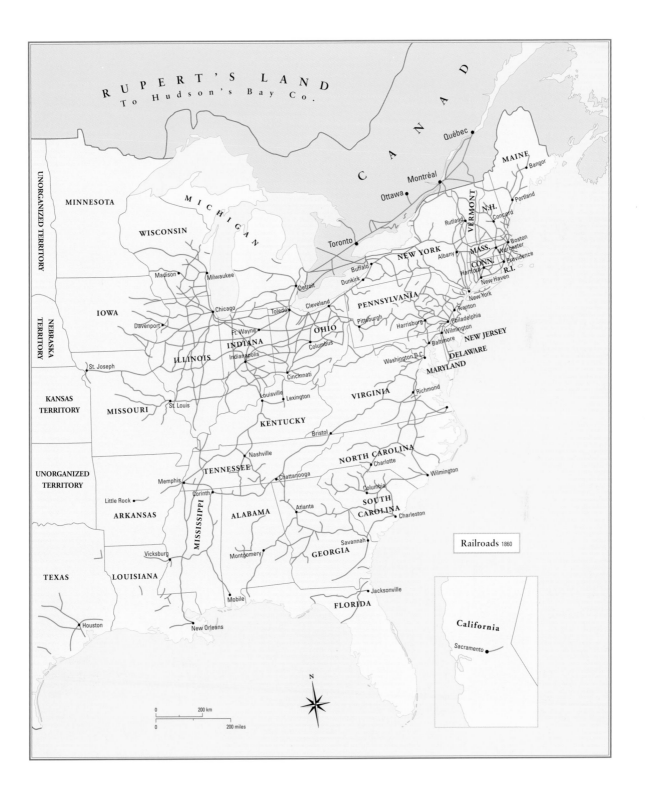

RUPERT'S LAND
To Hudson's Bay Co.

CANADA

Québec

MAINE
Bangor

MINNESOTA

MICHIGAN

Montréal
Ottawa

VERMONT
N.H.
Portland

WISCONSIN

Rutland
Concord

UNORGANIZED TERRITORY

Toronto

NEW YORK
Albany
MASS.
Boston
Worcester

Buffalo
CONN.
R.I.
Providence

Madison
Milwaukee

Detroit
Dunkirk

Hartford
New Haven

IOWA

Chicago
Toledo

Cleveland

PENNSYLVANIA

New York

NEBRASKA TERRITORY

Davenport

Ft. Wayne

Pittsburgh

Harrisburg

Trenton
Philadelphia

INDIANA

Columbus

Wilmington

NEW JERSEY

St. Joseph

ILLINOIS
Indianapolis

OHIO

Baltimore

DELAWARE

Cincinnati

Washington D.C.

MARYLAND

KANSAS TERRITORY

St. Louis

Louisville
Lexington

VIRGINIA
Richmond

MISSOURI

KENTUCKY

Bristol

UNORGANIZED TERRITORY

Nashville

NORTH CAROLINA
Charlotte

Wilmington

Memphis

TENNESSEE
Chattanooga

Columbia

Little Rock

Corinth

SOUTH CAROLINA
Charleston

ARKANSAS

MISSISSIPPI
ALABAMA
Atlanta

Savannah

Vicksburg

GEORGIA

Montgomery

TEXAS

LOUISIANA

Mobile

Jacksonville

FLORIDA

Houston

New Orleans

Railroads 1860

California
Sacramento

N

0   200 km
0   200 miles

THE BACKGROUND TO THE CIVIL WAR

RAILROADS WOULD BECOME A CRUCIAL ELEMENT IN THE WAR BETWEEN THE STATES, AND THE NORTH STARTED WITH AN ADVANTAGE, WHICH IT STEADILY DEVELOPED.

Although the Confederates were the first to take advantage of railroads, the Northern lines were ultimately the war-winner. They had about double the mileage and their technical condition was, on average, better; also they had more materials to cope with damage through wear and tear. Four-fifths of American industry was in the North, and this advantage was intensified after naval blockades prevented the South from importing

materials. Above all, however, in wartime the North finally succeeded in solving the problem of railroad organization and management, which the South failed to do.

In wartime, companies tend to declare their patriotism while at the same time putting their shareholders first, so that talk of self-sacrifice usually coexists with the pursuit of self-interest. The American railroads were no different, and sometimes their employees were no different. Although the Confederates won the First Battle of Bull Run by innovative use of rail transportation, this was in spite of

A breakdown of the free and slave populations of the United States in 1860-61.

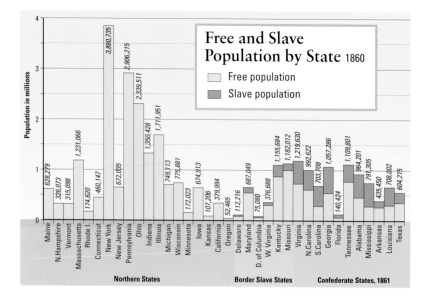

Free and Slave Population by State 1860
- Free population
- Slave population

The United States
January 1861

Free state

Slave state

Territory theoretically open to slavery after the Dred Scott decision of 1857

0   300 km

0   300 miles

an overtime ban by the enginemen. At another critical point, when the Confederate generals were desperate to move large bodies of troops, the railroad decided to raise its fares. Similar behavior was reported in the North.

Another managerial problem was that local commanders took things into their own hands, while understanding nothing of railway operation. In particular they failed to see the need for a prompt return of empty cars and did not understand how one unexpected demand could disorganize traffic for hours over hundreds of miles. The North solved these problems by taking a strong line. The United States Military Railroads (USMRR) organization could, and did, take over vital or recalcitrant companies while at the same time railroad managers were freed from military interference at the local level.

There were important economic differences between the South, the Northeastern states, and the Midwest—and immediately before the secession, many businessmen and politicians had made the point that their trade with each other was vital to their joint prosperity. The Northeast was industrial and urbanized, with an extensive transport network, including many railroads. Historically, the agrarian Midwest had been linked by road and rail to the ports and markets in the East, as well as the river network of the South.

Following Lincoln's election in 1860, seven southern slave states seceded from the Union to form the Confederate States of America. After the attack on Fort Sumter in 1861, four more states joined the Confederacy.

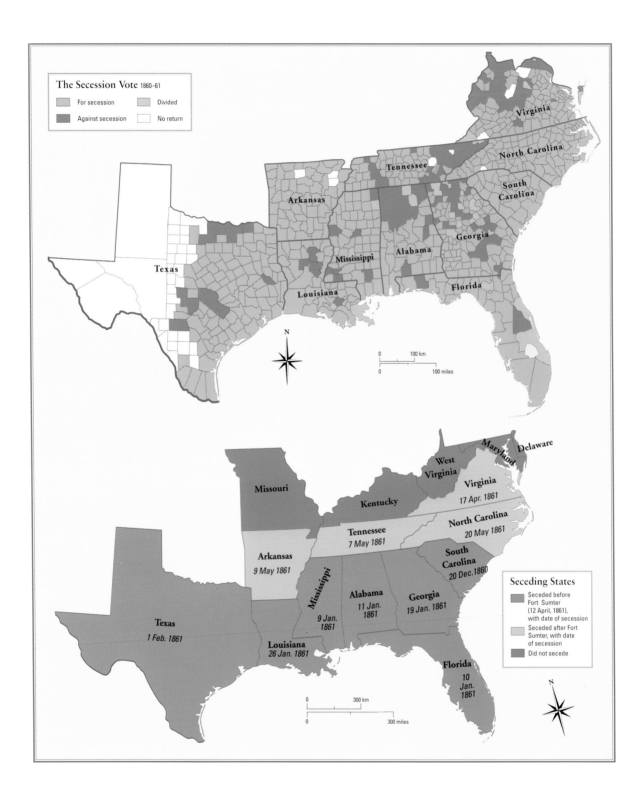

The Secession Vote 1860–61

For secession
Against secession
Divided
No return

Virginia

North Carolina

Tennessee

South Carolina

Arkansas

Georgia

Mississippi
Alabama

Texas

Florida

Louisiana

N

0   100 km
0   100 miles

Missouri

West Virginia

Maryland   Delaware

Kentucky

Virginia
17 Apr. 1861

Tennessee
7 May 1861

North Carolina
20 May 1861

Arkansas
9 May 1861

South Carolina
20 Dec. 1860

Mississippi
9 Jan.
1861

Alabama
11 Jan.
1861

Georgia
19 Jan. 1861

Texas
1 Feb. 1861

Louisiana
26 Jan. 1861

Florida
10 Jan. 1861

Seceding States

Seceded before Fort Sumter (12 April, 1861), with date of secession

Seceded after Fort Sumter, with date of secession

Did not secede

0   300 km
0   300 miles

N

NEGRO RECRUITS TAKING THE CARS FOR MURFREESBORO, TENN., TO JOIN THE FEDERAL ARMY.—FROM A SKETCH BY C. E. F. HILLEN.

On paper, the Union began the war with an enormous advantage over the South because it had over twice the railroad mileage—20,000 miles (32,200 km) of track compared to the South's 9,000 miles (14,840 km) of mostly lighter rail, while its two biggest railroads had more locomotives than the whole South. The South's system was also split into many separate small organizations, with crippling gaps in the network and, while most of the North's lines were at standard gauge 4ft 8 in (1.4 m), those in the South varied widely, forcing many more transfers. However, the North was not immune to the problem of a fragmented network, as was shown when the war was barely a week old. In 1861, Baltimore's two rail stations were widely separated, and as soldiers arrived from the North on their way to join the Army of the Potomac, they had to cross the city. When the Sixth Massachusetts Regiment disembarked and tried to transfer to the other station, its troops were attacked by Confederate sympathizers, forcing the soldiers to fire on the crowds.

As well as making it possible to wage war over a greater area than ever before, the railroads increased the scale of the conflict. For the equivalent weight of fuel compared to animal fodder, a railroad train of the era could carry 10 times the payload of a wagon pulled by draft animals. It could also deliver its payload at five times the speed. General Sherman's campaign of 1864 fielded 100,000 men and 35,000

African American recruits to the Federal Army board railroad cars bound for Murfreesboro, Tennessee in 1863.

Opposite page, bottom: After the Republican victory in the election but before the new administration took office, seven cotton states declared their secession and joined together to form the Confederate States of America.

animals whose supplies were all shipped by rail from Louisville to Atlanta. Sherman estimated that the single railroad track did the work of 220,000 mules and 36,800 wagons.

Naval units of the Union would seize many of the main rivers by 1862, making it easy for the Union Army to move its troops and munitions, and pinning those of the Confederacy into small regions. After the siege of Vicksburg in 1863, the Union controlled the Mississippi, making it impossible for Confederate forces to cross it, and cutting off the western Confederate states. Vicksburg, a fortress city on the Mississippi River, was typical of Southern towns in that it became a railhead for the Southern Railroad of Mississippi, down which General McCleland, one of the three Union leaders in the battle, would bring his troops. However, the defending forces were able to use the interior lines to move their own reinforcements, helping them to repulse the attackers.

All but two of the significant battles of the Civil War were fought in Confederate-controlled territory, almost half of them in Virginia and Tennessee. The first major land engagement, known as the First Battle of Bull Run, took place at Manassas, Virginia, on July 21, 1861, when inexperienced Union troops were routed by the Confederates, who advanced along the Manassas Gap Railroad from Gainesville to Manassas and encamped near Manassas Junction within 25 miles (40 km) of the capital. Manassas Junction was little more than a railroad crossing, but it was strategically important, with tracks leading to both sides' capitals of Richmond, Virginia, and Washington, D.C., as well as the Shenandoah. Despite the Confederate Valley victory, the South's forces were soon repulsed, and Manassas Junction remained in Union hands for much of the war. However, it was also the site of General Robert E. Lee's resounding victory over the Union forces in August 1862 at the Second Battle of Bull Run, after the Confederates broke through the encirclement of Richmond and drove General McClellan's Army of the Potomac back into the Virginia Peninsula.

The First Battle of Bull Run demonstrated that the Confederates had been quick to realize the strategic advantage of rail transport as a means of moving fresh troops rapidly up to the front from an area that was not under threat. The North had been slower to make use of its rail network. This was partly because the war was being fought farther south, and partly because the Northern rail companies were often more concerned with ensuring they were properly recompensed rather than supporting the war. All that changed when the Railways and Telegraph Act, passed on January 31, 1862, formally authorized Union forces to commandeer any railroad necessary to support military operations. The chief reason that the Act was passed was to pressurize the Northern railroads into cooperating. The United States Railroad Administration was formed to implement the Act. In fact, it rarely took over northern lines because its mere power to do so was enough to persuade managements to accept central coordination and control. When a Scottish railwayman, Daniel C. McCallum of the Erie Railroad, was put in charge, he and local railway managers, were given military rank so that they could not be pushed around by junior army officers. McCallum quickly established the Construction Corps for track repair and construction.

As a measure of its importance and the scale of its operations, by the end of the war, in Tennessee alone, the USMRR. was running two-thirds of the 15 private railroads that existed before the conflict. The existence of the USMRR. set the precedent for government control of the railroads in World War I.

At the end of hostilities, several railroad lines that had either been destroyed or abandoned were rehabilitated by the USMRR Department, the most famous being the Nashville & Chattanooga Railroad, which was completely rebuilt in 1865–6 and returned to its former owners.

The United States had an integrated railroad network with over twice the mileage of that in the Confederacy. The southern railroads used a variety of gauges, while the northern lines were all of standard gauge, giving the North a definite advantage.

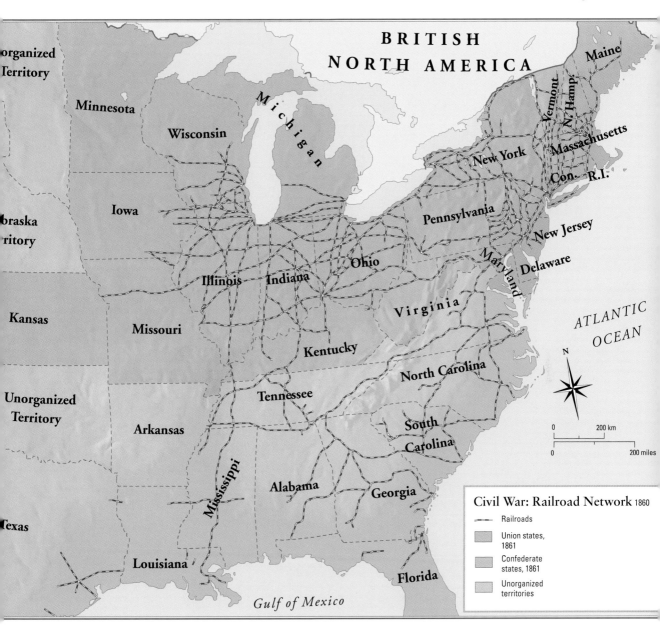

Civil War: Railroad Network 1860

- ⤍ Railroads
- Union states, 1861
- Confederate states, 1861
- Unorganized territories

RAILROADS AT WAR

IN WARTIME THE RAILROADS HAD TO PROVIDE TRANSPORTATION FOR TROOPS AND SUPPLIES, WHILE FREQUENTLY AT RISK OF VIOLENT ATTACK.

Men of the United States Army Railroad Construction Corps at work on the Orange & Alexandria Railroad at Devereaux station, near Manassas Junction, under the watchful eye of General Haupt (in the long black coat, right), in whose honor the locomotive was named.

Railroad tracks soon became prime military targets for raiders from both the North and South, and one of the strategic goals of many campaigns was to capture rail centers. Such attacks destroyed bridges and rolling stock as well as the rails themselves. Snipers were also stationed to attack locomotives, either by shooting the engineer or attempting to puncture a boiler. As a result, a few trains were armored, although full enclosure had a tendency to trap too much heat.

Because the early engines were relatively inefficient, they relied on stocks of wood and water being available at frequent intervals, as often as every 5 miles (8 km). A surprising hazard was suggested by military orders that prohibited soldiers from washing in the railroad water tanks because of the risk that soapy water would cause air locks in an engine's boiler. General Herman Haupt, the Union Army's chief of construction, arranged for stockpiles of railroad materials and prefabricated parts, including bridge sections, so that repairs could be made quickly. He also pioneered a system of transporting loaded rail cars by ferry, saving time in the process.

Both sides attacked the others' railroads. The Confederates twice

Railroads and the Civil War

- Union state
- Border slave state
- Confederate state
- Territory
- 4' 8 ½" (1.44 m) or 4' 10" (1.48 m) gauge railroad
- 5' gauge railroad
- Northern route
- Southern route

raided the Baltimore & Ohio Railroad at Martinsburg, West Virginia. In 1861, "Stonewall" Jackson's troops attacked the Baltimore & Ohio's workshops and engine house, where they destroyed 42 locomotives and removed another 14 partially dismantled units, using horses to drag locomotives and cars along dirt roads

Despite gauge differences, the railroads revolutionized warfare by their swift, sometimes unexpected, movement of troops, a foretaste of 20th century wars.

to the Confederate-controlled Virginia Central Railroad at Staunton, Virginia for use in the South. The Baltimore & Ohio Railroad was vulnerable because it had been built to the 5-ft (1.52-m) gauge.

Even though it was ultimately of minor strategic significance, the most famous railroad action of the Civil War was the Great Locomotive Chase, featuring the General, a 4-4-0 steam locomotive built by Rogers, Ketchum & Grosvenor in Paterson, New Jersey, in 1855. On April 12, 1862, in service on the Western & Atlantic Railroad between Georgia and Tennessee, the locomotive and a few railcars were hijacked by Northern spies, led by James J. Andrews, at Big Shanty (now Kennesaw, Georgia). Andrews and his men headed north, ripping up tracks and telegraph lines to sabotage the supply line to Confederate troops in Tennessee. Their plan had been to dynamite tunnels and bridges, then escape north to Union lines. However, using a variety of other transport—most notably the Texas, which he drove for over 50 miles (80 km) from Adairsville in reverse—the conductor of the General's train, William Allen Fuller, chased the raiders for 87 miles (140 km), until the General ran short of water and wood, and lost steam pressure. The Union spies were forced to abandon the train near Ringgold, Georgia, south of Chattanooga, and tried to escape on foot. Had Andrews not been pursued by Fuller, there is little doubt that his plan could have done significant damage to the Confederates. It was the second time that he had been unlucky. He had already tried to steal a train earlier that year, intending to destroy the strategically important bridge over the Tennessee River at Bridgeport, but that plan had been thwarted when his engineer failed to make a rendezvous. Captured soon after leaving the General, Andrews was court-martialed and hanged as a spy, as were half his men, although eight escaped from captivity and returned home.

The General itself was almost blown up when the Atlanta depot was destroyed by General Hood in 1864, but the locomotive survived to become a museum piece on the National Register of Historic Places. The events were dramatized in Buster Keaton's classic silent film, *The General* (1927), and a later Disney film, *The Great Locomotive Chase.*

James J. Andrews (c.1829-1862) and William Allen Fuller (1836-1905), two participants in the "Great Locomotive Chase" of 1862. Andrews, a Union agent during the American Civil War, hijacked a Confederate train named "The General" in Marietta, Georgia on April 12th. Fuller, the train's conductor, pursued the hijackers until they were apprehended and hanged.

JAMES J. ANDREWS   WILLIAM A. FULLER

The industrialized North had the advantage that damaged rails and rolling stock could easily be replaced, while the Confederacy's only locomotive works, in Richmond, were turned over to the manufacture of armaments. Advancing armies were forced to relay tracks that had been destroyed in action or sabotaged by the retreating soldiers. Some trains were converted for these engineering operations, but only one facility in the South was able to reclaim rails bent into "Sherman's Bow Ties."

The South's existing railroads had been built because they made economic sense. Now, new connections were being made because they made strategic sense. A good example was Florida where, before the war, the railroad network in the peninsula had no connection to other tracks in the South.

Farther north, work on the Atlantic & Gulf Railroad, running from Screven, south of Albany, was halted by the war, and in 1863, the Atlantic & Gulf Railroad merged with the Savannah & Albany, which ran east to Savannah. Late in the war, the Confederate government wanted to connect the Florida railroads with the rest of the network, so a spur was built from Dupont south to the Florida state line to link up with another spur running from Live Oak on the Pensacola & Georgia Railroad. Although this came too late to be of military importance, it usefully extended the Atlantic & Gulf's network when it acquired the extra track after the war. Pensacola, the first European settlement in what would become the United States, had weathered many changes of allegiance during its long history. It was evacuated early in 1862, leading to the seizure of the Alabama & Florida Railroad, part of which was replaced by the Mobile & Great Northern Railroad.

Other lines that were extended in 1862 included sections of the Alabama & Mississippi Rivers Railroad and the Northeast & Southwest Railroad. The following year, the Piedmont Railroad connected the North

Both sides used the railroads to move troops and supplies, so the trains and tracks became targets. Damaged by enemy action, this trestle bridge on the Orange & Alexandria Railroad in Virginia was quickly repaired by Union Army engineers, allowing the locomotive Firefly to pass safely over.

Carolina Railroad to the southern section of the Richmond & Danville Railroad at Danville, Virginia. In 1864, this would prove strategically important after the Petersburg Railroad—previously the only line connecting Richmond to the South—was cut off. Construction of other lines was abandoned owing to a shortage of money, even though some, like the Covington & Ohio Railroad, might have been valuable to the Confederacy.

The more industrialized North already had better rail connections and these assisted in the movement of supplies, arms, and munitions, but the Union Army also extended railroads, building a new section of the Nashville & Northwestern Railroad to bypass a stretch of the Tennessee River. More importantly, the Civil War was a major factor behind plans to

A large artillery piece mounted on a flatcar, with a wooden shield to protect the gun crew. While such arrangements provided mobility, they restricted the direction in which the cannon could be fired.

build the Union Pacific Railroad to the west. Closer to the battle zone, freight cars were widely used as artillery transportation to the front, and also as mobile gun platforms. Field guns were conventionally moved by horses, which had to be unhitched before the weapons could be deployed. Mounting a battery on flatcars meant that it could be fired without such a pause, or even while on the move. Guns were mounted so that they would recoil down the length of the car against restraining ropes. Some carried angled shields made of wood or metal to protect the gun crews.

Trains were often made up with the locomotive in the center, where it was less vulnerable to attack. Passenger cars or boxcars would be coupled to the locomotive, with flatcars at the ends. The latter carried troops or artillery where they would command the widest field of fire. Armored railroad cars were built. These looked like iron boxcars, the infantrymen inside being given apertures through which to fire, but their armor was only protection against small-arms fire. A later development had an artillery piece mounted on top to give it a field of fire all around the train. The final development of the "railroad monitor" had thick, angled armor and artillery resembling a modern tank, although turrets were not fitted until well after the Civil War.

Armor could protect a train from bullets and artillery shells, but the easiest target was the railroad track or roadbed. A damaged track would prevent forward progress until it was repaired, but would not wreck the train if the engineer were vigilant enough to stop in time. Far more deadly was a mine rigged to detonate when a train passed over it. Such devices, then known as "torpedoes," included specially constructed mines filled with gunpowder and a pressure-sensitive firing device, but artillery shells with percussion caps were sometimes used in this way. Where such hazards were expected, it was common practice to send a loaded flatcar ahead to detonate any hidden torpedo instead of risking the whole train. Another way to sabotage tracks and installations such as bridges, or even an

Opposite page: On 15–16 December 1864, General John B. Hood brought his reduced army before the defenses of Nashville, determined to force Sherman's Army out of Georgia, but was beaten by General George H. Thomas in the most complete victory of the war. In this photograph, believed to have been taken during the course of the battle, lines of United States Military Railroad locomotives stand ready for action.

United States Military Railroad engineers point out damage sustained by the locomotive Fred Leach during operations in Virginia. It received hits on the smokestack and tender.

oncoming train, was to pack an empty car or locomotive with explosives or set it on fire, then to send it on a collision course.

The war forced the development of many other specialized rail vehicles. Hospital cars for transporting the wounded were often converted from passenger cars, being fitted with double rows of stretchers in place of the bench seats, although some were purpose-built. Mobile medical cars were also made, providing surgical facilities on the move. Mobile field kitchens were developed as a way of efficiently feeding large numbers of soldiers.

At the Battle of Chattanooga, the Union sent 25,000 men and 10 batteries of cannon 1,200 miles (1,931 km) by rail from Virginia to Tennessee, to reinforce its army in just 12 days. The decisive impact of such troop movements was so great that commanders were known to shuttle empty trains back and forth in an attempt to deceive the enemy into thinking that reinforcements were being

A contemporary illustration of an armored boxcar.

sent to a particular destination. During the first week of the war, exactly this ruse had been used to bluff the Union troops into abandoning the shipyards in Portsmouth, Virginia, by repeatedly running the same train into and out of the town of Norfolk along the Norfolk & Petersburg Railroad.

The strategic importance of the railroad network was again clearly demonstrated in the spring of 1862, when Forts Donelson and Henry fell to the Union army, and the Confederate General Albert S. Johnston decided to evacuate Nashville, Tennessee.

Johnston was partly prevented from doing this when panicking civilians overwhelmed all southbound trains. He was, however, able to use the railroads to concentrate troops from all over the Confederacy at Corinth, Mississippi, the junction of the Memphis & Charleston and Mobile & Ohio lines.

In April, Johnston's army battled General Grant's Union troops near Shiloh Church. When Johnston was killed and his men were defeated, the Union gained control of the only railroad north of Vicksburg and west of Chattanooga, giving them an easy route east to within striking distance of Chattanooga and southward into Alabama. Grant defended the railroads around Corinth, Memphis, and Humboldt, but Confederate General Bragg launched raids against the Nashville & Chattanooga and Memphis & Charleston lines, as well as roads in Kentucky, with the effect of cutting Grant's supply line. This tactic delayed the Union Army and gave the Confederate forces time to move men by rail from Tupelo to Chattanooga.

Both sides in the war poured resources into the area using the railroads. The Union shipped in supplies to Murfreesboro, using the Nashville & Chattanooga Railroad, while the Confederacy brought in reinforcements from 1,000 miles (1,610 km) away in Virginia to supplement those who marched from nearby Mississippi. By September, Union forces were under siege in Chattanooga, where General Bragg had seized control of the supply routes. To relieve the starving troops, the North devised a plan to move in thousands of men from Virginia, finally succeeding in delivering Chattanooga and the rest of Tennessee into Union hands.

This experience helped to prepare General Sherman for his "March to the Sea," the campaign on Atlanta and Savannah. Realizing that his lines of supply would be under threat from Confederate saboteurs, he trained 10,000 troops in the art of railroad repair before he left Chattanooga. The troops became so skilled that damaged lines would commonly be returned to use within a day or two at most.

After the fall of Atlanta, when Sherman abandoned his supply line and continued the march to Savannah, as they progressed his men turned their attention to the systematic destruction of the railroads. A section of track was ripped up, and all the ties piled into a heap to make an enormous fire under the rails. When the rails had become red-hot, the troops bent them around a convenient tree, and also put a twist in them to ensure that they could not easily be straightened, giving birth to the term "Sherman's Bow Ties." This process made it virtually impossible for the Confederate forces to use the railroads to send men in pursuit of General Sherman and his troops, as he marched from the Georgia State Capitol and on through the Carolinas. General Grant was well aware that the South's shrinking industrial base made it increasingly difficult to reclaim the damaged rails or produce new ones.

Later, the railroads formed part of a strategy that ended the war after Lincoln made Ulysses S. Grant commander of all Union armies. In the belief that defeating the Confederates would only be possible by striking their economic base and supply lines, as well as their armies, and with the Confederate ports

blockaded since May 1861, Grant instructed Generals Crook and Averell to attack railroad supply lines in West Virginia. At the same time, other forces destroyed the agricultural bases in the Shenandoah Valley and Georgia. Toward the end of the war, the North was supplying its troops by the trainload, through its extensive rail network, while the Confederate Army, whose railroads had been almost completely destroyed, was starved of both food and munitions.

The strategic importance of the railroads to both sides is particularly clear from one incident during the spring campaign of 1864. General Crook, sent on a mission to destroy the salt works at Saltville, Virginia, met a sizable Confederate force near Dublin, Virginia. In what would become known as the Battle of Cloyd's Mountain, Crook's men routed the Confederate defenders, who were already on the run, until a train pulled into Dublin carrying 500 fresh Confederate cavalrymen from the force that had just defeated General Averell. Although Crook won the pitched battle that followed, it cost the Union almost 700 soldiers.

Crook then marched on Dublin, where he destroyed the railroad buildings and stores. To prevent further railroad movement, his men tore up sections of the tracks and burned the ties. Next morning, they marched east to capture the New River Bridge, a strategic crossing. Although the Union troops were halted by Confederate artillery on the opposite bank, the bridge was blown up and it collapsed into the river, after which the Confederates, cut off from their supplies, withdrew to the east.

General Grant's own overland campaign of 1864 was directed against Petersburg, Virginia, the port of which had been an important commercial center for transporting and processing cotton and raw materials. As railroad technology developed, Petersburg became established as the center linking

This giant mortar, known as The Dictator, was used in the Union seige of Petersburg. Weighing 17,120 lb (7,766 kg), it could throw a 13 in (33 cm), 200 lb (91 kg) shell over a distance of 2.5 miles (4 km). It was mounted on a special flatcar and operated on a branchline of the City Point & Petersburg Railroad.

Opposite page: General Sherman's army leaves Atlanta on its "March to the Sea," destroying the South's capacity to wage war by killing southern livestock, burning crops and tearing up southern railroads.

Opposite page: As the war progressed, the Confederacy used the railroads to move troops over 1,000 miles (1,610 km) to attack Grant at Chattanooga.

Locomotives of the United States Military Railroad, at City Point, Virginia, around 1864 after the seige of Petersburg. The important port blockaded by General Grant's troops can be seen in the background.

Richmond to the North, Farmville and Lynchburg to the west, and Weldon, North Carolina, to the south. It had been connected to the East when the 85 miles (137 km) of the Norfolk & Petersburg Railroad were completed in 1858.

Because of the port and the railroad, with its total of six locomotives, Petersburg became an important lifeline to the Confederate capital at Richmond, and General Grant decided that this link must be cut. On June 9, 1864, Generals Smith and Hancock began the siege of Petersburg, starting a 10-month campaign of trench warfare that ultimately led to General Robert E. Lee's surrender at Appomattox, and the end of the war itself in April the following year. The railroad was used to evacuate the entire Confederate Government staff from Richmond to Danville, Virginia, on April 2, 1865, less than a week before the surrender of Robert E. Lee.

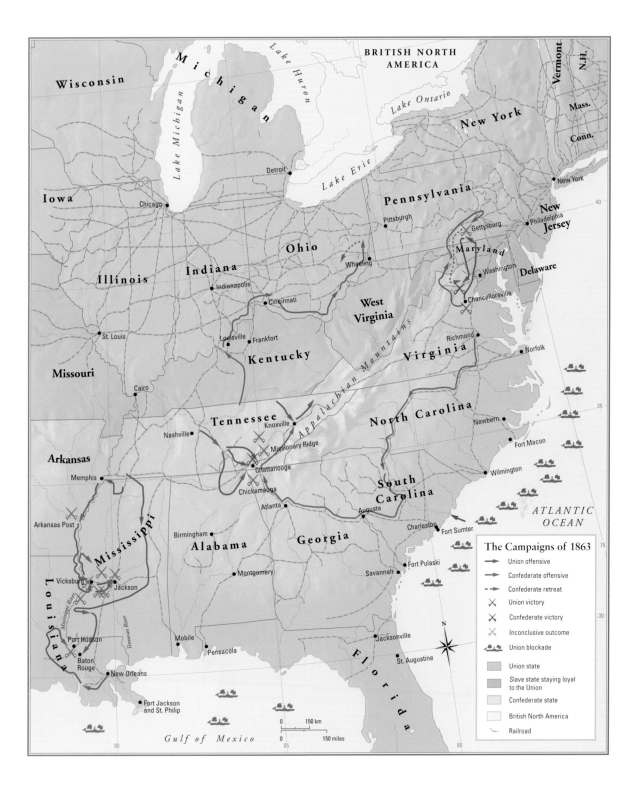

The Campaigns of 1863

→ Union offensive
→ Confederate offensive
⇢ Confederate retreat
✕ Union victory
✕ Confederate victory
✕ Inconclusive outcome
⛴ Union blockade

Union state
Slave state staying loyal to the Union
Confederate state
British North America
⌇ Railroad

Wisconsin

Michigan

Lake Michigan

Lake Huron

Lake Ontario

BRITISH NORTH AMERICA

Lake Erie

Vermont

N.H.

New York

Mass.

Conn.

Iowa

Detroit

Chicago

Pennsylvania

Pittsburgh

Gettysburg

Philadelphia

New Jersey

New York

Illinois

Indiana

Indianapolis

Cincinnati

Ohio

Wheeling

West Virginia

Maryland

Washington

Delaware

Chancellorsville

St. Louis

Louisville Frankfort

Kentucky

Richmond

Norfolk

Virginia

Missouri

Cairo

Tennessee

Knoxville

Nashville

Missionary Ridge

Appalachian Mountains

North Carolina

Newbern

Fort Macon

Arkansas

Memphis

Chattanooga

Chickamauga

Wilmington

Arkansas Post

Atlanta

Augusta

South Carolina

Charleston Fort Sumter

ATLANTIC OCEAN

Mississippi

Birmingham

Alabama

Georgia

Vicksburg Jackson

Montgomery

Savannah

Fort Pulaski

Louisiana

Port Hudson

Mississippi River

Tennessee River

Mobile

Pensacola

Jacksonville

St. Augustine

N

Baton Rouge

New Orleans

Florida

Fort Jackson and St. Philip

Gulf of Mexico

0   150 km
0   150 miles

STANDARDIZING THE RAILROAD GAUGE

THE CIVIL WAR EMPHASIZED THE NEED FOR COMMUNICATION BETWEEN EAST AND WEST. IT ALSO HIGHLIGHTED THE PROBLEMS CAUSED BY THE DIFFERENT RAIL GAUGES.

I t was national defense that led to the introduction of the Enabling Act in Congress, which was passed in the House of Representatives in May and approved by the Senate in June 1862. President Lincoln signed the Pacific Railroad Act on July 1, 1862. The Act empowered the Central Pacific Railroad Company to build a line from California eastward and appointed a new company, the Union Pacific Railroad Company, to provide a connection between a point on the western boundary of the State of Iowa and the 100th meridian (the exact point to be determined by the President), namely "...to the western boundary of the State of Nevada, there to meet and connect with the line of the Central Pacific Railroad Company of California." This was all due to be completed by July 1, 1874. The Act also provided for land grants and bond issues to help finance the railroad, which provided a strip of land 130 yds (119 m) wide along its whole length. In addition, there was a grant of 3,000 acres (1,214 ha) of land "to be freely selected by the railway authorities within 10 miles (26 km) of the tracks for every mile of line." There was still difficulty in raising money, so in July 1864, Lincoln doubled the land grants.

Although the President had signed the formal Enabling Act, there were disagreements and disputes from the start. The engineers wanted the new line to connect with the existing standard-gauge line east from Bellevue, Missouri, and started construction there, spending $100,000 before the president forced a stop. Lincoln specified Council Bluffs, Iowa, across the Missouri and opposite Omaha, Nebraska, as the Union Pacific railhead, and he was not prepared to change his decision.

California already had a 5 ft (1.52 m) gauge line east from San Francisco to Sacramento, and Lincoln supported its demand for that gauge on the new line. But Congress prescribed standard gauge through an Act that declared, "the gauge of the Pacific Railroad and its branches throughout the whole

Although standard gauge predominated among railroads of the North, in the South, 5 ft (1.52 m) gauge was commonly used. A number of other gauges were employed throughout the East. The need for a nationwide standardization became imperative.

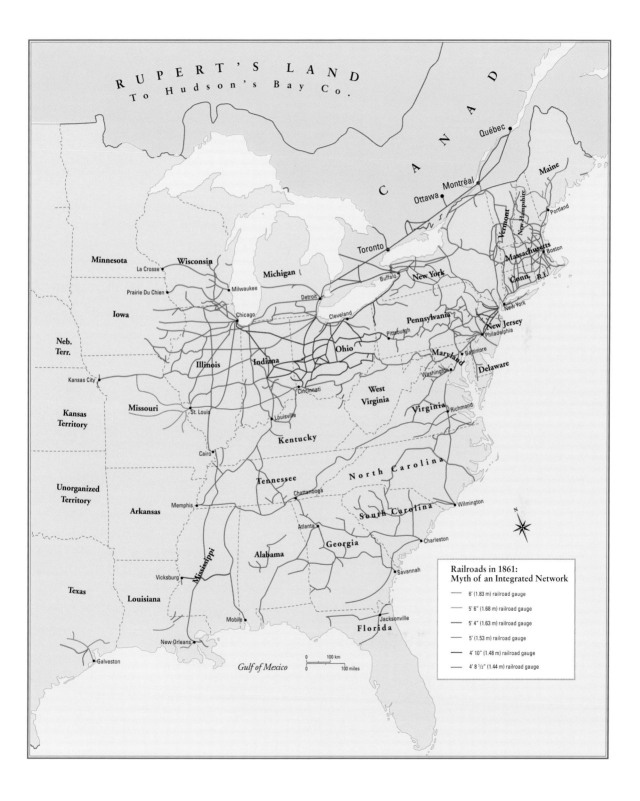

RUPERT'S LAND
To Hudson's Bay Co.

CANADA

Québec

Ottawa Montréal
Maine

Vermont New Hampshire Portland

Toronto Buffalo New York Massachusetts Boston
Conn. R.I.
New York

Minnesota Wisconsin Michigan
La Crosse Milwaukee Detroit Cleveland Pennsylvania New Jersey
Prairie Du Chien Chicago Pittsburgh Philadelphia
Iowa Maryland Baltimore
Neb. Illinois Indiana Ohio Delaware
Terr. Cincinnati Washington
Kansas City West Virginia Richmond
Kansas Missouri Virginia
Territory St. Louis Louisville
Kentucky
Cairo North Carolina
Unorganized Tennessee Chattanooga South Carolina Wilmington
Territory Memphis
Arkansas Atlanta Charleston
Georgia
Mississippi Savannah
Alabama
Texas Vicksburg Jacksonville
Louisiana Florida
Mobile
New Orleans

Galveston

Gulf of Mexico

0   100 km
0   100 miles

N

Railroads in 1861:
Myth of an Integrated Network

——— 6' (1.83 m) railroad gauge
——— 5' 6" (1.68 m) railroad gauge
——— 5' 4" (1.63 m) railroad gauge
——— 5' (1.53 m) railroad gauge
——— 4' 10" (1.48 m) railroad gauge
——— 4' 8 ½" (1.44 m) railroad gauge

extent, from the Pacific coast to the Missouri River, shall be, and hereby is, established at 4 ft 8 in (1.44 m)." This also officially established the standard gauge as the gauge for railroads throughout the United States, as it is today.

The rail gauge, as already noted, was standardized at 4 ft 8 in (1.44 m), and this enabled former isolated systems to be joined and rolling-stock standards to be established, although the process took quite a long time. It was not until 1886 that railroads in the South, almost all built to 5 ft (1.52 m) gauge, were converted to standard gauge.

While major existing railroads consolidated on the 4 ft 8 in (1,435 mm) gauge, there developed strong support for narrow-gauge lines, particularly the 3 ft (0.91 m) gauge. The Denver & Rio Grande Railroad is probably the best example. The Denver & Rio Grande was incorporated in 1870 and, with the mountainous terrain of Colorado and New Mexico to contend with, chose the narrow gauge because it was less costly to build than standard gauge. Locomotives and cars were smaller and cheaper, tracks could follow the contours and curves of mountainous terrain more easily, and the smaller rolling stock required smaller cuts and tunnels.

The original intention was to build from Denver, Colorado, south to Pueblo, west along the Arkansas River and over the Poncha Pass into the San Louis Valley, then south following the Rio Grande to El Paso, Texas. In 1877, there was the silver rush at Leadville, Colorado, and this resulted in skirmishes with the Santa Fe Railroad over the occupancy of Raton Pass and the Royal Gorge on the Arkansas River. The Denver & Rio Grande gave way and changed its ultimate goal to Salt Lake City.

While homesteaders received free land from the government, large tracts of land were granted to the railroads by the states and the federal government, with the goal of encouraging the railroads to construct their tracks where few people lived, and to help settle the country. The map of the Union Pacific Railroad Land Grant, below, shows a portion of Nebraska. It was published by H. R. Parge, Omaha, in 1880.

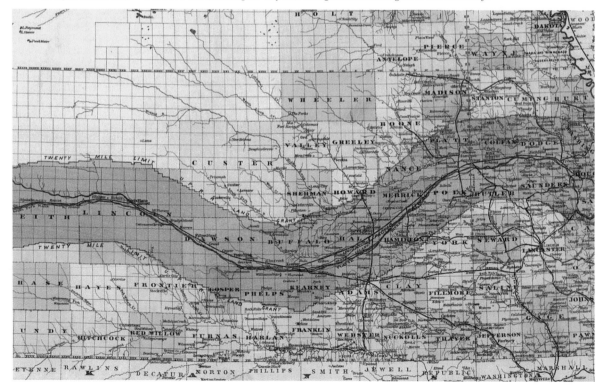

In 10 years, the Denver & Rio Grande had built lines between Denver and Pueblo, Leadville, Walsenburg, Alamosa, and Antonito to Chama, New Mexico. A year later, there was a line from Chama to Durango, and another from Salida to Gunnison. Within 30 years, many of the narrow-gauge lines were converted to either mixed gauge or standard gauge, although narrow gauge remained on some routes well into the 20th century.

The period following the end of the Civil War saw expansion of the rail tracks westward and the uniform adoption of the standard gauge. The few non-standard-gauge lines of the eastern states, including the 6 ft (1.83 m) gauge Erie Railroad, and the 5 ft (1.52 m) gauge lines of the South were converted to standard gauge by 1886. There remained many miles of narrower, mainly 3 ft (0.91 m) gauge tracks, however, chosen for reasons of economy and the local terrain: the trains could negotiate sharper curves than those of standard or broad gauge lines.

The Durango & Silverton narrow gauge railroad was founded by the Denver & Rio Grande Railroad in 1879. By July, 1882, the track to Silverton, Colorado, was completed. Constructed to haul silver and gold ore from the San Juan Mountains, this historic train has been in continuous operation for more than 126 years, carrying passengers behind vintage steam locomotives and rolling stock indigenous to the line.

Building the Union Pacific Railroad

THE CENTRAL PACIFIC BEGAN CONSTRUCTION OF THE FIRST TRANSCONTINENTAL RAILROAD AT SACRAMENTO, CALIFORNIA, ON JANUARY 8, 1863. THE UNION PACIFIC SET OUT FROM COUNCIL BLUFFS, IOWA, ON DECEMBER 2, OF THAT YEAR.

The task of providing raw materials for the construction of the Union Pacific Railroad was formidable. These included 6,250 ties and 50,000 tons (45,000 tonnes) of rails, which had to be carried over hundreds of miles by ox wagon, or by steamers on the Missouri River. As construction progressed, 30 rails at a time were conveyed to the end of the line by open railcars hauled by two horses; the final move to the end of the line was by a team of 10 men, five at each side of the car, who unloaded each length of rail and placed it in position. An average length of 2 miles (3.2 km) of railroad a day was constructed by these means. Construction westward to the Sierra Nevada was by groups of Irish laborers, and eastward from California by Chinese coolies.

On the plains, there were frequent attacks by Native Americans, who made building the railroads a hazardous operation. The tribes saw the railroads as a threat. Rails opened up new territory and were responsible for the virtual extinction of the buffalo (on which the whole economy of many Indian nations depended), destroyed the Native American hunting grounds, and led, ultimately, to their confinement in reservations.

Chinese laborers working on the Central Pacific line high in the Sierra Nevada, where snow added to their difficulties.

The construction gangs took everything they needed with them, and trains of special dormitory cars accompanied the construction teams. Every few miles, a new "end-of-track" construction town grew up, complete with saloons, gambling houses, and brothels operated by unscrupulous hangers-on, who saw a way of making easy money. Known as "Hell-on-Wheels," the traveling community would often revolt. On one occasion, an Army detachment from Fort Russell, Wyoming, had to be called in to restore order, resulting in the whole population being run out of the shantytown, permitted to return only when a measure of law and order had been re-established. The settlements were home to more than just the railroad builders. Major Henry C. Parry, traveling to Colorado noted, "I found as I passed through North Platte that the Indians had driven all the traders and miners in from the mountains." Massachusetts newspaper editor Samuel Bowles—the man credited with coining the phrase "Hell-on-Wheels"—wrote, "At North Platte [Nebraska] they were having a good time gambling, drinking, and shooting each other."

Working in the intense heat, teams of workers lay down track in Nevada as the Central Pacific Railroad progresses eastward. A telegraph line kept pace with the track. The hand-picked gang of Irish rail-layers, backed by a small army of trackmen, set an all-time record of 10 miles (26 km) of track, working from sunrise to sunset on April Day in 1869.

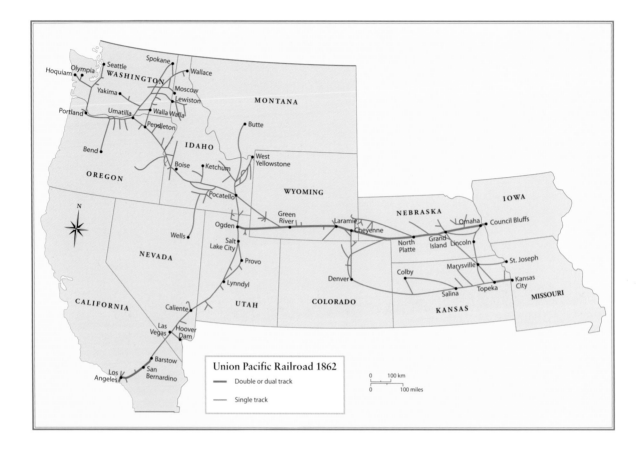

Union Pacific Railroad 1862
— Double or dual track
— Single track

After its meeting with the Central Pacific at Promontory Point, the Union Pacific Railroad spread northwest and southwest, laying tracks from Ogden, Utah, into Oregon and Washington, and across Nevada to Los Angeles, California.

Opposite page: The Union Pacific advertises the first passenger trains through to the Pacific, May 10 being the date of the "last spike" ceremony.

By 1867, the Union Pacific line over the Rockies was under construction, reaching its maximum altitude of 8,247 ft (13,272 m) at Sherman Hill, between Cheyenne and Laramie, Wyoming. However, this was not all. The Central Pacific company built its road along watercourses up the western slopes of the Sierra Nevada, performing incredible feats of engineering with Chinese labor and the crudest of tools—notably gunpowder. Instead of stopping at the Nevada state line, the Central Pacific pressed on across the flat plains of Nevada and into Utah, making for the Great Salt Lake.

Both companies pushed forward as fast as possible, eager to obtain grants for land. They met in early 1869 in western Utah, but neither company would acknowledge the existence of the other. They continued to build parallel lines in opposite directions. It was on April 9 that a deputation representing both sides met in Washington D.C. and agreed that the meeting point of the two roads would be at Promontory Summit, a few miles north of the Great Salt Lake. (By now, the two competing railroads had a 225 mile (362 km) overlap!) Congress swiftly approved the meeting point.

The inauguration ceremony on May 10, 1869, at Promontory Summit in Utah, included the driving of two spikes of silver and two of gold into a specially polished California laurel tie by Governor Stanford of the State of California, President of the Central Pacific, and Dr. Thomas C. Durant, President of the Union Pacific. Two trains had been brought up face-to-face, the Central Pacific's train with Jupiter, a wood-burner, and the Union Pacific's locomotive No. 119 from Omaha, a coal-burner, both of them eight-wheelers. Both locomotives were detached from their cars and moved forward until their cowcatchers touched, at which point bottles of champagne were broken in celebration. The photographer A.J. Russell recorded the ceremony for posterity. It is not known how many people attended the event—it may be as few as 500 or as many as 3,000 government and railroad officials and track workers.

The locomotives were then recoupled to their respective cars and moved in turn over the ceremonial tie. Then conventional materials were used to replace the ceremonial spikes and tie, after souvenir-hunters had torn the latter to pieces. Six more ties and two rails had to be replaced over the next six months.

At the ceremony, Governor Stanford, said: "This line of rails connecting the Atlantic and Pacific, and affording to commerce a new transit, will prove, we trust, the speedy forerunner of increased facilities. The Pacific Railroad will, as soon as commerce shall begin fully to realize its advantages, demonstrate the necessity of such improvements in railroading as to render practicable the transportation of freights at much less rates than are possible under [any system] which has been thus far [anywhere been adopted. ...] rates of speed that will answer the demands of cheapness; and time cars and engines will be light or heavy, according to the speed required and the weight to be transported. In conclusion, I will add that we hope to do ultimately what is now impossible on long lines: transport coarse, heavy and cheap products, for all distance, at living rates to trade. Now, gentlemen, with your assistance, we will proceed to lay the last tie and rail, and drive the last spike."

The Union Pacific had built 1,086 miles (1,748 km) from Omaha, and the Central Pacific 689 miles (1,109 km) from Sacramento in five years under the Congressional deadline. The "first total cost" was officially returned as $115,214,587.75—a good price for opening up the West.

In just under three decades from the opening of the first-ever American railroad, the rails extended from the Atlantic to the Pacific. Passengers and freight could now travel from

The inauguration ceremony at Promontory Point, Utah, May 10, 1869. With locomotives from both railroads nose to nose, silver and gold spikes were driven in to complete the first transcontinental railroad in the United States.

Opposite page: The Central Pacific's locomotive at the ceremony was named Jupiter. This fully working replica is on display at Promontory Point, long since bypassed by the railroad, which now takes a shorter route across the Great Salt Lake.

New York City to San Francisco, although at first such through traffic was chiefly freight. The railroad now connected New York with Philadelphia, Pittsburgh, Chicago, Omaha, Cheyenne, Ogden, Salt Lake City, Sacramento, and San Francisco. Track construction was rudimentary, by European standards, with rough-hewn wood ties laid either with minimal ballast or even directly on the soil or rock. Steel, flat-bottomed rails were laid directly on the ties and secured, for the most part, by spikes driven into the ties on each side of the rail. Tracks were normally unfenced, and undefended against cattle and other wild animals, as well as marauding Indians and the lawless. It made the use of powerful headlights and cowcatchers (not to mention armed guards at times) essential.

The electric telegraph was an essential feature of these early railroads and it was specified in the Enabling Act that the coast-to-coast operation was to be a continuous railroad and telegraph line. The telegraph was used as a crude signaling system, as the location of a train between depots had to be known before another train was dispatched. The telegraph was also a valuable asset to the many lonely townships along a route, providing contact with the outside world.

The Union Pacific had their locomotive No. 119 at the ceremony. It is represented at present-day Promontory Point by this magnificently colored, gleaming replica.

LANDMARKS IN LOCOMOTIVE DESIGN, 1860-80

TO KEEP PACE WITH THE EXPANSION OF THE RAILROADS AND THEIR EVER-INCREASING TRAFFIC, MOTIVE POWER HAD TO DEVELOP. IT DID THIS WITH THE HELP OF TECHNOLOGICAL INNOVATION.

Financial panics and the Civil War had reduced the number of locomotive constructors, but those who survived were in a strong position. Some railroads, like the Pennsylvania and the Reading, were building their own locomotives, and had developed design teams to produce engines specifically suited to their needs. There were still a number of independent builders, however, the two best known being Baldwin and the American Locomotive Company (ALCO). Other well-known names were Long & Norris of Philadelphia, Pennsylvania, Norris Brothers of Schenectady, New York, Sellers Brothers of Cincinnati, Ohio, and Eastwick & Harrison also of Philadelphia (and later of Aleksandrovsk, Russia).

The fundamentals of American steam locomotive design had been well established by 1870 and differed in some important respects from contemporary European practice.

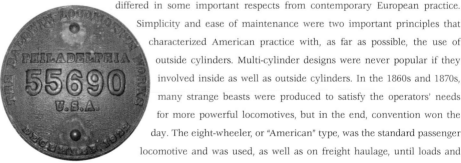

An example of a steam locomotive builders' plate, from Baldwin. These were carried on all locomotives, giving the builder's name, construction number, and the date the locomotive was completed.

Simplicity and ease of maintenance were two important principles that characterized American practice with, as far as possible, the use of outside cylinders. Multi-cylinder designs were never popular if they involved inside as well as outside cylinders. In the 1860s and 1870s, many strange beasts were produced to satisfy the operators' needs for more powerful locomotives, but in the end, convention won the day. The eight-wheeler, or "American" type, was the standard passenger locomotive and was used, as well as on freight haulage, until loads and gradients made the provision of more specialized types necessary. The first compound-expansion locomotive was built in the United States for the Erie Railroad. It was a rebuild of No. 122, by Shepherd Iron Works of Buffalo, New York.

The first official World's Fair in the United States, the "International Exhibition of Arts, Manufactures and Products of the Soil and Mine" opened in Philadelphia, Pennsylvania in spring 1876. The extravaganza celebrated the 100th anniversary of the signing of the Declaration of Independence, the country's emergence from reconstruction, and scientific, industrial and cultural successes. More than 10 million visitors attended—equivalent to about 20 percent of the population (although many were repeat visitors). On display in the Machinery Building were classic and new designs of locomotives, such as the new freight-hauling "Moguls" from Baldwin (whose stand is visible in the stereograph).

In 1866, the class name "Mogul" was probably applied for the first time to a 2-6-0 locomotive, fitted with a two-wheeled Bissell truck and constructed by the Taunton Locomotive Works, Massachusetts, for the Central Railroad of New Jersey. The Pennsylvania Railroad commenced building its own locomotives in their Juniata, Pennsylvania shops.

"Helpers" to assist trains over the steep gradients of the Alleghenies were built with more driving axles and, often, no carriers. Typical was James Millholland's 0-12-0 Pennsylvania, built in 1863 in the Reading's own shops. It was intended for pusher service for coal trains on the summit between the Delaware and Schuylkill rivers in eastern Pennsylvania, but it had to be rebuilt in 1870 as an 0-10-0

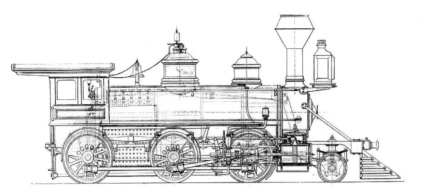

FREIGHT LOCOMOTIVE, "MOGUL" TYPE.

A technical drawing of a Baldwin "Mogul" 2-6-0 freight-hauling locomotive, which became a standard type during the 1880s.

Mitchell's Consolidation, the first 2-8-0 wheel configuration, was built by the Baldwin Locomotive Company in 1866.

for better curving ability, and was then provided with a tender.

Interest was soon shown in coupled eight- and ten-wheelers of more conventional design, and although the inferior tracks of the time often handicapped locomotives with long wheelbases, Alexander Mitchell, the master mechanic of the Lehigh Valley Railroad, drew up a design for a 2-8-0 freight locomotive fitted with a Hudson-Bissell truck. In 1865, Baldwin built it from Mitchell's drawings with some reluctance, predicting it would be a "colossal failure." Instead, the machine demonstrated its prowess by hauling a train of 100 empty coal cars weighing 340 tons (306 tonnes), up a 1 in 67 (1.5 percent) gradient near Delano, Pennsylvania. To commemorate the railroad's merger with a number of feeder lines, which included the Beaver Meadow Railroad, the Lehigh Valley christened the locomotive "Consolidation," which henceforward gave its name to the 2-8-0 configurations. Over 30,000 Consolidation workhorses were constructed in United States shops for many railroads over the following 45 years.

Encouraged by his success, Mitchell designed a 2-10-0 in 1867, of which two were built by James Norris's engine works at Lancaster, Pennsylvania. But the "Ant" and the "Bee", as they were named, were handicapped by poor tracks and derailed so frequently that they were converted to 2-8-2s. Much later, in 1897, Baldwin named some 2-8-2s for Japan's Nippon Railroad "Mikado," and this was the name by which the type was known. On the other side of the continent, big was also deemed to be beautiful.

In 1882 the Central Pacific Railroad built a 4-8-0 locomotive, "Mastodon," designed by the mechanical superintendent, A.J. Stevens, at its Sacramento, California shops to cope with the steep grades of the Sierra Nevada. It was capable of hoisting a 216-ton (240-tonne) train up a 25 mile (40 km) grade with a vertical rise of 3,900 ft (1,189 km)—an average gradient of 1 in 34, or 3 percent. Twenty more were built by Danforth-Cooke. Encouraged by their success, in 1883 Stevens designed a 4-10-0, El Gobernador, which weighed 66 tons (73 tonnes) without a tender—by far the largest American locomotive at that time. But the Central Pacific's trestles had to be strengthened to accommodate it, and it stood idle for a year. It turned out to be an unreliable machine, often breaking down in the High Sierras.

The first "rack" railroads were demonstrated by Sylvester Marsh in the United States and by Nicholas Riggenbach in Switzerland. On July 3, 1869, Marsh's Mount Washington Cog Railway opened in New Hampshire. It was recognized as the first cog (or rack-and-pinion) railway in the world by some six months. A cog railway has a special toothed rack rail, usually between the running rails. The trains are fitted with one or more cog wheels or pinions

that mesh with the rack rail. This enables the trains to climb steep gradients. Marsh's railway climbs Mount Washington in New Hampshire. The railway ascends the mountain from an elevation of about 2,700 ft (823 m) above sea level and ends at the summit of Mt. Washington, at an elevation of 6,288 ft (1,917 m). It is the second steepest rack railway in the world, with an average grade of over 25 percent and a maximum grade of 37.41 percent.

The 3-mile (4.8-km) long railway has always used a team of vintage steam locomotives, apart from an experimental diesel that was introduced between 1976 and 1981. The train ascends at 2.8 mph (4.5k/h) in about 65 minutes, and descends at 4.6 mph (7.4k/h) in about 40 minutes. Near the end of the decade, in 1869, other technical developments were coming to the fore. Experiments with compressed-air brakes (non-automatic) were enthusing George Westinghouse.

Few photographs exist of the muscular, 14-wheel, "El Gobernador," the 73-ton locomotive built by Central Pacific Railroad at its Sacramento, California shops. It was the only locomotive of the 4-10-0 wheel arrangement to operate on United States rails. When built, it was the largest railroad locomotive in the world.

"Peppersass," the vertical-boiler locomotive used to build Sylvester Marsh's Mount Washington Cog Railway in the 1860s, was wrecked in an accident in 1929, during which many passengers were injured and one—the photographer Daniel P. Rossiter—died when a cog tooth broke, causing an uncontrolled descent of the 25-ft (7-m) high trestle "Jacob's Ladder." Peppersass' boiler was not ruptured and, after being repaired, the historic old engine is now on permanent display at the cog railroad's base station.

The locomotive "Ammonoosuc," named after the ravine that lies on the west side of Mt. Washington, belches steam as it nudges its railcar up the 37.4 percent gradient of the trestle "Jacob's Ladder". The locomotive burns one ton (0.9 tonne) of coal and consumes 1,000 gallons (3.785 lt) of water on the 3-mile (4.8-km) ride, which generates the necessary energy to climb the 6,288 ft (1,917 m) mountain. Engine and coach are pulled up the mountain by a cog with 19 teeth, which mesh into the track's central rail. Two sets of ratchets are engaged during ascents, which keep the trains from moving backward at stops or in the event of an emergency, causing a distinctive "clinking" sound when going uphill.

Spreading railroad networks, 1865-79

AFTER THE END OF THE CIVIL WAR, THE UNITED STATES' RAILROADS CONTINUED TO EXPAND RAPIDLY, CONNECTING TOWNS AND CITIES ACROSS THE CONTINENT AND REVOLUTIONIZING COMMUNICATION.

I n terms of railroad expansion, the years between 1865 and 1879 witnessed considerable growth. America's expanding railroad network fed the growth of the cities. Railroads helped people move to the cities, and they transported the raw materials for industry. Cities flourished due to nearby resources: for example, Pittsburgh developed into a significant iron and steel manufacturing city because the surrounding area was rich in iron ore and coal. Other cities such as New York, Chicago and Kansas City also benefited from improved transportation of goods. In 1866, the Baltimore & Ohio Railroad leased the Central Ohio line from Bellaire, Ohio, through Newark to Columbus. The New York & Oswego Midland Railroad was incorporated to build a

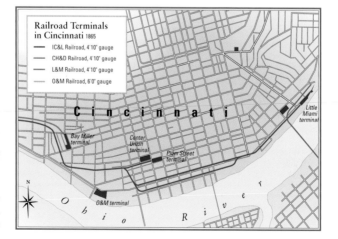

Cities benefited vastly from the expansion of the railroad network. By 1865, Cincinnati, Ohio, for example, was served by four different railroads, all operating on the 4 ft 10 in (1.47 m) gauge, with the exception of the Ohio & Mobile, which used 6 ft (1.83 m).

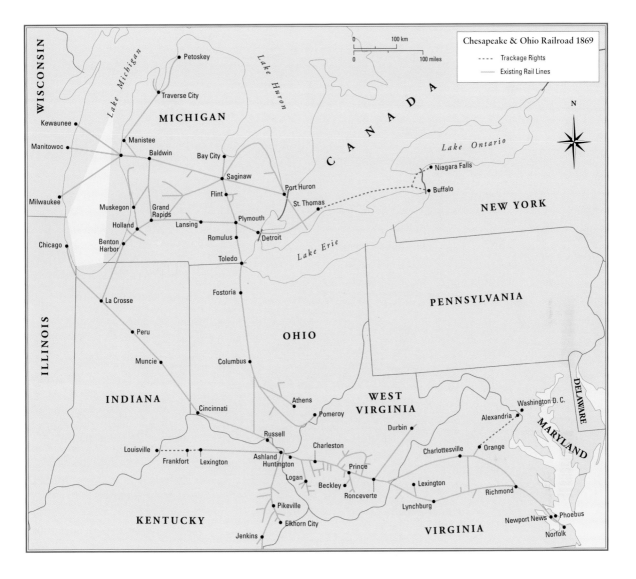

Chesapeake & Ohio Railroad 1869
- - - - Trackage Rights
───── Existing Rail Lines

line from Oswego, New York, on the shore of Lake Ontario, to the New Jersey state line, and thence to a terminal on the Hudson River. The Montgomery Railroad reconstruction began with a gauge conversion from standard to 5 ft (1.52 m). In 1867, the Illinois Central reached Dubuque, Iowa (Sioux City, 1870), and Cornelius Vanderbilt gained control of the New York Central Railroad.

Beginning the next year, Col. Cryus Kurtz Holliday turned the first shovelful of earth in Kansas City, Kansas, construction of the Santa Fe Railroad. This railroad began in 1860 as the Atchison & Topeka Railroad, with the intention of connecting Atchison and Topeka, Kansas with Santa Fe, New Mexico. Once connected to Santa Fe, it was renamed the Atchison, Topeka & Santa Fe. The railroad soon began to expand to the east and west, taking over other companies and building new tracks, until it reached

The Chesapeake & Ohio Railroad was formed in 1869, in Virginia, from many smaller railroads. It formed the basis for the city of Newport News and the coal piers—transloading facilities for coal between rail and ship—on Hampton Roads, and forged a rail link to the Midwest.

Grand Central Depot, seen here in 1880, was the forerunner of today's Grand Central Terminal, and was built between 1869-71. The train shed had two innovative facilities in United States railroads: the platforms were elevated to the height of the cars, and the roof was a balloon shed with a clear span over all the tracks. Cornelius Vanderbilt died on the same day a blizzard caused the glass roof to collapse.

Needles, California in 1883 and Los Angeles in 1885. By 1900 it was connected with San Francisco. At its largest, the Atchison, Topeka & Santa Fe Railroad covered more than 13,000 miles (21,000 km).

In 1868, the Lehigh & New England Railroad was inaugurated. It had been constructed specifically for the haulage of cement, slate, and anthracite from Hauto, Pennsylvania, to Campbell Hall, New York. Also that year, the Virginia Central and Covington & Ohio railroads consolidated as the Chesapeake & Ohio Railroad. The very first dining car to appear on North American railroads, named "Delmonico's," had its initial trip on the Chicago & Alton Railroad.

Existing tracks continued to be extended by this time, notably the Baltimore & Ohio Railroad, which, in 1869, had penetrated westward by leasing a line from Newark to Sandusky, Ohio, on Lake Erie. The Central of Georgia Railroad leased the South Western Railroad, and in so doing gained access from Macon westward to Columbus and then southward into Alabama at Eufaula. The Evansville, Terre Haute & Chicago Railroad

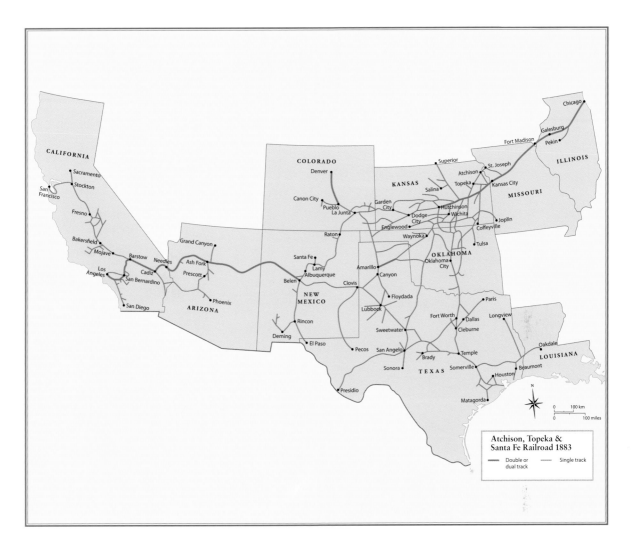

Atchison, Topeka &
Santa Fe Railroad 1883
—— Double or ——— Single track
dual track

was chartered, the Lackawanna Railroad leased the Morris & Essex Railroad to avoid using the Central of New Jersey tracks, while the New York, Ontario & Western Railroad opened its tracks from Oswego, on Lake Ontario, southward to Norwich, New York. The New York Central Railroad and the Hudson River Railroad were consolidated by Cornelius Vanderbilt as the New York Central & Hudson Railroad.

In 1869 Vanderbilt bought 23 acres (9.2 hectares) of land at the junction of 42nd Street and Fourth Avenue—a 45-minute journey from the center of the city—to house a rail depot for New York. The Grand Central Depot opened two years later, and included a facade which stretched 250 ft (762 m) along the street. The station was designed to bring the trains of the New York City & Hudson Railroad, the New York & Harlem Railroad, and the New York & New Haven Railroad together in one large station.

Vanderbilt had already constructed an impressive freight terminal for his railroad—a three-storey building decorated with a sculpture depicting various stages of his business career. Such was the growth

The Atchison, Topeka & Santa Fe became one of the largest and most well-known railroads in the United States. It was chartered in 1863, and portions of its main line from Chicago, through Kansas, New Mexico, and Arizona to California ran over the route of the original Santa Fe Trail. In 1996, it merged with the Burlington Northern to form the Burlington Northern Santa Fe.

The first transcontinental railroad was created by the meeting of two railroad companies. The Central Pacific RR set out from Sacramento, California, on January 8, 1863, while the Union Pacific RR struck out from Council Bluffs, Iowa, in December of that year. After a mammoth construction project, on May 10, 1869, both roads were joined at Promontory Summit, Utah, forming a 1,775-mile (2,856km) rail route across the country.

of the railroad, the New York terminal was expanded and renovated twice before 1900, and in 1902 plans for a new station for the latest electric trains—Grand Central Station—were being drawn up. That building opened in 1913 and continues to welcome rail passengers to New York today. Three problems doomed the old station—congestion, the suffocating smoke from the steam engines, and chaos in baggage transfer. Exacerbating the problems, work also commenced in 1869 on a new connecting railroad from Spuytn Duyvil—a subsection of the Riverdale section of the Bronx in New York City—to Mott Haven, the southernmost neighborhood in the South Bronx.

Over the following decade, competition between rival railroad companies and locomotive manufacturers began to become extremely intense, as the United States' transportation system continued to flourish.

Meanwhile, new administrative structures were appearing on the railroads, which in due course would become the corporate model for other big industries. The railroads were unprecedented in their size, and also in their fixed and operating costs. Moreover, if armies and navies are excepted, a railroad's labor force could be vastly in excess of what had hitherto been normal. Whereas the biggest US manufacturing enterprises might employ hundreds of workers, by the 1850s many railroads were employing thousands, and in the 1880s, tens of thousands. Moreover, those workers were spread over hundreds of miles so central administrators would rarely, if ever, see them at work; that obviously required new methods of supervision.

Added to this was that day-to-day railroad operation was costly and could be dangerous if badly done. Hence there was a succession of many and varied decisions to be made, like how many trains to operate over a given stretch, how many and what kinds of cars would be needed, and when to repair a given item of track or rolling stock. Then there were crucial longer-term decisions, like how much should be charged for each item of traffic. To do that required a knowledge of the cost to the railroad of performing a given function, so a new skill of cost-accounting was required.

It was probably the Baltimore & Ohio Railroad that introduced the important innovation of dividing management into separate operating and financial departments. It was the latter that dealt with accounting and helped a railroad's treasurer settle questions of fund-raising and the division of the revenue between profits and maintenance or repair. The operating department was responsible for the running of trains and the services needed to do that.

Soon the fast-growing Pennsylvania and Erie lines made their own contributions. The lines of authority down the system were defined for the several specialized managers, with particular attention paid to the prompt and accurate transmission of information up and down those lines. Because of the geographical spread of the railroads, the railway division became an operating unit. A railroad would have several of these, each headed by a divisional superintendent responsible for decisions and instructions for his division. His executives, while carrying out his instructions, would also report to their appropriate central officers on what they were doing as regards maintenance programs and other vital matters.

It was not long before another department appeared, the traffic department, whose job it was to deal with freight and passengers in all matters except their actual movement. Its main business was obtaining passengers and freight—drumming up business—and processing them before and after their carriage. In the 1870s, largely because increasing competition required it, the Louisville & Nashville Railroad refined its costing techniques, so essential for setting the most profitable tariffs while still attracting customers. The resulting statistical service was imitated by other railroads, and in due course by other industries. In due course it also became a not-always-popular way of evaluating the performance of managers.

When consolidations created super-large railroads, the divisional system was found wanting and the railway region, containing several divisions, was set up. The example was followed later by several big manufacturing companies, including General Motors, but was eventually abandoned by the railroads. The increasing role of the federal government and the tendency for decisions to be no longer one-off events but merely the observance of a set routine, together made it advantageous for railroads to return to a highly centralized departmental form of management.

COMMERCIAL RIVALS

BY 1870, THE RAILROADS WERE THE OVERWHELMINGLY
DOMINANT MEANS OF MEDIUM- AND LONG-DISTANCE
TRANSPORT FOR PASSENGERS AND FREIGHT. NOW CAME
AN INTENSE AND OFTEN BITTER RIVALRY BETWEEN
RAILROAD COMPANIES.

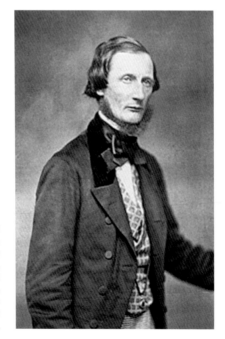

Cyrus W. Field (1819–92) had made a fortune by the age of 33. He pioneered the transatlantic telegraph cable in 1858. In 1884, the Canadian Pacific Railroad named the community of Field, British Columbia, Canada in his honor. Bad investments left Field bankrupt at the end of his life.

From a commercial point of view, by 1870 the die was cast and things did not change much in the running of the railroads until well into the 20th century. Wherever the rails advanced, the other carriers and coach firms retreated. Although the river steamboats were able to challenge the railroads on the big rivers, they could hold their own only on bulk carriage, not on speed. As time went on, locomotives developed the capability to become even faster.

The bitter rivalry that existed between transport companies for the domination of territory continued, and although the physical battles between rival concerns that had occurred over the previous three decades abated, they were replaced by more subtle, and often equally vicious, commercial battles. Many of the smaller railroads were consolidated into larger units; this was most pronounced in the New England states, where many railroads had grown up in the earlier years.

The first rail tunnel had been built through the Hoosac Range, part of the Western Massachusetts mountain range, in place of a canal tunnel that had been proposed some 50 years earlier. At the time of its completion, it was the second longest tunnel in the world (after the 8½ mile (13.7 km) long Mont Cenis Tunnel through the French Alps). The previously proposed canal route became a railroad to connect Boston, Massachusetts, with the Great Lakes at Oswego or Buffalo, New York. Begun in 1851 by the state of Massachusetts, the Hoosac (also called the Hoosic) Tunnel was not completed until 1875.

The project required the excavation of 1.8 m tons (2 m tonnes) of rock. First, a tunnel-boring machine was used, but it failed after excavating 10 ft (3 m). Builders resorted to hand digging, and later used the Burleigh Rock Drill, one of the first pneumatic drills. Tunneling also saw the introduction of large-scale commercial use of nitroglycerine and electric blasting caps.

Digging a central vertical shaft down through the mountain allowed tunnelers to expose two additional faces to excavate so that when the shaft was complete in 1870, workers dug outward from the center to meet the tunnels being dug from the east and west portals. Engineers built a 1,000 ft (305 m) elevator to hoist the excavated rock from the shaft.

The Hoosac Tunnel earned itself the nickname the "Bloody Pit"—and was considered to be haunted— due to the unhappy fact that 195 lives had been lost during its construction. Many of these deaths had been caused by the unstable nature of nitroglycerine.

This 1870 engraving, *The Great Race for the Western States*, caricatures the intense rivalry that developed between Cornelius Vanderbilt and Jay Gould, as the former attempted to gain control of the Erie Railroad from the latter. Vanderbilt is pictured saying "Now then Jim, no jockeying, you know!" while Gould replies "Let 'em rip, Commodore! But don't stop to water, or you'll be beat."

On its completion, the battle for control of the tunnel between six competing railroads resulted in a legislative committee proposal to consolidate all of them, which they all but turned down. The Fitchburg Railroad wanted to control the 4¾ mile (7.6 km) long tunnel, but the State would permit this only if the Fitchburg had its own route to the Hudson River. In the 1880s, the Fitchburg acquired three other railroads, including the Boston, Hoosac Tunnel & Western, and three branches. Ultimately, the Fitchburg became a part of the Boston & Maine Railroad.

The railroads were America's first big businesses, which meant that railroad promoters and managers had to work out entirely new approaches. In the 1850s, the problem of raising money had become acute; not only were there more projects chasing funds, but the size of the railroads was increasing. By the end of that decade at least ten railroads were capitalized at over $10 million, and there were a couple that reached $20 million. Railroads were expensive to build; just a mile of high-quality line could cost as much, say, as a new steamboat cost the railroads' rivals.

Following the earlier example of the canals, the first railroads had obtained much of their funding from their states, but this was restricted as taxpayers began to raise objections; in fact, some states were persuaded to amend their constitutions to forbid the funding of railroads. To some extent, local governments and cities filled the gap, and then the federal government helped by granting generous land grants to some of the new western lines. These land grants also became an issue (and still are, in history textbooks) although they assisted less than one-tenth of the railroad building. Local funding remained important, if only because it set the ball rolling on new projects.

But as time went on it was the private investor who provided the bulk of the capital. Many of these were local people who helped indirectly by buying the state and local securities that assisted the public authorities to finance the lines. Then they began to invest directly. Such local investors were special in

Jay Gould (1836–92) was seen by many as a railroad "pirate." A reckless speculator, by 1880 he owned 10,000 miles (16,000 km) of railroad route. He owned the Union Pacific Railroad and Western Union telegraph company.

Edward H. Harriman (1848–1909) was a successful stock broker who bought his first railroad in 1881. He took over the Union Pacific in 1890, the Southern Pacific in 1901, and the Erie Railroad in 1908.

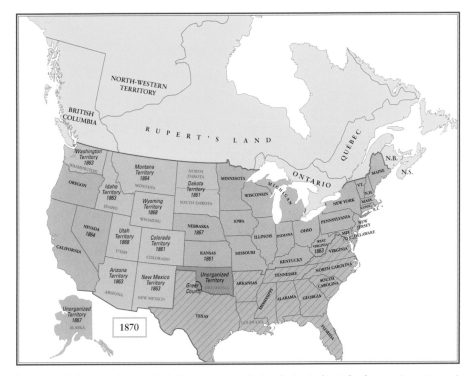

that they had their own interest in the line; its success in developing its hinterland was as important as its financial success. But local funding was rarely quite enough, and promoters went further afield to solicit funds. The distant investors they found, who tended to reside in the eastern states or Europe, were solely interested in getting a good return and did not really care about improving transportation.

The need to raise money led to the introduction of all kinds of new stock, notably including preferred stock, and also of new financial institutions. First it was local banks and local stock exchanges that provided the facilities, but with the increasing role of the distant investor more centralized institutions developed. At this time New York was in competition with Philadelphia and Boston, but its lead in financing railroads meant that it outpaced those two cities and its Wall Street became the nation's stock-trading center.

Simultaneously, the investment bank made its appearance with the function of bringing potential investors into financial contact with railroad projects. Such banks could inform potential investors of the merits of one or another investment. The investment banker thereby became an important and powerful figure, because he could recommend, or not recommend, investment in one or another railroad. He could therefore make or break a project and could have a strong influence on its promoters and managers. And when a railroad was bankrupt or nearly bankrupt such investment bankers could organize the rescue, often by fixing up amalgamations with other lines and thereby forwarding the process of creating big corporations that by the 20th century dominated the nation's transport system.

Americans tend to regard J. Pierpont Morgan as the greatest of these investment bankers and probably deservedly so, for from the 1890s he saved a number of lines that went on to become prosperous

By 1870, there was very little unorganized territory left. The country was steadily forming into a cohesive nation. In Canada, Rupert's Land had just been sold to the Canadian government, and the prairie provinces would be carved from it.

The Boston & Maine Railroad was originally chartered to connect Boston with Portland, but by a whole series of mergers it became a dense New England network, and also penetrated into Canada.

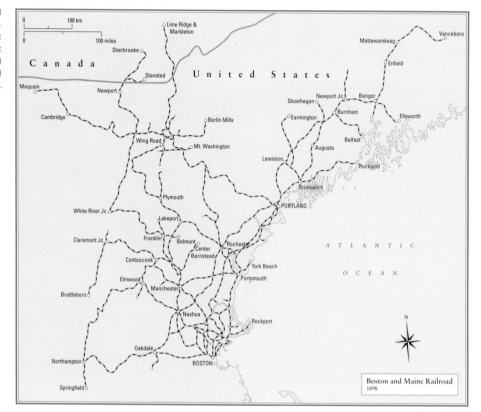

Boston and Maine Railroad
1898

components of the bigger systems. But he came only after a decade or two dominated by unscrupulous financiers who enriched themselves at the expense of shareholders and helped too often to build railroads that could never make a profit or indeed satisfy any real need. Famous names such as Daniel Drew, Cyrus Field, and Jay Gould implied not only railroad growth but also trickery. Cornelius Vanderbilt was somewhat more constructive but not without a tendency to bullying, violence, and deception, and Edward H. Harriman moved toward respectability and genuine usefulness.

Speculation by deception had arrived on the scene quite early. A repeated strategy was to promote railway-construction or landholding companies. Such companies would be formed by some or all of a projected railroad's directors who, in the case of a construction company, would make a contract for it to build the line with payment in the form of the railroad company's securities. They would then borrow money to build the line, using those securities as collateral. But they still had the power to dominate the railroad by virtue of those securities and they were free to raise the price of construction. Having virtually bankrupted the railroad by this, they still could walk away with a huge profit at the expense of the railroad's shareholders.

Often speculators could exploit state legislatures, but this was not always straightforward because one railroad project could persuade (or bribe) some law-makers while a competing railroad would work on others, and a given chamber could be split between two or more railroad parties. Eventually the public, and particularly railroad customers, became so enraged that regulation was put in place. This, at the same time, gave the judiciary greater power and influence. Railroad lawyers had a definite role in previous decades, but their importance was enhanced as regulation took hold.

It was distant farmers who really pushed for more regulation ball rolling. In the Midwest and West, for example, farmers were more dependent on railroads than in the East to move their products to market and railroads were fewer. The farmers complained that rates were unfair, with favored shippers receiving rebates. Rates were often higher where one railroad had a monopoly. As early as 1871, the state of Illinois passed legislation regulating freight rates and, in 1873, passenger fares. Minnesota did the same in 1874. By 1880, pressure for regulation had reached the national leveland resulted in the Interstate Commerce Act of February 1887, effective April 5, 1887.

The Interstate Commerce Commission (I.C.C.), the first president of which was Judge Thomas M. Cooley, was set up by the Act to regulate all railroads engaged in interstate commerce, even if they were located entirely within one state. Later, the Act also applied to motor carriers, water carriers (riverboats, barges, ferries, etc.) that are owned or controlled by railroads, and freight forwarders operating in interstate commerce. The Act stated that rates charged by the railroads had to be "just and reasonable," but unfortunately the members of the commission were unable to agree amongst themselves as to what was meant by "reasonable."

The Hoosac tunnel was the first railroad tunnel built in the United States. Its completion led to a battle between several railroads for control of it.

In exchange for land grants, the government stipulated that the railroads had to provide reduced-rate transportation for government property, mail, and employees. This provision continued well into the 20th century, by which time the government had received more than 10 times the value of the land it had granted. Railroads were forbidden to give preference, advantage, special rates, or rebates to any person, company, location, or type of traffic. They were not allowed to charge more for a short haul than for a long haul. Pooling (that is, sharing of revenue or freight) was forbidden, and railroads were required to publish their rates and give advanced warning of any change. In general, this was accepted until, in 1897, the Supreme Court ruled that the I.C.C. had no power to fix rates, which took most of the bite out of the clause requiring that short haul should cost no more than long haul.

In time, other acts modified the terms of reference, and the I.C.C. became more powerful, with widespread responsibilities, with the effect that the railroads increasingly found themselves commercially inhibited.

RAILROAD DISPATCH AND SIGNALING, 1870-1900

THE INCREASED SPEED OF TRAINS BROUGHT SAFETY PROBLEMS. FROM 1851, TRAIN DISPATCHING FROM A CENTRAL POINT HAD BEEN INSTITUTED, AND ALL RAILROADS SET ABOUT INSTALLING TELEGRAPH LINES.

The earliest United States railroad signal installation was on the New Castle & Frenchtown Railroad in 1832, consisting of peach baskets suspended from masts and raised and lowered by pulleys. Their position (high, middle, or low) and color (black or white), conveyed information to trains and stations, whose staff observed them with telescopes. This ball signal became widely used, its aspect for "proceed" giving the term "highball."

In the first decades of the 19th century, there was a gradual change from locomotives burning wood in favor of coal or anthracite, both of which were plentiful. Geographical development led to mechanical improvement and more sophisticated operating methods. Locomotives and rolling stock grew in physical size, and train weights increased. Trackbeds were improved and tracks re-laid to stand up to the heavier rolling stock and higher speeds that commercial pressures demanded. But after a disastrous accident between New York City and Philadelphia in 1863, when two trains met head-on—and there had been many such incidents—Ashbel Welch, president of the New Jersey Canal & Railroad Companies, instituted a system of block working.

Welch installed a system of signals on the line between New Brunswick, New Jersey and Philadelphia, Pennsylvania. Each signal consisted of a red banner that was dropped into view by a signalman through a

hole in a box the moment a train had passed. The track ahead was thus closed (blocked) until a message was received over the telegraph from the next station that the train had passed. The block was then cleared and the red banner was removed. The railroad formally adopted the system on March 27, 1865.

There were a number of places where tracks of rival companies crossed on the level, at grade. One such point was on the prairie outside Chicago, Illinois, known as Grand Crossing, where the Illinois Central tracks crossed those of the rival Southern Michigan. It was notorious as train drivers would race to get to the crossing before rival trains, and in 1853, a serious collision resulted in a wrecked locomotive and cars, 16 passengers dead, and many more injured. This caused the authorities to issue an edict that no train could enter a crossing with another road at grade until after it had stopped and the crossing was seen to be clear. This rule was made state law in Massachusetts in 1854, and most states followed suit so the law was soon extended to apply to most busy junctions.

This grade crossing rule led ultimately to the adoption of an invention of 1856 by the English engineer John Saxby, which eliminated this nuisance and led to the development of the modern signaling system.

Ensuring safety at a multitrack railroad crossing like this would be impossible without an effective signaling system. Greater Grand Crossing is an official community area of Chicago, Illinois, located on the city's south side. The neighborhood's name is the result of an 1853 right of way feud between the Lake Shore & Michigan Southern Railroad and the Illinois Central Railroad, which led to a "frog war" and a crash that killed 16 people.

In Saxby's invention, levers from a central tower operated signals and switches, the levers being interlocked to eliminate incorrect movements. This system was first installed in the United States in 1870 and meant that instead of having several men operating switches, with the ever-present problem of communication, the control of train movements came into the hands of one operator. Now trains could run safely through such crossings and junctions without the need to "stop, look, and listen."

The trial of the system worked so well that the first permanent installation was made at East Newark, New Jersey, in February 1875, on what had become the Pennsylvania Railroad. It was refined in the light of experience, and soon trains were detected by electrical track circuits, invented by Dr. William Robinson of New Jersey in 1872. An electric current was fed into sections of the rails so that the passage of a train over those sections caused an electrical relay to operate and either work a signal or release a lock to enable the signalman to operate a switch or signal. It was vital for the system to be fail-safe, and the presence of a train "shorted" the relay coil so that the relay was de-energized and its contacts completed an electrical lock. At the same time, a light was illuminated on a diagram to show the controller that a particular section of track was occupied.

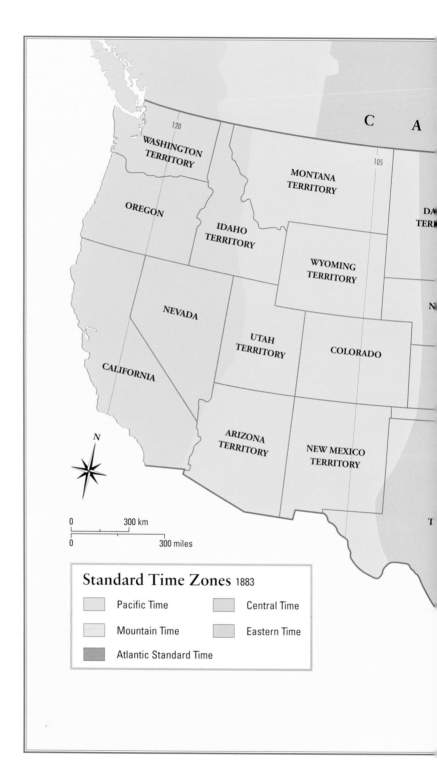

Standard Time Zones 1883

- Pacific Time
- Mountain Time
- Atlantic Standard Time
- Central Time
- Eastern Time

The General Time Convention of 1874 standardized time throughout North America, introducing time zones. These were adopted by the railroads in 1883, proving essential for the efficient operation of the railroads.

In the early 20th century, the "wigwag" was used at grade crossings. Its pendulum motion to signal the approach of a train—accompanied by a gong sound—was intended to mimic that of the crossing watchman swinging a red lantern from side to side, meaning, in railroad parlance, "stop."

In the early 1880s, compressed air was experimentally integrated with electric-circuit controls to operate switches and signals in complex switch interlocking arrangements. This meant that switches several miles away from any given control tower could be reliably operated in the correct sequence to establish a "safe route." By 1890, this all-American system was well established.

It took quite a long time for railroad chiefs to accept what many of them saw as obstructive: the costs of better signaling diverted funds from building new lines and money from investors' pockets; it was not until after 1885 that safe signaling enabled the "full stop" at grade crossings and junctions to be finally abolished. Productivity was improved by the passage of more trains through busy junctions, and time schedules were shortened. Gradually, signal systems and rules were standardized. It was largely the action of the railroads, through the General Time Convention of 1874—the body responsible for the introduction of a standard time and four time zones throughout the United States and Canada, which was finally adopted by the railroads in 1883—that rules were formulated for the harmonization of signaling, cars, train movements, and safety appliances. The rules were still only recommendations, rather than mandatory requirements—although non-observance was often not regarded favorably. The Convention became the American Railroad Association in 1891.

Mechanical signals themselves were initially of the rising and falling "ball" type, superseded by semaphore. The semaphore arm consisted of two parts: a blade, vane, or arm, pivoting at different angles, and a spectacle holding colored lenses, which moved in front of a lamp for night-time signaling. Vanes were combined or "somersault" types, in which the blade pivoted in the center, the arm separate from the spectacle. The blade projected horizontally in its most restrictive aspect; other angles indicated less restrictive aspects.

Semaphores are either "lower quadrant" or "upper quadrant" types. In the former, the blade pivots down for less restrictive aspects and in the latter, the blade pivots upward. It was common in the United States for train order signals to point the blade straight down to indicate "proceed." The color and shape of the blade were varied to show the type of signal and indication, for example, red, square-ended blades for "home" signals and yellow fishtail blades for "distant" signals. A third type, with a pointed end extending outward, may indicate "proceed at restricted speed after stopping." Semaphores were controlled through mechanical linkages from the tower by levers to move switches and signals. Signals were later operated by electric motors or hydraulically. They were designed to be fail-safe, so that if power is lost or a linkage broken, the blade moves by gravity into the horizontal position. Lower quadrant semaphores need counterweights to cause the blade to rise, which was one reason for a widespread switch to upper quadrant types.

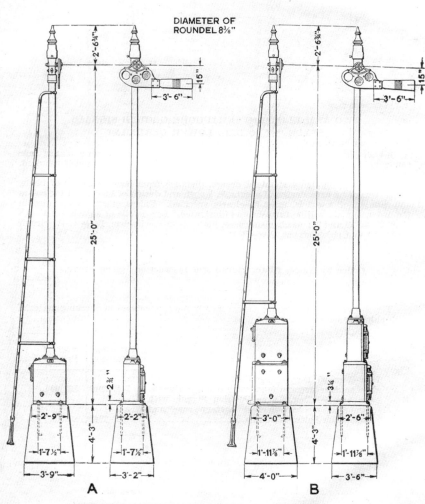

For many years, semaphore signals were used as a means of informing train crews about whether the train was cleared to proceed. Semaphore signals became the most widely-used form of mechanical signal, although they are now decreasing in number.

DIAMETER OF ROUNDEL 8⅜"

ONE ARM ELECTRIC SEMAPHORE GROUND SIGNALS
STYLE "S" 90 DEG. UPPER QUADRANT

ADVENT OF THE AIR BRAKE

INCREASED TRAIN SPEEDS REQUIRED BETTER BRAKES, SO HAND BRAKES WERE SUPERSEDED FIRST BY "SCREW-DOWN" MECHANICAL BRAKES, THEN BY STEAM BRAKES.

O riginally, passenger and freight cars were fitted with screw-down brakes, with brakemen riding the trains to operate them. Train speeds therefore had to be low enough to be able to stop in all conditions. To stop a train at a particular point needed good judgment. Each train carried an engine crew and a train crew of conductors and brakemen. When a train had to be stopped at a station, the engineer blew the steam whistle to alert the brakemen. The brakemen then ran along the tops of freight cars, jumping from car to car to apply the brakes and hope they had been given enough time to stop at the required point.

By the 1860s, a few applications of the European-style vacuum brake had been made on railroads on the Eastern Seaboard. The vacuum brake, which was dependent on atmospheric pressure, quickly lost effectiveness with increased altitude, so it had severe limitations on North American railroads. The most important improvement was the invention, in 1869, by George Westinghouse of the world's first continuous air brake. This was demonstrated between Pittsburgh and Steubenville, Ohio, on the Panhandle Railroad (the so-called Panhandle of West Virginia), later part of the Pennsylvania system. Compressed air, generated

Signaled by the engineer's whistle, the brakeman would walk the length of a train atop the cars—whatever the weather—to turn the brake wheel to apply the train's brakes. A brakeman's duties included ensuring the couplings between cars were correctly set, lining switches, and signaling to the train operators while performing switching operations.

by a steam-driven compressor and stored in a reservoir on the locomotive, was fed by a valve operated by the driver into a pipe that ran the length of the train. Cylinders on each vehicle pressed "shoes" onto the wheel tires. At the end of each car, a flexible pipe took the air to the next car. The trial installation prevented an accident when a farm wagon and horses became stuck on a grade crossing. The driver yanked the steam whistle cord to call the brakemen, then the air brake was applied. The train was brought to a safe stop and no lives were lost.

The "straight" air brake had three undesirable features. If one of the flexible pipes developed a leak, air escaped and all braking was lost. If cars became uncoupled on upgrades, only hand brakes could save them from rolling backward. In addition, with long trains, it took a considerable time for the air pressure to build up on the rearward cars. Two of these problems were solved in 1871 when Westinghouse invented the automatic brake with a fail-safe system. The air pipe was charged at a specific pressure all the time, and each car carried an auxiliary air tank and a triple valve, operated by a change in pressure in the main pipe. Any reduction of pressure in the pipe applied the brakes, while recharging the pipe to normal pressure released the car brakes.

With normal running conditions, all the auxiliary air tanks, air pipes, and flexible hoses were charged at the same pressure and formed a continuous system; the triple valves shut off the air to the brake cylinders. To stop the train, the engineer operated the control valve in his cab and reduced the air pressure in the train pipe. This caused the triple valve on each car to operate and allow air to flow

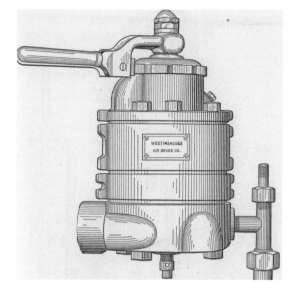

The control handle and valve used by the engineer to apply the train brakes in the Westinghouse air-brake system.

from the auxiliary tanks to the brake cylinders and so slow down or stop the train. The brakes were released by recharging the train pipe to normal pressure. This allowed the triple valve to void the air from the brake cylinders, at the same time equalizing the auxiliary tank pressure with the train pipe. The system has now been refined, but the fail-safe remains. Anything that results in a reduction of the air pressure in the train pipe will cause the brakes to be applied. The rupture of a flexible pipe, such as might be caused by a coupling breakage, will activate the brakes on all cars, bringing both the separated sections of the train to a stand. The brakes can then be released only manually on each car of the broken-away section of the train or by replacing the faulty flexible hose.

When in August 1871 a train out of Boston, Massachusetts, crashed, killing 29 passengers and injuring 57 as it plowed into the back of another train public and press denounced the directors of the railroad as murderers. The railroad reacted and the fitting of continuous brakes to passenger trains began, but it took another 20 years before they were fitted to all freight cars. Many railroads were reluctant to spend money, and mixed braked/non-braked trains resulted, with the "fitted" vehicles at the head. Regulations compelled car owners to fit through-brake pipes if not air brakes, so "mixed" trains could be run. Such trains presented an operating hazard on mountainous lines and braking was accompanied by bunching and surging as trains slowed, so that breakaways were not unknown.

In 1870, George Westinghouse had established a small works in Pittsburgh, Pennsylvania, with a work force of 105. By 1872, the Westinghouse automatic brake was in full production. Even so, with the link and pin couplers then in vogue, train separations were quite a common occurrence and the new brake took this into account. Passenger-train separations were considerably reduced and, by the late 1870s, most passenger rolling stock was equipped with some form of air brake. By the early 1880s developments were in hand to enhance the braking of freight trains and a new device was being fitted to freight vehicles: the brake cylinder pressure-retaining valve. This allowed safe operation on long grades and permitted the system to be recharged without having to release and re-apply the brakes.

ELECTRIC STREETCARS AND LOCOMOTIVES

COAL-FIRED, STEAM-POWERED STREETCARS WERE EXPERIMENTED WITH IN MANY UNITED STATES CITIES, BUT THEY PROVED TO BE UNSUITABLE FOR LARGE, CROWDED AREAS. THE SEARCH FOR A CLEANER, QUIETER, AND SAFER SOURCE OF POWER BEGAN.

Between 1870 and 1900, advances in technology saw steam heat and electric light replacing stoves and oil or gas lamps—a welcome move since wooden rail car construction was vulnerable to fires caused by overheated stoves or spilled oil. Automatic block signaling and the first electric locomotives appeared in the last 10 years of the 19th century. The standard eight-wheeler steam locomotive gave way to the rapid development of larger and more sophisticated types, as train weights and speeds increased with the introduction of much better and stronger tracks.

Electrical pioneer Thomas Edison produced a strange-looking electric locomotive in 1880 to demonstrate the practicality of electric traction, but the results were greeted with skepticism by steam. In 1888, however, the first practical electric streetcar appeared. Five years later, a four-wheeled electric locomotive was built and exhibited at the Columbian Exposition in Chicago, and by this time, a number of electric streetcar lines were already attracting the attention of those with the foresight to see this as the way forward.

Another unusual development was introduced by a partnership between two companies, Baldwin and Westinghouse. This was an electric locomotive that resembled a railcar without any visible means of driving it. The collaboration between the two companies was to continue until the second half of the 20th century. From these humble beginnings evolved the electric interurban railroad (the equivalent of today's light rapid-transit). The rolling stock was smaller than standard, and the rails ran partly in the

Opened in 1873, San Francisco's cable car system was an effective public transport system. Still in operation today, it is an icon of the city.

American inventor and businessman Thomas Alva Edison (1847–1931) developed many devices that influenced life around the world, including the phonograph and incandescent electric lamp. Applying the principles of mass production to the process of invention, he is credited with the establishment of the first industrial research laboratory, at Menlo Park, New Jersey. His company merged with a rival organization in 1892 to become General Electric.

The 1893 General Electric boxcab, displayed at the Chicago Exposition, was a new breed of locomotive in which machinery and crew areas are enclosed in a box-like superstructure. This electric boxcab was used on the New Haven Railroad, and is now on display in the Museum of Transport, St. Louis, Missouri.

street, partly on private rights-of-way. The emphasis was on local service, which main-line railroads found difficult and expensive to provide. Some traditional railroads encouraged neighboring electric interurban roads, but mainly, they ignored or treated them with open hostility.

The cable car, invented by Andrew Hallidie, seemed the ideal replacement for the horsecar. A remote power plant, which could drive a loop of cable beneath the street, to which cars could grip and haul themselves around, had many advantages and excelled on hills. In 1873, San Francisco was the first city to install a workable system, and its cable cars are now a public icon. Although expensive, cable cars were cheaper than horsecars to maintain, and every city wanted them. Systems were installed in the United States in Seattle, Chicago, New York, and Denver, in addition to Melbourne, Australia, and Wellington New Zealand. For a few years, the "gripman," as the driver was called, ruled the streets.

A buzz of activity produced dozens of competing electric-car designs, including battery powered cars, but none was wholly practical. William Siemens had some success in Germany with his cars, which ran sporadically just outside Berlin in 1881, but he used dangerous high-voltage track for power. In the United States, experimenters such as Leo Daft, who used electric locomotives, and Charles Van Depoele, who pioneered the use of the trolley pole to collect power from overhead wires, built lines that were almost profitable. It was Van Depoele who built the first city-wide electric streetcar system in the United States—in Montgomery, Alabama—after electrifying the city's horsedrawn Court Street Line in 1886. Thomas Edison also experimented with electric streetcars. Baltimore and Cleveland installed lines—and paid the price of frustrating unreliability. The early systems created unforeseen side-effects: hissing and static-ridden telephone lines, electrocuted cats and dogs, and burst water and gas pipes, caused by ground-circuit induced corrosion. Not one of the 10 lines running in 1887 had made any money for its host city or its investors.

All of the parts of this puzzle were put together by one man when, in the spring of 1877, Richmond, Virginia, had given a contract to build a 12-mile (19-km), 30-car streetcar line to a young ex-Navy officer and engineer, Frank Sprague. Although he was a successful builder of automobiles, he came fresh from a failed demonstration of electric-car technology to Jay Gould, a potential backer of a New York elevated trolley system. Sprague's naval experience and technical training prepared him for the type of trial and error needed to build a viable system. His motors, already good by the standards of the times, were combined with a "wheelbarrow" method of mounting to drive wheels that didnot shake them to pieces. He perfected a power regulator and controller that allowed up to 22 cars to start up at once, and a spring-mounted trolley pole topped the ensemble. Sprague's system worked. Although the line had to scramble to stay functional, it improved almost daily, until even people like Boston horsecar magnate Henry Whitney visited Richmond to investigate. They departed impressed, leaving Sprague with orders. Once Sprague set things in motion, the new system got under way as city after city rolled out its colorful new machines. Soon, even distant cities such as Florence, Italy had Sprague trolleys. His company was absorbed by General Electric, and although he stayed on for a while,

his name was removed from all patents and from the trolleys he had worked on, so except for rail and trolley enthusiasts, few know of him today.

Once practical trolleys were running in a few cities, local authorities everywhere from Canada to Mexico rushed to install them. Windsor, Ontario, was the first Canadian city with an electric streetcar system in 1886, followed by Vancouver in 1890, Winnipeg (1891), Montréal, Hamilton, and Toronto (1892), Edmonton (1908), Calgary (1909), and Regina (1911). Mexico's first trolley service began in 1890, when a line was built from Laredo, Texas, to Nuevo Laredo in Tamaulipas State. It was the world's first international electric streetcar line, and the first electric railroad in Latin America.

As cities electrified and built power plants, the extra infrastructure required to switch from horse-drawn cars to electric trolleys was minimal, for not only could existing track systems be used, but the horse-drawn cars themselves could have motors installed and be up and running on their old routes with minimal delays. This was hardly necessary, as new designs poured out of such firms as Stephenson and the Philadelphia-based J.G. Brill. The advances in motor design went on behind the scenes, and invisible—except to the technicians and mechanics—were new generations of motors and trucks that could be fitted to existing rolling stock.

Among the early trolleys, there were many different types of designs for interiors and exteriors. They ranged from luxurious heated Pullmans to open-sided cars. Most importantly, weight was no longer a drawback, but actually aided traction. However, the bare-essential interiors of horsecars, with their wicker or pierced-plywood seats, took on a gilded-age splendor, and their beautiful steam-bent tulipwood or birchwood sides were replicated in stamped metal or cast iron on the new electric cars.

By the 1900s, many cities across the United States boasted electric streetcar lines. Traffic on the roads frequently became clogged, as the slower-moving horsedrawn vehicles jostled with the colorful cars. This photograph, taken in 1909, shows a traffic jam without automobiles at the corner of Dearborn and Randolph Streets in Chicago, Illinois.

Master car builders' association

THE AMERICAN CIVIL WAR BROUGHT ABOUT A CONSIDERABLE INTERCHANGE OF ROLLING STOCK, PARTICULARLY OF FREIGHT CARS, WHERE TRACK GAUGES ALLOWED, AND IT SOON BECAME APPARENT TO CONSTRUCTORS THAT A DEGREE OF VEHICLE STANDARDIZATION WAS NEEDED.

Henry Bessemer (1813–98) was an English engineer and inventor. He was the first person in the world to develop a method of producing steel inexpensively.

The need for standardization in order to simplify the interchange of cars among railroads brought about the founding of the Master Car Builders' Association in 1867. In 1876, it established rules for the prompt interchange of cars, and of repairs to damaged and defective cars, with billing and payment for the repairs. The Association then went on to establish standards for other car parts that, for example, helped to reduce the enormous variety of axles and journal boxes at the time to five different types.

Another problem tackled by the Master Car Builders' Association was one that had arisen from the growth of the many unconnected railroads—that of the confusion of part names. In 1871, a publication called *The Railroad Gazette* was produced, which served as a dictionary, defining in words and pictures everything from "adjustable globe-lamp" to "yoke."

A British invention of 1856 had far-reaching effects in revolutionizing the process of rail manufacture. The introduction of Henry Bessemer's converter to steel-making resulted in the quantity production of stronger, more durable and less expensive steel rails. The widespread use of steel rails led to the development of bigger and heavier cars, longer trains, and more powerful locomotives. At the same time, with the interchange of rolling stock by the mid-1880s, the need was recognized for an acceptable, standard, continuous power-brake system. From tests organized by the Master Car Builders' Association, a quick-action, automatic air-brake system was developed in 1888 and subsequently adopted in 1889 as the American standard.

Bessemer's steel-making process relied on an egg-shaped device known as a converter. Molten pig iron was poured into this through the aperture in the top and air blasted through the base, which converted the iron into steel. The converter was then turned in its mounting so that the steel could be poured out. The process marked the beginning of mass steel production and provided the railroads with steel in large quantites for rails and other components.

Many variations of Janney's coupler were made, but the Master Car Builders' Association standardized the types in use, ensuring that all would intercouple.

The Westinghouse system was modified to allow air to be voided into the atmosphere, not only at the engineer's control valve, but also at every triple valve in a train. Trials conducted in 1886 at Burlington, Iowa, by the Master Car Builders' Association with three different types of brake, applied to strings of 50 boxcars weighing a total of 1,100 tons (1,000 tonnes), showed that the lag of 20 seconds or more in braking effect between the front and rear of the train gave unsatisfactory emergency stopping distances. The modified Westinghouse system improved this so much that there was only a one-and-a-half to two seconds' delay between the front and rear of the train. This was known as the quick-acting triple valve.

These tests also demonstrated the need for sweeping changes to car drawbars and couplings. Until that time, the standard coupling had been the combined drawbar, link, and pin coupling. As car and train weights increased, this type of coupling proved too weak, was dangerous to operate, and introduced a considerable amount of free slack in a long train. By the 1870s, passenger cars were already using some form of semi-automatic coupling—the Miller Hook was heralded as the greatest life-saving invention of the age—but even so, American draftgear was not designed generally to absorb energy, as was the case in Europe, where cushioned screw couplings and spring-loaded side buffers were the norm.

In 1868, Major Eli Janney invented (and in 1873 patented) an automatic knuckle-coupler that

A typical automatic coupler. The air hose for the train brake system can also be seen.

operated in the vertical plane. In the next decade, many other coupler designs of the same general type emerged. By 1889, there were around 80,000 freight cars in the United States, and 39 different varieties of coupler, the majority of which would not intercouple. It is thought that this was the single greatest factor responsible for the formation of the Master Car Builders' Association. The Association adopted automatic couplers in 1887 and, due to its efforts, the number of designs was reduced to 16 and, subsequently, to 12, all of which were able to intercouple.

The first truly automatic coupler was the Tower coupler, invented in 1892. It

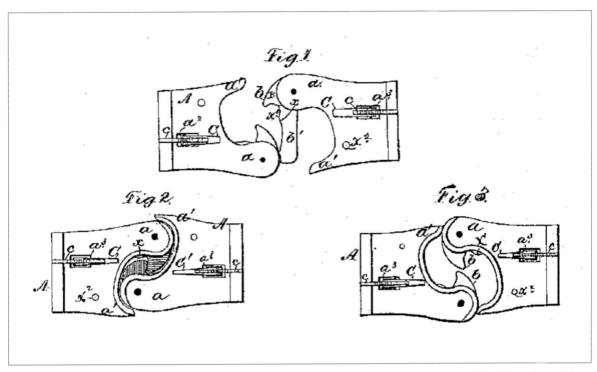

Fig. 1.

Fig. 2.

Fig. 3.

would couple and lock on impact (as indeed would many other designs), but it could also be unlocked and the knuckle thrown fully open by means of a lever at the side of the car.

Many railroads were slow to adopt automatic couplers and other safety devices until the Safety Appliances Act was passed by Congress in 1893. This made it mandatory, after January 1, 1898, for all cars used in interstate commerce to be equipped with couplers that were capable of coupling automatically by impact, and uncoupling without the need of trainmen imperiling themselves. Coupler development was stimulated as the result.

In the same period, the strength of freight cars was improved. Early freight cars had been made entirely of lumber. As early as 1829, the Delaware & Hudson Railroad had introduced anthracite coal traffic in New York State with wooden, open-top hopper cars, each running on two four-wheel trucks. This general type of car, updated, still appeared in the Car Builder's Dictionary in 1878, having a carrying capacity of 40,000–50,000 lb (18,150–22,680kg).

Boxcars of wooden construction averaged about 28 ft (8.5 m) in length and had a capacity of about 30,000 lb (13,600 kg). By 1888, the length had grown to about 35 ft (10.6 m), with a capacity of 50,000 lb (22,680 kg) and a tare weight of 24,800 lb (11,250 kg), giving an axle load, fully laden, of a little over 9 tons (8 tonnes). About this time, wooden frames gave way to wrought iron.

Tankcars had been used for the carriage of water and oil from early times; the first purpose-built tankcar went into service in Pennsylvania in 1865. The tank was made of riveted steel plates and was strapped to a wooden underframe with wooden cross-members. It had a typical empty weight of 28,000 lb (12,700 kg) and a capacity of 3,700 gallons (14,000 l).

Major Eli Janney invented this automatic knuckle-coupler in 1868. shown illustrated in the patent application of 1873.

Pullman and the new passenger cars

DEVELOPMENT OF THE PASSENGER CAR WAS PROCEEDING APACE. BETWEEN 1865 AND 1880 THERE WAS A TRANSITION FROM CARS THAT WERE LITTLE MORE THAN SMALL, UNCOMFORTABLE BOXES, TO DELUXE VEHICLES COSTING 10 TIMES AS MUCH TO PRODUCE.

LUXURY ON WHEELS

YOU TAKE YOUR HOTEL ALONG WITH YOU BY THIS ROUTE.

MEALS ENJOYED AT LEISURE

INTERIOR VIEW OF DINING CAR ON
CHICAGO & ALTON R. R. LINES
MEALS, 75 CENTS.

These luxury rail cars were intended to allow people to make long-distance journeys in comfort. Passage between adjoining cars when the train was in motion had been extremely hazardous in earlier types of cars, since the end platforms were narrow and completely open to the elements, and there were no buffers or tread plates between the end sills of the cars for passengers to step onto. Some early cars were fitted with various types of semi-automatic coupler, such as the Miller Hook, but there were no continuous brakes.

Car bodies were made of timber and were constructed in the form of a simple bridge truss, with a system of wrought-iron diagonal tension rods in the side framing. Support and control of vertical deflection was by wrought-iron truss rods under the floor. Brakes were primarily manual, and in the 1860s, some cars were equipped with elementary, non-automatic, vacuum brakes which were introduced from England. Westinghouse straight air brakes were fitted on some cars in the early 1870s. Speeds were relatively low and did not normally exceed 35–40 mph (56–64 km/h).

Passenger cars carried their own coal- or wood-burning stoves, although the luxury cars were equipped with circulating hot-air or hot-water systems

The Pullman Palace Company's "Holden" was, during the 1880s, an extremely plush and comfortable ride for its passengers. The ornate car was illuminated by oil lamps, and was heated in winter and ventilated in summer.

from Spear & Baker heaters. As early as 1856, a heating and ventilating system had been developed that introduced fresh air from the top of the car. Forced in as the train moved, air was passed through a plenum chamber, where it was heated by a stove. The warmed air was then distributed around the car through ducts in the ceiling. Cold air was removed through suction heads and returned to the stove for reheating. Steam heating from the locomotive was first introduced in 1883 on New York's Manhattan Railroad. Steam passed through pipes running around each car.

Wooden-truss construction continued to be used to the end of the 19th century, although it was developed so that the car sides, rather than the underframe, were used to support the weight of the car.

Opposite page: Railroad publicity made much of the luxury offered by their passenger cars for long journeys. This 1880s advertisement for the Chicago & Alton Railroad likens the dining car to a hotel, and offers the tempting delights of "Meals, 75 cents."

George M. Pullman (1831–97) originally trained as a cabinetmaker. After remodeling two cars for the Chicago, Alton & St. Louis Railroad, he went into the sleeping-car business, and developed it to such an extent that he had a virtual monopoly on the provision of sleeping and dining cars to United States railroads.

Elaborate wooden trusses or arch constructions were developed for use between the side sill and the belt rail, although truss rods continued to be used under the cars.

By the early 1890s, the automatic locking knuckle coupler with friction draftgear had been developed to the point where knuckle contours could be standardized. Henceforward, cars could be interchanged between different railroads, making it no longer necessary to change trains between one system and another. In 1887, the enclosed-end vestibule, invented by a Mr. Sessions, permitted passengers to walk safely through a moving train for the first time. This thereby encouraged the use of dining, lounge, and other special-purpose cars. At first, the vestibule was only between the step wells, but by 1893, it had been enlarged to cover the full width of the space between the carriages. In conjunction with the installation of automatic couplers, the construction used a metal faceplate with a canvas curtain to aid the transition of passengers and crew between adjacent cars.

Although George M. Pullman (1831-97) did not invent the sleeping car, he did improve and develop its design and construction to the point where it became a national institution. Pullman was a cabinetmaker from Brocton, New York, and after successfully remodeling (with his friend Benjamin Field) two Chicago, Alton & St. Louis cars in 1859, he decided to go into the sleeping-car business. In 1863, he set up his first works in Detroit, Michigan, and built a luxury car he named "Pioneer," which was larger and more luxurious than any other cars of the era. Legend has it that "Pioneer" formed part of the train that carried Abraham Lincoln's body home to Springfield, Illinois, in April 1865.

The Pullman Palace Car Company was chartered in 1867, and the first build totaled 48 cars. The company grew, acquiring cars from other operators, which it leased out to railroads, and moved to a larger plant near Chicago, Illinois. It went on to own all the sleeping cars on the Chicago & Alton

Pullman's cars were commonly named. This one bears the name of President Abraham Lincoln.

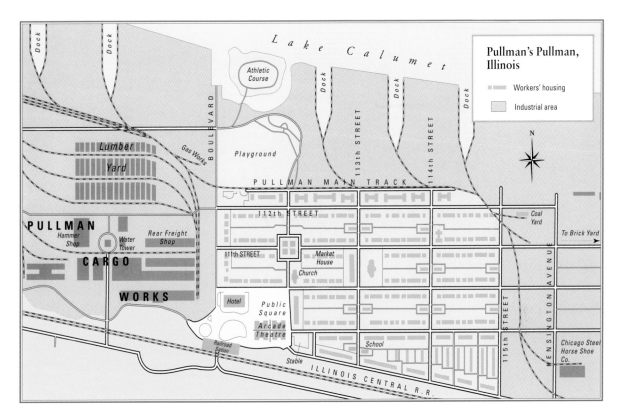

Railroad, the Burlington & Quincy Railroad, the Michigan Central Railroad, the Great Western Railroad of Canada, and the New York Central railroads. Pullman built the first "hotel car," a forerunner of the dining car, for the Great Western of Canada.

The entrepreneur entered into arrangements with railroads whereby he would provide the cars and staff, and the railroads would haul, light, and heat them. The railroad charged the regular coach fare for each passenger journey, with a supplement for a single berth or seat occupancy, which went to Pullman. Pullman was not the only sleeping-car operator—there were some 40 others in the United States during the second half of the 19th century—but ultimately all the others failed or were absorbed into his empire.

The Pullman Company was renowned for its standardization of both cars and service. Members of staff were trained from manuals that stipulated everything from the positioning of the pillows and the correct way to fold towels to the proper way in which to serve beer. The usual staff allocation per car was one African-American porter and one Filipino lounge attendant.

By the time George M. Pullman died in 1897, his company enjoyed a virtual monopoly of the sleeping-car services in the United States and ran dining- and parlor-car services as well. Its railroad car plant was the largest in the world and it was a pioneer in the building of steel cars. Later, it expanded into production of freight cars by buying other car builders. Pullman had also built the first model industrial town for his workers in Pullman, Illinois.

George Pullman created Pullman, Illinois, the first model industrial town, in 1880, on 4,000 acres (1.6 ha) of land he had bought, west of Lake Calumet, surrounding the Illinois Central Railroad. At the center of the town was his car business. The housing boasted "modern" conveniences by 1880s standards, including indoor plumbing, sewage, and a gas works. During the Depression of 1893-94, Pullman reduced wages and hours, prompting a notorious strike. The company sold its non-industrial property, and all the housing had been bought by 1907.

SPREADING NETWORKS AND CANADA, 1870-90

IN THE 20 YEARS FROM 1870, UNITED STATES RAILROADS HAD SPREAD ACROSS THE COUNTRY, AND A SECOND LINK EXISTED TO THE PACIFIC. IN CANADA, SIGHTS WERE ALSO SET ON BUILDING A TRANSCONTINENTAL RAILROAD TO CONNECT BRITISH COLUMBIA IN THE WEST WITH THE EASTERN PROVINCES.

A look at a United States railroad map of 1890 shows four main transcontinental lines, plus other connecting lines and a very dense network of railroad lines in the East and around the Great Lakes, with minor networks in Colorado and Utah. With the original transcontinental route from Omaha, Nebraska, to Sacramento, California completed, thoughts were directed to the development of other routes on the basis of those proposed in previous years. Several rail routes to the Pacific were constructed during the 1880s: the Santa Fe Railroad and Southern Pacific Railroad met at Deming, in southwestern New Mexico, in 1881, and three more routes were completed in 1883. The Santa Fe now had its own route across northern New Mexico and Arizona, while the Southern Pacific completed its line from New Orleans, Louisiana to Los Angeles, California. At the same time, the Northern Pacific opened its line through the Rockies from Duluth, Minnesota to the Pacific at Portland, Oregon. Competition was such that the Union Pacific Railroad also set its sights on the Northwest, and in 1884 it opened a route from Ogden, Utah through Idaho to Portland.

The first trans-Canada route was opened by the Canadian Pacific in 1885. The Dominion of Canada was created on July 1, 1867, but British Columbia, in the west, did not join the other states until 1871.

Canada's first railroad, the Champlain & St. Lawrence, opened in 1836 and ran between the St. Lawrence River and St. John's, Quebec, at the head of open-water navigation on the Richelieu River, which flows from Lake Champlain. Other lines followed.

By the time British Columbia joined the Dominion in 1871, it had been promised a railroad by the Canadian government to link it with the rest of the country. Since other lines were not interested, the Canadian Pacific Railroad was incorporated in 1881 to build a western extension from Callander, Ontario to the Pacific at what is now the main city of British Columbia, Vancouver.

The builders of the trans-Canada railroad had to cross 1,300 miles (2,090 km) of wilderness, 1,000 miles (1,600 km) of prairie, and 500 miles (800 km) of difficult terrain in the Rockies. While construction of the line along the shores of Lake Superior was difficult enough, national sentiment prevented a detour through United States territory. Construction of the route over the Rockies was a formidable challenge, involving gradients of 1 in 22 (4.5 percent). The line was opened on November 7, 1885. In June 1886 the first through train from Montréal via Ottawa to the Pacific was run. As Montréal was an Atlantic seaport, the subsequent regular trains were the only true transcontinental services in North America.

In 1885, the majority of the population was spread thinly along the border with the United States. The Canadian Pacific Railroad provided a vital link with British Columbia in the West, helping to create a unified nation.

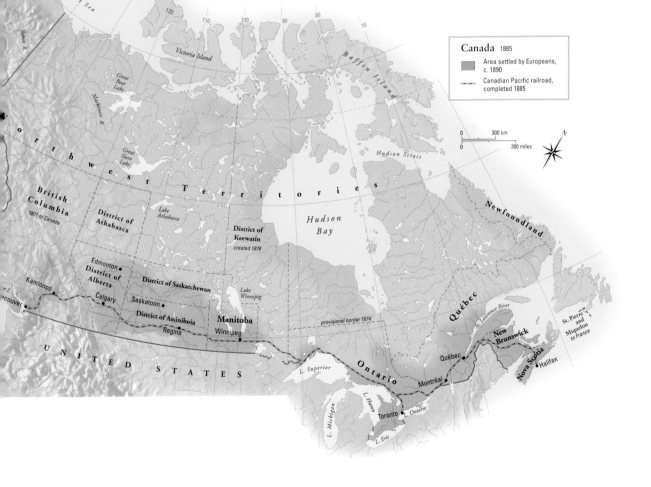

Canada 1885

▨ Area settled by Europeans, c. 1890

┄┄ Canadian Pacific railroad, completed 1885

Railroads, 1890

Thunder Bay

Québec

Duluth

Montréal

Portland

Ottawa

Boston

Milwaukee

Toronto

Detroit

Buffalo

New York

Chicago

Cleveland

Davenport

Philadelphia

Columbus

Pittsburgh

Baltimore

Indianapolis

St. Joseph

Cincinnati

Washington D.C.

Kansas City

St. Louis

Richmond

Nashville

Charlotte

Chattanooga

Wilmington

Memphis

Columbia

Corinth

Little Rock

Atlanta

Charleston

Savannah

Vicksburg

Montgomery

Jacksonville

Mobile

uston

New Orleans

In the decade between 1880 and 1890 the United States railroad network had increased by more than 70,000 miles, as more towns and cities became served by branch lines. The network was also continuing to spread farther westward. Canada now had a coast-to-coast rail link, and the standard gauge had been imposed.

N

0   200 km

0   200 miles

The last spike of the Canadian Pacific is driven in by Donald Smith, the financier who had done much to raise the funds. The Governor-General was intended to perform this ceremony with a silver spike, but he was unable to attend so an iron spike was substituted.

The Canadian Pacific was not the first long-distance line. Its celebrated engineer, the Scotsman Sandford Fleming, came to the job only after constructing the 840-mile (1353 km) Intercolonial Railway, which linked Montréal to Halifax in Nova Scotia. It was at this period that Canadian railway mileage began to increase dramatically. But this extra mileage was only partly accounted for by those two lines, however romantically they may have appeared to the public then and since. Certainly they had political significance, tying together the enormous landmass of Canada into something approaching an integrated nation. But their appearance coincided with the building of thousands of miles of lesser lines.

Needless to say, in this extensive and lightly populated country it was single track lines which predominated. Even a hundred years later the only significant lengths of double track in Canada would be Canadian National's main line from Montréal to Toronto and onward to Sarnia, Ontario, the northern part of the Canadian Pacific's line from Montréal in the same direction, and 400 miles in the praires (Winnipeg – Fort William) built to satisfy the farmers' need for an uncongested grain outlet.

Another geographical feature of Canada is that about 15 percent of its territory is island, and the railways found themselves providing ferries, even train ferries. For years the railway-operated ice-breaking ferry to Cape Breton was a key link in Nova Scotia, and there was a train ferry connecting Prince Edward Island with New Brunswick. At the other end of the country, freight cars from Vancouver to Vancouver Island were moved by barge, and soon after the Grand Trunk Pacific reached Prince Rupert in 1914 there would be a freightcar ferry service to Ketchikan in Alaska. By 1890, the eastern lines extended from Windsor, Ontario through Montréal, over the national frontier into Maine, and onward to St. John, New Brunswick. The future Canadian National Railways would later be formed by merging five major companies: the Intercolonial, National Transcontinental, Canadian Northern, Grand Trunk Pacific, and Grand Trunk Railways

The Intercolonial began operations between Halifax, New Brunswick, and Rivière du Loup, Québec province, in 1876, taking in the operation of the Grand Trunk's line from Rivière du Loup to the west of Levis, across the St. Lawrence from the city of Québec, in 1879. The National Transcontinental was built in the first decade of the 20th century. It provided a direct route from Moncton in New Brunswick to Winnipeg via Québec City, through mainly desolate country. It was expensively built and an obvious

The Canadian Rockies were a formidable barrier to a Canadian transcontinental Railway. There were few routes by which they could be crossed.

The Grand Trunk Railway's No 40, built by the Portland Company (Maine) in 1872, would later become Canada's last wood-burner.

Victoria Bridge, spanning the St. Lawrence River at Montréal, under construction in the early 1850s. The structure was finally opened in 1859 but the cost of building it was so high that the Grand Trunk Railroad was obliged to ask the government to bear most of the cost.

loss-maker to all except its investors and political proponents. The Canadian Northern began in the 1890s, when William Mackenzie and Donald Mann merged a series of other projects. The Grand Trunk Railway was incorporated in 1852 and included the former Champlain & St. Lawrence Railroad. By 1856, it was operating between Levis and Windsor, Ontario. Three years later, it opened the Victoria Bridge across the St. Lawrence at Montrèal.

When Canada became a Dominion in 1867, it was proposed to extend the Grand Trunk Railway west to the Pacific, and east to New Brunswick and Nova Scotia at public expense. Public opinion was against the proposal, and in the end, the Grand Trunk Railway built south to Chicago, Illinois, which it reached in 1880. It used the tracks of several short lines it purchased, then the Michigan lines were connected to the rest, first by ferry and in 1890 by the St. Clair Tunnel. By 1890, the Grand Trunk Railway owned a majority interest in the Boston & Maine Railroad, and went on to expand in the first few years of the 20th century. It would not be until 1914 that the Grand Trunk Pacific Railway would run its first train from Winnipeg to Prince Rupert on the Pacific.

An engineers' inspection train stops for a photograph, on the Canadian Pacific Railway in 1889.

GROWTH OF THE MEXICAN RAILROADS, 1860-90

AFTER A SLOW START, RAILROAD CONSTRUCTION GAINED MOMENTUM IN MEXICO, FOLLOWING THE OPENING OF THE NATION'S FIRST INTER-CITY LINE IN 1873. JUST OVER A DECADE LATER, THE COUNTRY HAD A GROWING NATIONAL NETWORK AND LINES CONNECTING IT TO THE UNITED STATES.

José de la Cruz Porfirio Díaz Mori (1830–1915) was a Mexican-American War volunteer, French Intervention hero, and president of Mexico from 1876 to 1880 and from 1884 to 1911. He actively encouraged the growth of the railroads in Mexico.

Mexico's railroad network began with a line linking the capital, Mexico City, with the port of Veracruz on the Gulf of Mexico. The first step toward building this line came in 1837, when the government awarded a concession for its construction to Francisco de Arrillaga, a trader from Veracruz.

Progress was painfully slow, however, so the government withdrew de Arrillaga's concession and, in 1842, awarded one to the commission responsible for roadbuilding in the Veracruz region. But by 1850, the commission had completed just 7 miles (11.5 km) of the line, from Veracruz to El Molino, so the government again withdrew the concession.

Revolutions and government changes held back construction, but after the execution of the French-sponsored Emperor Maximilian and the institution of Benito Juarez's republican presidency, a British syndicate found the money to complete the railroad. The Mexican Imperial Railway Company (Compañia Limitada del Ferrocarril Imperial Mexicano, later Ferrocarril Mexicano) completed the construction of the railroad in late 1872, and the 270-mile (433-km) line was inaugurated on January 1, 1873. From

Veracruz the line rises from sea level to 8100 ft (2,469 m) on the Mexican Plateau. The resultant severe grades around Orizaba later prompted the electrification of some sections, where electric locomotives were used until, eventually, diesels took over.

Ferrocarril Mexicano built a number of branch lines to connect the line between Mexico City and Veracruz with nearby towns, but for a while connections with United States railroads were discouraged by the Mexican government. To counterbalance the company's monopoly, concessions or subsidies were granted to railroads prepared to construct alternative lines between the Gulf and the interior. But Mexico could not afford to ignore the United States for long, so two lines connecting the border with Mexico City were built with the aid of concessions. The principal line, from El Paso, Texas across the Rio Grande through Ciudad Juárez, was built by Santa Fe interests as the Mexican Central (Ferrocarril Central Mexicano) and completed in 1884. One of the cities along the line's route was Aguascalientes, and in 1897, the Mexican Central and the Mexican government chose this city as the site for the country's main railroad engineering depot. This depot, the General Workshops for the Construction and Repair of Machines and Rolling Stock, was completed in 1903. At its peak, it covered an area of about 200 acres (81 ha) and employed more than 7,000 workers. It was also the center for training railroad workers, not just from Mexico, but from all over Central America, becoming known as the "Railroad University."

Work on the second international line to Mexico City, from Laredo, in eastern Texas, began in 1881. It was built to the narrow 3-ft (0.91 m) gauge as the Mexican National (Ferrocarriles Nacionales de

Below: Locomotive crossing Gorge of Metlac on the Veracruz railroad, Mexico c. 1882.

Overleaf: The Mexican railroads acquired much of their rolling stock second-hand from US railroads. This twelve-wheel parlor car was operated by the Chihuahua Pacific Railway in the 1950s.

Watched by one of the crewmen, Mexican locomotive No.124 emerges from the mouth of a tunnel in the Tamasopa Canon, and prepares to negotiate the tight curve around a giddyingly steep stonebuilt grade.

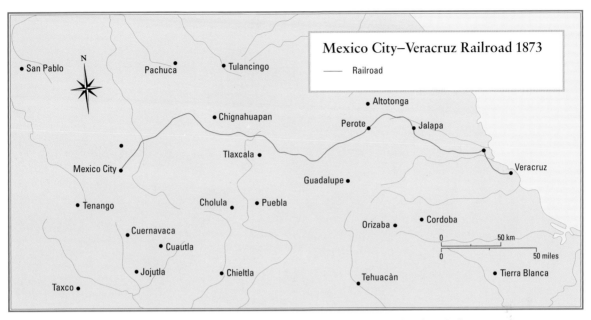

Mexico City–Veracruz Railroad 1873

—— Railroad

San Pablo • Pachuca • Tulancingo • Altotonga • Chignahuapan • Perote • Jalapa • Tlaxcala • Veracruz • Mexico City • Guadalupe • Tenango • Cholula • Puebla • Cuernavaca • Orizaba • Cordoba • Cuaútla • Jojutla • Chieltla • Tehuacàn • Tierra Blanca • Taxco •

México) by General William Jackson Palmer, builder of the Denver & Rio Grande Railroad, and reached Mexico City in 1888.

Later, the line had branches in the North from Monterrey to Matamoros on the Gulf of Mexico, and, farther south, from Acámbaro to Uruapan. A third line, the Mexican International (Ferrocarril Internacional Mexicano), was completed in 1892 and ran from Durango in central Mexico to the border town of Piedras Negras, then across the Rio Grande to Eagle Pass, Texas.

A new and different Mexican National Railways (Ferrocarriles Nacionales de Mexico, or N de M) appeared in 1908, a merger of several lines, mainly US-financed. The biggest of these was the Mexico Central, and most were standard gauge, although there was also the 3-ft (0.9-m) gauge line from El Paso to Mexico City, which tried to behave like a mainline railroad, with smart sleeping and observation cars running into its own San Lazaro terminal in Mexico City. The N de M was Mexico's main railroad for most of the 20th century, finally disappearing in the massive privatization of railways in the 1990s. In its later years it could boast, among other things, of possessing the newest locomotive roundhouse in North America, at Valle de Mexico, a suburb of Mexico City.

Although the N de M converted some narrow-gauge lines to standard gauge, it maintained quality on the narrow gauge, even building a new station at Pueblo in the 1950s. The daily train from Pueblo into Mexico City had a scenic route along volcanic slopes as far as Cuatla, where engines were changed for the stiff grades to Ozumba, after which there was a gentle descent into Mexico City. The distance covered was 192 miles (310 km), probably a record run for the narrow gauge in North America. Apart from the quite heavy passenger traffic, the line carried considerable freight, serving a sugar refinery, a brewery and forestry.

A notable US-owned railroad was the Sud Pacifico de Mexico which, as its name suggested, was built by the US Southern Pacific RR. This had links with yet another railroad, the Chihuahua Pacific, whose

The first railroad in Mexico ran between Mexico City and the port of Veracruz on the Gulf of Mexico. After a number of false starts, it finally opened in 1873.

An early-model American Locomotive Company road-switcher, evidently in need of maintenance, acquired by the Ferrocarril del Pacifico when it began its dieselization program.

scenic line was later transformed into a tourist attraction. The Southern Pacific sold the Pacifico to the Mexican government in 1951, whereupon its name was changed to Ferrocarril del Pacifico. It would be one of the first Mexican lines to be fully dieselized, although its more useful steam locomotives were transferred to the N de M.

In the southeast of Mexico, the first line of the United Railroads of Yucatán (Ferrocarriles Unidos de Yucatán, or UdeY) was opened in 1881. UdeY developed into a system of narrow- and standard-gauge lines linking much of the state of Yucatán with its capital, Mérida, with a line into the neighboring state of Campeche. On the Pacific Coast, the grandly named Pan-American Railway (Ferrocarril Panamericano) linked the standard-gauge network south of Mexico City with the town of Tecún Umán just over the border in Guatemala.

By 1910, Mexico had most of its national railroad network in place, built with the active encouragement of President Porfirio Díaz, who ruled the country from 1876 to 1880 and from 1884 to 1911. Díaz had embarked on a program of modernization in an attempt to bring Mexico up to the level of a modern state. He was keen to see steam machines and technological appliances being used in industry, and the construction of factories in Mexico City, and actively invited and encouraged foreign investment. This policy resulted in the rise of an urban proletariat in Mexico, and the influx of foreign capital (principally from the United States). Díaz's plans included the building of railroad and telegraph lines across the country. Under his presidency the amount of track in Mexico increased tenfold; many of these rails

1877 map of the first railroad line from Mexico City to Veracruz, Mexico, with additional lines between Apizaco and Puebla and between Jalapa and Veracruz. .

remain in operation today without remodeling. In less than 40 years, it had constructed some 12,000 miles (20,000 km) of track, often over difficult terrain across deserts, through rainforests, and across hills and mountains that called for many high bridges and long tunnels.

The Mexican railroads had a notably high mortality rate in their not infrequent accidents, although reporting of accidents was so haphazard that the number of fatalities is sometimes uncertain. Many of their accidents are better described as catastrophes. In 1881 a troop train fell when a bridge collapsed, with fire adding to the horror, killing more than two hundred. In 1895, near Mexico City, a pilgrims' special train fell off a cliff's edge with many deaths. Soon after, Mexico plunged into civil war, bringing not only more accidents but sabotage as well. In 1912 a troop train was mined with the presumed loss of hundreds of lives. In 1915 another troop train came lethally to grief, and the same year a train carrying soldiers' families fell into a chasm near Guadalajara, but an accurate death toll was never published. There were reports of a passenger train entering a tunnel that a local commander had blocked with a burning freight train; again, details are scarce.

After the civil war mortality dropped to a more normal level (and it might be noted that US railroads for decades also had a safety record that was far from unblemished). But in 1945 another pilgrims' train had a head-on collision with a freight train, killing about a hundred passengers. And as late as 1972 the train crew of another pilgrim special, later said to have been intoxicated, exceeded speed limits and derailed the train at a cost of more than two hundred lives.

Farmers versus the Railroads, 1866-90

FARMERS BEGAN TO SUFFER FINANCIALLY FROM THE DEMANDS FOR UNFAIR RATES AND OTHER DISCRIMINATORY PRACTICES AT THE HANDS OF THE BIG RAIL CORPORATIONS, WHICH WERE SWALLOWING UP THE SMALLER, LOCAL LINES.

Oliver Hudson Kelley (1826–1913) was the "Father" of the Order of Patrons of Husbandry. Born in Boston, Massachusetts, he moved to the Minnesota frontier in 1849 and became a farmer. He felt the need to gather together farmers and their families in a fraternal organization, and in 1867 he formed the "Grange."

At the end of the long and costly American Civil War, farmers faced a range of social and economic problems that made their rural lives dismal. The seller's grain market that had existed during the war had disappeared as supply began to outweigh demand. The price of crops fell, and farmers who had borrowed heavily during the prosperous war years to expand their businesses were unable to repay their debts. Carpetbagging was rife as the Northerners took advantage of the Southerners during postwar reconstruction. These problems were not limited solely to the devastated Southern states; many farmers in the North had been left physically disabled as a result of combat and were unable to work on the land, or had lost family members who were vital to their farm's workload. The national depression that began in 1873 exacerbated matters.

The root of the farmers' problems, as they saw it, lay in the devious and greedy railroad magnates. While the farmers had actually helped to fund the establishment of railroads during the 1850s, they had subsequently witnessed the smaller regional lines being bought out by the larger corporations based in distant places such as New York. The railroads set rates for haulage that were not prompted by a competitive market, but through agreements secured with other railroads, giving the farmers no choice: to transport their crops, they were obliged to pay the rates.

In 1866, Oliver Hudson Kelley, a Minnesota farmer, agricultural writer, and member of the Masonic Order, was commissioned by President Andrew Johnson to carry out a survey of agricultural conditions

The railroads made it easy for farmers to send their produce to markets in the East. At the same time, the presence of railroads encouraged agriculture within reach of their tracks.

The Railroads: Getting Agricultural Products to Eastern Markets 1890

Over 90 people per square mile

Wheat growing

Corn growing

Railroad

Shipment of grain, 1890, in thousand tons:

3,450

1,500

380

Wheat   Corn

in the Southern states. He was horrified to see the farmers so beleaguered, and determined to do something to alleviate their woes. On December 4, 1867, having forsaken farming for a job in the Post Office Department in Washington, D.C., Kelley established the Order of Patrons of Husbandry, known simply as the "National Grange." Joining Kelley were six other founders: four Washington government officials, a banker, and a minister. Although some of the seven had an agricultural background, none was actively involved in farming. The Grange was set up as a fraternal, socio-economic organization that would act on behalf of the farmers, their families, and their interests, which Kelley envisioned as encompassing all the rural areas of the United States.

Grange members were able to meet in township halls to discuss their problems, many of which were centered on the railroads and their middlemen. The railroads, it was stated, deliberately withheld vital information from farmers, such as the amount of grain held in storage, and some were known to cheat when weighing crops. They would frequently levy transportation charges that were more per ton for short hauls than for longer ones. The fledgling Grange made a name for itself as a railroad reformer, although this was not its original intention. In 1870, for example, the Illinois Grange won a constitutional amendment that gave the state control over the railroads. The following year, the State Legislature fixed

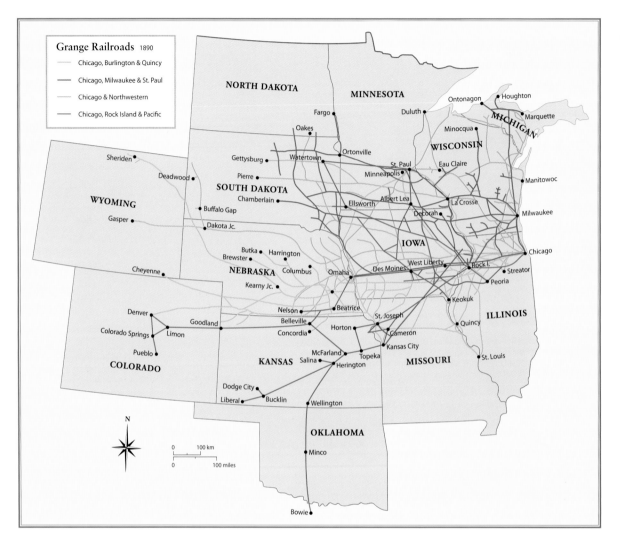

Grange Railroads 1890

— Chicago, Burlington & Quincy

— Chicago, Milwaukee & St. Paul

— Chicago & Northwestern

— Chicago, Rock Island & Pacific

Railroads that operated in the Midwest were most affected by the Granger Laws.

a constant rate for freight and passenger trains. The Granger Laws dictated rules the railroads had to adhere to and regulated the charge for grain elevators. In 1873, the Texas Grange was organized with the prime intention of fighting for railroad legislation. Half of the delegates that were elected to the Texas Constitutional Convention of 1875 were members of the movement. After the convention, railroad companies were forbidden from buying or controlling competing lines, and cities were prevented from issuing bonds to pay for the construction of railroads. Rates and fares were fixed by the legislature.

After the nationwide financial panic of 1873, growth in the membership of the Grange increased dramatically, and by 1874 there were some 268,368 paying members. By 1875, this had increased to 850,000. The organization was most strongly represented in Illinois, Minnesota, Iowa and Wisconsin—states where many railroad regulations were imposed. During its battles with the railroad companies, the Grange was sued by its adversaries, with many cases being heard in the United States Supreme Court.

Numerous rulings were given in favor of the Grange. As the organization grew, it began to take on more of an economic role. It established cooperative grain elevators and mills, and set up buying cooperatives, cutting out the middlemen and so reducing prices. Critics, however, claimed that the Grange itself had become a middleman.

Although much of the Grange's activities were aimed against the railroads, this was by no means its sole purpose, a concept reinforced in a report to the executive committee in 1874, which stated, "Unfortunately for our order, the impression prevails to some extent that its chief mission is to fight railroads and denounce capitalists. It is a work of time to remove these erroneous impressions, and to prove that we do not wage a meaningless aggressive warfare upon any interest whatever..." The group had interests in mail delivery, and in the 1870s, campaigned for rural free delivery (RFD); by the turn of the century, the scheme was widespread. It was staunchly pro-temperance; it railed against tobacco products, and argued for a system of progressive federal income tax.

As time progressed, however, it seemed that the movement attracted many of the individuals it sought to control: it was thought that new enrollments secretly had allegiance to the middlemen and the railroads, and that many were hoping to secure discount prices. Membership of the Grange dropped during the late 1870s, and its political influence became minimal. By 1879, there were fewer than 250,000 members, and during the 1880s, there were little over 100,000.

Grain elevators were important to the storage and shipment of grain. Invented in 1842 in Buffalo, New York, by Joseph Dart, who had earlier developed a steam-powered mechanism (a "marine leg") for scooping grain out of the hulls of ships directly into storage silos. Early grain elevators and bins were constructed of wood and prone to fire; later types were constructed of steel or reinforced concrete. The elevator's silos, bins, and tanks were emptied by gravity flow, sweep augers and conveyors—blended and weighted—into railroad cars or barges, or, later, trucks, and shipped to the end users of grain, such as mills.

THE LAND GRANT ISSUE

THE RAILROADS CONTINUED TO EXPAND DURING THE 1880S, ENCOURAGED BY THE FEDERAL GOVERNMENT. LUCRATIVE LAND GRANTS WERE MADE AVAILABLE TO ENABLE THE RAILROADERS TO PROGRESS WITH BUILDING.

Without assistance from the United States government, railroad construction between 1860 and 1900 would certainly have been greatly curtailed. Land grants were made available by Congress to the railroad companies, since private banks were afraid that the railroad companies would need a long time to pay off their debts and were reluctant to lend them money. To remedy the situation, railroads received millions of acres of public land, which they sold to make money, enabling them to lay their tracks. Four out of the five United States transcontinental railroads were built with this type of assistance from the government.

The land-grant bills made government gifts of public land to the railroad companies in exchange for laying track in specified areas. As the value of land increased, both the railroads and the government gained financially. The railroad companies would then sell their profitable lots of land and use the proceeds to pay for materials and labor with which to continue their expansion. By this method, the construction of the railroads became entwined with the sale of land, and provided a substantial amount of the capital required to finance future railroad projects. Land sales were encouraged in the United States and Western Europe through advertising by the railroads. In this way both immigration and westward migration were accelerated by the development of the railroads.

The first major railroad land grants had resulted from the 1862 legislation that allowed the transcontinental railroad to come into being. The Union Pacific and Central Pacific railroads had been granted 400 ft (122 m) rights-of-way as well as 10 square miles (25.9 sq km) of land for every mile (1.6 km) of track built. While this amount of land seemed substantial, the parcels did not share a common border, being laid out in a checkerboard design. Seen on a map, the railroad track would snake across this

Opposite page: As a result of its land grants, the Burlington & Missouri River Railroad in 1872 posted this enticing advertisement, offering "Millions of Acres" for sale in Iowa and Nebraska, on 10 years credit, at 6 percent interest and "low prices." It goes on to offer "extraordinary inducements on freight and passage afforded to purchasers and their families."

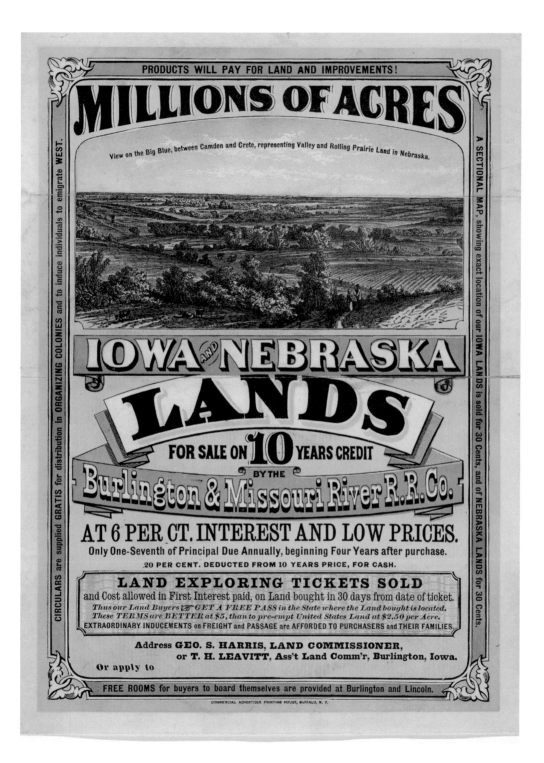

PRODUCTS WILL PAY FOR LAND AND IMPROVEMENTS!

MILLIONS OF ACRES

View on the Big Blue, between Camden and Crete, representing Valley and Rolling Prairie Land in Nebraska.

IOWA and NEBRASKA LANDS

FOR SALE ON **10** YEARS CREDIT

BY THE

Burlington & Missouri River R.R.Co.

AT 6 PER CT. INTEREST AND LOW PRICES.

Only One-Seventh of Principal Due Annually, beginning Four Years after purchase.

20 PER CENT. DEDUCTED FROM 10 YEARS PRICE, FOR CASH.

LAND EXPLORING TICKETS SOLD

and Cost allowed in First Interest paid, on Land bought in 30 days from date of ticket.

Thus our Land Buyers ☞ GET A FREE PASS in the State where the Land bought is located.
These TERMS are BETTER at $5, than to pre-empt United States Land at $2.50 per Acre.

EXTRAORDINARY INDUCEMENTS on FREIGHT and PASSAGE are AFFORDED TO PURCHASERS and THEIR FAMILIES.

Address **GEO. S. HARRIS, LAND COMMISSIONER,**
or **T. H. LEAVITT**, Ass't Land Comm'r, Burlington, Iowa.

Or apply to

FREE ROOMS for buyers to board themselves are provided at Burlington and Lincoln.

COMMERCIAL ADVERTISER PRINTING HOUSE, BUFFALO, N. Y.

(left margin) CIRCULARS are supplied GRATIS for distribution in ORGANIZING COLONIES and to induce individuals to emigrate WEST.

(right margin) A SECTIONAL MAP, showing exact location of our IOWA LANDS is sold for 30 Cents, and of NEBRASKA LANDS for 30 Cents.

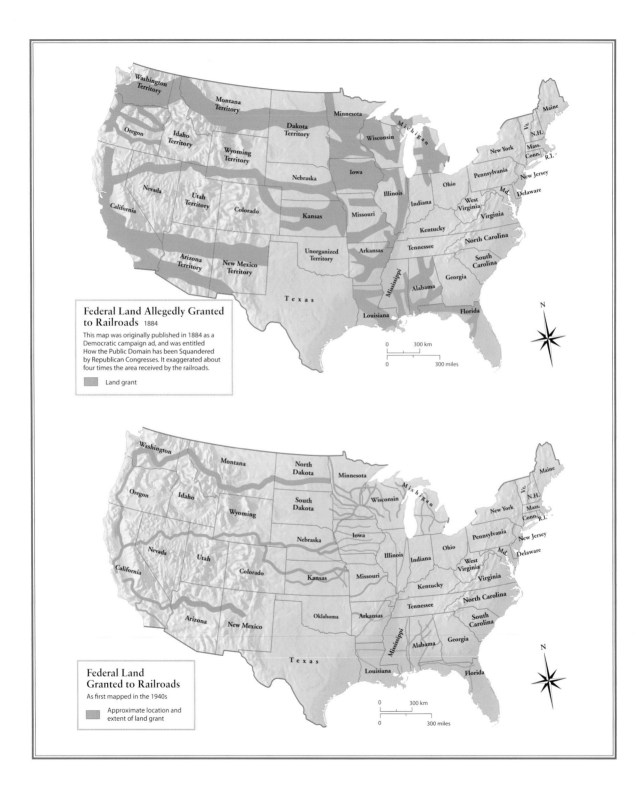

Federal Land Allegedly Granted to Railroads 1884

This map was originally published in 1884 as a Democratic campaign ad, and was entitled *How the Public Domain has been Squandered by Republican Congresses.* It exaggerated about four times the area received by the railroads.

Land grant

Federal Land Granted to Railroads

As first mapped in the 1940s

Approximate location and extent of land grant

checkerboard, with parallel lines drawn 10 miles (16 km) to the left and 10 miles (16 km) to the right. The railroads were given the odd-numbered sections on each side of the railroad right-of-way, meaning they would have 5 square miles (13 km²) of land on each side of the track.

Shortly after the completion of the first transcontinental railroad in 1869 with the meeting of the two railroad companies at Promontory Point, land grants ceased to be public policy. Many people had voiced dissent at the long-term sense of giving away so much land to private companies. Between 1850 and 1870, more than 129 million acres (52 million ha)—seven percent of the continental United States—had been ceded to just 80 railroad companies. Most of that land lay west of the Mississippi, and the value of the grants totaled more than a staggering half billion dollars.

The responsibility for surveying and mapping the areas of the land grants fell to the United States General Land Office. Hundreds of maps of the United States and individual states and counties were produced, indicating the precise parcels of granted land and showing the railroad rights-of-way. These land-grant maps were also used by speculators to advertise railroad lands that were to be made available for sale to the public. In the late 1860s, most western railroads had established land departments and bureaus of immigration—many of which had offices in Europe—to sell land and promote foreign settlement in the western United States.

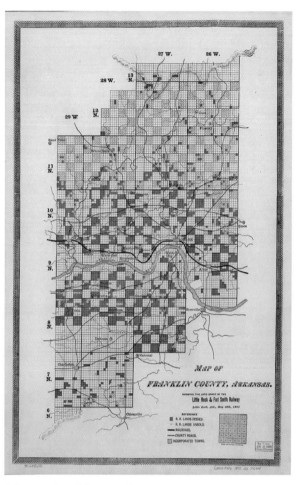

This large-scale grant map, of Franklin County, Arkansas, dated 1893, shows the typical checkerboard pattern of railroad land grants. The dark shaded areas were granted to the Little Rock & Fort Smith Railroad. Maps such as this were used by land speculators to advertise railroad lands that were made available for sale to the public.

The government land-grant maps themselves had misrepresented the true size of the granted areas, however, and it is likely that intense competition between speculators led to them distorting their railroad maps. For example, the Illinois Central Railroad had been granted land along its path in 1850. John W. Amerman's book, *The Illinois Central Rail-Road Company Offers for Sale Over 2,000,000 Acres Selected Farming and Wood Land* (New York, 1856) shows an outline map of Illinois with the Illinois Central Railroad highlighted by a heavy black line; stations are shown spaced along the line, suggesting the proximity of towns along the tracks, which was misleading. During the early 1880s, scale, area and the routes of the railroads were manipulated to create a false impression in favor of the railroad companies.

The land-grant topic was highly political and controversial. In 1884, a Democratic Party campaign advertisement, entitled *"How the Public Domain has been Squandered by Republican Congresses,"* exaggerated by about four times the amount of land that had been made available to the railroads.

Despite the criticism of the land grants, they helped to bring West and East together so that goods could be sent to market more cheaply, shipping costs were reduced, and thousands of jobs were created as a result of both railroad construction and the new settlements.

LOCOMOTIVE DEVELOPMENTS, 1880-1900

TOWARD THE END OF THE 19TH CENTURY CAME ADVANCES IN SCIENCE AND TECHNOLOGY, ENABLING THE DEVELOPMENT OF MORE ADVANCED LOCOMOTIVES.

As steam locomotives grew larger, so their consumption of fuel and water increased. There had always been a plentiful supply of fuel, since the United States had huge reserves of wood and coal, even so, thought was given to possible alternative fuels. The first regular use of oil as a fuel for locomotives seems to have been in Russia in 1882, when Thomas Urquhart, superintendent of the Gryaz-Tsaritsyn Railroad, developed a suitable system and, by 1885, 143 engines had been converted to burn oil. American engineers kept an eye on developments in Europe, and those features that were considered to be suitable for American conditions were tried or adapted and developed for their particular needs. For example, valves for the distribution of steam in the cylinders had always presented problems with lubrication and wear. Piston valves were introduced successfully on the North Eastern Railway in England in 1887, and were in use in the United States by 1898.

The growing size of locomotives meant that more coal and water had to be carried if more frequent or longer water-replenishment and refueling stops were not to cancel out any gains in speed made possible by increases in power. In Europe, fuel economy for other reasons had led to experiments with compound expansion, in which steam was fed to one or more cylinders at boiler pressure, and then exhausted to another cylinder or cylinders for further expansion. Theoretically, steam exhausted from one cylinder at about half boiler pressure could exert the same force on another piston of twice the surface area.

In 1889, 33-year-old Samuel M. Vauclain was general manager of the Baldwin Locomotive Works—his father was one of those who had built the locomotive Old Ironsides. He invented the "tandem compound" system which used high- and low-pressure cylinders mounted one behind the other. By 1893, he had

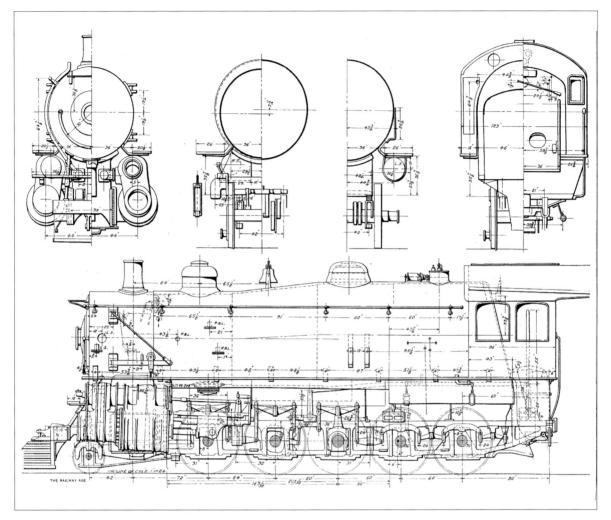

THE RAILWAY AGE

refined the system sufficiently for the Atchison, Topeka & Santa Fe Railroad to take delivery of the first of an order for 86 successful 2-10-2s.

Other types of compounding were developed, the most successful probably being that conceived by Alfred de Glehn in France, and first used in 1886. His system employed four cylinders, two outside the frames at high pressure, and two low-pressure cylinders between the frames. Two similar systems were developed in the United States, one by Vauclain and another by Francis J. Pitkin of the American Locomotive Company (ALCO). Both claimed savings of up to 20 percent in fuel.

Meanwhile, other engineers were showing interest in the possible use of electric traction, particularly on mountain lines with long tunnels and on other lines with tunnels, within city limits, where smoke from steam locomotives could prove a health and safety hazard.

At the end of the 19th century, railroads were firmly established, and travel by train could be accomplished in reasonable comfort from the Atlantic to the Pacific in under six days.

With the dawn of a new century came a change in locomotive design to reflect technological discoveries and give a more modern appeance to rolling stock. This technical drawing shows the Atchison Topeka & Santa Fe's Decapod Tandem Compound engine, built by ALCO around 1902.

Camelbacks and high wheelers

THE "CAMELBACK," WITH ITS CHARACTERISTIC WIDE FIREBOX, WAS A POPULAR LOCOMOTIVE. IT WAS DEVELOPED IN 1877, WHEN JOHN E. WOOTTEN OF THE PHILADELPHIA & READING RAILROAD IMPROVED THE STABILITY OF A WASTE-ANTHRACITE BURNING LOCOMOTIVE BY PLACING THE GRATE ABOVE THE REAR DRIVERS ON A 4-6-0.

In Wootten's design, the cab was placed above the firebox, and the fireman stoked the grate from an unprotected platform on the tender. A machine of this type was sent to Europe, but owing to restricted tunnel clearances in France and Italy, the cab had to be moved forward and lowered. Thus was born the "camelback,"

An example of a 4-6-0 camelback built by the Baldwin Locomotive Works for the Central Railroad of New Jersey.

also known as the "Mother Hubbard." The wide firebox became known universally as the Wootten firebox, and was used worldwide. Various designs of camelback were built, but a second, rudimentary cab had to be provided, usually mounted off the end of the firebox, to protect the fireman. The design lasted well into the 20th century, used on some very large locomotives.

With reliable brake systems, it was possible to run at higher speeds, and by the late 1880s the thoughts of engineers turned to maximum speeds as high as 100 mph (160 km/h). To keep piston speeds at reasonable levels, designers increased the diameters of the driving wheels. Locomotives with these taller drivers were known as "high wheelers," most were 4-4-0s, and a few were 4-4-2s, but all were more sophisticated than the standard American type. Typical high wheelers were those turned out to the designs of William Buchanan of the New York Central & Hudson River Railroad.

The most famous of the New York Central's high wheelers was No. 999, which hauled the crack Empire State Express. On May 10, 1893 No. 999, with a light train, covered a measured mile of slightly downhill track west of Batavia, New York, in 31.2 seconds—a speed of 112½ mph (181 km/h). This was claimed as a record, but was later the subject of much controversy. Nonetheless, No. 999's 80-in (61-cm) drivers and 24-in (61-cm) piston travel undoubtedly gave it the potential for very high speeds.

The ultimate example of a camelback. This massive 0-8-8-0 articulated locomotive was one of three built by ALCO for the Erie Railroad in 1908. Two firemen were needed to stoke the huge grate. It weighed 205½ tons (185 tonnes).

A pair of Baldwin 4-4-2 camelbacks built for the Atlantic City Railroad in 1896 regularly ran the 55.3 miles (89 km) between Atlantic City and Camden, New Jersey at an average start-to-stop speed of 70 mph (113 km/h) and could develop 1,450 hp at that speed.

The advance of technology was nowhere more widely evident than in motive power. Toward the end of the 19th century, the steam locomotive was evolving rapidly. Following the introduction of continuous train brakes and stronger couplings, it was growing in size, which enabled the operation of much longer and heavier trains. This, in turn, led to the need for more powerful "pusher" locomotives on the long, steep grades of the Alleghenies in the East, and the Sierra Nevada, the Rockies, and their outliers in the

While the engineer of a camelback locomotive enjoyed the protection of the cab, the fireman had to make do with a rudimentary shelter at the rear.

West. In freight and pusher service, the greater the number of driving wheels, the better the traction; and, as speeds were low out of necessity, small wheels gave high pulling power. On the other hand, passenger-train speeds were becoming ever faster and loads much less, so that large driving wheels were the order of the day. Some high wheelers had drivers as tall as 86 in (218 cm). But it was the details that were improved—to reduce maintenance, increase power output, reduce fuel consumption, and so on. The external appearance of locomotives was changing, as well, with the advent of larger-diameter boilers.

American locomotives could be built large because the physical dimensions of the early railroads were not inhibited by tunnels and bridges to anything like the extent they were in Europe, and in Britain in particular. There is little doubt that Russian railroads were strongly influenced by American engineers and built locomotives of much the same dimensions; their choice of the 5 ft (1.52 m) gauge was no coincidence.

Be that as it may, by the end of the 19th century locomotives in the United States were rapidly increasing in size and power. Ten driving axles became popular for freight locomotives, particularly pushers, while for passenger trains, the ten-wheeler locomotive replaced the eight-wheeler. The 4-4-2, or "Atlantic," was popular, as the addition of the trailing axle permitted a wide firebox of the Wootten type and a correspondingly larger boiler. By the turn of the century, the salient characteristics of the American steam locomotive were established and being used to the full.

A 4-4-2 high wheeler of the Pennsylvania Railroad. The large-diameter driving wheels allowed locomotives to run at high speeds while keeping piston speeds at an acceptable level.

RISE AND FALL OF THE ELECTRIC INTERURBANS

IN THE 1890S, THE USE OF ELECTRIC STREETCARS SPREAD FROM THE CITIES TO RURAL AREAS WITH THE INTRODUCTION OF "INTERURBAN" NETWORKS OR, AS THEY WERE KNOWN IN CANADA, "RADIALS."

The Yakima Valley Transportation Company Interurban Railroad opened in 1907, connecting Yakima, Selah and Wiley City, Washington. Its passenger service ceased in 1947, but the line ran freight until 1984. The City of Yakima acquired a portion of the track to run as a tourist operation by Yakima Valley Trolleys.

The interurban trolley seemed such a powerful idea, particularly in the American Midwest. The steam railroads had no interest in connecting small towns with any kind of frequent service, for the large locomotives took a long time to stop and then get up to speed again. Trolleys, on the other hand, were suited to quick stops and starts, smooth acceleration, and long runs at high speed. The later American interurban cars appeared unstoppable—majestic machines that could out-accelerate a steam locomotive. They were an intimidating 3 ft (91 cm) higher than a streetcar and twice as heavy.

The technology was easily adaptable to long distances. Using low-loss, high-voltage lines to transmit the power, and step-down transformers and rectifiers spaced along the track to feed the accustomed 600 volts dc to the car, power losses were kept to a minimum. The first of the interurbans, in Sandusky, Ohio and Portland, Oregon in 1893, folded quickly, largely because hardware and reliability still presented problems. Nevertheless, pressure mounted for the construction of new interurban lines.

Not only did large stretches of the country need to be tied together, but people were convinced that their town was "nowhere," a backwater, unless it had an interurban connection. So the networks grew and grew from the Midwest, where Ohio alone had nearly 3,000 miles (4,800 km) of track, and it was possible to take a 217 mile (349 km) trip between Cincinnati and Toledo. The Northeast and the South were also affected, with property values rising everywhere, and the giant railroad companies started to acquire control of the upstart interurbans. In the West, where such men as Henry E. Huntington and his Pacific Electric streetcar company were building furiously, it was possible in Los Angeles in 1905 to make a profit of 60 percent on property held for just a month. By 1913, plans to construct a grand interurban connection from New York to Chicago, which would be called the "Air Line," were complete. Two beautifully appointed cars were built for the Air Line and stock was sold, but the line was never built.

It cost more and more to bring each new passenger into the system and, as city centers grew more congested,

the 60–70 mph (95–110 km/h) speedsters had to crawl through town. Most ominous of all, roads were improving and interurban passengers were growing ever more vulnerable to the siren call of the automobile. In their short golden age, the interurbans had been magnificent machines though, with names like the Orange Limited, the Muncie Meteor, and the Red Devil. They are all gone now. The only remaining interurban run in the United States is the South Shore Line, which uses modern rolling stock and connects South Bend, Indiana to downtown Chicago, Illinois.

One of the best known of the early interurban lines was the Chicago, North Shore & Milwaukee Railroad. Beginning in 1891 as the Waukegan & North Shore Rapid Transit Co., a trolley line for the city of Waukegan, 36 miles (58 km) north of Chicago, Illinois, it was extended south to Lake Bluff and became the Chicago, North Shore & Milwaukee Electric Railroad when extended farther to Chicago.

The year 1895 saw the first haulage by electric locomotives of main-line trains on standard gauge. The Baltimore & Ohio Railroad tunneled under the city of Baltimore, while the sections between the Waverley and Camden stations—about 3 miles (5 km)—were electrified by the Westinghouse Electric Company in 1895 to eliminate the smoke nuisance created by steam locomotives. At first, a conventional train, including a coke-burning locomotive with steam shut off and the valve gear in mid-gear, was hauled by pairs of Bo + Bo electric motors through the tunnel sections. This was the forerunner of the Baltimore Belt System. The electrification was at 600 volts dc on the overhead system. Instead of a contact wire, because of the high current demand, an overhead rail supported from insulators was provided and current was collected by a pantograph arm with a shoe that ran along the rail. The locomotives were of the "steeple-cab" type with four gearless traction motors. This pickup system was later replaced by a third rail.

The technology used to run electric streetcars was applied, in the early 20th century, to interurbans connecting cities and towns—transporting freight and passengers. In urban areas they ran on the tracks of existing streetcars; between towns, new tracks were laid on their own rights-of-way. Interurban lines were prolific in the Midwest. People could ride from upstate New York to Wisconsin on a connecting interurban line. In the 1920s, when automobiles became more popular, the interurbans began to lose popularity and, within the next 20 years, all but disappeared.

THE ADAPTABLE STREETCAR

FROM THE 1890S TO THE MID-1920S, STREETCAR NETWORKS GREW IN NUMBERS AND IN SIZE, AND THE STREETCARS BECAME BIGGER, FASTER, SAFER, AND MORE COMFORTABLE.

In the early years of the 20th century, the small, four-wheeled vehicles that had replaced the horsecars were themselves succeeded by longer, heavier cars carried on pairs of four-wheel trucks, and wooden bodies were replaced by steel. Another innovation, not always welcomed by the passengers, was the trend for those networks that operated cars with open-sided bodies to phase them out in favor of designs with fully enclosed bodies and glazed windows. In the early days of the trolley, there was little difference in comfort between closed and open cars, because on both types the open platforms at front and rear had little more than a waist-high dashboard for weather protection. Nevertheless, when summer came the public wanted open cars, and even in Canada, the closed cars would be put into storage and out would come the "breezers."

Many companies possessed two fleets of streetcars, one open and one closed. The transit lines hated the expense and inefficiency of this, but they were partly to blame. To increase passenger revenue, they

had encouraged people to take weekend and vacation excursion tours and special trips. How many people at the beginning of the 20th century had any other way to feel the cooling rush of air as they took a spin through meadows and woods at a galloping 15 mph (24 km/h) on a hot July day? Streetcar companies financed and built parks at the ends of their lines to encourage leisure traffic. These "trolley parks" were often fanciful places with picnic grounds, bandstands, dance halls, games fields, scenic railways, or roller coasters, lit and powered by electricity from the same sources that supplied the trolleys. There was Luna Park, Washington, D.C., Overlook

Open streetcars known as "breezers" were a welcome relief in the hot summer months. This car ran on 8th and Central Avenues, Minneapolis, Minnesota, in 1894. Its curtains could be drawn to shield against the sun, or if the weather was less clement. The driver, however, stood on an open platform at the front.

Park, Ohio, with its automated piano, Willow Grove Park, Pennsylvania, with its Electric Fountain, lit at night by multicolored electric lights, and countless others. Ravinia Park, Illinois even had the Chicago Symphony Orchestra.

Despite this, the companies hated the open cars, although they loved the revenue they brought in. The open benches and full-length step rails also encouraged people to leap on and off cars while they were in motion, so increasing accident rates. Worst of all, from the companies' point of view, passengers could avoid the conductor and "beat the fare." As fare collection plans evolved in the closed cars, the open cars disappeared from all but the hardiest tourist lines.

As much as the public loved open cars, the trolley companies resisted demands to provide two sets of cars for good and bad weather, or even to have two sets of bodies, as was tried in Baltimore and a few other places. In Baltimore, the Union Railway & Electric Co. thought it the height of efficiency to buy one set of trucks and wheels, and two sets of bodies for its new fleet in 1902. Thus 110 enclosed bodies sat idle in spring and summer until each fall they replaced the airy, awning-bedecked open car bodies. To overcome the problem of having so much expensive equipment lying idle for half the year, several designs—called "convertibles"—attempted to combine the best features of both open and closed bodies.

Some of the earliest attempts to obviate the need for two fleets of cars, or two sets of bodies, were the half-and-half designs known as "California" cars, such as those still in use on San Francisco's cable-car system. The flaw in the design was that on sunny days everyone wanted to be outside, but when it rained, people huddled inside, so half the car's capacity was always unused.

As with many of the innovations in streetcar design, the true convertible seems to have had its beginnings in Canada. In Toronto in 1904, cars were designed with removable side panels that could be changed in the sheds. Some single-ended cars were built as "nearside convertibles," with only one side (the one away from traffic) removable. Others were more flexible and could be changed quickly "in case of a change in the weather." Brill had one with straight-sided panels that slid up into the roof. There was also the Duplex design, which used curved sliding panels; these last were known as semiconvertibles.

Open cars and convertibles were both phased out during World War I. The dangers of boarding open cars, especially as traffic, and the transportation companies' preoccupation with fare-dodging increased, meant that only a few tourist-type open or convertible cars continued into the 1920s and 1930s. One exception was in New York City, where the convertible cars remained in day-to-day service throughout Brooklyn until after World War II. Perhaps the secret of their longevity was the open metal grille work that replaced the windows in summer and kept passengers from losing an arm or leg in the brutal New York traffic.

Some streetcars, such as the San Francisco cable cars still in use today, were half-and-half varieties, offering fully enclosed seating at one end, or open benches at the other. However, during inclement weather, passengers tended to desert the open seating and huddle in the enclosed section.

TROLLEY MAP OF

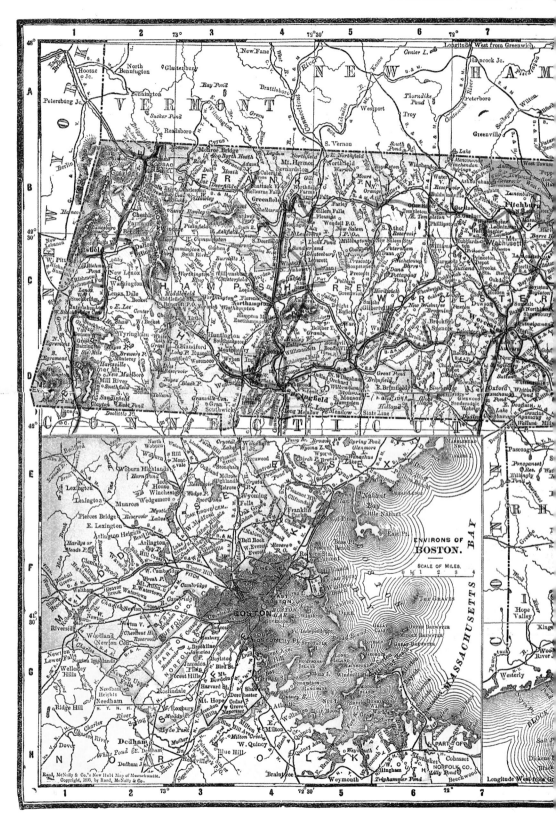

HUSETTS

A 1912 map of Massachusetts showing the extent of the trolley system. This widespread system of routes was replicated across the country and made it possible to travel, for example, from New York to Portland Maine, or Chicago to Minneapolis, by trolley alone. All the passenger needed was time, and a nickel for every stage of the journey.

RAILROADS TO THE PACIFIC 1893–1900

AFTER THE ORIGINAL RAILROAD TO THE PACIFIC WAS COMPLETED IN 1869, OTHERS FOLLOWED, HELPING TO OPEN UP VAST SWATHES OF LAND, PARTICULARLY IN THE NORTHWEST WHERE SEVERAL RAILROAD COMPANIES VIED FOR BUSINESS.

President Lincoln signed the Northern Pacific Railroad's charter in 1864, but the first northern transcontinental line was not completed until 1883. The line ran from Duluth, Minnesota, to Seattle, Washington State. In the 1970s, the Northern Pacific became part of the Burlington Northern.

By 1890, the Union Pacific/Central Pacific line across the United States, which had become known as the "Overland Route," had been joined by three more railroads to the Pacific coast. These were the Northern Pacific and the Southern Pacific Railroads, both completed in 1883, and the Atchison, Topeka & Santa Fe Railroad, completed in 1888.

The Northern Pacific route began at the twin cities of Minneapolis and St. Paul, in Minnesota, and headed westward through southern North Dakota and Montana. It ran parallel to the border with Idaho before crossing to Spokane, Washington. Then it passed through the Cascade Mountains, dropped

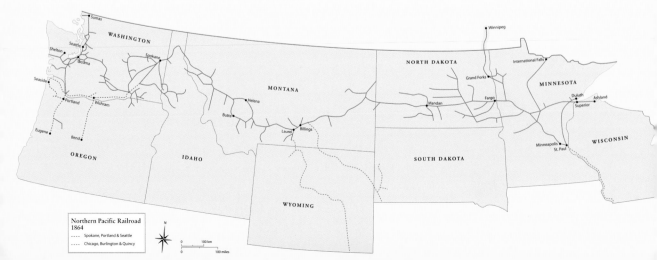

Northern Pacific Railroad
1864
- - - - Spokane, Portland & Seattle
- - - - Chicago, Burlington & Quincy

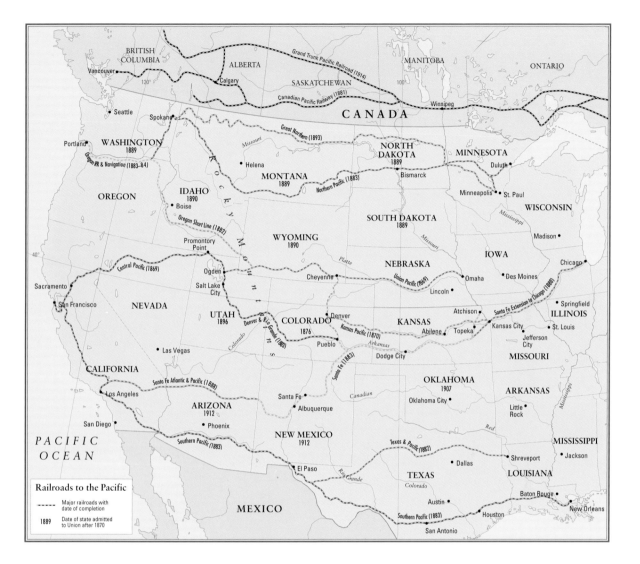

down into Portland and on to Seattle. The line was built with government subsidies and massive land grants, which included all of present-day Yellowstone Park. It was not the most direct of routes to the Pacific Northwest, however, and it had many steeply graded sections that tested the mettle of the early locomotives.

Many hundreds of miles to the south, the Southern Pacific ran all the way down through California from San Francisco to Los Angeles, then across into Arizona where its route ran near the border with Mexico. The railroad stayed close to the border as it passed through New Mexico and across Texas into Louisiana, finally reaching New Orleans. The Southern Pacific played a major role in developing California, since it enjoyed a near monopoly on north–south traffic, and it became very influential in state affairs, as it had politicians from both parties in its pocket. In 1885, the Southern Pacific Railroad took over the

By 1893, when the Great Northern Railroad was completed, linking Minneapolis and St. Paul with the West Coast, there were several routes to the Pacific, all of which played major roles in opening up the western states to migrants from the East.

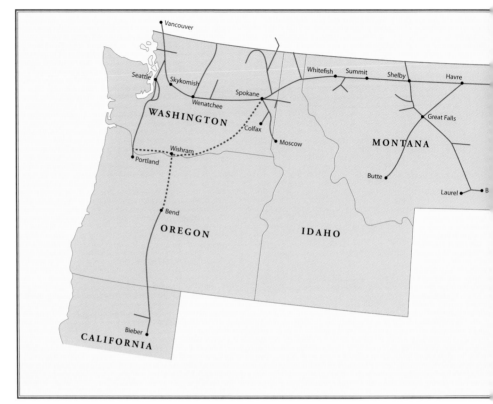

Central Pacific's portion of the Overland Route. On two occasions, the Southern Pacific came to the aid of the population of California: in 1905, following the Imperial Valley floods, and a year later, after the San Francisco earthquake.

Westward from Chicago, the Atchison, Topeka & Santa Fe Railroad (known simply as the Santa Fe) provided a truly great route to the Pacific coast. It ran through Dodge City, Kansas, Albuquerque, New Mexico, and on to Los Angeles, California, crossing seven states, three time zones, and three great mountain ranges. The total route length was 2,223 miles (3,577 km). The Santa Fe went on to become probably the best-known railroad in the United States, running such famous trains as the steam-hauled Chief and the diesel-powered Super Chief. At the peak of the steam era, during World War II, when an efficient service of very heavy trains running across the country to the West Coast was a national necessity, only two locomotives were needed for the entire journey, which took two days.

One of the original syndicate involved in building the Canadian Pacific Railroad was James Jerome Hill, who had substantial business interests in the United States. He had urged that the Canadian Pacific be routed south of Lake Superior, into United States territory, to link up with those interests, but he was outvoted. As a result, he resigned from the project and set about promoting a rival transcontinental line in the United States, which became known as the Great Northern. This railroad had its headquarters at

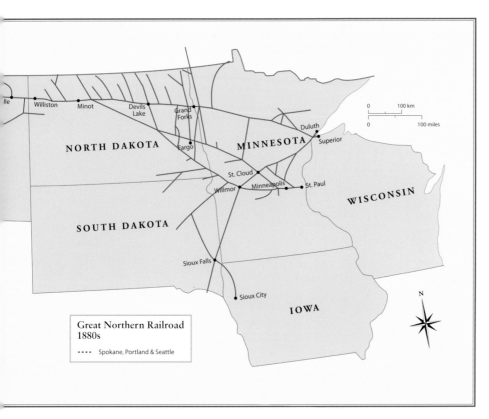

Great Northern Railroad
1880s

•••• Spokane, Portland & Seattle

Minneapolis/St. Paul, Minnesota. Work began in 1887, with a route being forged across northern North Dakota, Montana, and Idaho. Meanwhile, the western portion of the line was built from Seattle across Washington State and up into the Cascade Mountains. The onset of winter in 1892 made the work in the mountains arduous, but on January 6, 1893, the two tracks met in the snow high in Stevens Pass.

In addition to competing with the Canadian Pacific, the Great Northern Railroad also had a rival in the shape of the Northern Pacific Railroad. The Northern Pacific was saddled with debt and heading for bankruptcy following the stock market plunge of 1893, which set off five years of financial panic. By 1900, James Jerome Hill's banker, J.P. Morgan, had hatched a plan to take over the Northern Pacific and hand it to Hill to run along with the Great Northern. Morgan and Hill also took over the Chicago, Burlington & Quincy Railroad, combining all three under the Northern Securities banner. Eventually, Hill's railroad activities would earn him the name "the Empire Builder," which later would be applied to a Great Northern Railroad.

The Union Pacific Railroad completed its Oregon Short Line across Idaho to Portland, Oregon in 1884, while in August 1893, the Minneapolis, St. Paul & Sault Ste. Marie Railway (Soo Line) linked the twin cities of Minneapolis and St. Paul with Portal on the border between North Dakota and Canada. This provided a connection with the Canadian Pacific and a through route to Vancouver.

James Jerome Hill (1838–1916), pictured around 1890. From Wellington County, Upper Canada (now Ontario), he relocated to the USA to build the Great Northern transcontinental railroad. "What we want," Hill said, "is the best possible line, shortest distance, lowest grades, and least curvature we can build. We do not care enough for Rocky Mountains scenery to spend a large sum of money developing it." Hill planned the route himself, traveling on horseback.

Consolidation and legal issues, 1900-10

THE FIRST THREE DECADES OF THE 20TH CENTURY SAW CONSOLIDATION RATHER THAN EXPANSION, ALTHOUGH SOME NEW RAILROADS WERE BUILT.

In 1900, Arizona, New Mexico, Oklahoma, Alaska, and Hawaii were still classed as territories. The part played by the railroads in encouraging growth in the first three at least must have contributed to their eventual elevation to full statehood.

The industrialized Northeast's dense network of large and small railroads had grown faster than anywhere else in the country, although in other regions some were catching up rapidly. The railroads were the single most important factor in the development of modern America. As large railroad corporations grew and became more powerful, it suited them either to acquire smaller roads or to squeeze them out of business. Many of these had serious financial problems and were glad to be rescued by more prosperous concerns.

In 1901, the Baltimore & Ohio, the oldest United States railroad, had a large slice of its stock acquired by Pennsylvania Railroad, and Leonor F. Loree was installed as president. He immediately began a major program of route improvement, which included reducing grades and curves, and doubling many miles of track. He also secured a large interest in the Reading Railroad, which in turn brought in the Central Railroad of New Jersey, already under Reading control. The Central passed fully into control by the Pennsylvania after a few years.

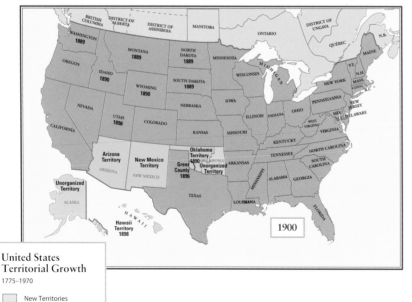

United States
Territorial Growth
1775–1970

☐ New Territories

☐ Canadian Territories

■ US States

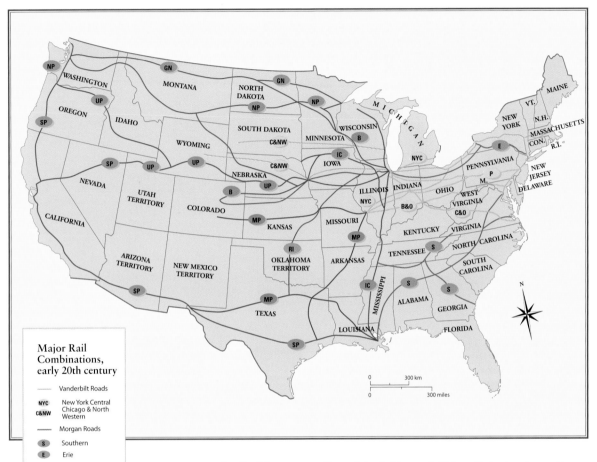

Major Rail Combinations, early 20th century

——		Vanderbilt Roads
NYC **C&NW**		New York Central Chicago & North Western
——		Morgan Roads
S		Southern
E		Erie
——		Pennsylvania Group
P		Pennsylvania
B&O		Baltimore & Ohio
C&O		Chesapeake & Ohio
——		Harriman Roads
UP		Union Pacific
SP		Southern Pacific
IC		Illinois Central
——		Hill Roads
GN		Great Northern
NP		Northern Pacific
B		Burlington
——		Gould System
MP		Missouri Pacific
——		Rock Island System
RI		Rock Island

In 1910, Daniel Willard became president of the Baltimore & Ohio Railroad. In the same year, Baltimore & Ohio Railroad acquired the Chicago Terminal Transfer Railroad, which was renamed the Baltimore & Ohio Chicago Transfer Railroad. Further acquisitions extended the Baltimore & Ohio Railroad area of operations from New York City in the East to Chicago in the North, and St. Louis, Missouri in the West. By 1929, Baltimore & Ohio Railroad operated 5,658 miles (9,105 km) of railroad and owned 2,364 locomotives.

The fact that competition was so great had a side effect for the railroads generally. The struggle for traffic forced down rates to a point where the strongest companies could make a profit. Although there were agreements to maintain rates, these were just pieces of paper—there was practically no limit to the rebates extorted by the shippers and their agents under threat of diverting traffic to other carriers. There was discrimination and undue preference in the most insidious and corrupting form. While many

During the early part of the 20th century, many United States railroads merged or were taken over by more prosperous companies. The major consolidations are shown on this map.

Alexander Cassatt, President of the Pennsylvania Railroad, and other major railroad executives worked to strengthen the Commerce Act, preventing unscrupulous carriers from giving preferential rates to particular customers or for certain types of traffic.

By 1900, the total length of United States railroads had grown to 192,556 miles (309,880 km). The densest part of the network remained in the industrialized Northeast.

industries prospered by these practices, the railways suffered proportionately.

In the 10 years to 1900, the number of freight cars had increased by 64.5 percent and locomotives by only 29.5 percent, indicating better utilization as well as increased locomotive haulage capacity. Passenger cars too had increased, but only by 41.2 percent. The figures indicate the intensive development that had been characteristic of American railroads over the decade. The demand for increased transport along established lines encouraged the laying of double tracks. There was considerable investment in improving facilities, easing gradients, and realigning routes, which was made possible by reducing or withholding dividends to stockholders.

Earnings from both passenger traffic and freight were low, and attempts by the carriers to increase these rates to compensate for mounting expenses in 1900 brought more protests to the Interstate Commerce Commission and to Congress. The so-called Elkins Amendment to the Commerce Act strengthened its provisions, forbidding special rates, rebates, or other devices granting undue preference to any individual or type of traffic. In addition, the publication of tariffs was made obligatory, and any practice on the part of carriers to transport any article at a lower rate than that named in the tariffs was prohibited under penalty.

While Senator Elkins gave his name to the legislation, it was in fact a joint effort on the part of railway executives under the leadership of President Cassatt of the Pennsylvania Railroad to root out the demoralizing and destructive practices of unscrupulous corporations, which threatened to disgrace the transportation system and lead it to financial disaster.

Railroads, 1900

In 1906, the ICC got what it wanted. On June 20, Congress approved the Hepburn Bill, which gave it authority to prescribe rates in place of those that, after complaint and hearing, it pronounced unjust, unreasonable, or discriminating. Even so, a year later, although railroad managers had accepted the act in

Work began on the first railroad in Alaska in 1903, with 50 miles (80 km) of track being laid north from Seward on the coast. In 1910, another 71 miles (114 km) were added. Four years later, Congress voted to fund construction and operation of the railroad through to Fairbanks, at an estimated cost of $35 million. The Alaska Railroad was finally completed in 1923, when President Warren G. Harding drove in the golden spike at Nenana, one of the state's largest cities at the time.

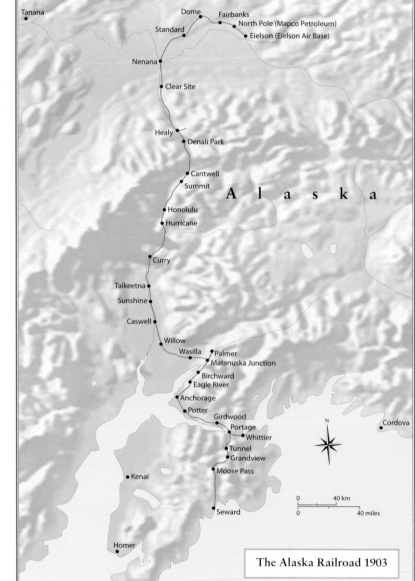

The Alaska Railroad 1903

good faith, little progress had been made in implementing it, and suits were filed questioning the right of Congress to delegate to any tribunal the authority to establish an interstate rate.

It was not until 1910 that the position was finally clarified, and the Commission received almost absolute authority over the rate-making phase of railroad management. Not only was it authorized to suspend rate increases until the circumstances had been investigated, but the act imposed the burden of proof on carriers to justify any proposed rate advances.

The immediate effect of this was to put the brakes on expansion and construction. New mileage in the six years following the passing of the Act showed a drop of 34 percent compared to the six years before. Receipts from freight dropped by $30 million a year.

The effects of stringent regulation were not the only things to affect the railroads as again, for the fifth time in eight decades, they were caught in the middle of financial panic in the fall of 1907. In the very heyday of their usefulness, the railroads found themselves in a situation that lost them $300 million, or over 11 percent of earnings, in one calendar year. Prompt and drastic retrenchment was essential, which reduced the payroll by nearly 18 percent in 1908. The recovery of the national economy and the railroads from this financial panic was not complete until 1910.

Stringent regulation would also have a lasting effect on the railroads' fortunes. Altogether, the first three decades of the century saw many changes in the railroads of the United States as a result of the regulations, together with natural disasters, a world war, and government policies that resulted in financial failures, mergers, and company buyouts.

By 1900, United States railroads were working 192,556 miles (309,880 km) of single track and 14,074 miles (22,649 km) of auxiliary track (lengths of double line, passing loops, etc., which indicates the increased volume of traffic over some routes), and had 52,154 miles (83,931 km) of sidings, giving a total track length of 258,784 miles (416,461 km). In addition, they operated 37,663 locomotives, 34,713 passenger cars, and 1,365,531 freight cars.

The harsh winter climate of Alaska can make keeping the tracks clear a difficult task. One solution was the steam powered blower, such as the White Pass snowplow, built in 1899 in Skagway, Alaska.

REROUTING, 1900–04

FINANCIAL PROBLEMS BESET THE SOUTHERN PACIFIC AND UNION PACIFIC RAILROADS, AND AS PART OF THE REVITALIZATION PLAN, THE TRACKS WERE IMPROVED TO ACCEPT HEAVIER ROLLING STOCK.

Railroads had grown in importance, while the mileage covered by their operations and the traffic were also requiring physical growth. The early tracks and trains had been small and relatively light, but by the turn of the century the sheer volume of traffic meant that the permanent way and bridges (particularly trestles) needed strengthening, many curves needed straightening, and gradients required easing. In some areas, new alignments, cutoffs, and even abandonment of some parts of routes were necessary.

A prime example was the original transcontinental route, which had been completed in 1869. It was soon found that little revenue was generated by through traffic from the East, and although local traffic produced much of the income, this was still modest, since development of the country was slow at first. As a result, the railroad was starved of revenue and passed into administration. Then Edward H. Harriman took the railroad in hand and used his extraordinary energy to make it pay.

Only 30 years after they were completed, the Union Pacific and Southern Pacific had to pay a huge price for the speed and cheapness of the original work. As early as 1869, a Federal commission had criticized the route of the Central Pacific through the Sierra Nevada: "The curvature was excessive and needlessly sharp. Throughout a large portion the ascents and descents had been multiplied needlessly. Grades of 70 to 80 ft (21-24 m)/mile (1.3 percent to 1.5 percent) had been introduced where one of 53 ft (16 m)/mile (1.0 percent) would have sufficed, and grades of 53 ft (16 m)/mile where one half that rate of ascent was required. In the Humboldt Valley between Lake Humboldt and Humboldt Wells, the difference in elevation of a little over 1,100 ft (335 m) had been overcome by ascents and descents amounting to 6,232 ft (2,000 m) in a distance of 290 miles (467 km)."

In fairness, it should be remembered that the track had been completed seven years ahead of estimate and, at the time of construction, facilities were crude. It was also claimed: "A good deal of improvement was purposely left to the future, when traffic developments should justify the expense."

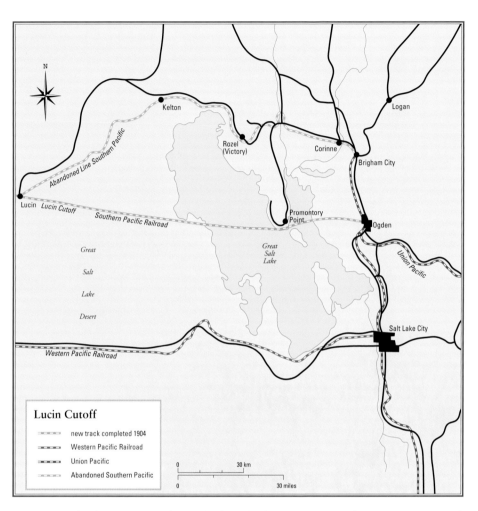

The Lucin Cutoff ran in almost a straight line from Ogden to Lucin, across the Great Salt Lake, cutting out the heavily graded section that ran around the north of the lake, which was expensive to operate. In doing so, however, it isolated the historic meeting place of the Union Pacific and Central Pacific railroads at Promontory Point.

By 1900, "developments" in traffic made the task of reconstruction and improvement essential. This involved tearing up and replacing much of the old track, abandoning some sections altogether to construct new ones, additional tunneling to ease gradients and curvature, and replacement of wooden trestles by steel bridges.

The original route between Summit, in west Omaha, and Lane ran for 21 miles (34 km). Even though the two towns were only 12 miles (19 km) apart, the land between them was rolling and partly unstable. The Omaha Cutoff, which replaced the original track, runs in a straight line, and to keep it as level as possible, construction involved excavating 2.8 million cu yds (2.14 million cu. m) and filling about 4.0 million cu yds (3.0 million cu. m) of embankment. At one point, the embankment is 65 ft (20 m) high and, at just over a mile long, it required 1.5 million cu yds (1.1 million cu. m) of earth. Another fill, across Little Papillon, took the track 89 ft (27 m) above the floor of the valley and was 3,100 ft (945 m) long.

Perhaps the best-known rerouting project is the Salt Lake, or Lucin, cutoff across the Great Salt Lake, in Utah, completed in 1904. This saved 43 miles (70 km) over the original line around the northern end

At the point where the causeway crosses, the Great Salt Lake is 30 miles (48 km) wide. The causeway itself rises 17 ft (5 m) above the water, while the width at the top is 16 ft (4.8 m). Construction was carried out by 3,000 men, working night and day, the bridge being built in two sections from opposite shores of the lake and meeting in the middle. A steamboat, the Promontory, was floated on the lake to tow barges with supplies and provisions for the construction camps.

Originally, engineers envisaged that the track for the Lucin Cutoff would be carried across the Great Salt Lake on a long wooden trestle bridge. In the end, however, only 12 miles (19 km) of trestle were built; the remainder of the causeway was an earth embankment. Even so, over 38,000 wooden piles were used, equating to a section of forest 2 miles (3 km) square.

of the lake, which was heavily graded with many curves. Unfortunately for history, it removed the track from the original point connecting east and west at Promontory summit, about 30 miles (48 km) west of Brigham City, where there is now a commemorative museum and the meeting place is designated the Golden Spike National Historical Site. The last spike ceremony is reenacted there regularly. The original line was finally abandoned and the rails lifted in 1942.

From Sacramento, California eastward, the line had to climb the western flank of the Sierra Nevada, and from Roseville, the climb was 7,000 ft (2,134 m) in 140 miles (225 km) to Donner Pass, about 30 miles (48 km) west of the Nevada state line. Bridges were strengthened and track realigned to ease gradients and curvature. The ruling gradient was reduced to 1 in 42 (2.4 percent), although some sections were still as steep as 1 in 38 (2.63 percent). Protection of the track from avalanches needed a total of 40 miles (64 km) of snow sheds and 39 tunnels. Track was relaid to take the heavier rolling stock necessitated by Edward Harriman's revitalization program.

In less than 30 years, the transcontinental railroad changed the nature of the country through which it passed and helped open up the West. Omaha became the third-largest packing station for meat products in the country. Fremont, 30 miles (48 km) northwest of Omaha, grew from nothing into a thriving city. The prairie became a great agricultural region as well as an exporter of livestock and minerals. Lexington, on the Platte River, grew on the site where South Cheyenne Indians had burned a freight train in 1867, and Laramie, Wyoming became a mining center with railroad workshops. Some 200 miles (322 km) to the west, Green River became the junction for the northward route via Idaho, to Portland, Oregon and Seattle and Spokane in Washington.

EASTERN CITY ROUTES

IN THE EAST, COMPETITION FOR PASSENGERS BETWEEN THE MAJOR CITIES WAS INTENSE, NOWHERE MORE SO THAN ON THE NEW YORK–CHICAGO ROUTE. PUBLICITY-CONSCIOUS RAILROADS INTRODUCED NAMED LUXURY TRAINS, AND THE IDEAL OF "CHICAGO IN 24 HOURS" FROM NEW YORK WAS SOON BETTERED.

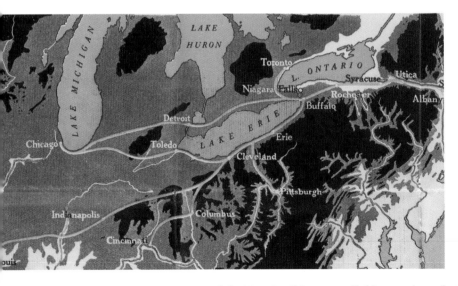

Many early railroads followed rivers and watercourses because they meant easy grades. The New York Central enjoyed this benefit on its route to Chicago.

The New York Central Railroad had its Empire State Express, while the Pennsylvania Railroad had the Pennsylvania Limited. The Vanderbilts controlled the New York Central Railroad, and the president of the Pennsylvania was Alexander J. Cassatt. To say that there was considerable rivalry between them is an understatement but, fortunately, they confined their hostility to undercutting each other's rates and rival services.

The New York Central & Hudson River Railroad and its ally, the Lake Shore & Michigan Southern Railroad, operated the Water Level Route, so-called because it ran for the most part in sight of water (notably the Hudson River) and therefore was relatively easily graded. Its route distance between New York and Chicago was 961 miles (1,547 km). The rival "mountain" route of the Pennsylvania Railroad negotiated 1 in 50 (2 percent) grades and climbed to 2,193 ft (668 m) across the Alleghenies, but it had a shorter route of 912 miles (1,468 km) and moreover, called at Philadelphia on the way. An overall average speed of 40 mph (64 km/h) does not seem much by today's standards, but it was very creditable in the last few years of the 19th century. Stops along the way were necessary, since locomotives had to be changed, water replenished, and attention given to train service requirements.

In New York City, the two railroads had separate stations: the New York Central had its Grand Central Terminal (remodeled and enlarged in 1900) in Manhattan while the Pennsylvania Railroad's terminal was across the Hudson at Exchange Place, Jersey City. They shared the same terminal in Chicago, however, on La Salle Street. The rivalry became intense when, in 1902, the New York Central introduced a new luxury train called the Twentieth Century Limited, which cut the time between the two cities to 20 hours at an average of 48 mph (77 km/h).

Built by ALCO, this 4-4-0 high wheeler, No. 999 of the New York Central, was said to be the first steam locomotive to have exceeded 100 mph (160 km/h) when in service hauling the Empire State Express.

The inaugural train on June 15, 1902 consisted of only five wooden-bodied cars—two sleepers, a diner, a buffet car, and an end-platform observation car. It was hauled by a high-wheeler of the same type as the speed-record holder, No. 999 (which resides today in the Chicago Museum of Science and Industry). On the day the Twentieth Century Limited was inaugurated, it was challenged by the Pennsylvania Railroad, which introduced the Pennsylvania Special, running its 912 miles (1,468 km) also in 20 hours at an average of 45.6 mph (73 km/h).

While both trains left New York City from different stations in different directions, sharing the same station in Chicago caused the most rivalry. Since they both departed from La Salle Street at the same time (12.40 pm) for the journey to New York on parallel tracks, there was usually a race over the first few miles to Gary, Indiana.

One of the impressive Hudson (4-6-4) type locomotives built by A L CO in the 1930s for the New York Central and used for hauling the Twentieth Century Limited, among others.

So successful were these trains that patronage grew quickly. By 1903, two trains for each road were often necessary. Special rolling stock was built, steel cars being introduced in 1903 and upgraded at regular intervals as one railroad attempted to outdo the other. Trains became longer and heavier, so larger steam locomotives were soon required.

The New York Central terminal in Manhattan was approached by tunnel. Some 700 trains in and out of Grand Central every day produced considerable smoke nuisance, and by the early

Chicago's La Salle Street station, destination for the rival express services from New York, operated by the New York Central and the Pennsylvania.

1900s, the pollution had given rise to serious concern. This was compounded in 1902 by a serious accident in the approach tunnel, when a train overran a stop signal obscured by smoke, and 15 people were killed. In 1903, the New York legislature passed a law prohibiting the use of "smoking locomotives" south of the Harlem River (effectively south of 125th Street) after July 1, 1908. The railroad had to act or it would be barred from its prestigious and conveniently located Manhattan terminal. The railroad chose electrification.

The Baltimore & Ohio Railroad had earlier used electric locomotives in its tunnels running under the city of Baltimore, while the New Haven Railroad had electrified some of its Connecticut branch lines on the third-rail system at 600 volts dc. This was the system chosen for the lines into Grand Central.

A total of 35 electric locomotives was built by the American Locomotive Company (ALCO) and General Electric and delivered in 1906. Electric haulage was introduced a year later, the changeover point being Wakefield. In 1913, electrification was extended to

Locomotive No. 999 of the New York Central hauled the Empire State Express to a record speed of 112 mph (179 km/h).

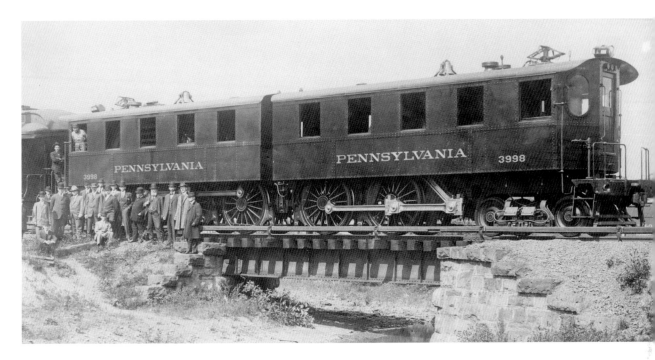

Harmon, some 33 miles (53 km) from New York City on the east side of the Hudson River, where steam locomotives were exchanged for electric, and vice versa, and where a large locomotive depot was built. The New Haven Railroad, which shared Grand Central Terminal, had a changeover point also on the east side of the river a couple of miles (3 km) away at Croton. Electric multiple-unit cars were introduced on local services.

Pennsylvania's terminal in Jersey City meant that travelers on this line to New York had to complete their journey by ferry. In 1900, the "Pennsy" acquired the Long Island Railroad and, after a study of possibilities for bridges and tunnels, in 1904 it began construction of Pennsylvania Station on Manhattan Island. Sited between Seventh and Eighth Avenues and 31st and 33rd Streets, it was in a good position. A twin tunnel was constructed under the Hudson as well as four single tunnels under the East River, which, together with a double-track main line across the Hackensack Meadows, connected the new terminal to its road east of Newark, New Jersey. All these lines were electrified, again on the 600 volt dc, third-rail system. The new Pennsylvania Station was opened in 1910 and electric haulage in and out of the terminal began, with steam locomotives being changed for electric, and vice versa, at a station called Manhattan Transfer, where it was also possible for passengers to make cross-platform interchange with the Hudson subways.

On November 24, 1912, the Pennsylvania Special was renamed Broadway Limited. The name was coined, not to honor the entertainment industry, but in recognition of the fact that much of the route between New York and Chicago was quadruple track—a subtlety that was probably lost on most travelers. Both roads were obliged to introduce steel rolling stock, since wooden cars were banned from using the tunnels.

A crowd poses in front of the Pennsylvania Railroad car, No. 3998. This was the largest electric locomotive in the world, when it was first introduced during the early 1900s to run through the subway line into New York City.

Natural disasters

NORTH AMERICAN RAILROADS HAD TO FACE STORMS, FLOODS, AND WINTER SNOW. THEY ALSO HAD TO CONTEND WITH EARTHQUAKES AND LANDSLIDES.

Many railroad lines followed watercourses, with the tracks often only a few feet above the normal high-water level, making them vulnerable to flooding, while others endured washouts and destruction by torrential rain in the hills and mountains. Lines west of the Mississippi followed or crossed many rivers that could turn into rushing torrents, irrespective of the season. The Mississippi itself has been responsible for much railroad destruction.

When the San Francisco earthquake of 1906 devastated the city, the railroads also suffered—but not so seriously, and they played a significant role in the rescue work. On the first day of the disaster, the railroads delivered food from Los Angeles by special fast freight, and moved 1,073 carloads of refugees away from the city. Between April 18 and May 23, the Union Pacific and Southern Pacific together took in 1,603 carloads of supplies and carried out 224,069 refugees, absorbing costs that amounted to over $1 million.

In his *Short History of American Railways* (1925), Slason Thompson wrote: "The bears of the stock exchange in New York did not fail to take note of the calamity. The psychological tremor that struck San Francisco was felt across the continent and shook more than $1 billion of market value out of railroad securities. Between April 17 and May 20 the shares of the leading companies sold off all the way from 6 to 48 points. Industrial stocks showed their sympathetic sensitiveness to anything affecting the railways by even greater losses."

Railroads have also played their part in dispensing first aid, and sometimes other forms of assistance, to the injured in almost every state, and mostly have been taken for granted for being willing rescuers.

An earthquake caused severe damage to San Francisco in 1906, but help was at hand from the railroads, which shipped in supplies and evacuated refugees to safety—despite the fact that many of the tracks had been badly warped and rendered impassible by trains.

Above: North Shore locomotive (since Northwestern Pacific did not take over the line until 1907) on the morning of the 1906 earthquake at Point Reyes Station.

Left: After the earthquake in San Francisco came the conflagration, as fires swept through the city. Helpless citizens could only stand by and watch. This photograph clearly shows the cable car track in the center of the devastated road.

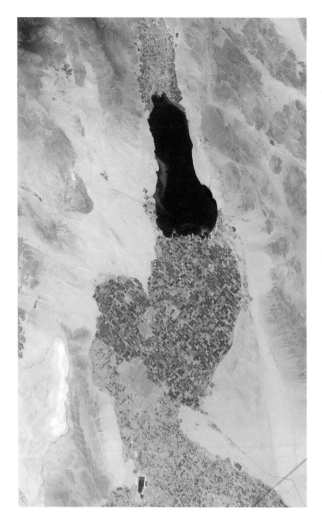

The Salton Sea today, as seen from a satellite orbiting the earth. The floods that led to its formation threatened the fertile Imperial Valley. Thanks to the help of the Southern Pacific Railroad, the valley was saved.

Another illustration is the way the Southern Pacific saved Imperial Valley after the floods of 1905.

Today, Imperial Valley is known as a rich section of southern California, famed for its glorious climate and golden harvests—both agricultural and mineral. Geographically, it is a depression in the earth's surface about 100 miles (161 km) long and 35 miles (56 km) wide, which was once covered by water to a depth of 300 ft (91 m) at its deepest part. Originally, this area was part of the Gulf of California, but in time the Colorado River formed a barrier of silt, leaving the upper stretch a great salt lake. Slowly, the water evaporated and an arid basin, called the Salton Sink, remained. There is geological evidence that from time to time in the past, the Colorado has broken through the barrier, and the process that formed the Sink has been repeated several times over.

In 1902, a canal was dug from the Colorado River at Pilot Knob, opposite Yuma, Arizona. The Sink was renamed Imperial Valley, and 400 miles (644 km) of ditches were dug to irrigate 100,000 acres (40,470 ha) of land. The railway, a branch of the Southern Pacific, arrived in 1904, bringing with it more than 10,000 settlers, and numerous townships were established. The capacity of the canals and ditches quadrupled, and by the beginning of 1905, 120,000 acres (48,564 ha) of reclaimed land were under cultivation. The soil was so rich that it would produce almost anything. The air of the valley was so dry that men could work in a shade temperature of 120°F (49°C) without exhaustion.

Nobody seems to have realized that the bottom of the valley was far below the level of the Pacific Ocean. In 1904, silt from the Colorado clogged up the canal and the California Development Company cut a new intake from the river, but failed to provide head-gate control. In February 1905, it flooded, but not seriously. A second flood followed shortly afterward and in March the volume of water, increased by the rapid melting of snow, enlarged the size of the intake. The breach increased in size so rapidly that no amount of plugging with piles, brushwood, and sandbags was of any use. Water flowed into the valley through a breach 100 ft (30 m) wide at the rate of 90,000 cu. ft (2,547 cu. m) a second—a new Salton Sea was forming.

As the valley filled, the town of Salton, parts of the nearby Indian Reservation, and a long section of the Southern Pacific Railroad was flooded. The Southern Pacific Railroad mounted a lengthy rescue operation, during which the railroad poured in a great deal of money and resources to achieve a successful conclusion—a feat as remarkable in its way as its operations during the San Francisco earthquake. The flooding was finally checked in 1907 by a dike, built with the aid of railroad cars that

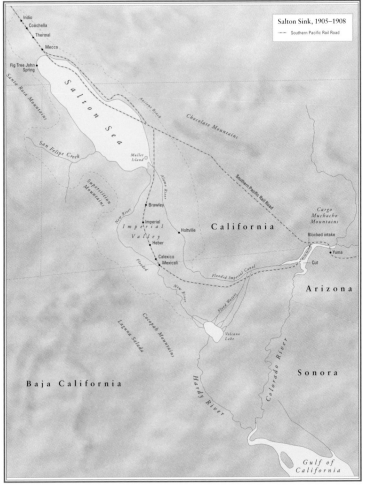

Salton Sink, 1905–1908
— · — Southern Pacific Rail Road

dumped boulders into the floodwaters. The Southern Pacific spent $3.1 million on rescuing Imperial Valley, and although Congress was urged by both President Theodore Roosevelt and his successor, William Howard Taft, to reimburse the claim in some measure "for coming to the rescue of the Government at the instance of President Roosevelt in a great emergency," as Taft put it, the claim was never honored. In January 1911, the Senate House Committee on Claims reported a bill appropriating $773,000, but it was not taken any farther. In 1916, it was claimed that the farmers in the Imperial Valley expected to earn a sum equivalent to the interest on $500 million.

To quote Slason Thompson again: "In this splendid piece of rescue work the Southern Pacific simply added to the long list of sacrifices American railroads have made for the communities they serve, only to experience the traditional ingratitude of republics."

Another disaster befell the cities, towns, and settlements in the state of Ohio in March 1913. Floods inundated an area of about 315 sq. miles (816 sq. km), with the city of Columbus at its center, when 7 to 8 in (18 to 20cm) of rain fell in four days, following wind damage that had already disrupted telegraph and telephone communication in the area. The Pennsylvania Railroad probably suffered most, but other railroads also affected by the floodwater were the New York Central, "Big Four," Erie, Baltimore & Ohio, Hocking Valley, Wabash, and many of the other small railroad companies that served the flooded area. This time, the direct monetary loss was estimated at $300 million. Again, this sum of money was never reinbursed.

The lack of head-gate control on the new canal intake from the Colorado River led to the flooding of Imperial Valley in 1905. In the process, a long section of the Southern Pacific Railroad was inundated and a new Salton Sea was formed.

Presidents William Howard Taft (top) and Theodore Roosevelt (above) urged Congress to reimburse the Southern Pacific Railroad for its great efforts in saving Imperial Valley, but with little success.

NEW CONSTRUCTIONS, 1906–10

IN THE EARLY PART OF THE 20TH CENTURY, MUCH NEW CONSTRUCTION WAS CARRIED OUT BY THE NORTH AMERICAN RAILROADS AND MANY MAJOR CITIES SAW THE ERECTION OF MAGNIFICENT TERMINAL BUILDINGS.

In 1906, the New York Central began constructing a tunnel to replace the ferry that had long been its only way to run trains from Detroit across the Detroit River into Windsor, Ontario. The river is over half a mile (0.8 km) wide and in places is 50 ft (15 m) deep, with an uneven bottom and a mph (3 km/h) current. To avoid steep approach gradients, the decision was made to construct a tubular tunnel on the riverbed rather than a bored tunnel beneath it.

To provide a graded bed for the tubes, the river was dredged at that point to a depth of 74 ft (22.5 m) below the lowest surface level. Sections of tube measuring 260 ft (79 m) long were constructed 5 miles (8 km) upstream, loaded on pontoons that were launched sideways, and floated downriver to be sunk into position. Supreme accuracy was essential so that sections could be placed and joined to form a continuous tunnel. The internal diameter of each concrete-lined tube was 23 ft 4 in (7.1 m), and they were encased in concrete so as to form in cross-section a solid rectangle, the function of which was to exclude water completely.

The magnificent Pennsylvania Station, with its classical facade, was built on Manhattan Island in 1910. It was a massive building, covering an area of 28 acres (11 ha). Trains approached through tunnels under the river and were electrically hauled for that portion of the journey.

The tunnel opened on October 16, 1910 and, together with the approaches, measured 2.4 miles (3.9 km) in length. To avoid smoke and ventilation problems, trains were hauled through the tunnel between Detroit and Windsor by electric locomotives operating from 600-volt dc third-rails. Six were delivered initially in 1909 by General Electric, which was responsible for the whole scheme. As far as is known, the tunnel has never developed any structural defects.

The new (1910) Pennsylvania Station in New York City has been described as one of the great monumental edifices of the world, with the part visible from the streets designed to classical proportions. The work of reaching Manhattan began across the Hudson at Harrison in the New Jersey hinterland. The double-track Hudson River tunnels were built at a depth of 97 ft (30 m) below mean water level, but the line emerged at Manhattan's 10th Avenue to enter the main terminal building. The tunnels were about 9 ft (3 m) below mean water level at the highest point. For the Long Island Line trains, there were four tunnels under the East River, which emerged on the Long Island shore in Queens.

The station and yard covered an area of 28 acres (11 ha) with 16 miles (26 km) of tracks and siding space for 386 cars. There were 21 standing tracks in the station and 11 island platforms, with the capacity of the tunnels feeding the station estimated at 144 trains per hour. The station was opened to traffic in September 1910, nine years after the franchise was granted by the City of New York. It was demolished in 1966.

Pennsylvania Station was one of a number of great stations built in that era. On June 4, 1911 the Chicago & North Western opened its new station in Chicago on Madison Street and Canal and Clinton Streets, moving its passenger services from the old Wells and Kinzie Street site on the north side to the west side of the city. The total cost was $23.75 million.

Twelve railway systems united to provide Kansas City Union Station with the list including all those railroads entering Kansas City in 1906. When the scheme was first promoted, it provided a new belt line around the northern end of the city, with the station on an entirely new site. The main buildings and train shed covered 18 acres (7 ha), an area exceeded only by the Pennsylvania and Grand Central stations in New York. The station was not a terminal as such, since the tracks ran right through.

A contemporary illustration from Century magazine showing the excavation of the new Grand Central Terminal, New York, in 1907.

Above: At the turn of the 20th century, the Kansas City Terminal Railway erected a new terminal building south of the central business district, above and away from the floodplain of the previous location. Jarvis Hunt's design had a main hall for ticketing, and a perpendicular hall extending over the tracks for passenger waiting. The Beaux-Arts station opened on October 30, 1914, the third-largest railroad station in the country.

The interior of the Pennsylvania Station, showing the complex, vaulted, glazed roof. The station contained 11 island platforms and 21 standing tracks.

Another grand station to be built was the Union Passenger Station on Massachusetts Avenue in Washington, D.C., which was completed and opened on November 17, 1907. Built by the Washington Terminal Company in agreement with the Baltimore & Ohio Railroad and a subsidiary of the Pennsylvania, the terminal was for the joint use of the Southern, the Washington Southern, the Chesapeake & Ohio, and "such other companies as might be admitted to the use of its facilities and connections." Expenses and revenue were to be charged separately against the tenant companies in proportion to their use. Under Act of Congress, all other railroad stations in the city were abandoned, together with their approaching tracks.

Above: Grand Central Terminal in New York. This picture would have been made in about 1918 when the station was only a few years old. Later it would be surrounded, almost submerged, by tall buildings.

The grandiose interior of New York's Grand Central Terminal, with its ornate moldings, imposing windows, and the magnificent four-faced clock on top of the information booth, its most recognizable icon. Each of the four clock faces are made from opal, and both Sotheby's and Christie's have estimated its value to be $10-20m.

Legislation and losses, 1900–16

DESPITE THEIR APPARENT OPULENCE, AMERICAN RAILROADS
WERE BEING SLOWLY STIFLED IN THE FIRST DECADE OF THE
20TH CENTURY AS TOUGH REGULATIONS AND INCREASING
COSTS CUT THEIR INCOMES.

By 1910, restrictive legislation, both state and federal, together with increasing materials and labor costs, were slowly but surely eroding the railroads' ability to pay their way. Between 1900 and 1910, everything affecting their operation had increased in price, except the one thing they all had to sell: transportation. This had been fixed by legislation. By contrast, all their essential commodities increased by an average of a little over 2 percent per annum. Any other industry would have added these increases to their selling prices, but being unable to do so, the railroads incurred additional expenses of $250 million over the decade. An application to the Commission for increased rates was denied in 1911, owing to a misinterpretation of railroad profits, dividends having been counted twice. There was also an optimistic anticipation of heavier traffic, which did not materialize. An increase in expenses did come about, however, and the next few years showed a marked shrinkage of net income.

About this time, a number of the leading personalities involved in the development the railways were lost. Alexander J. Cassatt, president of the Pennsylvania Railroad since 1899, died in 1906 at the age of 66 before he could see the completion of his crowning glory. He had great foresight and remarkable gifts as a railway engineer and executive. His monument was the great double-track tunnel under the Hudson River, the magnificent Pennsylvania Station, the four tunnels under the East River, and the great steel-arch bridge over "Hell Gate" that connected with the New Haven road, all in New York City. The monument erected to him in Pennsylvania Station bore the inscription: "Alexander Johnston Cassatt, President, Pennsylvania Railroad Company, 1899–1906, whose foresight, courage, and ability achieved the extension of the Pennsylvania Railroad System in New York City."

Opposite: The Southern Railway was one of four trunk lines created by Edward H. Harriman's reorganization of the southern railroads following the financial panic of 1893.

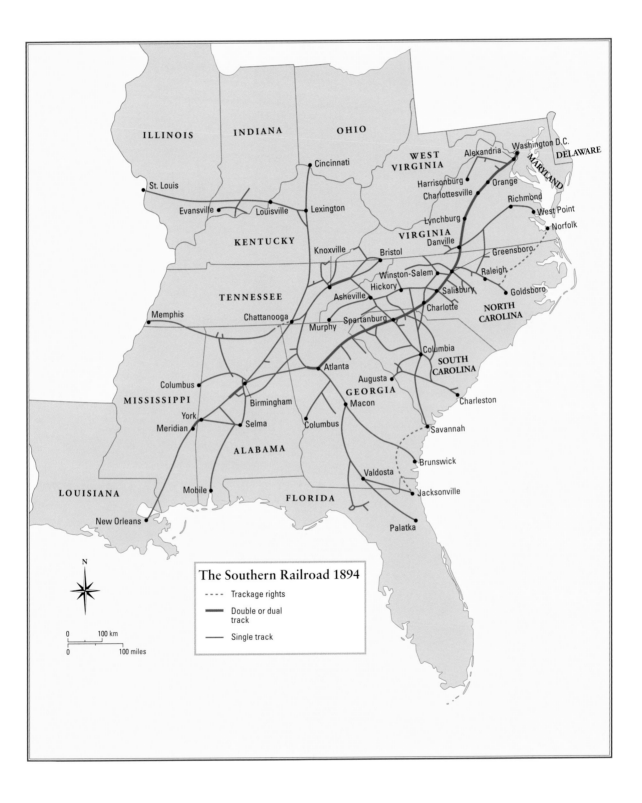

The Southern Railroad 1894

- - - - Trackage rights

━━━ Double or dual track

──── Single track

0   100 km

0   100 miles

Completed in 1916, New York's Hell Gate Bridge is a steel arch railroad bridge spanning the East River, and connecting Astoria in the borough of Queens with Randalls and Wards Islands. Originally, it carried four tracks (two passenger and two freight), but today has only three.

Edward H. Harriman died in 1909 aged 61. It has been said that wherever he touched a piece of railroad property, the result was an improved and more profitable service to the public at reduced rates. There was one exception: the Chicago & Alton Railroad, which he left rehabilitated and improved—but impoverished.

He is remembered for the reconstruction of the Union Pacific line. The most difficult task facing his engineers was the easing of the gradients on the section of line over the Black Hills in South Dakota. His board had laid down a maximum gradient of 43 ft (13 m) to the mile (1.6 km), 1 in 123 (0.81 percent). This involved constructing a new line over all manner of natural hazards. In addition, curves were eased on each side of Sherman summit, which itself was lowered 247 ft (75 m) by boring a 1,800-ft (549-m) tunnel, and the 6,000-ft (1,829-m) long Aspen tunnel was constructed. Oakes Ames, who directed part of the route, said: "To undertake the construction of a railroad, at any price, for a distance of nearly 700 miles in a desert and unexplored country, its line crossing three mountain ranges at the highest elevations yet attempted on this continent, extending through a country swarming with hostile Indians, by whom locating engineers and conductors of construction trains were repeatedly killed and scalped at their work; upon a route destitute of water, except as supplied by watertrains, hauled from 100 to 150 miles, to thousands of men and animals engaged in construction; the immense mass of material, iron, ties, lumber, provisions and supplies necessary to be transported from 500 to 1,500 miles—I admit might well, in the light of subsequent history and the mutations of opinion, be regarded as the freak of a madman if it did not challenge the recognition of a higher motive."

Harriman was responsible for the reorganization and consolidation of minor railroads south of the Mason-Dixon line. This involved most of the southern lines that had suffered in the financial panic of 1893 following the collapse of the stock market to make four trunk lines: the Southern, the Atlantic Coast Line, the Louisville & Nashville, and the Seaboard Air Line. Together, they operated 20,000 miles (32,200 km) of track. He also helped to place the Illinois Central in the forefront of railroad progress.

James Jerome Hill died in 1916 at the age of 78. He was known as the Empire Builder, a title earned by his work through the whole of the Northwest from Lake Michigan to Puget Sound in Washington State. He was involved in two transcontinental projects, the Great Northern and Northern Pacific systems, and laid the foundations for their consolidation with the Chicago, Burlington & Quincy Railroad.

Another personality to pass away in this decade, at the age of 75, was Edward Payson Ripley, president of the Atchison, Topeka & Santa Fe. The passing of these men perhaps signified the end of an era.

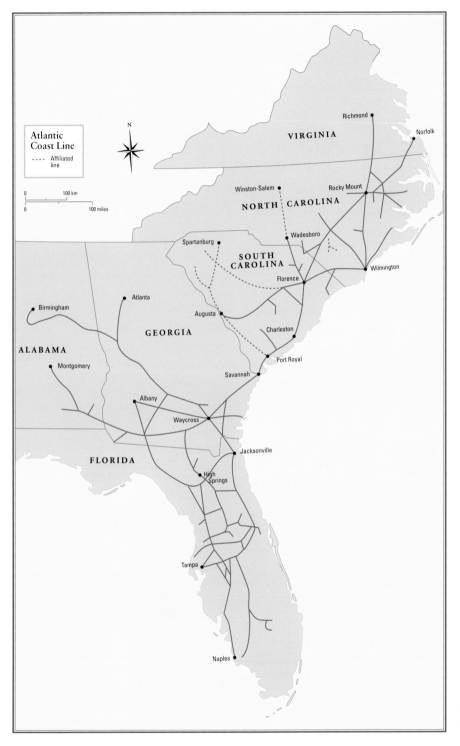

Atlantic
Coast Line

- - - - Affiliated
line

0   100 km

0   100 miles

N

VIRGINIA

Richmond

Norfolk

Winston-Salem

Rocky Mount

NORTH CAROLINA

Wadesboro

Spartanburg

SOUTH
CAROLINA

Florence

Wilmington

Atlanta

Birmingham

GEORGIA

Augusta

Charleston

ALABAMA

Montgomery

Port Royal

Savannah

Albany

Waycross

Jacksonville

FLORIDA

High
Springs

Tampa

Naples

Another railroad that owed its
existence to Edward H. Harriman was
the Atlantic Coast Line.

GROWTH OF THE STEAM LOCOMOTIVE, 1900-28

AROUND THE TURN OF THE CENTURY HEAVIER LOCOMOTIVES WITH EIGHT OR EVEN TEN COUPLED WHEELS APPEARED.

In the 1860s and 1870s, the classic American eight-wheeler (4-4-0) was giving way in passenger haulage to the 10-wheeler, and in freight haulage to the "Mogul" (2-6-0) and "Consolidation" (2-8-0) types. Around the beginning of the 20th century, these were replaced by the "Atlantic" (4-4-2), "Pacific" (4-6-2), and "Mountain" (4-8-2) types for passenger trains. The "Mikado" and, later, "MacArthur" (2-8-2) and "Santa Fe" (2-10-2) types took over freight haulage.

Other wheel arrangements were also used on freight and banking (pusher) locomotives. A two-wheel trailing truck was provided underneath the firebox, which had grown in size, to give a larger grate for more power output. By the 1920s, the demand for yet more power resulted in even larger fireboxes, which required four-wheel trailing trucks for support. Among the best-known designs representing these types were the "Hudson" (4-6-4), "Berkshire" (2-8-4), "Northern" (4-8-4), and "Texas" (2-10-4), their names giving an indication of the railroads for which they were first developed.

With the introduction of steel for freight car frames, and the adoption of automatic couplers and automatic air brakes, longer and heavier trains became possible, which suited the American market. By the early 1900s, 5,000-6,000 ton (5,500- and 6,600-tonne) trains became the norm on many lines, trains being up to a mile (1.6 km) long. With long, single-track stretches of road, it was beneficial to run the longest possible trains between any two points. This called for extremely powerful locomotives.

An I1S 2-10-0 Decapod heavy freight locomotive built for the Pennsylvania Railroad by Baldwin.

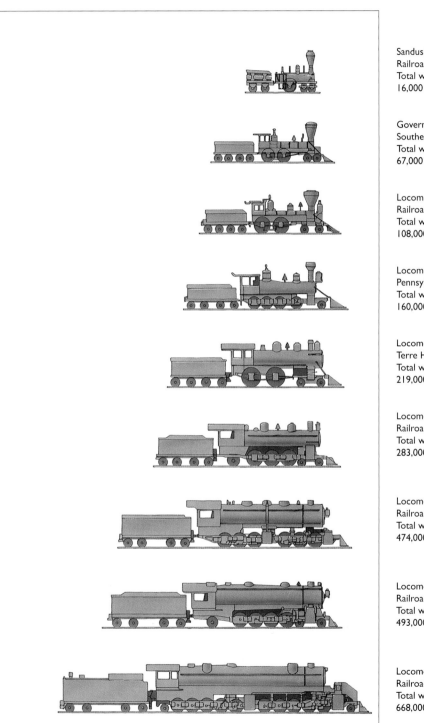

Sandusky built for Mad River & Lake Erie Railroad in 1837.
Total weight of loaded engine and tender 16,000 lb (7,257 kg).

Governor Merey built for Michigan Southern Railroad in 1851.
Total weight of loaded engine and tender 67,000 lb (30,390 kg).

Locomotive built for Hudson River Railroad in 1860.
Total weight of loaded engine and tender 108,000 lb (49,000 kg).

Locomotive built for New York, Pennsylvania & Ohio Railroad in 1880.
Total weight of loaded engine and tender 160,000 lb (72,574 kg).

Locomotive built for St. Louis, Vandalia & Terre Haute Railroad in 1895.
Total weight of loaded engine and tender 219,000 lb (99,336 kg).

Locomotive built for Missouri Pacific Railroad in 1902.
Total weight of loaded engine and tender 283,000 lb (128,336 kg).

Locomotive built for Baltimore & Ohio Railroad in 1904.
Total weight of loaded engine and tender 474,000 lb (215,000 kg).

Locomotive built for Chesapeake & Ohio Railroad in 1911.
Total weight of loaded engine and tender 493,000 lb (223,621 kg).

Locomotive built for Baltimore & Ohio Railroad in 1904.
Total weight of loaded engine and tender 668,000 lb (303,000 kg).

A 2-8-0 Consolidation freight locomotive. These locomotives were true workhorses of the railroads during the late 19th and early 20th centuries.

As train weights increased, so the problem of steep gradients became more acute. Making headway uphill was not the only problem: it was often difficult to stop a long, heavy train on the steepest downhill gradients. Pusher locomotives had been employed since early times on the mountainous lines, and some had been specially developed for that purpose. In 1900, it was quite common to find two at the end of a long, heavy coal train as well as a "helper" at the head. Invariably, these were of the small-wheeled type, and their number of axles grew as their duties became more onerous. Even with the newer upgraded tracks, the weight had to be spread as much as possible. While the pioneering Stourbridge Lion of 1829 weighed 8 tons (8.8 tonnes), Baldwin's Santa Fe (2-10-2) of 1903 weighed 143½ tons (158 tonnes).

For most North American railroad men, the ideal locomotive should be big, powerful, rugged, and mechanically simple. As the locomotive increased in size, its appetite for fuel and water grew—as did its tender. No steam locomotive is complete without its tender (unless it is a tank locomotive, which carries its fuel and water on the same frame). Originally, tenders were kept as small as possible, because they were a non-revenue-earning load. The simple tender carried on two four-wheel trucks soon became too small to allow a train to complete its journey without frequently stopping for water.

An 0-6-6-0 articulated freight locomotive built for the New York Central Railroad. Big, rugged locomotives of this type had great hauling capacity. They often took the place of two locomotives on heavy freight trains, providing a saving in crews and fuel.

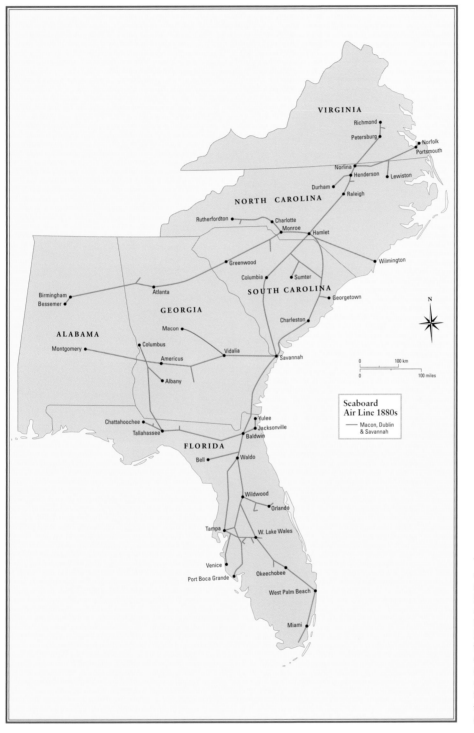

VIRGINIA
Richmond
Petersburg
Norfolk
Portsmouth
Norlina
Henderson
Lewiston
Durham
Raleigh
NORTH CAROLINA
Rutherfordton
Charlotte
Monroe
Hamlet
Wilmington
Greenwood
Columbia
Sumter
Birmingham
Bessemer
Atlanta
SOUTH CAROLINA
Georgetown
GEORGIA
Charleston
ALABAMA
Macon
Montgomery
Columbus
Americus
Vidalia
Savannah
Albany

N

0   100 km
0   100 miles

Seaboard
Air Line 1880s
— Macon, Dublin
& Savannah

Chattahoochee
Yulee
Jacksonville
Tallahassee
Baldwin
FLORIDA
Bell
Waldo

Wildwood
Orlando

Tampa
W. Lake Wales

Venice
Okeechobee
Port Boca Grande
West Palm Beach

Miami

The Seaboard Air Line was
created in the 1880s by the
consolidation of the Seaboard &
Roanoke Railroad with several
other small lines in the Carolinas.
Eventually, over 100 lines were
incorporated in its system. By
the mid-20th century, it had
over 4,100 miles (6,600 km) of
route. It merged with the Atlantic
Coast Line in 1967 to form the
Seaboard Coast Line, then joined
the Chessie System in 1980 to
create CSX Corp.

The "Pacific"-type locomotive built by ALCO in 1924 still had a double-truck, eight-wheel tender, and it could carry 15 tons (13.5 tonnes) of soft coal and 10,000 gallons (36,850 l) of water. This was a more or less standard size of tender for the era. By way of contrast, the Northern Pacific 2-8-8-4 Mallet of 1928, also built by ALCO, had a tender with a capacity of 27 tons (24 tonnes) of coal and 21,200 gallons (80,242 l) of water, carried on two six-wheel trucks. (Of course, a Mallet of that size was almost the equivalent of two "Consolidations.")

By 1917, the number of locomotive builders in the United States had been reduced to three: the American Locomotive Company (ALCO), Baldwin Locomotive Works, and Lima Locomotive Company. The last had its roots in a locomotive builder established in 1880, Carnes, Agather & Company, with a works in Ohio. It also produced sawmill equipment and, since logging railroads had particularly light and rough tracks, it added a special articulated type of locomotive invented by a Michigan lumberman, Ephraim Shay. These were double-truck locomotives, usually with double-truck tenders, all the wheels—including those of the tender—being driven through bevel gears from a longitudinal shaft, which was connected flexibly to each end of the crankshaft of a two- or three-cylinder vertical engine. The Shay

The 4-8-4 was the classic heavy general-purpose locomotive of the final decades of steam traction. This Canadian National example is being prepared for night service at Turcot Yard in Montréal.

locomotive was particularly flexible, coping with the dips and rises of the hastily laid, uneven track of logging outfits far better than any conventional locomotive.

Lima began building conventional locomotives in 1912, from which time they became the company's chief product. When the federal government took over the railroads in December 1917, representatives of the three builders formed a committee of the United States Railroad Administration (USRA) to develop 12 standard types of locomotive for wartime service. These included a six-wheel switcher, a "Santa Fe," a "Pacific," a "Mountain," and two Mallets—a "light" 2-6-6-2 and a "heavy" 2-8-8-2. The only previous example of a "Mountain" (4-8-2) had been built in 1911 by ALCO's Richmond, Virginia plant for the Chesapeake & Ohio Railroad.

The USRA locomotives were good, pleasing, well-proportioned designs. They had a large number of interchangeable parts and, being mass-produced, they came off the production lines fast with low unit costs. In less than two years, 1,830 were turned out by the three manufacturers. This example of efficient design and standardization made good economic sense—but it was swiftly abandoned when the railroads were returned to private control in 1920.

This was the big-locomotive era, but at first the pace was slow. It took a good few years to recover from the effects of the panic of 1907. There had been two lean years in 1911 and 1912, then in 1913 operating revenues grew, aided by a 5 percent rate increase in the Central territory in 1914.

The 2-8-2 configuration was most often called a Mikado (sometimes nicknamed "Mike"), but also referred to as a MacArthur type. The arrangement allows the firebox to be placed behind, instead of above, the driving wheels, permitting a large, wide and deep firebox. This example is the Pennsylvania Railroad locomotive No. 520, shown here on display at the Pennsylvania Railroad Museum, Strasburg, Pennsylvania.

Shay locomotives were designed to climb steep grades, swing around hairpin curves and negotiate the temporary tracks of logging operations. Unlike standard steam locomotives, Shays are driven by direct gearing to each wheel, which allows the smooth, even flow of power. Shays also had to be powerful enough to haul heavy loads from the woods to the mill. In 1911, West Virginia led the nation with more than 3,000 miles (4,828 km) of logging track. All that remains are 11 miles (17.70 km) at the Cass Scenic Railroad State Park, restored as they were in the early 1900s. Shay No. 2, shown here filling up at a water tower, is a "Pacific Coast" type—the only one used east of the Mississippi—a souped-up, 70-ton (63 tonne), three-truck Shay. It features superheat, a bigger firebox, lower gear ratio, steel cab, and steel truck frames.

THE MALLETS, 1904–20

A SIGNIFICANT EUROPEAN DEVELOPMENT IN LOCOMOTIVE DESIGN BEGAN TO INTEREST AMERICAN ENGINEERS. THIS WAS THE ARTICULATED LOCOMOTIVE, INVENTED BY ANATOLE MALLET.

The Swiss-born, French-educated Jules Anatole Mallet (1837-1919) was a high-achiever: striving to design a workable system of compounding (using the same steam in two successive cylinders) he managed to develop the system of locomotive articulation that took his name and was widely used in the USA. This was at a time when the practice of increasing tractive power by adding extra driving axles could be pursued no further because a long rigid wheelbase had difficulty in negotiating curved track. Ten driving wheels were viable, but the few 12-coupled designs that were built had problems. The solution was to split the driving wheelbase into two pivoted sections. Mallet's idea was to pivot just the leading set of wheels and cylinders and, because the pipe carrying the steam to the leading cylinders would need to have a flexible joint that could lead to leakages, he decided that the rear cylinders should be high-pressure, feeding bigger leading cylinders with used and therefore lower-pressure steam. Tried successfully on small tank locomotives in France, tender versions soon appeared in Germany and Switzerland in the 1890s, just in time to interest American locomotive engineers who were wondering how to meet the demand for ever more powerful freight locomotives. Canada never showed much interest in this idea, possibly because of the extra complication and hence heavier maintenance cost. Like several US railroads, the Canadian lines

One of three Mallets supplied to the Erie Railroad by ALCO. The fire grate of these locomotives was so large that they had to be built as camelbacks.

preferred to retain their conventional designs, using two on a train when necessary. It was J.E. Muhlfeld, the Baltimore & Ohio's superintendent of motive power, spurred on by the Baltimore & Ohio's president, who introduced the Mallet locomotive to the United States. This was to have far-reaching consequences.

This restored 2-6-6-2 Mallet type locomotive was built in 1928 by Baldwin for the Weyhauser Lumber Company in Washington State. Today, it sees service on a tourist line in the Black Hills.

The Baltimore & Ohio was working trains of 2,000 tons (1,800 tonnes) over the Alleghenies, and three "Consolidation" locomotives were needed—one hauling, two pushing—to work such a train over the Sand Patch gradient. Muhlfeld calculated that he could use a Mallet to replace two of the locomotives and crews, and reap the benefits of higher thermal efficiency with compounding. He designed an 0-6-6-0 Mallet and ordered it from the American Locomotive Company (ALCO). It was delivered in 1904—just in time to be exhibited at the St. Louis Exposition. At the time, it was the largest locomotive in the world (if only briefly) and weighed 167¼ tons (151.7 tonnes).

Muhlfeld's Mallet incorporated a number of firsts. It introduced United States railroads to the Walschaerts valve gear (until then, Stephenson's link-motion had been the normal type), it employed steam-assisted reversing gear and (later), it was fitted with an early form of mechanical stoker. On test on the Sand Patch grade, No. 2400 easily accomplished the task normally undertaken by two "Consolidations" and burned a third less coal. Indeed, one authority on articulated locomotives claimed a 38 percent saving between 1905 and 1910 using Muhlfeld's Mallet.

Having no separate guiding axles, No. 2400—affectionately known as Old Maud by its crews, after a fabulously strong strip-cartoon mule of the period—was unstable at speed, so it was confined to pusher work until something even bigger came along. Then it was relegated to switcher work, where it remained in service until 1938.

Baldwin Locomotive Works was not slow in recognizing the benefits of Mallet locomotives, and even profited from a lesson learned from the operation of Old Maud on the Sand Patch grade. While it clearly demonstrated the potential of the articulated, compound-type locomotive for sustained running with heavy trains, it was clear that guiding wheels were needed. In 1906/7, Baldwin built 30 2-6-6-2 Mallets for the Great Northern Railway's Cascade Division, which operated through the Rockies. They were designed primarily for head-end service between Spokane and Leavenworth, Washington, but five were reserved for helper service.

Next in the field was the builder of Old Maud, ALCO, who delivered to the Erie Railroad three of the biggest Mallets ever made. These too had no leading axle, and were 0-8-8-0s weighing 205½ tons (185 tonnes). So big was the firebox of these locomotives that they were built as camelbacks, the cab being close behind the stack, which was not appreciated by the engineers. Two firemen had to be provided to feed the 100 sq. ft (9.3 sq. m) of grate—a grate area of about 50 sq. ft (4.6 sq. m) was considered to be the limit of firing for one fireman—and they rode in a very rudimentary shelter behind the firebox. These locomotives were used on the road up to Gulf Summit grade, east of the Susquehanna, Pennsylvania.

The French engineer Jules Anotole Mallet was responsible for the concept of the articulated, or duplex, locomotive. It effectively combined two locomotives in one, ideal for hauling heavy trains.

A Mallet articulated locomotive with its two engine units fed from a single boiler, the forward unit being pivoted. This example was built by Baldwin in 1911 and photographed still at work in Mexico 50 years later.

The use of two firemen was not economic and gave rise to the invention of the mechanical stoker. A design was developed for the Pennsylvania Railroad in 1905, but it was about 1920 before satisfactory models were in general use. The Archimedes' screw provided the answer. Placed in a trough or pipe, the spiral screw was driven by a

This 0-8-8-0 Mallet type of the New York Central Railroad is of conventional design. Note the massive cylinders.

small steam motor and carried coal from the locomotive's tender to the grate. One slight disadvantage of mechanical stokers was that only small-size coal could be used, but means were soon found to obtain the necessary size of coal by grading.

As one road adopted the Mallet, so others with severe gradients soon followed suit, and it was not long before even bigger locomotives were being built. Simple rather than compound expansion was preferred. Another attraction, of course, was that train weights and lengths could be increased if Mallets were used for head-end power, with another Mallet as pusher on steep grades. The limit to the size of locomotive was the restriction placed on the diameter (and length) of the boiler that could be accommodated. Some rather strange beasts appeared, but in the end these gave way to reason. In all, it is estimated that approximately 3,100 Mallet locomotives were built for service on American railroads.

To some extent, the spectacular success of the various Mallet designs overshadowed the steady progress made in improving the "conventional" steam locomotive during the same period. Boiler efficiency was increased by a number of devices, but the invention of the superheater in 1897, by the German engineer Wilhelm Schmidt, was probably the greatest advance in this field.

At best, the steam locomotive is not very efficient at converting energy into power, but the superheater enables much better use of the steam generated in the boiler. The superheater allows the temperature of the steam to be raised without increasing its pressure and, hence, to expand more in the cylinders, so producing more work for the same volume of water evaporated. Increases of 25–30 percent in power output over a similar unsuperheated locomotive can be obtained.

The superheater consists of a reservoir divided into two compartments. The first compartment receives steam from the boiler, feeding it through tubes that run back and forth in the boiler flues. Here the heat of the gases increases the temperature of the steam, which then is fed into the second chamber for supply to the cylinders. Schmidt return-bend superheaters were generally adopted from about 1910.

In Europe, locomotives were developed with inside cylinders as well as outside cylinders, but the extra complication was never popular on North American railroads, since it required more maintenance, which often was more difficult. In the 1920s, there was some interest in three-cylinder locomotives, but again the extra complexity forced their discontinuance. Mallet locomotives were the exception, but all their cylinders were external. The Mallet compound had extra complications and was avoided by some railroads, simple expansion being preferred.

CAR DESIGN, 1900–25

THE PROJECTED OPENING OF THE MANHATTAN TERMINALS, WHICH WERE APPROACHED BY RELATIVELY DEEP TUNNELS, AND THE INCREASING COST OF LUMBER, PROMPTED THE DESIGN OF MORE FIRE-RESISTANT PASSENGER CARS IN 1904.

By the time the Pennsylvania Railroad decided to abandon wooden cars on grounds of safety, suitable lumber was becoming scarce and had increased in price dramatically, so the change to steel cars also made a lot of sense economically. By 1907 a practical design had been developed and tested, and large-scale production began. In fact, by 1913, no more wooden cars were being produced for domestic service. Despite this, the wooden car was slow to disappear, and even in 1920 some 60 percent of the nation's car fleet was still made of lumber, and a few wooden cars remained in commuter service as late as the 1950s.

One result of the introduction of steel cars was a dramatic increase in train weight. Cars were longer—up to 80 ft (24 m)—and although they looked very similar to the wooden cars they replaced, the designs involved the fitting of massive underframe support sills. Added to this was the use of concrete floors for fire resistance, cast-steel endframes, and cast-steel, six-wheel trucks with massive wrought-steel wheels. The result was a very heavy car of 80–90 tons (72–81 tonnes), which would last 50 or more years in service. This all taxed motive power and increased fuel costs. During the 1920s, an effort was made to reduce car weights by replacing steel with aluminum, but this was largely confined to commuter cars. Heavyweight steel cars remained for a long time on long-distance trains.

The pot-bellied stove, with which passengers had a love-hate relationship for most of the 19th century, gave rise to many suggestions and inventions. There were several unrewarding experiments with furnaces in each car supplying a central heating system (a practice that was adopted in Russia and has survived into modern times). The success of steam heating in large buildings and the

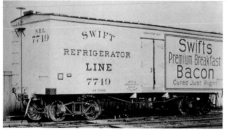

Many specialized freight cars were developed. This is an early refrigerated boxcar.

appearance of larger locomotives that had more steam in reserve led to trains being provided with central heating systems fed by pipe from the locomotive. This improved safety, for the old stoves had caused many lethal train fires, especially in derailments and collisions. Kerosene train lighting was another cause of conflagrations. Gas-mantle lighting supplied by a gas tank under each car improved matters but was still a potential danger. At the beginning of the 20th century electric lighting appeared and was grandly advertised. Initially, generators placed in baggage cars and powered by small steam engines provided the current (and a lot of smoke), but in due course under-floor batteries recharged by generators powered by the car axles were generally adopted.

Freight cars too were growing in size and weight. In 1900, the standard open-top hopper car was constructed from riveted steel plates and had a capacity of 50 tons (45 tonnes), a weight when empty of 21 tons (19 tonnes), and a volume of 2,035 cu ft (57.6 cu. m). Between 1912 and 1925, the coal car grew from 50 through 70 to 100 tons (45 through 63 to 90 tonnes) capacity. The 100- ton (90 tonne) car had an empty weight of 30 tons (27 tonnes), giving a weight on each axle of 32½ tons (29.3 tonnes)—a punishing load on rail joints, even though freight train speeds at the time were relatively low, at around 35 mph (56 km/h). A wide variety of freight cars was in use: flatcars, boxcars, tankcars, refrigerated boxcars, gondola cars, and covered hopper cars. Boxcars came in various sizes, but typically were of 40–50 tons (36-45 tonnes) capacity and up to 60 ft (18 m) long.

Refrigerator cars were already in existence in 1878, and at first they used water-ice as the refrigerant. Automated ice-bunker systems had been developed by the early 1900s and could carry a 30-tonne (27 ton) load plus 5 tons (4.5 tonnes) of ice. A car of this type weighed up to 65 tons (58.5 tonnes).

Steel railroad cars were much safer than their wooden predecessors, but they increased train weights considerably.

INDUSTRIAL TURMOIL

THROUGHOUT THEIR HISTORY, UNITED STATES RAILROADS HAVE BEEN INVOLVED IN LABOR DISPUTES, BUT THE WORST OCCURRED TOWARD THE END OF THE 19TH CENTURY AND IN THE YEARS FOLLOWING WORLD WAR I.

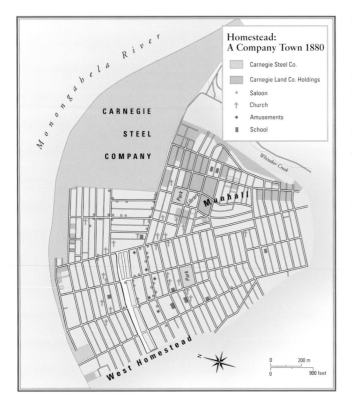

Homestead:
A Company Town 1880

Carnegie Steel Co.
Carnegie Land Co. Holdings
○ Saloon
† Church
♦ Amusements
■ School

I n the early 1890s, workers in United States industry were forming unions to protect their rights. Many employers of the time had little respect or sympathy for their employees, and tried their utmost to keep wages low. Not surprisingly, this led to discontent among workers, and on occasion they expressed that discontent by walking off the job, sometimes with violent consequences. In 1892, for example, a failure to agree terms between management and workers at the Carnegie Steel plant in Homestead, just outside Pittsburgh, led to a 13-hour gun battle between strikers and strikebreaking Pinkerton detectives. Three detectives and seven steel workers lost their lives. Eventually, the National Guard was called in to quell the trouble. Workers were evicted from their company-owned homes and many were arrested. Such tactics broke the strike and prevented union organization within the steel industry for 40 years.

In June 1893, the Stock Market crashed, setting off what became known as the Panic of 1893, which led

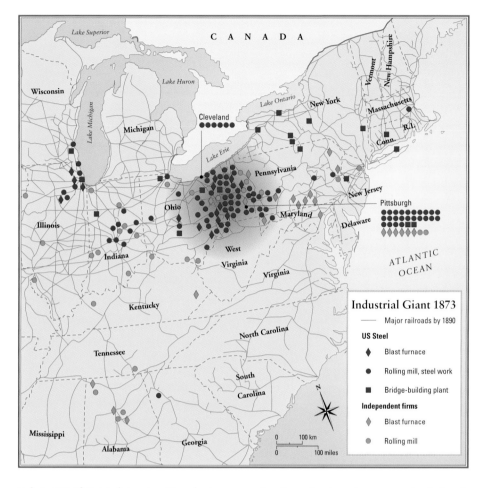

Industrial Giant 1873

— Major railroads by 1890

US Steel

◆ Blast furnace

● Rolling mill, steel work

■ Bridge-building plant

Independent firms

◆ Blast furnace

● Rolling mill

By 1900, aided in no small part by the railroads, the United States had become an industrial giant. The major steel manufacturing plants were centered on the Northeast, where the proliferation of roads ensured easy transport of raw materials and finished products.

to five years of severe depression. Many businesses went under and vast numbers were put out of work, so that over half of United States railroads became bankrupt. At George Pullman's sleeping-car plant in Chicago, 2,000 of the workforce were dismissed, and the remainder faced a reduction in hours and an average cut in wages of 25 percent. The company was also its workers' landlord, having built a town for its employees alongside the plant. Despite the reduction in wages, Pullman refused to reduce their rents to make life a little easier.

Finally, on May 11, 1894, Pullman's workers walked out. Many were members of the American Railway Union (ARU), and they turned to its leader, Eugene Debs, for help. At first, Debs sought to arbitrate between the strikers and Pullman, but the company would not meet the union. The ARU called for a national boycott, which came into effect on June 26, instructing its members to keep the mail moving, but to leave Pullman cars idle.

Within three days, the strike had spread throughout the railroad industry, involving 50,000 workers. Matters took a turn for the worse when a union meeting at Blue Island, Illinois erupted into violence, the strikers derailing a locomotive and destroying railroad yards. In response, the government obtained an

The Carnegie Steel plant at Homestead, near Pittsburgh, Pennsylvania, dominated the town. In 1892, there was a strike by workers over pay and conditions, which led to a bloody confrontation with Pinkerton men hired to break their blockade. In time, the workers returned, but to lower wages and longer hours. Andrew Carnegie, owner of the plant, was roundly condemned for his treatment of the steel workers and spent much of the rest of his life making philanthropic gestures to atone.

injunction against the strike, allowing federal troops to be sent in to protect the mail. Far from defusing the situation, this prompted angry strikers, again at Blue Island, to obstruct the tracks with baggage cars. The strikers' violent behavior turned public opinion against them, and following the arrest of Debs and other union leaders, the strike collapsed on July 11, with the only stipulation that workers be rehired in their previous jobs. In fact, many were not taken back. Moreover, Pullman workers were forced to sign agreements that they would not join a union on pain of dismissal.

Between 1898 and the beginning of World War I, many railroads recovered from the hard times of the Panic of 1893. During the war, the railroads had been under the control of the United States Railroad Administration, which had increased railroad workers' wages substantially. The railroads were returned to private ownership in 1920—with a huge deficit, rolling-stock shortages, and high labor costs. Another economic turndown after the war compounded the problems. With falling prices, the railroads sought to reduce wages, seeing the labor surplus caused by the depression as a means of breaking the power of the unions.

To pressurize its workers, the Pennsylvania Railroad contracted out some locomotive repair work to Baldwin, even though its own shops could have handled the work. Other railroads followed suit. Then, in June 1922, the Railway Labor Board (RLB) allowed a 7 percent reduction in shopworkers' wages and when it came into effect on July 1, railroad workers across the country walked out. It was the beginning of the Great Railroad Shopworkers Strike of 1922. Within three days, the RLB had given permission to the railroads to hire strikebreakers, promising government protection. The railroads housed the strikebreakers

Soldiers from Company C of the 15th United States Infantry, tasked with protecting the United States mail during the Pullman Boycott, pose with the train in which they patrolled the tracks.

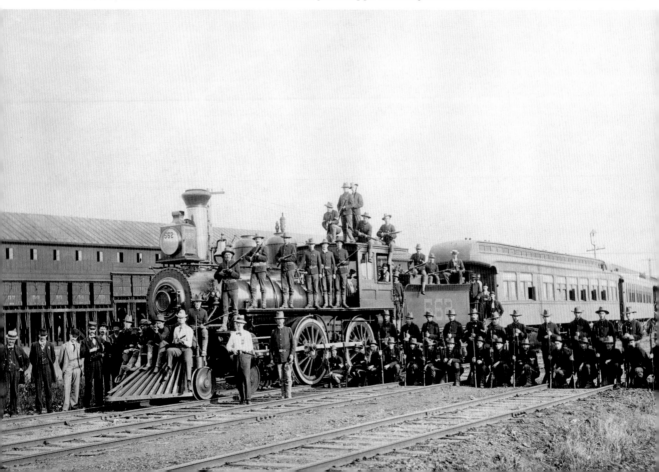

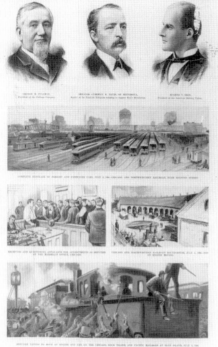

in barbed-wire compounds protected by armed guards. These became the focus of abusive confrontations between strikers and "scabs." The confrontations escalated from abuse to violence. Then, on July 8 came the news that strikers had been shot and killed in Buffalo and Cleveland. Groups of strikers began beating up strikebreakers and subjecting them to mock lynchings. There were shootings too.

The government obtained injunctions to make support of the strike a criminal offense. Federal marshals, sent to arrest strikers, were stoned. Trains were sabotaged, equipment damaged, and there were bombings. In one town in Texas, martial law was declared. When federal troops put down the trouble, more were sent to other railroad shop towns in Texas.

By August, with much rolling stock in a poor state of repair, crews were refusing to operate trains they considered unsafe, while their unions were threatening to bring everything to a halt. Finally, using interference with the United States mail as a reason, the government obtained an injunction that made it a criminal offense to interfere with trains and equipment, to prevent their repair, intimidate others, to congregate near railroad facilities, or to ask anyone to stop work. So wide-ranging was this injunction that it broke the strike, albeit gradually. It ended in 1928, when the last strikers returned to work on the Pennsylvania Railroad. The outcome of the strike was the Railway Labor Act of 1926, which stipulated that both sides in a dispute should go through a rigorous mediation procedure in an effort to prevent strikes. No more would labor disputes end in violent confrontations and even murder, but rather they would be entrusted to the argument of lawyers.

Above left: These contemporary sketches record some of the individuals and events of the Pullman Boycott in and around Chicago. Top, left to right: George Pullman, Cushman Davis, and Eugene Debs. The scenes show a blockade of railcars, individuals applying to become deputies at the United States marshal's office, a roundhouse, and deputies trying to move a car at Blue Island.

Above right: A contemporary illustration showing troops confronting rioters during the Pullman Boycott—with disastrous consequences.

Transcontinental Railroads, 1900–20

Railroads extended the reach of their lines on both sides of the Canadian border, and more tracks were laid to the Pacific coast.

The Northern Securities grouping of the Great Northern, Northern Pacific, and Chicago, Burlington & Quincy railroads, planned by banker J.P. Morgan and railroad pioneer J.J. Hill, finally came to fruition in 1901. The inclusion of the Burlington, as the Chicago, Burlington & Quincy was known, gave the Great Northern and Northern Pacific access to Chicago and many other cities in the Midwest, as well as in the East. The other transcontinental railroads also had their own preferred partners among the Midwestern grange railroads. The Union Pacific, for example, had a connection with the Chicago & North Western, and the Southern Pacific worked with the Rock Island, while the Santa Fe had its own grange lines. There was one major grange line that did not have any kind of transcontinental connection, however, and that was the Chicago, Milwaukee & St. Paul Railroad, which was known simply as the St. Paul in those days, but subsequently became more famous as the Milwaukee Road.

The way things were shaping up, it looked as though the St. Paul would be surrounded and cut off from routes to the Pacific coast. Moreover, finding a new, viable route to the Northwest appeared a difficult prospect as the Great Northern and Northern Pacific had taken the best. Even so, in 1905, work began on the St. Paul's Pacific Extension. The railroad already had a line that ran from Minneapolis/St. Paul to Aberdeen in northern South Dakota. This was the jumping-off point for the new route. Track was laid across the southwestern corner of North Dakota and into Montana, passing through Miles City and across the Continental Divide to Butte. Because the Great Northern and Northern Pacific had already

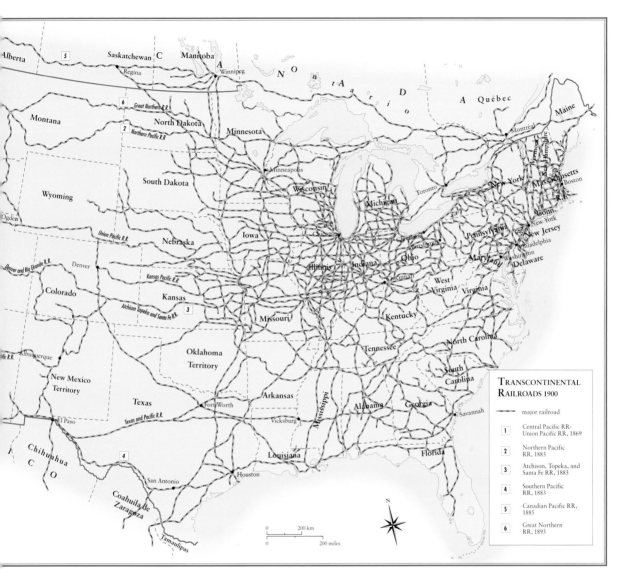

TRANSCONTINENTAL
RAILROADS 1900

— major railroad

1 Central Pacific RR–
Union Pacific RR, 1869

2 Northern Pacific
RR, 1883

3 Atchison, Topeka, and
Santa Fe RR, 1883

4 Southern Pacific
RR, 1883

5 Canadian Pacific RR,
1885

6 Great Northern
RR, 1893

occupied the only suitable gap between the Selkirk and Bitterroot Mountains, the St. Paul was forced to push its way through the Bitterroots, boring numerous tunnels and building endless soaring trestle bridges. More engineering challenges presented themselves as the railroad crossed the Cascades through Snoqualmie Pass. The line continued across Washington State to Seattle, while at Tacoma, the St. Paul built a seaport so that ships could berth alongside waiting freight cars. The line was completed in 1909, a golden spike ceremony being held at Garrison, Montana. As with other transcontinental lines, the St. Paul opened up the country it ran through. It encouraged settlers to fill the new towns along its route, opening land offices in the eastern states and in Europe. Thousands flocked to the new lands, which seemed to hold out so much promise. That promise was fulfilled for a few years, but in 1917 Montana entered a

By 1900, the eastern half of the United States was crowded with railroads, while there were many transcontinental lines providing a choice of east–west links. Finding another route to the Pacific, particularly in the Northwest, was a difficult prospect for the Chicago, Milwaukee, St. Paul & Pacific.

Southern Pacific train No. 2 at Elko, Nevada, in around 1910, hauled by one of a series of Pacific locomotives built by Baldwin from 1904. On most railroads, train numbers 1 and 2 were bestowed on the company's best service.

prolonged dry spell and crops began to fail. Many farmers lost their livelihoods. A couple of decades later things would get worse: the Great Depression was just around the corner.

The St. Paul was not faring well either. Its port at Tacoma had not attracted the business expected, while the Great Northern and Northern Pacific had a stranglehold on connections west of the Twin Cities; they insisted that any traffic bound for their yards on the Pacific coast be passed to them at St. Paul to be hauled west. Only in Butte, Montana, and Washington State could the St. Paul interchange cars with another major railroad, the Union Pacific. Moreover, 600 miles (966 km) of the line had been electrified, and the company was locked into a deal with the Montana Power Company that obliged it to buy a certain amount of power, whether it needed it or not. The Pacific Extension had been financed with loans, and the repayments were crippling. Eventually, in 1925, the Chicago, Milwaukee & St. Paul became bankrupt. It resurfaced in 1928, then fell victim to the Great Depression in 1935, not appearing again until after World War II.

In the meantime, to extend the transcontinental network, other lines were constructed. For example, in 1907 the Union Pacific completed a connection between Los Angeles and Salt Lake City in Utah. In 1909, the Western Pacific was completed between Salt Lake City and Oakland, California.

In 1904, following a suit by the government, the Supreme Court had ordered that Northern Securities be broken up, although the Great Northern and Northern Pacific retained a 48 percent share each of the Burlington and continued to cooperate closely. That cooperation included building the Spokane, Portland & Seattle Railway, and extending their lines to Portland.

Another major transcontinental railroad grouping had come about in 1900, when E.H. Harriman had put the Union Pacific and Southern Pacific under common management. Like Northern Securities, however, the Supreme Court took a dim view and ordered that they be split, which occurred in 1913.

In Canada, meanwhile, two rivals of the Canadian Pacific had struck out west-northwest from Winnipeg, both heading for Edmonton, Alberta. The Canadian Northern (started in 1899) and the Grand Trunk Pacific (begun in 1903) strove to open up different parts of the intervening country, but they were never very far apart. The Canadian Northern ran abreast of the Canadian Pacific in the canyons west of Kamloops and eventually reached Vancouver, while the Grand Trunk Pacific continued northwest through virgin territory to Prince Rupert. Both of these railroads, and the lines connecting with them

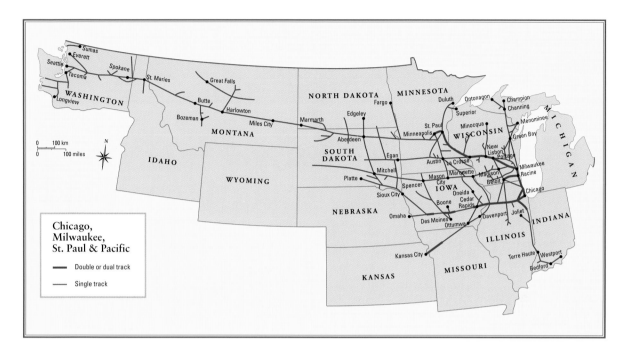

Chicago,
Milwaukee,
St. Paul & Pacific

— Double or dual track

— Single track

from the East at Winnipeg, fell into financial difficulties and were kept going during World War I by substantial government loans. In 1922, all of these lines were amalgamated with the Grand Trunk and the Intercolonial to form the huge Canadian National Railways, a publicly owned company that worked alongside the privately owned Canadian Pacific.

The Chicago, Milwaukee, St. Paul & Pacific Railroad pushed its line westward from Aberdeen in South Dakota. After reaching Butte in Montana, it was forced to forge a route through several mountain ranges on its way to Seattle in Washington State.

During an icy blizzard, the first double header steam train prepares to go through the Chicago, Milwaukee, St. Paul & Pacific Railroad pass, and cut through the Bitter Root Mountains, Idaho, in 1909, transporting a carload of workers with little more than shovels.

RAILROADS DURING WORLD WAR I, 1914–18

DURING WORLD WAR I, THE UNITED STATES RAILROAD TRAFFIC INCREASED MASSIVELY AND THE GOVERNMENT TOOK CONTROL.

Although mounting artillery pieces on railroad flatcars made them easy to move, it did restrict the direction in which they could be aimed.

Opposite page: A World War I propaganda poster urging railroad shop workers to contribute to the war effort by keeping locomotives running.

The first effect of World War I on the American economy was to create a remarkable boom in exports, from which the railroads were able to benefit by means of considerable increases in the amount of freight they carried. In the first months of the war there was a massive increase of 260 percent in the freight that was exported via the railroads, and then a further 37 percent by the time the United States entered the war in 1917. The Commerce Law prevented the railroads from reaping the true benefits of this increase in traffic, however, unlike profiteers in industry, who lost no time in increasing their prices and thereby doubling or even tripling their profits.

During the course of the war, the prices of locomotives doubled, the cost of passenger cars rose by 18 percent and of freight cars by 50 percent, while the price of fuel rose by over 80 percent. On August 29, 1916, Congress passed an act authorizing the president, in time of war and "through the Secretary of War," to assume total control of the transportation system. America entered the war on April 6, 1917, and five days later a group of senior railroad executives led by Daniel Willard, President of the Baltimore & Ohio Railroad, pledged their cooperation in the war effort and created the Railroad War Board (RWB). Among the problems the board had to face were labor difficulties caused by employees rushing to join the army, and a huge amount of freight for the war effort that choked every eastern rail yard and port.

President Woodrow Wilson (top) ordered that the railroads be placed under the control of the government during World War I. This was done through the United States Railroad Administration; Wilson's son-in-law, William G. McAdoo (above) was appointed Director General of Railroads.

By 1916, United States railroads had a combined route length 254,037 miles (408,822 km).

Railroads, 1916

A large group of new recruits to the US Army about to depart from Woodhaven, Long Island, circa 1918.

The War Board tried hard, especially in regard to the near-crisis caused by an enormous expansion of traffic to the eastern ports, which had developed in 1915 when Britain and France placed huge orders with American industry. Freightcars became very scarce. There was no planning, if only because there was nobody with authority to carry out plans. An extreme example is the hold-ups that occurred when new shipyards were built at Philadelphia. Trainloads of building supplies were rushed to the site without any attention paid to priorities and, moreover, there were no unloading facilities; within a few weeks thousands of precious freightcars were congesting Philadelphia's tracks, waiting to be unloaded. The War Board did some useful things: ensuring that all freight trains moved at the same speed to increase line capacity, pooling open-top freightcars, and transferring locomotives from the less-busy railroads to the hard-pressed. But the old practice of routing freight over a railroad's own tracks (to increase revenue) even when there was a shorter route by another railroad, could not be stamped out until the government took full control. Although the war left the US railroads in a sad physical shape, without government control things would have been far worse. The decision finally to take control was speeded by labor unrest (railroad workers resented the new high wage rates of the new war industries; they thought they were

equally deserving). To this was added the blizzards of December 1917, which brought many vital lines to a standstill. Government control was imposed on December 26, 1917.

President Woodrow Wilson explained this takeover as "…not because of any dereliction or failure on their part…but only because there were some things which the government can do and private management cannot." Most of the evidence suggests he was right.

President Wilson placed the nation's railroads under the control of the government through the United States Railroad Administration (USRA) agency, appointing his son-in-law, William G. McAdoo, then Secretary of the Treasury, as Director General of Railroads. Some years before, McAdoo had been in charge of construction of the Hudson & Manhattan Railroad, now the Port Authority Trans-Hudson (PATH), between New York City and Hoboken and Newark, New Jersey.

Among other acts, McAdoo replaced many railroad managers with federal managers, eliminated all competition between railroads, and awarded a flat increase of $20 per month to all employees who earned less than $46 a month. At the same time, it was decreed that the railroads should accept the average of their net operating income for the three-year period ending June 30, 1917, "as just and reasonable compensation." The fact that the lean year to June 30, 1915, had been included effectively robbed the railroads of at least $100 million a year while the guarantee lasted.

Additionally, the USRA ordered and assigned to the railroads more than 2,000 new locomotives and 50,000 freight cars of a standardized design.

Railroad passenger cars were converted into makeshift mobile hospital wards to care for the war wounded.

When America entered World War I, there were some 240,000 miles (386,232 km) of track in the United States. Rolling stock and railroad rights-of-way were being taxed to their utmost, and while there was a shortage of around 117,000 freight cars, some 700 miles (1,127 km) of double track were added, together with a large number of new and enlarged freight yards.

Federal control of the railroads came to an end on September 1, 1920, when they reverted to fully regulated, private operation. The result of nearly three years of government management, however, was an enormous deficit. The country's railroads were then desperately short of rolling stock, while their labor costs had risen significantly.

The USRA's net operating income for the 26 months of control fell short of the guaranteed payments by an incredible $714 million and damage claims amounted to an additional $677 million.

One beneficial legacy of the war years and governmental control of the country's railroads were the 12 standardized locomotive designs to which wartime and postwar locomotives were built—some even as late as 1944.

A novel form of military transport, this highway truck has had its conventional wheels and tires replaced by flanged steel wheels.

ICC REGROUPING AND ELECTRIFICATION, 1903–30

ATTEMPTING TO EVEN OUT COMPETITION AFTER WORLD WAR I, THE INTERSTATE COMMERCE COMMISSION PREPARED A PLAN TO COMBINE THE RAILROADS INTO A NUMBER OF GROUPS. MEANWHILE, ELECTRIFICATION SEEMED ATTRACTIVE.

In 1920, Congress asked the Interstate Commerce Commission (ICC) to prepare a plan for grouping the railroads while at the same time preserving competition and existing routes of trade. The aim was to create some 19 groups from existing railroads in such a way that the cost of transportation on competing routes would be the same—or, to quote the ICC, to "equitably parcel out the weak sisters."

It was 1929 before the commission published its recommendations. Broadly, they were that subsidiaries would remain with their parent companies, short lines would be assigned to the connecting trunk line, and affiliates of the Canadian roads would remain with either Canadian National or Canadian Pacific; a few railroads were assigned to joint ownership of more than one system. The plan would have resulted in the following main railroad companies: Boston & Maine; New Haven; New York Central; Pennsylvania; Baltimore & Ohio; Chesapeake & Ohio-Nickel Plate; Wabash-Seaboard Air Line; Atlantic Coast Line; Southern, Illinois Central, Chicago & North Western, Great Northern-Northern Pacific, Milwaukee Road, Burlington; Union Pacific; Southern Pacific; Santa Fe; Missouri Pacific; Rock Island-Frisco.

Nobody was happy; after much agonizing and many proposed changes, some of which were the result of altered circumstances, Congress withdrew its original request in 1940.

In Canada, although the Canadian Pacific was thriving, other companies were not. For this they were themselves largely to blame. Most shareholders of Canadian railways were not Canadians, and they were interested more in dividends than in development. The inability of the companies to compromise in the discussions leading up to the laying of the second transcontinental line was blamed for its high cost

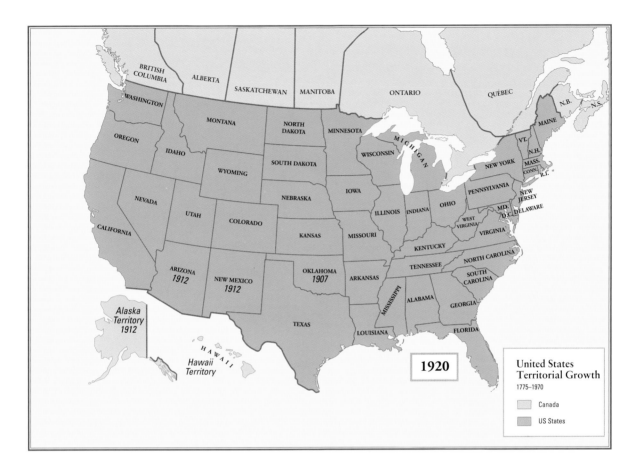

of construction (although overcharging and veiled corruption seem to be equally important). The long-established Grand Trunk was doing badly, and was not without its scandals.

The unusual Canadian solution was a railway system that was half private and half state-owned. (The word "nationalization" was avoided: at this time the specter of Bolshevism loomed large in some circles). The Dominion government acquired the shares of the loss-making companies to form, in 1923, Canadian National Railways, ultimately responsible to the Canadian parliament. Many feared it might fail, while others hoped it would—and thereby prove that state ownership could not work.

Electrification had never played a major part on American railroads (apart from some special tunnel schemes) and was confined mainly to mountain sections or urban areas, where it could be justified by traffic density. Following the New York Legislature Act of 1903, the New Haven Railroad chose to electrify from Woodlawn, New York to New Haven, with alternating current at 11 kilovolts, 25 Hz, single phase with overhead conductors. Before the turn of the century, the New Haven, which was a heavy-duty, high-traffic-density railroad, had electrified some branch lines using low-voltage direct current. To work into the New York terminal, its electric locomotives were designed also to operate from 600 volts dc with a third-rail pickup. Electric operation began in 1907. It was eminently successful and later extended.

By 1920, growth in the western United States, encouraged by the existence of the railroads, ensured that Arizona, New Mexico, and Oklahoma were granted statehood.

Hopper car built for the Soo Line's mineral traffic.

The Butte, Anaconda & Pacific Railroad was a mining railroad serving the copper mines at Butte, Montana. By 1911, it employed a considerable amount of electrical plant in the mines and decided to electrify its rail operations to take advantage of the economy of electric traction. The system of electrification was 2,400 volts dc with overhead conductors. It opened in 1913 and continued for many years.

In 1915, the Norfolk & Western electrified 56 miles (90 km) of line in the region of Vivian and Bluefield, in the southwest corner of West Virginia, to remove the need to run steam locomotives over 2 percent grades and through the Elkhorn Tunnel, both of which were severe obstacles to steam operation. Electrification produced an increase in line capacity and lasted for 35 years, by which time a realignment had obviated the need. The system was alternating current at 11 kilovolts, 25 Hz, single phase.

In 1925, the Virginian Railroad began electric operation between Roanoke, Virginia and Mullens, West Virginia, a section notoriously difficult for steam operation, which in 1916 was worked unsuccessfully by the 377-ton, 2-8-8-8-4 triple Mallet. Electrification enabled heavier trains to be run twice as fast as steam. Again, the system was alternating current at 11 kilovolts, 25 Hz, single phase.

Electrification in the mountainous region of the Continental Divide was an attractive proposition, and in 1916 the Milwaukee Road put 30 electric locomotives into service on freight, followed by another 12 on passenger trains. The first section, from Harlowtown, Montana to Avery in northern Idaho was followed by the section from Othello, Washington to Tacoma, with a northward branch to Seattle. In nine years, the

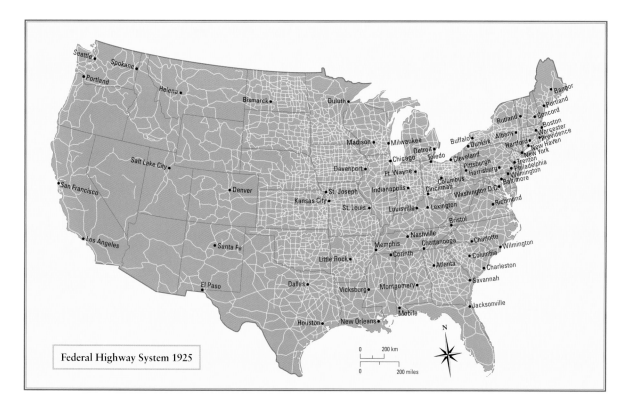

Federal Highway System 1925

0   200 km

0   200 miles

N

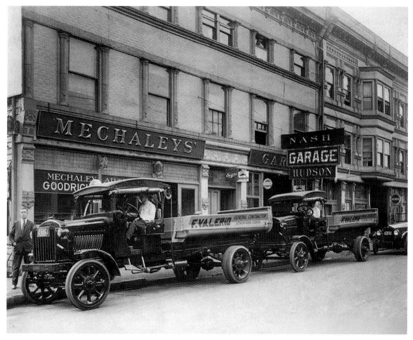

As the 1920s progressed, the railroads had to face competition from automobiles and trucks. A spreading highway system meant that they no longer had a monopoly on passenger and freight traffic.

The advent of the motor truck and development of the highway system caused severe problems for the US railroads. Much freight traffic was lost to the trucking companies.

Milwaukee Road produced savings of $12 million over steam operation. In this case, the system chosen was 3,000 volts dc.

The Pennsylvania terminal line into New York City was electrified initially (1910) with third-rail direct current, at the time principally to conform with its subsidiary company, the Long Island Railroad. In 1915, the Pennsylvania electrified the line from Philadelphia to Paoli, Pennsylvania on the alternating-current system at 11 kilovolts, 25 Hz, single phase. With electrification from New York to Washington, D.C. and Philadelphia to Harrisburg, Pennsylvania, in mind, the single-phase system was extended to Wilmington, Delaware and Trenton, New Jersey. The line into New York City terminal was switched to alternating current to meet the line from Philadelphia. With the exception of suburban services in the New York City area, no further electrification took place until after World War II.

Mention has been made of the growth of the interurban railroads during the early part of the 20th century. Some were successful, and were enlarged and extended. However, the interurban did not enjoy a monopoly for long; the automobile and the extension of paved highways began to make inroads into the interurbans' business for short journeys. The majority of interurbans did not last much beyond 1930. In an attempt to fight back, many railroads formed bus and truck subsidiaries and some even entered the airline business. But times were about to become worse—the Great Depression was on its way.

The production-line manufacture of automobiles, pioneered by Henry Ford's Model-T, put the nation on wheels and hit the railroads' passenger traffic hard. In fact, they never recovered.

Specialized freight car belonging to the Minneapolis, St. Paul & Sault Ste. Marie RR (Soo Line): a slatted boxcar for moving livestock.

FARE DODGERS AND SAFETY CARS, 1920s

TOWARD THE END OF THE 1920S, STREETCAR OPERATORS WERE LOSING INCOME THROUGH FARE-DODGING, WHILE PASSENGER NUMBERS WERE BEGINNING TO DROP. NEW INNOVATIONS IN CAR DESIGN WERE SEEN AS THE ANSWERS TO THEIR PREDICAMENT.

The costly problem of fare-dodging, which had plagued the streetcar operators for years, was addressed by two important innovations—pay-as-you-enter (PAYE) cars and Peter Witt cars. Today, it is hard to imagine any other fare-paying method than giving the money for the fare (or showing your transit card) to the driver. Almost all local buses are one-man operated and it is almost as if there was never any other way. When PAYE was first introduced, in Montréal, Canada in 1904, the idea that a passenger should pay when getting on to a streetcar was revolutionary, but by 1915, the idea had spread to Toronto and soon followed in most parts of North America. Of course, open cars did not lend themselves to the PAYE method, which requires passengers to board only through the front entrance, and this was another factor that led to their being phased out.

The second fare payment innovation was the idea of Peter Witt, the commissioner of street railways in Cleveland, Ohio. Immediately after World War I, Witt designed a fare-paying scheme and car layout that became standard among many streetcar companies as they sought the most efficient way of getting passengers on and off the cars. This type of car and its cousin, the nearside car, were designed so that people entered a large holding area at the front of the car and left from the center, where the conductor stood. The best seats were in the rear, and to get to them, passengers had to pass the conductor and pay their fares. This logical pattern greatly reduced boarding delays and, as a result, Peter Witt cars spread throughout the world. In North America, cities such as Toronto, Buffalo, Baltimore, and Philadelphia had them, but Milan, Italy is the last city to use them in large numbers, which it still does.

TO. COURTESY TTC (2003)

Peter Witt cars, particularly the smaller, later versions, used the most modern techniques to reduce weight and increase comfort and safety. The cars had such features as steel-arch-roof bodies with improved ventilation, air-operated doors, and better motors and performance.

Introduced in 1916, the Birney Safety Car was seen by many operators as the salvation of the streetcar industry, which was under increasing threat from its new competitors, the automobile and the motor bus. The car's safety features included interlocked doors, which prevented the car from starting if a door remained open or a passenger was stuck.

By the late 1910s, despite the phasing out of open-bodied cars and the reduction in fare-dodging as indicated above, many streetcar systems were struggling for survival. While Henry Ford's Model "T" and its ilk put millions of ordinary people on the road, costs and wages were rising as passenger numbers leveled off. In addition, the motor bus was rapidly gaining in popularity and becoming a serious rival to the streetcar. The industry, with some equipment now 15 or 20 years old, was also suffering from what today would be called an infrastructure problem. So when Charles Birney designed a new type of car for trolley operator Stone & Webster, which promised to solve these problems, manufacturers and transit companies alike rushed to place orders.

The new Birney Safety Car was a clever mixture of modern and antique. Recalling the days of the horse-drawn car, when some companies introduced small one-horse cars called "bobtails" as an economy move, the Birney reverted to a short-wheelbase, single-truck layout for minimum weight and low unit cost. New

Peter Witt, Commissioner of Street Railways for Cleveland, Ohio, designed this form of car, in which passengers entered at the front and left from the center. That way, they could not avoid passing the conductor.

To prevent accidents with pedestrians, Birney Saftety Cars were fitted with a device similar to a locomotive's cow catcher. In this demonstration right, it can be seen how the device would prevent a pedestrian from being run over, while nevertheless taking a tumble.

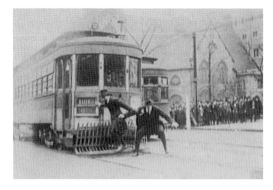

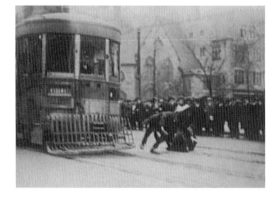

Open streetcars made it easy for passengers to hop on and off—and easy for them to dodge paying the fare. They could be dangerous too.

technology included the smooth-arch roof and a stressed-steel-skin construction that routed structural loads through external body panels, thereby reducing the weight and bulk of the frame. A key strategy was one-man operation, which was achieved by the use of the new deadman switch on the controller, and by an interlock on the doors so that the car could not move if they were open. Smaller wheels and high-efficiency, compact motors allowed for a lower overall height. On paper, at least, it seemed a surefire winner, and thousands of Birney Safety Cars were made between 1916 and 1921.

Although the wide, low, well-rounded design gave the cars the appearance of competence, in practice they fell short. The passengers were the first to notice its rocking, porpoising ride because of the short wheelbase and light weight, which led the public to name the cars "Galloping Gerties" and "Rocking Horses." Because only one of the two doors would usually be in use at a time, boarding congestion was a constant irritation. The companies found that their problems had been staved off only temporarily by the new cars. Although possibly understandable, it was both shortsighted and naive to believe that a transformation in public attitudes as fundamental as that brought about by the automobile and the bus could be countered by some tinkering with the hardware.

Following their arrival in the 1880s, electric streetcars quickly became the dominant form of urban and interurban transportation. By the 1920s, however, their supremacy was under serious threat from the rise of the automobile and the motor bus. In 1920, almost every city in the United States with a population of more than 10,000 had streetcars. The number of street railway companies had grown to more than 1,000, and annual passenger numbers had risen from around 410 million in 1890 to

more than 13.7 billion. During this period, the only serious threat to the dominance of the streetcar had come from jitneys—shared-ride taxi services operated with automobiles or small motor buses that ran along fixed routes for a fixed fare of one nickel, or jitney. The first large-scale use of jitneys began in Los Angeles in 1914, and by the end of that year, the city had more than 800 in service. The jitney craze then spread quickly throughout the United States, and by the end of 1915, the number in use nationwide had topped 62,000.

The streetcar companies, some of which had lost up to half of their passengers to jitneys, reacted swiftly, successfully lobbying their local and state authorities to regulate the operation of these unwelcome rivals. The restrictions placed on the jitney operators included minimum route lengths and hours of operation, limits on routes allowed, and compulsory public-liability insurance, which typically cost them 25–50 percent of their net earnings. The effect on the jitneys was so rapid and dramatic that by the end of 1916 there were only 6,000 of the vehicles still operating.

For the streetcar companies, however, the problems created by the jitneys were merely a foretaste of worse troubles ahead, in the form of competition from the automobile and the motor bus. During the 1920s, automobile ownership in the United States—encouraged by rapidly improving vehicle design, falling prices, and paved roads—rose from 8.1 million to 23.1 million. Meanwhile, bus passenger numbers had grown steadily from near negligible in 1920 to more than 2 billion in 1929. Thanks to this growth in automobile and bus usage, and in some cities the expansion of subway and elevated railway systems, annual streetcar passenger numbers began to fall in 1923 and, by 1929, they had dropped to about 11.8 billion and clearly were in long-term decline.

The interior of a Birney Safety Car, showing its basic wooden bench seating. Limited passenger capacity made them unsuitable for busy routes and rush hour service, and the public began to deride them as flimsy.

Jitneys—unregulated, shared-ride taxi services—caused serious problems for the streetcar companies. Running on fixed routes with a single fixed fare, they took up to half the passengers from some companies. When regulations were put in place to control their operation, however, many soon disappeared.

THE GREAT DEPRESSION AND RECEIVERSHIP IN THE UNITED STATES, 1930s

THE RAILROADS WERE NOT IMMUNE FROM THE EFFECTS OF THE DEPRESSION, AND TO MAKE MATTERS WORSE, THEY WERE FACING STIFFER COMPETITION FROM THE AUTOMOBILE AND AIRLINES. IT WAS NOT UNTIL THE POSTWAR BOOM OF THE 1940s THAT THEY BEGAN TO RECOVER.

During the Depression years, unemployment soared as companies went out of business. The unemployed headed westward, to California, in the hope of finding work, many "riding the rails" for free by jumping on to freight cars. In the late 1930s, this man traveled with his family and all their possessions in bundles, headed for Toppenish, in the Yakima Valley, Washington, in search of a new life.

The Great Depression, which began with the Stock Exchange crash in October 1929, did not result in an immediate, complete economic collapse, but went in a series of dips and temporary recoveries until the economy reached its low point in 1933. An enduring image of the human cost of the Great Depression is of transients "riding the rails" in search of a new future. At its peak, the army of jobless totaled four million, and hundreds of thousands of these chose to cross the United States in search of work on the great rail networks, such as the Great Northern, Union Pacific, Southern Pacific, and Pennsylvania railroads, many

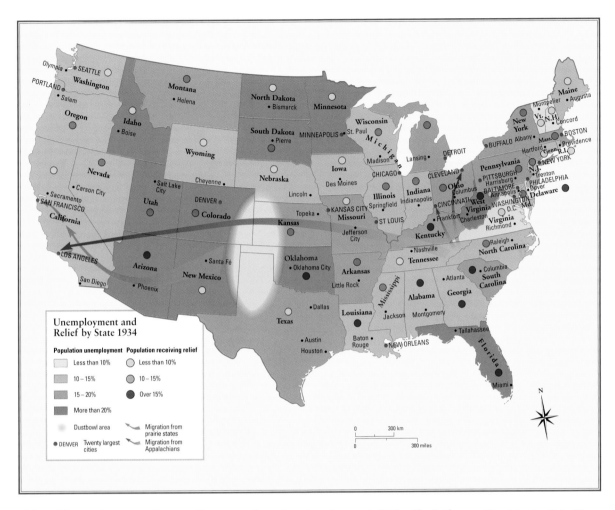

Unemployment and Relief by State 1934

Population unemployment
- Less than 10%
- 10 – 15%
- 15 – 20%
- More than 20%

Population receiving relief
- Less than 10%
- 10 – 15%
- Over 15%

Dustbowl area

● DENVER Twenty largest cities

Migration from prairie states
Migration from Appalachians

0   300 km
0   300 miles

of them following the seasonal harvests. For vast numbers, the only option was to hitch a "free" ride on a freight car. The chances of being caught and ejected were high—in 1932, the Southern Pacific alone recorded 683,457 trespasses—but for many desperate itinerants, the cost was even higher. According to the Interstate Commerce Commission's annual reports, during the decade 1929–39, 24,647 trespassers were killed and 27,171 were injured on the nation's railroads.

The Depression's financial costs to the railroads were also high, since there was a huge decrease in revenues from both passengers and freight. The results were clear at the Baldwin Locomotive works, which, together with ALCO, accounted for most of the United States locomotive building business. As the Depression began to bite, Baldwin's chairman robustly stated, "I have seen the grass, at times, grow six in (15 cm) high in the Baldwin Locomotive works. It is not six inches (15 cm) high now. Therefore, why worry?" In 1932, however, Baldwin sold only six locomotives. In 1929, it had been considered among the most solid of companies, with assets of over $20 million. In 1934, its assets had dwindled to under $3.5 million, and the company was having trouble meeting its interest payments.

The catastrophic effects of the Great Depression in the 1930s are starkly revealed in this map, which traces the dire state of unemployment and governmental relief, and the reaction of desperate people on the move in search of work.

President Hoover had refused to listen to the advice of his Treasury Secretary, Andrew Mellon—"Liquidate labor, liquidate stocks, liquidate the farmers, liquidate real estate..."—since he did not believe that the government should provide direct state aid. Instead, he promoted the idea of "voluntary cooperation" between business and government. However, when it became clear that recovery would take much longer than first thought, Hoover put in place a series of programs that were intended to combat the economic and social problems. These included the Emergency Relief Organization, the National Credit Corporation, and the Reconstruction Finance Corporation, which gave billions in aid to state

In the throes of the Depression, dust storms wreaked ecological and agricultural havoc on the American and Canadian prairies. A result of decades of intensive farming without crop rotation among cotton, corn and grain farmers, the storms promoted erosion, which was exacerbated by severe drought. As hundreds of tons of topsoil were blown off barren fields, dust clouds blackened the sky all the way to Chicago. An exodus set out from Texas, Arkansas, Oklahoma, and the surrounding Great Plains— many riding the rails—with over 500,000 Americans left homeless. Canadians fled to urban areas such as Toronto. The photograph shows the most devastating storm approaching Stratford, Texas, in 1935, after which the region became known as the Dust Bowl.

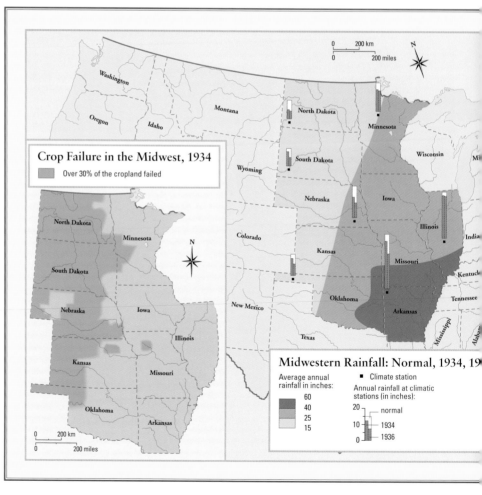

Crop Failure in the Midwest, 1934

Over 30% of the cropland failed

Midwestern Rainfall: Normal, 1934, 19

Average annual rainfall in inches:

- 60
- 40
- 25
- 15

■ Climate station

Annual rainfall at climatic stations (in inches):

20 — normal
10 — 1934
0 — 1936

and local government, and made loans to banks, mortgage associations, and other businesses, including the railroads. He also encouraged public works with the aim of creating jobs. As part of this policy, there was an acceleration of the construction schedule of the Boulder Canyon dam, ultimately to be known as the Hoover Dam.

When Hoover's measures failed to improve matters, it was seen as proof that the government needed to take a more active role in the economy to aid recovery. President Roosevelt, newly elected in 1932, blamed the power of big business for causing an unstable economy. His New Deal proposed the remedy of empowering farmers (with aid programs) and labor unions, and increasing taxes on corporate profits. Despite this, the effects of the Great Depression continued throughout the 1930s and until well after the outbreak of World War II. From 1935, however, Roosevelt's Works Progress Administration (WPA), which was formed with the aim of putting people back into work, employed millions of Americans on federal funded projects. Almost three-quarters of this was construction work. The WPA built 650,000 miles (1,046,000 km) of highways and streets, 78,000 bridges, and 700 miles (1,127 km) of airport

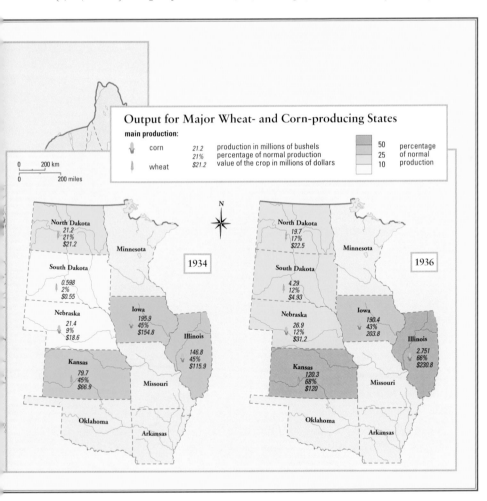

Output for Major Wheat- and Corn-producing States

main production:

corn   21.2   production in millions of bushels
        21%   percentage of normal production
        $21.2   value of the crop in millions of dollars

wheat

50   percentage
25   of normal
10   production

In the mid-1930s, a reduction in rainfall in the Midwest caused serious problems for farmers. Crops failed and livelihoods were destroyed, all adding to the westward move of population.

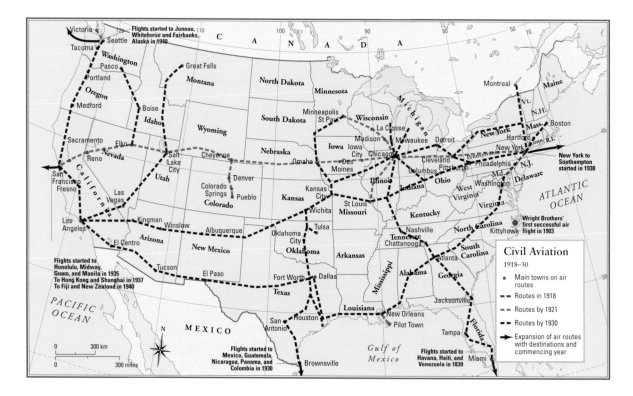

runways. It also constructed 125,000 public buildings and sports facilities, as well as many sewers, dams, and other utilities.

The Great Depression hit the railroads every bit as hard as industry generally. They were doubly affected, however, because of the increased attraction of road and air transport. The effect was inevitable. Business declined so there was less freight and even fewer passengers. Services were cut, so locomotives and cars were put into storage (some were even scrapped). Many railroad corporations became bankrupt, including such major railroads as the Frisco (St. Louis-San Francisco), Missouri-Illinois, Milwaukee Road, and New Haven. The strongest railroad companies survived, but in a weakened state. By 1939, close to one-third of the United States' total mileage of track belonged to companies in receivership. Their future fortunes were mixed. The Frisco came out of receivership in 1947, a result of its receipts being boosted by revenues from increased traffic during World War II. The Missouri-Illinois Railroad was taken under the control of the Missouri Pacific in 1929, when the latter was reorganized, and emerged from bankruptcy in 1944, merging with the Mississippi River & Bonne Terre Railroad in 1945.

The New York, New Haven & Hartford Railroad eventually swallowed up nearly all the railroads in Connecticut, Rhode Island, and southeast Massachusetts, and was a primary connection between many places and New York City. It was a heavy-duty, intense-traffic railroad, more in the European style than American, operating a suburban service out of New York, and had electrified its main line in the 1920s. Despite four-fifths of New Haven's stock being owned by the Pennsylvania Railroad, and the fact that it had an interest in the Boston & Maine Railroad, the Depression played its part here, too, the company

Airports Constructed or
Improved by WPA,
to June 1941

becoming bankrupt in 1935. Reorganization involved pruning much of its branch-line network and upgrading plant and rolling stock on the main line. In 1938, it introduced "piggyback" services—double stacking containers on flatcars—and it switched to diesel power for many of its main-line trains. Traffic increased considerably during World War II, but it was not until 1947 that the New Haven Railroad completed its reorganization. Hardly had this happy state of affairs been reached when, in 1948, control passed into the hands of Frederic C. Dumaine, Patrick B. McGinnis, and others. The New Haven's fortunes quickly plummeted to new and greater depths. Experienced executives were dismissed and new management was hired, leading to turmoil. McGinnis assumed the Presidency in 1954; in 1956, he became president then, in 1962, chairman of the Boston & Maine Railroad, resigning in 1963.

Many battles raged between stockholders and management, and some dubious accountancy (which had valued the road at over double its worth) was exposed when McGinnis departed for the Boston & Maine Railroad in 1956. It took another six years to get the New Haven back into shape, and seven years more before it was healthy enough to be involved in a merger with the Penn Central. McGinnis' financial dealings culminated in a prison sentence for receiving kickbacks on the sale of Boston & Maine Railroad's streamlined passenger cars, ending his career in railroading. Many other railroads were involved in similar financial wrangles, but these examples illustrate the kind of problems besetting railroads in the late 1930s and during the post-war era.

Among the tasks undertaken by the WPA during the 1930s was the construction or improvement of airports across the country. These all helped boost air services, at the expense of the railroads.

STREAMLINED STEAM

DESPITE THE DEPRESSION, MANY UNITED STATES RAILROADS TOOK ON NEW ROLLING STOCK, IMPROVED THEIR OPERATING PRACTICES, AND INTRODUCED PRESTIGE INTER-CITY TRAINS.

Although the Depression hit many railroads hard, there were still success stories. The Union Pacific, for example, enjoyed impeccable credit in the capital markets throughout the Depression, being able to afford new locomotives and even new, streamlined diesel trains, despite the fact that it connected only 36 communities of 10,000 people or more. Even among the harder-hit railroads, the picture was not all gloomy: along with bankruptcies, reorganizations, and mergers, there were improvements in operating methods, new construction techniques, upgrades of tracks, new signaling, and ever larger and more powerful locomotives.

One major railroad that made it through the Depression without going bankrupt was the Pennsylvania. Having made an early start on electrifying its main artery from New York City to Washington, D.C., it completed the conversion of its New York terminal to high-voltage alternating current in 1933. In 1935, electrification was extended through Baltimore, Maryland and Washington to Potomac Yard in Alexandria, Virginia. It was farther extended in 1938 from Paoli to Harrisburg, with the intention of going on to Pittsburgh, Pennsylvania.

The New York Central leased the "Big Four"—Cleveland, Cincinnati, Chicago & St. Louis—in 1930, and it weathered the Depression as well. The New York City Railroad continued to develop its prestige passenger services, and its crack train, the Twentieth Century Limited, was so popular that it frequently ran in many sections. The record number had been achieved just before the Depression, when on January 7, 1929 it ran in seven sections, carrying a total of 822 passengers. Now it included sleeping

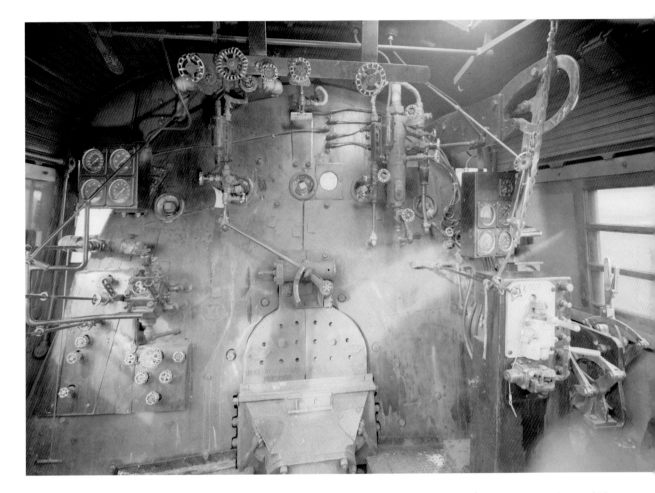

cars, with single rooms, barbers, fresh- and salt-water bathrooms, valet and ladies' maid services, and manicurists. On-board stock-market reports were available, as were the services of a stenographer.

New Pullman cars were introduced with single and double rooms, some with drawing-room accommodation, restaurant cars, club lounges, and a rear observation lounge. An express parcels and post-office car was included as required.

From 1927, motive power for the New York City's main passenger trains had been provided by a new design of 4-6-4 steam locomotive by ALCO. The type was developed with successive batches until by 1948 there were 275 in total, all except 10 having been delivered by ALCO. The latter were built by Lima and allocated to the Boston & Albany Railroad, which had been leased by the New York Central in 1900. In 1932, the New York City to Chicago schedule was cut to 18 hours, in 1935 to 16 hours, and in 1936 to 15 hours.

Meanwhile, the Pennsylvania's rival Broadway Limited continued to prosper. Through the 1920s, the train was hauled mainly by 4-6-2 Pacifics of the famous K.4 class, until they were replaced by electric locomotives as far as Harrisburg, Pennsylvania in 1938. In 1926/7, more powerful steam 4-8-4

Streamlining was often superficial cladding on the exterior of a locomotive. This glimpse inside the cab of the Norfolk & Southern Railroad locomotive No. 611 reveals a confusing mass of valves and controls for brake and throttle, and rather stark conditions for the engineer.

Opposite page Built by ALCO and based on the lightweight 4-4-2 Atlantic type, the streamlined locomotives opperated by the Milwaukee Road made the fastest regular running during the steam era. They were used to pull the *Hiawatha* expresses inaugurated in 1935.

This strikingly streamlined Hudson class locomotive was designed by Henry Drefuss and built by ALCO for the New York Central Railroad. It was used to haul The Twentieth Century Limited express during the 1930s.

M.1 locomotives, built in the company's own Altoona shops, took the express over the Alleghenies between Altoona and Pittsburgh, negotiating the Horseshoe Curve. From Pittsburgh, a K.4 would take the train on to Chicago; similarly, on the run to New York City, a K.4 would take over at Altoona.

The Chesapeake & Ohio Railroad introduced a new, all-air-conditioned train, the George Washington, which ran between Washington, D.C., Newport News, Virginia, Louisville, Kentucky, and Cincinnati, Ohio. Clearly, the race was on to win as much traffic as possible. In this period, and following World War II, it was fashionable to name principal trains. There were many examples, such as the Panama Limited (Illinois Central Railroad), Chicago–New Orleans; Overland Limited (Chicago & North Western/Union Pacific/Southern Pacific), Chicago–San Francisco; Super Chief (Santa Fe), Chicago–Los Angeles; Daylight (Southern Pacific), San Francisco–Los Angeles; City of Salina (Chicago, Burlington & Quincy Railroad), Kansas City–Salina, Kansas; The Flying Yankee (Boston & Maine/Maine Central), Boston–Bangor, Maine; and Twin Cities 400 (Chicago & North Western), Chicago–St. Paul and Minneapolis, Minnesota, which had the proud boast, "400 miles in 400 minutes!"

In the 1930s, streamlining was the fashion in industrial design, and many railroads attempted to update the look of their trains with streamlined locomotives, along the lines of the diesels. The public associated diesels with state-of-the-art passenger services and considered steam to be old-fashioned. While not all railroads could afford the luxury of these fine, but expensive, trainsets, publicity-conscious managements began to employ the new breed of industrial designers to give their trains a modern appearance. Among the most famous associated with railroads of the early 1930s were Henry Dreyfuss, Raymond Loewy, and Otto Kuhler, who respectively styled the New York Central's the Twentieth Century Limited, the Pennsylvania Railroad's Broadway Limited, and the Milwaukee Road's Hiawatha in an attempt to give steam power an up-to-date, sophisticated image in the face of the diesel threat. Loewy was particularly associated with the striking appearance of the R-1 and GG-1 electric locomotives, but his talents were also applied to steam locomotives, notably the duplex, high-speed T.1 4-4-4-4.

The Milwaukee Road was reorganized in 1925 and was now the Milwaukee, St. Paul & Pacific Railroad, but in 1935,

it declared bankruptcy again. Despite this, the 1930s and 1940s saw the railroad involved in several notable developments. One was the introduction of Hiawatha, the 100 mph (160 km/h), steam-powered streamliner that operated between the cities of Chicago, Milwaukee and St. Paul. The train was a great success, and Hiawathas were introduced on other routes. The Milwaukee's own shops produced the cars for the Hiawathas; indeed, they built most of the company's freight and passenger cars, and many of its locomotives. Again, the postwar boom helped to bring the Milwaukee Railroad out of bankruptcy.

Otto Kuhler styled the 4-6-4 Hudson, which had driving wheels of 7 ft (2.13 m) in diameter, for the Milwaukee Road's Hiawatha. For a time, this seemed to be an effective answer to the high-speed, lightweight diesel streamliners. These and similar designs of steam locomotive for other roads were used until the last days of steam, when diesels replaced them, particularly where grades were encountered with heavy passenger trains.

Much of the so-called streamlining on both diesel and steam locomotives was bogus, being little more than styling to create a new image, with little attention being paid to aerodynamics. As a result, much of it "aged" very quickly—rather as last year's styling gimmick does in the automobile industry—and was soon discarded, particularly if it hampered access for maintenance.

One of 10 streamlined locomotives designed for Canadian National's Chicago-Toronto-Montrèal international service.

ALTERNATIVE MOTIVE POWER

RAILROADS WERE FORCED TO SEEK COST-CUTTING MEASURES, ONE OF WHICH WAS TO REPLACE STEAM WITH MORE ECONOMIC FORMS OF MOTIVE POWER.

With the industrialization of the Eastern states and the ever-expanding programs of road building and improvement, many former railroad passengers opted for personal transportation in the form of the automobile. The first to feel the effect of this were the railroads' branch and secondary lines, which had always carried lighter loads than the mainlines. This was not true of the less-industrialized states of the Midwest, whose railroads were confident that they could continue to attract a commercially viable flow of passenger traffic. They reckoned they could do this if "limited-stop" trains were introduced. To achieve this, however, it would be necessary either to increase the water-carrying capacity of existing locomotive tenders, or to abandon steam locomotives in favor of internal-combustion-engined trains. There was a limit to the former option, while the latter form of motive power needed to be developed.

In the 1920s, a few railroads had experimented with vehicles powered by internal-combustion engines—some with diesel switcher locomotives, but many more with self-propelled passenger vehicles (railcars). The latter were mainly gas-electric passenger cars, one of which would usually replace a two- or three-car local train and would be operated by a smaller crew. There was also a saving in maintenance on these services because such a car needed less servicing and was instantly available. By 1930, there were many such cars, the most successful of them built by the Electro-Motive Company of Cleveland, Ohio, which had manufactured around 500 of them between 1922 and 1929. Electro-Motive built the cars and their transmission systems, while power was provided by Winton gasoline engines.

Another company involved in the development of self-propelled railcars was formed by Harry P. Edwards in 1917. The Edwards Railway Motor Car Company, based in Sanford, North Carolina, ceased motor car construction in 1942, but by then it had manufactured over 130 rail cars, sold to 50 different railroads in 19 different countries in the Western Hemisphere. Edwards cars were simple, well built, and rugged, with a low purchase cost. There were two basic styles—the 1920s Model-20, and a 1936 streamlined Model-21, reminiscent of the Zephyrs. Only a handful of the company's cars survive today.

By 1936, there was a relatively small number of various types of diesel-engined locomotives ranging from switchers to road diesel units. The first three diesel-electric locomotives in the United States were switchers, built in 1918 by General Electric. One went to the Jay Street Connecting Railroad, one to the United States Army, and one to an industrial concern in Baltimore, Maryland. Commercial success came in 1924 following a tour with a demonstrator by GE/Ingersoll-Rand. This resulted in the production by ALCO/GE of five locomotives, the first of which, No. 1000, was sold to the Central Railroad of New

Jersey in October 1925. Several factors made diesel locomotives desirable. In an ailing industry where cost savings were needed, a unit that could run nearly continuously, be operated economically, and comply fully with local smoke-abatement laws was seen to be just what the railroad managers needed for switching and transfer work. By 1936, there were 200 such locomotives operating on railroads across the United States and Canada.

If switchers were so desirable, what about road locomotives? The first experimental road locomotives in North America were built by the Canadian Locomotive Company, of Kingston, Ontario, in 1925 for

Built by Electro-Motive Corporation during the 1920s, the Doodle Bug was a self-propelled passenger car suitable for interurban use. It had a gasoline engine and electric transmission.

the Canadian National Railroad and were powered by four- or eight-cylinder motors built by Beardmore, of Glasgow, Scotland. In 1929, one of these twin-unit locomotives made a passenger trip from Montréal to Vancouver to demonstrate its long-range capability. It completed the 2,937-mile (4,727-km) run in 67 hours.

The first two diesel-electric locomotives in the United States were delivered to the New York Central in 1928 and 1929, one for freight and one for passenger haulage in the Putnam division. The first suffered a succession of failures, but the second performed better, although neither of these experimental locomotives was wholly satisfactory. The railroad men, fiercely loyal to steam power, did not care for them, and there was also a lack of adequate service and maintenance facilities.

Perhaps the most important event in American diesel locomotive history came about by the lucky collaboration of Hal Hamilton and Carl Salisbury. The former founded the Electro-Motive Engineering Company of Cleveland, Ohio, while the second was chief engineer of the Winton Engine Company, also of Cleveland, which had built the successful gas-electric, self-propelled railcars mentioned earlier. A third person, also a significant contributor in the field of electric transmission was Richard (Dick) Dilworth, who later had a major influence on the design of diesel-electric locomotives. He became chief engineer of the Electro-Motive Company on January 1, 1926, and was an active contributor to the development of these units until he retired in 1952.

The self-propelled, diesel powered railcar West Virginia Central M-3, affectionately known as Salamander, was built in 2000 by the Edwards Railcar Company (reformed in 1997), from original Edwards drawings of 1922. The 48-seater travels two scenic routes on the lofty Cheat Mountain at Cheat Bridge, West Virginia.

DIESEL-ELECTRIC LOCOMOTIVES, 1930-44

DIESEL-ELECTRIC LOCOMOTIVES WERE IDEAL FOR THE STREAMLINED PRESTIGE TRAINS OF THE 1930S AND PERFORMED WELL IN FREIGHT SERVICE.

General Motors Corporation purchased the Winton Engine Company in June 1930 and, in December 1930, the Electro-Motive Company, which would become General Motor's Electro-Motive Division. This was the beginning of the story of diesel-electric traction in the United States. Despite a number of efforts to introduce alternative forms of power, diesel-electric was the chosen system in the 1930s, and it has remained the most practical form of motive power for locomotives to this day.

In 1933, Ralph Budd, president of the Chicago, Burlington & Quincy Railroad, visited the Chicago World's Fair and was impressed by the Winton diesel engines he saw powering the Chevrolet model assembly plant. At the time, he was engaged in the design of a high-speed, lightweight, self-propelled train, and this engine was just what he needed. It was the right size, had a low specific weight, and developed the right output. The Chicago, Burlington & Quincy design was for a three-car, articulated unit, the cars being constructed from stainless steel, and it was intended to run long distances at higher than usual speeds. Called the Pioneer Zephyr, the train employed a modified design of Winton's 8-201A eight-cylinder, two-stroke engine with electric transmission from General Electric, and was capable of over 110 mph (177 km/h). It was built by the Edward G. Budd Company and delivered to the Chicago, Burlington & Quincy on April 18, 1934.

The Pioneer Zephyr weighed only 97 tons (88 tonnes) and was immediately successful in drawing public attention to a new era. Generally, this train is considered to be the single most important factor in introducing the diesel-electric locomotive to road passenger service in the United States. After a short trial period, on May 26, 1934 it ran from Denver, Colorado to Chicago, Illinois, a distance of 1,015 miles (1,634 km), in 13 hours, 4 minutes, and 58 seconds—with an average speed of 76½ mph (123.3 km/h)—

The streamlined diesel-electric Pioneer Zephyr was a striking sight. The train played a major role in introducing diesels into passenger service.

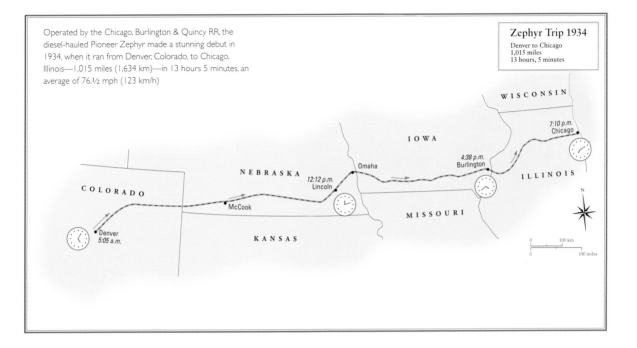

Operated by the Chicago, Burlington & Quincy RR, the diesel-hauled Pioneer Zephyr made a stunning debut in 1934, when it ran from Denver, Colorado, to Chicago, Illinois—1,015 miles (1,634 km)—in 13 hours 5 minutes, an average of 76.½ mph (123 km/h)

Zephyr Trip 1934
Denver to Chicago
1,015 miles
13 hours, 5 minutes

WISCONSIN

7:10 p.m.
Chicago

IOWA

ILLINOIS

Omaha

4:38 p.m.
Burlington

NEBRASKA

12:12 p.m.
Lincoln

COLORADO

MISSOURI

McCook

N

Denver
5:05 a.m.

KANSAS

0   100 km

0   100 miles

Coming or going, the Pioneer Zephyr was a striking looking train. Its bodywork, as shown in the rear observation car, was formed from highly polished stainless steel.

exceeding 100 mph (160 km/h) at several points on the journey. It entered regular service between Lincoln, Nebraska and Kansas City, Missouri in November 1934. Later, in 1938, a fourth car, a Dinette, was added.

The innovative Union Pacific Railroad had already ordered a three-car, articulated, streamlined train, which was even lighter than the Zephyr, since its construction made extensive use of aluminum. It was built by the Pullman Standard Car Company in Chicago, and weighed 85 tons (77 tonnes). Named the City of Salina, it made an extensive tour in February 1934. Apparently, it was not quite what was wanted, as shortly after a longer articulated train was built, consisting of a power car and six trailers, two of which were sleepers and one a day car. This was also powered by a Winton engine, a V-12 201A of 900 hp, but later this was changed to a V-16 201A of 1,200 hp. Then the train was named the City of Portland. In all, seven generally similar units were built between 1934 and 1936. Only the first had a single engine: the second had a 900 hp booster engine, and the remaining five had 1,200hp booster engines. Another six units followed in 1937, all with a single 1,200 hp engines.

Meanwhile, in 1935, the Burlington Road had added two more three-car trainsets and two four-car sets. Eventually all carried names, with the Flying Yankee, which ran between Boston, Massachusetts, and Bangor, Maine, probably the best known in the East. All the Zephyrs have been preserved in railroad museums. Gradually, power cars began to lose ground to locomotives, but, in whatever form, diesel-electric power began to take a firm hold, especially in prestige expresses. Other famous named trains introduced in this period included the New Haven Railroad's Comet, Baltimore & Ohio's Royal Blue, Santa Fe's Super Chief, and Chicago & North Western/Union Pacific's City of Los Angeles.

In May 1935, Electro-Motive completed a prototype passenger locomotive with a total rating of 3,600 hp. It was a twin-unit, meaning two separate, identical 1,800 hp halves coupled together. Each unit weighed 120 tons (108 tonnes) and had two 12-cylinder, 900 hp 201A engines with electric transmission. Although a successful demonstrator, it had a short life and was retired in 1938. A similar single locomotive for the Baltimore & Ohio, built in August 1935, had a much longer life and was used to haul the Royal Blue, which ran between New York City and Washington, D.C. In 1937, it passed to the Alton, when one driving-cab end was restyled. Later, it became the property of the Gulf, Mobile & Ohio Railroad on merger in 1949. Subsequently, it was restored to its original design and livery.

When in late 1935 a 3,600 hp, twin-unit locomotive was introduced, this set the scene for the concept of the multiple-unit passenger locomotive, which became the standard for many years. It was the forerunner of the E-series, which developed from 1,800 hp to 2,400 hp per unit over the next 19 years. In the same year, General Motors began construction of its diesel locomotive manufacturing plant at La Grange, Illinois, where it developed its own version of the Winton engine, with a simplified design, tailored to locomotive work, which became the Electro-Motive Division 567 series of 8-, 12- and 16-cylinder engines.

Diesel locomotives soon showed that they could accelerate faster than steam locomotives, take curves at higher speeds, and run greater distances without service stops. Moreover, if they were good for passenger trains, they would be equally good, if not better, for freight, so attention turned to the development of freight units for long-distance haulage. In 1939–40, the first Electro-Motive Division freight locomotive made a national tour of a number of railroads, including the Santa Fe.

The freight demonstrator was a four-unit, 5,400 hp (4 x 1,350 hp) locomotive. On its maiden trip, it took 66 cars from Kansas City, Missouri to Los Angeles, California, efficiently and economically. Known as the model FT, the first were ordered by the Santa Fe Railroad, being delivered in 1941. Although wartime restrictions limited production, by 1945 no fewer than 555 A-units and 541 B-units had been delivered, most semi-permanently coupled as A + B pairs.

The diesel-electric locomotive seemed to be the answer to the railroad man's prayers. The first railroad to turn to diesel-electric freight locomotives was the Santa Fe. With long runs through desert country, it had always had water-supply problems for its steam locomotives. Apart from a relative shortage of water, much of what there was led to problems with scale and other deposits which built up in the steam locomotive boilers, and led to increased maintenance costs and downtime. Diesel fuel was also relatively cheap, while the efficiency of diesel locomotives was high—about three times the typical 6–7 percent efficiency of comparable steam locomotives. So it was not surprising that the Santa Fe purchased

Built by Pullman for the Union Pacific Railroad in 1934, the City of Salina was a three-car articulated train that made extensive use of aluminum in its construction.

The first United States railroad to turn to diesels was the Santa Fe. Its Electro-Motive Division F7 locomotives were ideal for the terrain in which the railroad operated, and hauled famous passenger trains such as the Super Chief and El Capitan. This locomotive sports the company's distinctive Warbonnet paint scheme, and its famous "Indian Head" logo.

the first 68 FT diesel-electric locomotive models from the Electro-Motive Division at General Motors.

One drawback, however, was initial cost—a little over twice that of a comparable steam locomotive. Another was the railroads' considerable existing investment in servicing plant, repair facilities, coal depots, and water supplies for steam locomotives, not to mention the men and materials needed to keep a large fleet of steam locomotives running. However, there was no escaping the fact that with steam locomotives went dirt and pollution: they threw out large quantities of smoke and cinders.

The diesel-electric manufacturers began their marketing campaigns well before World War II. Fuel and operating economies were highlighted, as was the reduction in servicing facilities required. The high purchase price was countered by the claim that savings in operational costs would recoup more than the price difference over a very short period. This could easily be demonstrated with switchers: with their higher availability, fewer diesel-electric locomotives—probably only half the number of steam—would be needed to do the same amount of work. Passengers would be won back, they thought, by the vision of new, fast, clean motive power that did not shower them with cinders. In this way, the United States, rapidly becoming a nation of automobile drivers, would be attracted back to the railroads.

Even so, some steam railroads were skeptical and a few even remained opposed to the very idea of diesels. Soon after World War II, however, many of the smaller railroads and most of the larger ones had succumbed. Among the few that held out against diesels was the Norfolk & Western Railroad, a coal hauler from the Appalachian coalfields to the port of Norfolk, Virginia. The company designed and built its own locomotives at Roanoke, Virginia, and many of those, it claimed, were more than a match for the diesels.

Before World War II, other manufacturers besides General Motors had begun manufacturing diesel-electric locomotives. ALCO and its Schenectady, New York, neighbor, General Electric, produced a large range of switchers and line locomotives using ALCO diesel engines and GE electrics. Baldwin combined with Westinghouse to build a similar range. Finally, toward the end of the war, Fairbanks-Morse—a company based in Beloit, Wisconsin—entered the field with its novel, two-stroke, opposed-piston engines.

Economy and low price went together, which was understood by General Motors. From the start, the company saw the advantage to the railroads of highly standardized products, and the flexibility to meet haulage demands by running relatively small locomotives coupled in two, three, or four units as the occasion demanded. This was also understood by the ALCO-General Electric combination, but Baldwin still adhered to the time-honored railroad tradition of custom design; consequently, its products were more costly and often cumbersome.

Opposite page: An early Electro-Motive Division diesel freight locomotive, built for the Atchison, Topeka & Santa Fe Railroad, being washed down before being put back into service during World War II.

Fairbanks-Morse also introduced a line of standardized locomotives for all applications, but they were late arrivals, appearing in August 1944. Their lightweight, opposed-piston engine had been supplied almost exclusively to the United States Navy during World War II and, although it had been very well regarded by Navy engineers, it was never taken up by the railroads in large quantities.

HEAVY STEAM, 1930-50

DESPITE THE CHALLENGE FROM DIESEL ENGINES, STEAM FREIGHT LOCOMOTIVES WERE BECOMING BIGGER AND INCREASINGLY POWERFUL, BUT WORLD WAR II ACCELERATED THEIR REPLACEMENT.

A s freight trains grew in weight, so locomotive power was increased to meet the need for heavier haulage, and to avoid double-heading, except where it was necessary to use helpers on severely graded lines. By 1950, the Mallet-type articulated locomotive was well established as a freight hauler over the more mountainous lines, but perhaps the first popular freight locomotives for heavy hauling at relatively low speeds were initially the 2-8-0, then the 2-10-2.

The first 2-10-2s were built for the Santa Fe Railroad, and from then on, the wheel arrangement was known as the "Santa Fe" type. It was developed in two ways: one with a four-wheel trailing truck as a 2-10-4, or "Texas," to support a larger firebox, and the other with a four-wheel leading truck for greater stability as a 4-10-2, or "Overland." Some three-cylinder "Overlands" were built for the Union Pacific and Southern Pacific. The last "Texas," produced by Baldwin for the Santa Fe Railroad in 1938, had the highest piston thrust of any steam locomotive, and with 6 ft 2in (1.9 m) driving wheels, it was capable of reaching high speeds.

A notable and rare type for North America was the "Union Pacific." This was a three-cylinder 4-12-2, of which 88 were built by the American Locomotive Company (ALCO) for the Union Pacific from 1926–30. It was an interesting design for two reasons: it was a rare example of a non-articulated, multi-cylinder locomotive, and it represented the limits of a rigid driving wheelbase—30 ft 8 in (9.4 m). Also, it had a rare American example of Nigel Gresley's combination valve gear. The long wheelbase restricted its use to roads with only moderate curvature. "Union Pacific" locomotives were operated for 10 years on main-line work, subsequently being relegated to lesser duties.

For general-purpose freight, the 2-8-2 (called "Mikado" until 1941 and "MacArthur" thereafter) and its development, the 2-8-4 ("Berkshire"), were built in large numbers. The Louisville & Nashville Railroad took its final delivery of "Berkshires" as late as 1949.

In 1930, Baldwin Locomotive Works delivered this 2-10-4 Texas-type locomotive to the Santa Fe for freight work. Known as Madam Queen, it remained in service until 1953.

This 4-6-6-4 "Challenger" has been preserved by the Union Pacific Railroad for special events. The class preceded the larger "Big Boys" and was remarkable for its capabilities at the higher speeds.

Articulated locomotives were built mainly to provide greater power for roads with special characteristics, particularly heavy grades with severe curvature. They were the largest and most powerful steam locomotives to be built, but there were only about 2,800 of them spread over 22 main-line railroads. The first examples were compounds and were restricted largely to helper or yard work, since they were unable to work at acceptable speed on main lines. In articulated locomotives, the rear, fixed engine worked at boiler pressure, exhausting steam into the front, pivoted engine. Not being physically coupled, the front and rear engines tended to get out of "phase," and the exhaust from the high-pressure engine was choked by the low-pressure engine.

The Union Pacific's "Challenger" 4-6-6-4s of 1936 were probably the outstanding design. Intended for freight, they were capable of passenger train haulage as well. Union Pacific operated 105 "Challengers," and a further 149 had been built for six other roads by the early 1940s. While they were sometimes used on passenger trains, their main duty was to haul heavy freight trains at speeds approaching those of passenger trains. One Union Pacific "Challenger" has been preserved in running order and is used occasionally on long-distance excursions.

The ultimate in articulated steam locomotive design was achieved with the aptly named 4-8-8-4 "Big Boy." This was a 1941 design, also for Union Pacific, and again from ALCO. Over the next three years, 25 of these immense locomotives were built. They were the largest steamers of all, more than 130 ft (39 m) long, 16 ft 2 in (4.9 m) high, and (with tender) weighing 552 tons (492 tons) (the tender alone weighed over 150 tons (137 tonnes). They developed no less than 7,000 hp and could generate a starting tractive effort of 135,375 lb (61,406 kg). The "Big Boy" was an express freight locomotive, designed to run at up to 80 mph (129 km/h), and to take 100-car trains over the formidable Sherman Summit. At times, the trains

A 4-6-6-4 "Challenger" and 4-8-8-4 "Big Boy" of the Union Pacific double heading a freight train on Sherman Hill, Wyoming in the mid-1940s.

were so heavy that two of these giant locomotives were needed to maintain speeds in the region of 40 mph (64 km/h) up "The Hill."

To satisfy their large appetites, these and the later "Challengers" were provided with 14-wheel tenders of a novel design, carrying 28 tons of coal and 24,000 gallons (90,840 l) of water. They were intended principally for the long, heavy drag from Cheyenne, Wyoming up through the Wasatch Range in Utah, and on to Salt Lake City. Each "Big Boy" cost $265,174. Today, a few have been preserved in railroad museums as awe-inspiring examples of the ultimate in steam locomotive size and power.

To quote from Henry B. Comstock's delightful book, *The Iron Horse*: "The engines were deliberately 'overbuilt' to withstand the punishment of 80 mph (128 km/h) speeds, and during World War II they occasionally topped 70 mph (112 hm/h) with heavy troop trains. However, they were at their vocal best when they drummed up Weber Canyon out of Ogden, Utah, punctuating each beat of their exhaust with a towering black exclamation mark."

The Pennsylvania Railroad and United States Railroad Administration (USRA) apart, standardization of design was almost nonexistent in the steam era. Most railroads considered that their own designs were necessary to meet their own particular requirements. To quote E. Thomas Harley, from an article published by the American Society of Mechanical Engineers (ASME) in 1979: "It has been said, with some overstatement, that the steam locomotive standard was 'N.T.A.' (no two alike). Be that as it may,

American Railroads and Builders provided what the United States required, locomotives that were relatively crude and simple, yet powerful and reliable. Nevertheless the United States. built the largest and most powerful steam locomotives ever produced."

The steam locomotive fleet reached its peak at 70,000 in 1924, then steadily dwindled. There were 40,000 in 1944, and only 29,000 by 1949, when commercial steam locomotive production ceased in the United States. The last steam locomotive in regular service on a road carrier dropped its fire for the last time in 1960. Of those remaining in 1949, only 8,000 had been built after 1925, suggesting that the diesel-electric mainly replaced worn-out steam locomotives at or near the end of their economic lives, and not a large number of modern, high-capacity steam locomotives, as has been suggested.

Locomotive No. 4449 is the only surviving example of the Southern Pacific Railroad's powerful GS-4 class of steam locomotives. The GS-4 is a streamlined 4-8-4 (Northern) type; the GS is said to stand for "Golden State," a nickname for California, where the locomotive was operated in regular service, or "General Service." Built by the Lima Locomotive Works in Lima, Ohio for the Southern Pacific in May, 1941, it received its bold red-and-orange paint scheme for the Daylight passenger trains, which it hauled for most of its career. The locomotive was retired from active service in 1957 and placed on static display in Oaks Park, Portland, Oregon. In 1974, it was restored to operative use in the second American Freedom Train, which toured the United States for the American Bicentennial celebrations. Since then, No. 4449 has been operated as an excursion service throughout the continental United States.

RAILROADS DURING WORLD WAR II, 1939-45

DURING WORLD WAR II THE RAILROADS BECAME THE TRANSPORTATION BACKBONE OF THE NATION, MOVING VAST QUANTITIES OF WAR TRAFFIC WHILE AT THE SAME TIME MAINTAINING REGULAR PASSENGER AND FREIGHT SERVICES.

Following the outbreak of World War II in Europe, the American government's Neutrality Act of 1937 was altered to permit war materials to be sent to the Allied nations fighting Germany. At home, steps were taken to build up the army and navy. All this increased both freight and passenger traffic, but, unlike during World War I, no steps were taken to exercise federal control over the railroads. Even when the Japanese bombing of Pearl Harbor on December 7, 1941, prompted the United States' entry into the conflict, the railroads remained in control of their affairs and were able to direct their best efforts where needed.

Overall, freight traffic doubled and passenger business quadrupled, much of the extra freight traffic being the movement of war materials from factories to ports on both sides of the continent. In addition, the railroads took on the shipment of oil to east-coast refineries following attacks on coastal shipping by German submarines. It was said that a troop train set off for an embarkation port every six minutes, while a freight train carrying war materials left every four seconds.

The greatest burden fell on the lines leading to the Pacific coast. To aid the passage of a far greater number of trains than

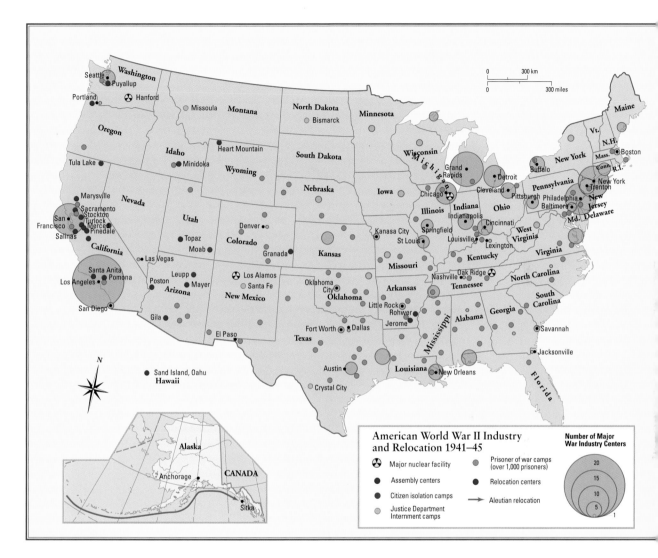

American World War II Industry and Relocation 1941–45

☢ Major nuclear facility
● Assembly centers
● Citizen isolation camps
○ Justice Department Internment camps
● Prisoner of war camps (over 1,000 prisoners)
● Relocation centers
→ Aleutian relocation

Number of Major War Industry Centers

20
15
10
5
1

that for which they were equipped, the technology of modern signaling, in the form of Centralized Traffic Control (CTC), was applied to great advantage. One problem faced by all the railroads during the war was a shortage of manpower as thousands of skilled men and women left their jobs with the railroads for military service. The Southern Pacific alone lost 11,000 in this way, and over 1,300 men and women of the Pennsylvania Railroad never returned, having lost their lives during the conflict.

Traffic peaked around the beginning of 1943, then dropped gradually until 1946. Motive power, particularly for freight, was stretched to the limit, and although there was a shortage of steel, the War Production Board permitted some new building. To save time, however, construction was restricted to locomotives of tried and proven designs or, at most, limited developments of existing types.

During World War II, the railroads experienced a significant rise in freight and passenger traffic as they shuttled personnel, materials, and munitions around the country. Passenger traffic increased four-fold, and included the movement of prisoners-of-war and internees.

Opposite: The railroads were vital for transporting huge numbers of military personnel across the country to embarkation ports on the Pacific and Atlantic coasts.

One design chosen by the Pennsylvania Railroad was the Chesapeake & Ohio's "Texas" (2-10-4) freight locomotive, of which 125 more were built, the work being shared between the Pennsylvania's own Juniata shops and Baldwin's between December 1942 and December 1943. Many regarded them as the finest freight locomotives ever to have run on the Pennsylvania.

The switcher diesel was well established by the outbreak of war, and the first generation of passenger and freight diesels was already being built. The construction of passenger diesels was halted between 1940 and 1944, although diesel freight locomotives and switchers continued in production.

At the end of World War II, in the summer of 1945, the owners of railroad companies could breathe a sigh of relief. They had weathered 15 difficult years, first with the Depression and then with the war. They had done a magnificent job moving men, supplies, and munitions, all the while handling regular passenger and freight traffic. In the public eye, the railroads' role had been amply reinforced by war as the backbone of transportation. Most people assumed—as did the railroads—that this situation would remain, at least for the foreseeable future.

Above: In addition to personnel, the railroads moved vast amounts of war materials and equipment. Here, Sherman tanks are given a rousing sendoff as they leave the factory on flatcars.

Opposite page: As they had done in World War I, the railroads turned to women to keep the trains running when many of their male employees had left to enlist. These "wipers" of the Chicago & North Western Railroad clamber aboard a giant H-class locomotive in Clinton, Iowa.

Above: A freight train hauled by a Santa Fe locomotive gets ready to leave the Corwith Yard, Chicago, for the West Coast in the winter of 1943.

The Chicago & North Western Railroad classification yard, Chicago, Illinois, in 1942. Yards such as these were vital to the shipment of war materials.

Opposite page: With the railroads being such a vital part of the war effort, the locomotive shops were kept busy night and day.

Sulphur being loaded on to railroad cars at Hoskins Mound, Texas, 1942. The railroads were essential for carrying raw materials to the factories during the war.

Returning servicemen, however, having made sacrifices overseas, saw things differently. Their dream was a job, a family, and an automobile. The automobile manufacturers, released from wartime restrictions, responded and sales soared. Demands for highway improvements were voiced and seen by politicians as a vote-catcher, so there was a boom in highway construction. Tax funds for new highways became plentiful, and truckers took to the new highways, capturing short- and medium-haul business from the railroads, whose deliveries were less favorable.

Internal air traffic also began to increase, while the aircraft manufacturers, who had benefited from advances in technology brought about by the war, produced airliners like the Douglas DC-7 and the Lockheed Constellation, both developments of highly successful wartime transport planes. The cost per passenger seat fell below that of prewar prices, and flying gained a "popular" image. Meanwhile, the truckers' success encouraged them to enter the long-haul business, particularly for the carriage of light manufactured goods using articulated (tractor and semi-trailer) vehicles. Gasoline was cheap, made possible by the vast production of the Texas, Oklahoma, Louisiana, and California oilfields, plus the newly tapped reserves of the Middle East, which helped trucking companies and airlines to lower their rates and become very competitive with rail.

Diesel engines needed far less by way of servicing compared to steam locomotives. Here, a Santa Fe Electro-Motive Division is being prepared for another run of the Super Chief express.

Below: Freight cars as far as the eye can see; the Chicago & North Western's Proviso Yard, 1942.

OIL-BURNING, CAB-FORWARD LOCOMOTIVES, 1900-60

NORMALLY, STEAM LOCOMOTIVES WERE COAL-FIRED, BUT IN THE OIL-PRODUCING REGIONS OF THE UNITED STATES, RAILROADS BENEFITED FROM SWITCHING TO OIL. THIS ALTERNATIVE FUEL ALSO LED TO SOME INTERESTING LOCOMOTIVE DESIGNS, NOTABLY THE "CAB-FORWARD" OF THE SOUTHERN PACIFIC.

The Southern Pacific's "cab-forward" locomotives were developed for hauling heavy freight on the steeply graded line between Sacramento and Donner Summit.

Although coal was the normal fuel for steam locomotives, there had also been interest in using oil, but it was not until the American oilfields began to produce large surpluses in the late 19th and early 20th centuries that the price became attractive. Railroads with access to the oilfields of the South and West now began to take an interest. Even so, many railroads were slow to adopt oil as a fuel for steam locomotives, because it required much more careful handling. The regular steam-locomotive firebox could be adapted to burn oil without difficulty, but special burners and firing techniques had to be developed. On the other hand, some railroads were forced to burn soft coal from local coalfields. One such railroad was the Chesapeake & Ohio, and photographs of many of its trains are notable for the large volumes of black smoke emitted by the locomotives when working hard.

In addition to the ready availability of fuel oil to some railroads, there were other advantages of burning oil in steam locomotives. Oil has greater calorific value than coal. Moreover, whereas in a coal-fired locomotive, the fire itself gradually became clogged with ash, reducing its heat output, with an oil-burner, this did not occur, as no dirt or dust was produced. The locomotive cab also remained cleaner,

A double-headed freight train is hauled through Altamont Pass by Southern Pacific AM-2 Mogul 4-6-6-2 "cab-forward" locomotives in 1936. The cab was placed at the front of the locomotive to prevent the crew from being asphyxiated by the exhaust gases as the train ran through the many snow sheds on the line.

and the fireman had time to help the engineer by keeping a lookout for obstructions on the track. On a coal-burner, when the firedoor was opened at night, the glare could distract the engineer, which did not happen on an oil-burner.

The tender of an oil-burning locomotive normally had the same overall design as that of a coal-burner, except that the oil was contained in a large tank. As a rule, this would be mounted at the rear, with the water tank toward the front.

The principle oil-producing regions were Texas, California, the Gulf, Oklahoma, and Kansas, and the railroads of these areas began to switch to oil-burning locomotives. The Southern Pacific was one of the first railroads to turn to oil in the early 1900s, with the Santa Fe soon after.

Were it not for oil, the famous Southern Pacific "cab-forward" locomotives would not have been possible. In all, 250 of them were built. The first AC-4 was a conversion from a Baldwin 2-8-8-2. Later, a four-wheel truck was substituted to improve curving. There were also some AM 2-6-6-2s. In the class names, "AC" stands for "articulated Consolidation," and "AM" for "articulated Mogul." Both types were Mallet locomotives. They provided an effective answer to the problem of heavy haulage over the "Hill"—the tortuous stretch that climbs the western slopes of the Sierra Nevada in California, between Sacramento and Donner Summit, close to the Nevada state line. This section abounds in a succession of snow sheds—20 miles (32 km) or more of them—and has a ruling grade of 1 in 37.7 (2.7 percent). On the line through the Cascades between Eugene and Klamath Falls, Oregon and Redding, California, many single-line tunnels existed and in these conditions, enginemen on chimney-first locomotives were in danger of asphyxiation. Even diesels can get a little short of breath on this line!

The last cab-forward locomotive, No. 4294, was withdrawn from traffic by the Southern Pacific Railroad in 1958, having entered service in 1944. Today, it is preserved in the California State Railroad Museum at Sacramento.

Postwar problems, 1945-60

AFTER WORLD WAR II, FALLING TRAFFIC, WORN-OUT ROLLING STOCK, RISING COAL PRICES, OVERMANNING, AND HIGH WAGE DEMANDS MADE LIFE DIFFICULT FOR THE RAILROADS, AND HOPES WERE PLACED ON THE DIESEL LOCOMOTIVE.

In 1944, railroads handled nearly 80 percent of passenger-miles between cities. By 1950, this had dropped to 47 percent, and by 1960, to 29 percent. Freight did not fare quite so badly but, nonetheless, it was down from 69 percent in 1944 to 44 percent by 1960. What had gone wrong? There were several reasons for this drop in traffic. With the end of the war in sight, railroad managers had made smug assumptions that business would continue more or less as usual. Investment in track, locomotives, and rolling stock had not kept pace with demand, however, and a substantial amount of the locomotive fleet was old and worn out, representing a major cost sink, which the war had exacerbated. Very few locomotives had been built between 1942 and 1945.

Coal prices were jacked up by strikes in the Appalachian coalfields. This increased fuel costs for railroads from the East through the Midwest, the latter having higher haulage costs to add to the higher fuel bill. Railroad workers demanded higher wages, with every railroad union bargaining for higher pay and walkouts in most grades. By 1951, there were still almost as many railroad employees as in 1944, yet although railroad revenue had fallen steadily during this period, employees' wages had risen by as much as 53 percent. Something had to change. In fact, attitudes and employment levels had not altered much since the early years of the century. Despite the universal use of reliable continuous brakes, the numbers of trainmen differed very little in 1950 from 1905.

The diesel locomotive loomed as a serious challenge to steam. Many railroads were quick to see the diesel-electric's advantages, while others would fight almost to the death to keep steam. In the main, the big locomotive builders fell into the latter category, even though American Locomotive Comapny (ALCO) had a lucrative arrangement with General Electric (GE) for diesel-electric work and Baldwin acquired Lima Locomotive Works in 1950. There could be no doubt that a wholesale switch to diesel power would bring sweeping changes. It would offer greater flexibility in operation, and much less labor-

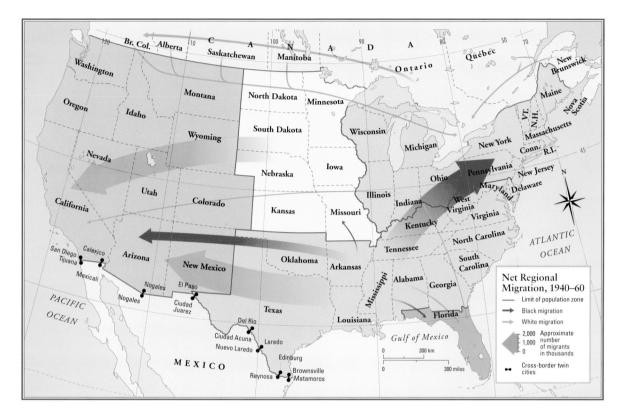

Net Regional
Migration, 1940–60
— Limit of population zone
→ Black migration
→ White migration
2,000 Approximate
1,000 number
0 of migrants
in thousands
•—• Cross-border twin
cities

intensive servicing and maintenance work. It also promised much greater standardization in locomotive design and manufacture. As we have seen already, many railroads stuck to the conviction that they were best served by locomotives designed specifically for their needs. Undoubtedly, this was true with steam locomotives, but for diesels, it was quite another story.

In the road diesel field, the Electro-Motive Division of General Motors enjoyed a virtual monopoly for a number of years. It researched railroads' needs very thoroughly and came up with a very flexible concept: the relatively low-powered unit that could be coupled to one or more similar units to form one high-powered locomotive, which could be operated by a single crew. A great deal of experience had been obtained during the war, which demonstrated what diesels could do.

The Santa Fe's president, Fred Gurley, was probably the diesel's greatest salesman. In a speech in 1946, he said of the diesel, "Time does not permit a discussion of all its virtues; sufficient to say it is the best which man's ingenuity has produced for our service." *Life* magazine took this up in 1947 and, with a big photospread, made the observation, "Last year 90 percent of the locomotives ordered by railroads were diesels." Except for the Norfolk & Western, which continued building its own steam locomotives until 1953, the last steamer on United States railroads was ordered in 1947.

However, the diesel-electric protagonists had a big battle on their hands. The change to diesel power would not only affect machines, but also people and their jobs. In the eyes of the American locomotive industry, General Motors was an outsider. How could it possibly know what the railroads really needed

Population movements have always had an effect on the railroads. Trains have carried migrants from one part of the country to another in search of perceived better opportunities. Moreover, the resulting increases and decreases in local populations have led to changes in demand for railroad services. Over the period between 1940 and 1960, there have been major movements from the poorer areas of the South to the more prosperous Northeast and West Coast.

Built by ALCO between 1941 and 1960, the RS-1 four-axle, diesel-electric locomotive had the longest production run of any diesel in the United States. By its side is a restored Fairmount railcar.

to run their businesses? But with an outsider's eye, General Motors could see very well what was needed to pull the railroads out of their doldrums. It rejected design collaboration, refusing to be a party to the traditional railroad-company/locomotive-supplier relationship. Indeed, on one famous occasion, when a railroad wanted to help in the development of a diesel locomotive, General Motors refused its offer to underwrite the cost of testing. When asked why, the company replied, "So you fellows won't tell us how to build it."

Standardization in high-volume production—General Motors's basic manufacturing credo—would be impossible if each individual customer wanted a different locomotive design. High volume meant efficient production methods, low production costs, low material costs—and low prices to customers. Electro-Motive Division had already shown that, with the flexibility conferred by electric transmission, a good general-purpose, diesel-electric locomotive could successfully handle a much wider variety of traffic over many different routes, grades, etc., than any steam locomotive. That being the case, customized design was no longer necessary.

One famous episode in American railroad history calls to mind Henry Ford and the Model "T," of which he is alleged to have said, "You can have it any color you like, so long as it's black." A certain

An Electro-Motive Division BL2 four-axle road switcher built by General Motors. The letters "BL" stood for "Branch Line," indicating that the locomotive was intended for light traffic and switcher work.

railroad persisted in asking for a series of design alterations to the diesel it wished to order, so General Motors finally delivered an ultimatum: "We'll build you a locomotive. You tell us what color you want it painted and we'll be responsible for everything else. We'll send you the locomotive without charge, with one of our men in it to supervise. You run the locomotive for six months. At the end of that time, you send us either the locomotive or the money." Six months later, the railroad paid—and ordered five more locomotives of a standard Electro-Motive Division specification.

The big three locomotive builders all went into the diesel business. Baldwin—now known as BLH, following its merger with Lima and Lima-owned Hamilton in 1950—built standardized diesel-electric switchers, mainly with Westinghouse electrical equipment. BLH ceased building locomotives in 1956, by which time it had produced around 3,000 for the American market. It fell into the trap of trying to satisfy the demands for custom design, and did not survive.

On the other hand, ALCO understood the need for a high degree of standardization and, while its arrangement with General Electric for transmission equipment endured, it became an effective competitor to Electro-Motive Division. ALCO saw the need for high-horsepower units and pioneered the 2,000 hp locomotive, which could be used singly or in multiples for both main freight and passenger work.

The first was put into service on the New York, New Haven & Hartford Railroad in 1941, working the Shore Line between Boston, Massachusetts and New Haven, Connecticut. The New Haven had been one of the pioneers among eastern railroads in the use of diesel locomotives, its first switcher entering service in 1931. This was the first 600 hp switcher to be manufactured by ALCO-GE.

General Electric (GE) broke off its partnership with ALCO in 1952. Although the latter continued using GE electrical equipment for a time, as did its offshoot, Montréal Locomotive Works (MLW). It built its last diesel in 1969.

The final diesel builder to enter the field was Fairbanks-Morse in 1944. It had made gasoline-engined railcars early in the century, but now produced an opposed-piston diesel engine with a good power/weight ratio of particular interest to railroads. It built complete diesel-electric locomotives with General Electric or Westinghouse electrical equipment in its shops near the Illinois state line at Beloit, Wisconsin. Its first 1,000 hp switcher went to the Milwaukee Road on August 8, 1911. Fairbanks-Morse F-M assembled both switchers and road diesels for a number of years, but dropped out of the United States market in 1958.

General Electric had been early in the market, but concentrated chiefly on the smaller industrial switcher market, being well occupied otherwise with electric locomotives and multiple units. It produced a four-unit set that operated on the Erie Railroad as a test laboratory during 1954–5, after which it was sold to the Union Pacific. Two of the units originally had 1,200 hp engines, while the other two had 1,800hp power plants. For UP service, all were equipped with 2,000 hp engines.

Erie-Lackawanna General Electric U25B 2504 and coal silos. Port Jervis, New York.

General Electric did not begin building large locomotives seriously until 1959, when it introduced the U25B road switcher of 2,500hp, having sold 10 road switchers of 1,800 hp to Mexico in 1956. Today, it is the only serious competitor to Electro-Motive Division .

By 1960, it is estimated that approximately 34,000 diesel-electric locomotives had been built for United States railroads, with a further 3,500 for Canada and Mexico.

The diesel locomotive was probably the catalyst for a host of changes that railroad managements knew had to be made including the cost of labor to operate trains, which remained high. Steamers required a crew of two for each locomotive used on a train, and fuel and watering facilities were needed at frequent intervals on every line, and each had to be manned. Servicing and repairs were much more labor-intensive for steamers than for diesel-electrics. The switch from steam to diesel would be revolutionary, not least in its effect on the size of the workforce. There was much hardship, and there would have been even more if train crews had been reduced still further. The unions fought tooth and nail to keep communities together where sometimes the livelihoods of whole townships were bound to the railroads.

Passenger and Freight Car Evolution, 1920-50s

RAILROADS PUT PRESSURE ON PASSENGER CAR BUILDERS TO PRODUCE LIGHTER AND MORE COMFORTABLE VEHICLES. HOWEVER, THE PASSENGER MARKET WAS COLLAPSING. FREIGHT CARS MEANWHILE BECAME LARGER AND MORE SPECIALIZED.

By the 1920s, some 100,000 travelers slept in Pullman beds every night. The heavyweight passenger cars were built like tanks and offered a service life of 50 or more years. During the worst part of the 1930s Depression, however, the Pullman company was losing money heavily. People were traveling less and, at the same time, the interstate highway construction program, funded by the taxpayer, was eating into the rail passenger business.

Change was forced on Pullman and other railroad car builders by the need to cater for higher speeds with more comfort over longer distances. Only under heavy pressure from the railroads did Pullman modify its rigid attitude and concede that it had to move away from building very heavy cars. It did introduce private-room accommodation, but it was slower to build lighter vehicles. The advent of the experimental diesel trains in the early 1930s showed that passenger cars could be made from something other than ¼-in (6-mm) steel plate. Lightweight aluminum and stainless steel, together with carefully designed trucks, brought weight down but even so, providing such amenities as air conditioning and its power supply left the new streamliner cars still in excess of 60 tons (54 tonnes) apiece. The large-scale introduction of air conditioning began in 1930, and by 1936, there were some 5,800 cars so equipped.

Railway Post Office cars were fitted with a hook to collect the mail bag as the train sped through a station.

Another notable device that began to appear in the 1930s was the disc brake, which the Budd Company began marketing in 1938–39, although it was not in general use until the mid-1950s. Disc brakes were quieter than shoe brakes and saved on wheel wear.

In 1940, the United States Department of Justice filed a complaint against Pullman's monopoly of the sleeping-car business. This had been tolerated by the railroads because Pullman's pool of cars could be moved around the country to wherever they were most needed. In 1947, Pullman was forced to separate its car building from its operating division, creating Pullman Inc., Car Builder. The sleeping-car operation, the Pullman Company, was sold to the 57 railroads over which it ran its cars.

No other major innovations appeared until the 1950s. While 3,000 new cars had been ordered in 1945–46, they were essentially copies of earlier models; even by 1950, only 15 percent were lightweights. At the time, economic conditions did not favor a full-scale replacement of cars and as passengers deserted the railroads for the automobile and air travel, few new cars were ordered. Long-distance travel was still in demand, however, and continued for the next decade. In 1957, the Pennsylvania began operating its own parlor cars, and one by one, the other railroads pulled out of the Pullman operation. In 1958, when the New York Central started to run its own sleeping cars, the first commercial jet airliners, which would take most business away from Pullman, went into service.

Among many attempts by the railroads to lure passengers back was the dome car, which gave passengers a panoramic view of the most scenic parts of a route. They were few in number, however, as were the Santa Fe's "Hi-level" cars. By 1955, the passenger market had collapsed generally; new car construction was stopped and obsolescent vehicles retained. It was a dismal picture, symbolized at the end of 1960 by American Car & Foundry quitting the market altogether.

Although it could have been better, freight traffic held up fairly well, with bulk traffic, the kind of haulage suited to rail, retaining a fair market share. Again, steel had replaced lumber in the construction of freight cars in the early 1930s, and welded-steel structures were being designed and adopted for hopper cars to reduce dead weight. It was possible to increase the payload from 70 to 82 tons (63-74 tonnes) within the gross rail load limit of 210,000 lb (95,256 kg) in force at the time. Since then, there has been an increase in payload as rail load limits have been raised in the wake of stronger tracks.

High-capacity flatcars were introduced in 1933, enabling road vehicles to be transported great distances. From the 1950s, the flatcar grew to a length of 89 ft (27 m); at the same time, autorack and "piggyback" carriers were introduced. Boxcars grew to a length of 86 ft (26 m). Various devices were introduced to cushion loads from shunting and other knocks. Many other special-purpose cars have been introduced, with tankcars particularly reaching a capacity of 12,000 gallons (45,420 l) by 1960. The range of special freight cars is interesting in its diversity. For example, there are cars for hauling hot metal, steel billets, poultry, pickles, vinegar, milk, livestock including horses, cattle, and pigs, military equipment of all kinds, atomic waste, and bridge components.

Tankcars for carrying milk were just one innovation among many when it came to the design of freight cars.

The dome car provided a high-level observation point, giving passengers a panoramic view of the passing countryside.

Bulkhead flatcars had sturdy end-walls, to prevent loads shifting beyond the ends of the car. Loads typically carried were lumber, pipe, and steel slabs.

The New Interurbans, 1930-41

DESPITE THE INROADS OF THE AUTOMOBILE AND MOTOR BUS—AND THE IMPACT OF THE WALL STREET CRASH OF 1929, AND THE GREAT DEPRESSION THAT FOLLOWED IT—THE TROLLEY BUILDERS, AND THOSE INTERURBAN OPERATORS WHO HAD NOT SWITCHED TO BUSES, WERE NOT GOING TO GIVE UP WITHOUT A FIGHT.

For a decade or two the interurban performed an appreciated service. Affection which people felt for it was transferred, after its demise, to thousands of enthusiasts. Many small investors put their savings into it. But in retrospect it was not a good investment. Advancing technology made it, and advancing technology destroyed it, and its window of prosperity was very short, beginning perhaps in the 1890s and ending with the 1930s. It was especially important in the Midwest, which had a web of quite long lines.

Street and interurban trolleys probably peaked in 1923, when there were about 14 billion passengers carried. But because of early line closures the peak total mileage was probably in 1917, when they measured about 45,000 miles. Interurban trains could move at high speeds, sometimes over distances of several hundred miles. They carried mail and a few of them ran dining cars and even sleepers. Some operated freight trains.

Their proponents, then and now, believed that they disappeared, if not because of bad management, then because gasoline, motor bus and road-building interests combined against them. In fact, there is some truth in all these beliefs, but really the interurban disappeared because the internal combustion engine, hard-surfaced roads, and rubber tires combined to produce an unbeatable competition. At that time, ecology did not come into the equation.

And not everybody loved it. The railroads in particular were not gladdened by it, for it took valuable traffic from them by virtue of its low fares, frequent service, and the ability to stop where the passengers wanted. The railroads tried to lobby state regulatory commissions in their favor, but failed.

The interurbans, like the mainline railroads, had frequent, lethal accidents. As with the main lines, many of these occurred because the railroad builders had, whenever possible, crossed highways at grade rather than build bridges. In the early days it was farmers or their livestock who were the typical victims; later it was the occupants of automobiles and highway commercial vehicles. Because the interurban cars advanced with less visible and audible commotion than the steam train, they were correspondingly more likely to catch the careless wayfarer.

Interurbans were lightly built and their safety procedures far from perfect. So right from their start they killed not only wayfarers, but their own passengers too. As early as 1899 the new and hurriedly-built Bridgeport to Shelton, Connecticut ran a Sunday trolley that jumped the track as it entered a trestle bridge, fell, and somersaulted to land on its roof; few of the 30-odd passengers survived. In 1910 there were two disasters. On the Fort Wayne and Wabash Valley line there was a head-on collision that killed 30, and not far away the Illinois Traction Company also had a head-on collision, killing 36. Rear-end collisions were much rarer, except when very frequent services were run. This was the case in the 1920 disaster that befell the Lackawanna & Wyoming Valley line, when one train crashed into the rear of another, with comparatively little bloodshed until a third drove into the wreckage at speed, killing 16.

The basic problem was that most interurbans, though they had copied the rudiments of railway safety regulation, did so in a sometimes superficial way. Moreover the mainline block-signalling system was almost non-existent, and instead the traditional train order system of traffic management was used–often in a highly informal manner.

A very sad accident occurred in 1950. A wealthy enthusiast had bought a 12-mile length of the Milwaukee Electric System and successfully resuscitated it, but the fatal head-on collision of two excursions finally put an end to it.

Streetcar design had changed little during the 1920s, but by the end of the decade the industry realized that higher standards of vehicle performance and passenger comfort would be essential if it wanted to avoid extinction. In 1931, the J.G. Brill company produced a series of ten high-speed railcars, known as Bullet cars because of their radically streamlined noses. The Bullet car, probably the first trolley ever to be tested in a wind tunnel, was Brill's bid to revolutionize the high-speed interurban market. It was the first American trolley to sell streamlining to the traveling public, and was introduced after tests by the aerodynamicist Professor Felix Pawlowski, of the University of Michigan, claimed a 42 percent

The bankrupt North Shore Line turned to the streamlined Electroliner to revive its fortunes in the early 1940s.

Built by the St. Louis Car Company, the Electroliner was an articulated four-car trainset that did much to generate renewed interest in interurbans.

increase in efficiency resulting from its streamlined shape and aluminum body. One of the largest customers for Bullet cars was the Philadelphia & Western Railroad, which put them in service at the end of 1931. Even as the Depression decimated the interurban lines, Philadelphia & Western Railroad traffic increased, for the public loved the new cars and their speeds of up to 85 mph (137 km/h). The Philadelphia & Western Railroad's successor, the Southeastern Pennsylvania Transportation Authority (SEPTA), continued to run them on its Red Arrow Lines, and they spent a phenomenal 60 years on the main line. The Philadelphia & Western Railroad's Bullet cars never ran as trolleys, because they drew their power from a third rail, not from overhead wires, but they probably traveled farther, faster, and more profitably than most other streetcars.

Another notable attempt to revitalize interurban streetcar travel began in 1938, when the St. Louis Car Company (SLCC) started work on its Electroliner vehicles. At the time, the major railroads were beginning the transition from steam to diesel and introducing new locomotive designs called streamliners. Stealing a bit of thunder from these eye-catching models, the sleekly streamlined, articulated, four-car Electroliner was designed specifically to revitalize the bankrupt North Shore Line. The North Shore Line had its origins in 1891 as a trolley line in Waukegan, Illanois, which was soon extended, as the Chicago & Milwaukee Electric Railway, to Evanston and then Chicago. In 1908 it reached Milwaukee and bankruptcy almost simultaneously, and bankruptcy was its condition for much of its life. This did not, however, prevent the operation of a very smart service of electric trains between the two cities, running at up to 70 mph (113 km) and boasting both parlor and dining cars. With its low fares, the line took a good deal of traffic from the two competing mainline railroads. Much of its enterprise could be attributed to the takeover of the line by Samuel Insull in 1916, at which time it was finally renamed as the Chicago North Shore and Milwaukee.

Insull was an Englishman who became private secretary to Thomas Edison, and later branched out into electric company investments. In 1914 he started to buy up trolley lines, and was responsible for the modernization of several interurbans, especially in Indiana. His interests collapsed when, during the Depression, a bank refused to renew a loan. An unholy alliance of newspapers and enemies then launched a campaign against him, making him a scapegoat of the Depression. He fled the country, was dragged back from Turkey, and taken to what was intended as a show trial but ended with his acquittal. He died soon after of a heart attack.

The North Shore Line acquired new tracks in the 1920s, but was hit by the Depression and, once again, was declared bankrupt in 1932. But it continued to provide a good service and could still be regarded as perhaps the model interurban. The Electroliners helped it, and so did the influx of traffic during World War II. But it was abandoned in 1963, by that time owned by a big corporation that found its losses good for tax purposes.

When the shovel-nosed Electroliner went into service in 1941, it far exceeded expectations, and passenger numbers on the line doubled in one year. It was a huge leap forward for interurban lines, and among the improvements it offered were true air conditioning, soundproofing, and hydraulic shock absorbers. There was even a luxurious bar, where passengers could munch Electroburgers while cruising at 90 mph (145 km/h) as the 1,000 hp of the Electroliner's eight motors whisked them toward Chicago's Loop. Only two Electroliners were built, however, and when the North Shore Line gave them up in 1963, Red Arrow Lines of Philadelphia took them over. There, renamed Liberty Liners and in the same livery as the Bullet trains of 1931, they ran until 1979. After they were retired, they were acquired by museums—one is now at the Rockhill Trolley Museum in Rockhill Furnace, Pennsylvania, while the other is at the Illinois Railway Museum in Union, Illinois.

One of the big interurbans has survived, although nowadays it hardly resembles the traditional model. The Chicago to South Bend, Indiana line was acquired by Insull in 1925, and renamed Chicago South Shore & South Bend Railroad. After Insull retreated in 1932 the new owners decided on a reconstruction that amounted almost to conversion into a standard railroad, instituting interline ticketing and developing its freight services. The freight service finished in 1981, but in the same decade new passenger rolling stock rejuvenated the line.

THE LAST GREAT STREETCAR

IN 1929, OVER 50 LEADING MEMBERS OF THE STREETCAR INDUSTRY GOT TOGETHER TO PLAN A MODERN, STANDARDIZED REPLACEMENT FOR NORTH AMERICA'S AGING AND DIVERSE FLEET OF TROLLEYS. THE RESULT WAS THE PCC, A STREETCAR THAT BECAME A WORLDWIDE FAVORITE AND IS STILL IN USE TODAY.

Alongside their development of new interurbans, Brill and the St Louis Car Company (SLCC) were active in the production of new urban streetcars. Brill introduced its Master Unit streetcars in 1929, and the two companies shared the production of 20 streamlined cars for the Capital Transit Company of Washington, D.C., which were delivered in 1935. More importantly, both companies were members of an industry consortium called the Electric Railway Presidents Conference Committee (ERPCC), which was set up in 1929 to develop a modern, standardized streetcar design. Headed by Dr. Thomas Conway, who had ordered the Brill Bullet cars for the Philadelphia & Western, its membership consisted of 28 streetcar-operating companies and 25 manufacturers.

After five years of intensive effort, the committee completed a total redesign of every component of the streetcar. Mechanical improvements concentrated on smooth, rapid acceleration and a whisper-quiet ride. As for the exterior skin, it was to be expected that the "dream streetcar"—known as the PCC (a shortened form of ERPCC)—would take the aerodynamically inspired streamliner shape. Steam locomotives of the day had received the same treatment from such industrial designers as Norman Bel Geddes and Raymond Loewy, as had many other vehicles and home appliances. Although they were far from the perfectly aerodynamic teardrop shape, the PCC prototypes resembled nothing else then running on United States trolley tracks. As a fitting inaugural gesture for this new breed of streetcar, Frank Sprague, the man who had started the whole business in 1877, rode in a prototype PCC car shortly before his death in 1934.

SLCC and Pullman-Standard rushed them into production and the first to be delivered was Brooklyn 1001, which went into trial service with the Brooklyn and Queens Transit Company, New York, in May

1936. The first to enter actual revenue service was Pittsburgh 100, the second PCC to be built, which was delivered to the Pittsburgh Railways Company two months later. For a streetcar designed by a committee, the PCC streamliner was overwhelmingly successful, and production totaled more than 5,000 in North America, where SLCC made 3,966 and Pullman-Standard 1,057. Another 15,000–20,000 more were manufactured under license by factories in Europe, and hundreds still run on routes throughout the world more than 70 years after their debut. Philadelphia, San Francisco, and Boston have some, as do several cities in Europe and in Latin America. PCC technology also formed the basis of rapid-transit trainsets for urban railroads in Boston, Brooklyn (New York), Chicago, and Cleveland.

National production priorities during World War II halted most assembly lines for automobiles, buses, and home appliances, but trolleys, which consumed no scarce gasoline or rubber tires, remained in production and regained a measure of importance in city transportation systems. Pullman-Standard kept its PCC production lines open, but shortages of raw materials meant that the chrome trim in the interiors had to be abandoned, paint being used instead, and some of the rubber inserts that gave PCC cars their quiet ride were omitted. Pullman-Standard simplified the interior trim and eliminated a few compound-curved metal panels for ease of manufacture, but these cars still gave sterling service for the duration of the war and long after.

First tested in 1934, PCC cars were long used in North America and elsewhere. This example carries the colors of the Newark, N.J. system.

When you enter a PCC car today, it is disconcerting to see a driver's seat like that of a bus, with accelerator and brake pedal, and a petite speedometer, but no steering wheel, only a row of switches across the dashboard. The foot pedal replaced the old hand controller, resulting in much smoother acceleration. There were three discrete brake systems on the PCC: a regenerative brake, which fed stopping energy back into the power grid, a compressed-air system, and an emergency magnetic system, which clamped down on the tracks. A 19-ton (17-tonne) vehicle needed all the stopping power it could muster, especially in the fall, when wet leaves littered the tracks. The wetness was not a problem—it actually improved steel-to-steel friction—but the leaves were worse than sheet ice, as any veteran driver would attest.

The later, postwar PCCs, called all-electric because they had electric "fail-safe" brakes instead of air brakes, had an additional row of "standee" windows running along the top of the car. Because of the rakish "chopped and dropped" windows on earlier PCCs, standing passengers could not see their stops. The new windows, which helped to overcome this problem, were allegedly copied from those of the buses of the time. This was only fair, because buses had borrowed heavily from the PCC in their styling. Also of note on these newer PCC cars was a long dorsal pod containing ventilating fans, which, curiously, were never used by the PCCs operated by the Toronto Transportation Commission. The fans were removed, but the pods were left in place.

Toronto operated more PCCs by far than any other Canadian city. In all, 745 streamliners saw service there between 1938 and 1995, and in the 1950s, the city was operating the largest fleet of PCCs in the world. Some PCCs were produced for Toronto by SLCC and Canadian Car & Foundry, acting in partnership. Others, built by SLCC and Pullman-Standard, were bought secondhand from United States cities, such as Louisville, Cincinnati, Cleveland, Birmingham, and Kansas City. All were similar in size—slightly less than 47 ft (14.4 m) long—and, of course, used the nonstandard Toronto wide gauge of 4 ft 11 in (1.5 m). Most of the earlier, prewar cars and those that had been acquired secondhand were disposed of in 1983.

Later examples of the PCC had a long pod on the roof containing ventilating fans.

Although it had been a member of the ERPCC, Brill opted out of PCC production, preferring to develop its own new streetcar, the Brilliner. Intended as a competitor for the PCC, the Brilliner was launched in 1938 and had bodywork styled by Raymond Loewy. Brill sold only 40 of them, however, including 25 to Atlantic City and 10 to Philadelphia's Red Arrow Lines. The Atlantic City Brilliners remained in service until 1955, while those in Philadelphia—which were the last streetcars Brill ever built, in 1941—ran for more than 40 years until their retirement in 1982.

The PCC was the most successful of all streetcar designs, and in many cities it helped to slow the conversion from streetcars to buses, but the long-term decline in streetcar patronage continued unabated. In the United States, annual passenger numbers were down to just under 6 billion by 1940, less than half of what they had been in 1920. They rose again to around 9 billion during World War II (when fuel and tire rationing hit private automobile use), but dropped rapidly after the war, slumping to under 4 billion in 1950, and just 133 million in 1980, by which time only a handful of North American cities were operating regular streetcar services.

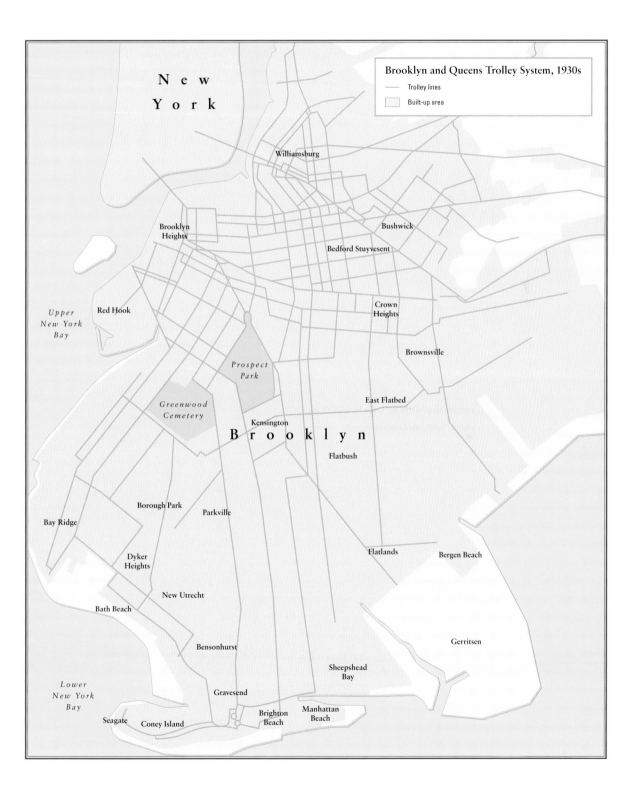

Brooklyn and Queens Trolley System, 1930s

— Trolley lines

☐ Built-up area

New York

Williamsburg

Brooklyn
Heights

Bushwick

Bedford Stuyvesent

Crown
Heights

Red Hook

Upper
New York
Bay

Prospect
Park

Brownsville

Greenwood
Cemetery

East Flatbed

Kensington

Brooklyn

Flatbush

Borough Park

Parkville

Bay Ridge

Flatlands

Bergen Beach

Dyker
Heights

New Utrecht

Bath Beach

Bensonhurst

Gerritsen

Lower
New York
Bay

Sheepshead
Bay

Gravesend

Seagate

Coney Island

Brighton
Beach

Manhattan
Beach

The growth of commuter traffic

SEEKING NEW KINDS OF TRAFFIC, AS ALWAYS, THE RAILROADS ENCOURAGED THE GROWTH OF A COMMUTING POPULATION, BUT THIS DID LITTLE FOR THEIR PROFITS.

The Long Island Railroad, acquired by the Pennsylvania Railroad in 1900, benefited from a suburban boom in the 1920s, but in most years ran at a loss.

Urbanization and suburbanization went hand in hand, and suburbanization and commuter railroading were mutually supporting; indeed, the possibility of rail service into the cities encouraged developers to offer inviting home sites away from the stresses of city life, and the growth of such home sites in turn encouraged the provision of rail services into and out of the cities. Everybody seemed to benefit: the new home buyers, the builders and developers, and, of course, the landowners. A situation soon arose when even the rumor of an impending rail line or service could lift land values drastically. However, for the railroads the benefits from this seemed doubtful.

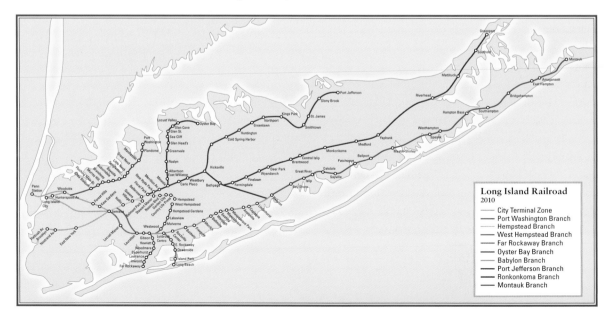

Long Island Railroad
2010

—— City Terminal Zone
—— Port Washington Branch
······ Hempstead Branch
—— West Hempstead Branch
– – Far Rockaway Branch
–O– Oyster Bay Branch
······ Babylon Branch
—— Port Jefferson Branch
—— Ronkonkoma Branch
—— Montauk Branch

Providing facilities in the form of stations and trains just to handle the peak morning and evening traffic of the working day was not necessarily profitable, even though trains were heavily loaded. But the railroad companies in those early decades did not worry about this. If they thought about it at all, they believed that, given time, the situation would improve. Some tried to develop off-peak traffic, and around big centers such as New York, where there were many attractions for the leisured, this could work. To encourage the frequent traveller, passengers could commute a week's or a month's trips into one period ticket, giving a lower rate per trip. The masses of people, mainly workers, who took advantage of this were described as commuters, a term that soon became a widely used sociological term.

In the beginning, providing a commuter service meant simply installing a few extra stations on an existing line into the city, and using old locomotives and coaches. Later, some railroads built lines specifically for commuters. There were even companies that were almost exclusively devoted to commuter traffic. One such was the Long Island Railroad, serving commuters east of New York and soon enjoying such a very high traffic density that it became (and remained) America's busiest passenger railroad. It had rolling stock specifically for commuter use. Some other railroads took the same course

A Metro-North electric commuter train leaves New York City in 1983. Metro-North was established to take over commuter services formerly operated by the New Haven and New York Central railroads.

The last significant steam-hauled commuter service was that of the Canadian Pacific at Montréal. Here, former mainline locomotives handle the evening rush.

when their commuter traffic developed into heavy flows, for the use of old long-distance stock, with its low-density seating and capacious washrooms, meant fewer seats per foot or per ton of vehicle.

As early as 1905 the Long Island had an electrified line and was running America's first all-steel passenger cars. It was not long before other United States lines, including the New York Central and New Haven, were also operating electric services, although this early start was really caused by the need to avoid smoke in the tunnels leading to Grand Central Terminus. In Canada, Montréal's electrification of the line northward through Mount Royal Tunnel had similar motivation.

Avoidance of smoke was also one of the arguments used in favor of the elevated railway, whose tracks straddled city streets. In fact, for the higher-floor residents of apartments, this made the nuisance worse as steam trains bustled past just a few feet from their front windows. Few elevated lines survived, although Chicago still has its elevated Loop, which nowadays is more of an electric light-rail operation, fulfiling functions which are elsewhere entrusted to underground transit railroads. A short elevated line, with the unusual track gauge of 5 ft 2½ in (1587 mm), also survived in Philadelphia under the auspices of the South Eastern Pennsylvania Transport Authority (SEPTA), which is one of many North American transit authorities set up to coordinate bus and light rail, as well as short-distance rail services, in this case those previously offered by the Pennsylvania and Reading railroads.

John Pierpont Morgan, when he was in control of the New Haven Railroad, took the unprecedented step of electrifying from the start a new suburban line out of New York to Westchester. Expensively

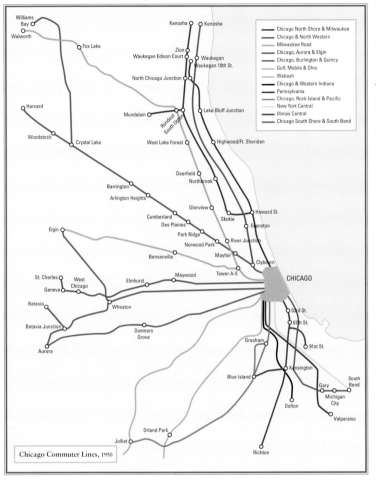

Chicago Commuter Lines, 1950

Legend:
- Chicago North Shore & Milwaukee
- Chicago & North Western
- Milwaukee Road
- Chicago, Aurora & Elgin
- Chicago, Burlington & Quincy
- Gulf, Mobile & Ohio
- Wabash
- Chicago & Western Indiana
- Pennsylvania
- Chicago, Rock Island & Pacific
- New York Central
- Illinois Central
- Chicago South Shore & South Bend

engineered (the final cost was well above estimate, some of the money just seemed to mysteriously disappear), the venture was a failure. It drew a few passengers from other lines but traffic levels were never enough to pay back the huge investment cost. It opened in 1912 and was sold for scrap after its closure in 1937. Where services were not intensive, railroads tended to use hand-me-down steam locomotives until

Chicago commuter lines connected to the suburbs from the city center for commuters needing to reach the city.

the latter were replaced by standard diesel locomotives. In the late 1950s, the last two North American steam commuter services, the Grand Trunk from Detroit and the Canadian Pacific from Montréal, were using locomotives that had only recently hauled heavy long-distance trains. There was one steam locomotive specifically conceived for commuter and transit services, this was the "Forney Tank" designed by Matthias Forney. Originally intended to replace streetcar horses in 1872 (when horses were succumbing to an epidemic), it was soon taken up by railroads. It was a "double-ender," running in either direction without the need to be turned for the return trip. The absence of a tender enabled this, and water supplies were carried in a tank behind the cab. The last Forneys were hauling commuters for the Canadian National until the late 1950s.

By that time the Canadian National's Montréal commuter services had been reduced to this one steam route and the electrified lines under Mount Royal. Canadian Pacific had been the first company to think of suburban services, having built a "suburban spur" from its Montréal—Ottawa main line to serve Pointe Fortune, 50 miles from Montréal in 1893. This spur was not a great success and the service was

Steam commuter trains lasted until 1958 at Detroit. Grand Trunk Western locomotives stand ready to leave for Pontiac.

subsequently cut back to Rigaud, 40 miles away, and this became well used and a permanent asset to the city. Later the Grand Trunk provided a service to Vaudreil, which was in part-competition with the Canadian Pacific's line. This service would be the last haunt of the Canadian National's "Forney Tank"

locomotives. However, this service came to an end in 1965, leaving the Canadian National to concentrate on its quite dense electric service into the northern suburbs via Mount Royal. After 1950 railroads began to look for ways of shedding their commuter services. Plain abandonment usually required state agreement, which was usually not forthcoming. Eventually, services received subsidies from local authorities, with the latter going on to establish transit and local transport commissions to take over entirely. When this happened, the passenger initially only noticed that the locomotive had received a new coat of paint and logo. Quite typical was the history of San Francisco's line to San Jose. This had originally been built by a local company in the 1860s, but had soon been taken over by the Southern Pacific Railroad, which attempted to make it useful and profitable enough to double-track. This doubling was achieved in 1904 and the service continued for some decades, with passenger numbers reaching a peak during World War II. After that, multiplying automobile ownership, together with local authority highway-building, soon made the line into a heavy loss-maker. Southern Pacific tried to discontinue the service. This was disallowed, but eventually the California Department of Transport provided a subsidy and, by the end of the century, the line's modern bi-level trains were bearing the Caltrain logo.

A late-surviving "Forney tank" locomotive hauls a Canadian National commuter train at Montréal in 1957.

Short lines and regionals

ALMOST A THIRD OF FREIGHT STARTS OR FINISHES ITS JOURNEY ON A SHORT LINE. HUNDREDS OF SUCH LINES STILL EXIST AND THEY HAVE A LONG HISTORY.

In the beginning, all lines were short lines, but some grew into major railroads, while others were absorbed by the latter. Over the decades, the number of short lines grew, reaching a peak before World War I when they numbered more than 1,000. That was a running total, for throughout the railway age these railways appeared, disappeared, or changed their name or ownership at a rate so rapid that it is hard to accurately gauge how many there were at any given time, despite the existence of national and state short line associations to which most of them belonged. Identification is additionally hampered by the very names of these companies which, apart from changing from time to time, may consist of the names of places which a line never touched, although it might once have hoped to do so.

The names of these lines were unknown to the wider public, but in the areas they served they were a familiar and sometimes treasured part of daily life. The archetypal short line was, and is, a single track passing through unspoiled countryside and carrying one or two trains a day linking a small community or an isolated business to the outside world, usually by exchanging traffic with a major railroad. Management might consist of perhaps one or two persons, accessible to all, and total staff would be in the tens rather than the hundreds or thousands. The fate of the townships served was intimately bound up with the well-being of the line; a line could fail if an important client closed down, and a failed line could mean hardship for many people and businesses in the places it served. But this intimacy was

A Providence & Worcester Railroad locomotive exchanges cars on former New Haven trackage at Old Saybrook, Conn.

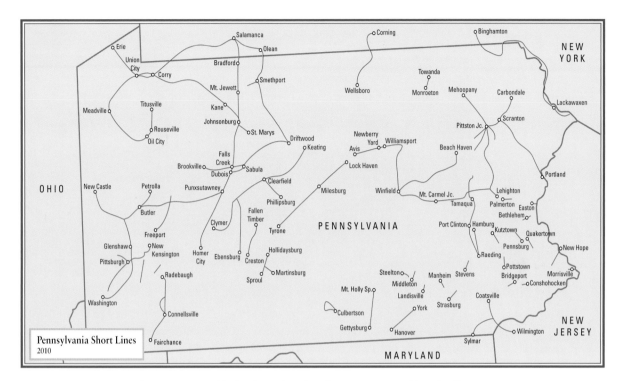

Pennsylvania Short Lines 2010

Pennsylvania is well provided with short lines. This map shows them in 2010.

also a strength for, managed and often owned by local people, a short line operator was able and willing to study the needs of its clients and, furthermore, provide a service more personal than that which might have been offered by a large company.

Such lines have continued to exist, but they are only part of the wide range of rail companies that fall into this classification. In the USA and Canada "short line" is an official category, not a mere description. In 1911, when the Interstate Commerce Commission introduced the Class I, Class II, and Class III classification, a short line fell into Class III (having an annual revenue of less than $100,000). Over the years definitions changed. Nowadays federal bodies rate a Class III as having less than $32 million operating revenue, while the Association of American Railroads defines a Class III as having less than 350 miles and revenue of less than $40 million. In Canada short lines are defined as Class II.

Short lines may be divided into those whose main role is to fetch or deliver freightcars from adjoining mainline railroads, for which they receive a flat fee or a portion of the overall tariff, and those that link two elements of an industrial process, for example, a coal mine with a nearby power plant. In recent years, the short line tourist railroad has appeared, either using defunct tracks or sharing them with other short line traffic, with some lines handling freight on weekdays and tourists on weekends. Historically, most short lines have been owned by non-rail companies for the benefit of an industry, but such lines also carried general traffic.

On the eve of the Staggers Act of 1980 (which would change the picture somewhat), a survey of 200 of the most prominent short lines revealed that more than half were fully owned by non-railroad companies. Usually, these were owned by a local industry, willingly or unwillingly. The unwilling were

One of the Chicago Belt Railroad's many switchers extricates a car from an industrial track.

those businesses for whom a line was the only available, or cheapest, form of transport available. There were elevator companies in Illinois, for example, for whom ownership of a short line was essential for the outward transportation of their grain because truckers were too expensive. A number of other short lines were wholly, or more often partly, owned by the larger railroad companies. States and local municipalities also owned some, as did a few individuals.

Among the lines owned by railroad companies were the several belt or terminal railways. These were lines jointly provided by one or more railroads in a given city to provide a common-use switching and interchange service. Some of the belt railways, linking sorting yards of the several railroads, could develop into big enterprises placing them outside the category of small railways; they might have short mileages, but the tonnage moved could be enormous. The Chicago Belt Railroad was perhaps the most substantial of these lines. It was started in 1882 by a consortium of the railroads serving Chicago (with subsequent mergers it is now owned by six Class I railroads). It has a quite small route mileage of 28 miles (46 km) but its track mileage is around 300 miles (483 km) thanks to its switching and sorting tracks. Not only does it serve the participating railroads, but also the many industrial enterprises that decide to locate themselves along it.

Scores of short lines are now devoted to the running of tourist trains and heritage trains. The luckiest or best-endowed of these use steam locomotives, usually restored by the long and expensive efforts of volunteers. Most are small operations, hitting local headlines only on special occasions when they run Santa Claus specials or feature Thomas the Tank Engine. On the other hand, some are large and well-known. The Silverton and the Cumbres & Toltec narrow-gauge lines in Colorado and New Mexico are among these. Steamtown at Scranton, Pennsylvania, is noted for its large stock of old locomotives, its working roundhouse, and opportunities offered to the public of work-experience holidays.

Regional Railroads
2010

| 0 | 200 km |
| 0 | 200 miles |

N

Possibly the best known is the Strasburg Railroad in Pennsylvania, whose origins go back to the beginnings of the American railway age. It has claimed to be the oldest surviving railroad in the United States because it was chartered in 1832, although the date of its first trains is not known, and it still retains its original name. The claim of being the oldest short line was also made, until its demise in 1981, by the Skaneateles Railroad in New York State, which is actually known to have been up and running in 1840. In 1901 a competing tram service obliged the Strasburg Railroad to end the operation of passenger trains, although a single daily mixed passenger and freight train continued to run. However, in 1957, the owners decided to abandon the line after bad floods. It was thereupon purchased by enthusiasts, who ran their first freight train that year and in 1958 embarked on the venture of offering heritage trains for tourists

Main regional railroads in 2010. Off-map is the 110-mile narrow-gauge White Pass and Yukon RR, which connects Skagway, Alaska, to the Yukon via northern British Columbia.

over 4 miles (7 km) of line. The first steam locomotive, a former Canadian National six-wheel switcher, was acquired in 1960 and several other vintage locomotives and rolling stock were acquired later, and the line subsequently prospered.

The Staggers Act, which made it easier for the Class I railroads to divest themselves of unwanted lines, provided opportunities for new short line companies to take over such railways. Labor laws and other railroad regulations were less burdensome for short lines, and this alone could make a branch line viable on transfer from a major railroad.

Since these lines provided useful traffic for the big railroads, the latter did what they could to help the new owners. A quite unusual situation developed in 1981 when the short line Iowa Railroad took over the former main line of the Rock Island Railroad eastward from Omaha: part of its route included sharing trackage rights with the mainline Milwaukee Railroad, the latter using the line in the daytime and the Iowa Railroad using it at night.

One of the Strasburg Railroad's early tourist trains, hauled by a former Canadian National switcher.

When sizable divisions were thus hived off, the newly independent lines were too big to be classed as short lines and became regional railways, usually categorized as Class II roads. They joined an existing collection of regionals, many of them long established and prosperous, with others that were the remains of former Class I railroads that had been demoted. The Providence & Worcester is a not untypical representative of the long-established regionals, having begun operations in 1847. Serving parts of Massachusetts, Connecticut and Rhode Island, it fell into the hands of the New Haven Railroad in 1892 and hence of the Pennsylvania Railroad when the New Haven was itself absorbed. It became independent again, just in time to avoid inclusion in the ill-fated Penn-Central conglomeration, and in the 1980s was operating 371 miles (597 km) of route with 14 locomotives. It has continued to prosper.

A feature of the post-Staggers period has been the further development of holding companies owning and operating several short or regional lines. Among them have been Genessee & Wyoming, Guilford Transportation Industries, and Rail America. The first of these was a salt-hauling short line until the Staggers Act gave it the chance to acquire scores

of short lines in the United States; later it also bought lines in Canada, the Netherlands and Australia. Guilford, which took over the lines of the former Boston & Maine and Maine Central railroads among others, was renamed Pan Am Railways in 2006, having acquired the name and logo of the famous but defunct airline. Rail America owned scores of short lines as well as the former Class I Florida East Coast, which no longer qualified as a major railroad despite its efficient long-haul business.

In Canada the short line picture was similar to that of the United States, although short lines were less numerous. Canada early on had a number of regional railroads, although they were not described as such. Some were sponsored and supported by provincial governments like the Ontario Northland, Northern Alberta and British Columbia railways. In Québec the Québec North Shore and Labrador has long functioned as a carrier of iron ore down to the St Lawrence; its construction began in 1951 and it was soon a heavy-duty railway passing 230-car ore trains, which had to cease running in winter because of the ore's propensity to freeze. Not having a Staggers Act, Canada waited until the 1990s before experiencing a proliferation of short line and regional railways as the Canadian National and Canadian Pacific sought to rid themselves of unprofitable lines. In Eastern Canada, in particular, lines were handed down to new companies. The Canadian Pacific decided to divest itself of all its lines east of Montréal, giving rise to several new companies. In the west, the Northern Alberta Railways was broken up. It had been built largely to serve the grain-growers and had been a loss-maker, although admirably serving its purpose of supporting agriculture. It was split up but after several changes of ownership it was taken over by Canadian National.

As commuter services decline, a new regime enters

THE POST-WAR YEARS FOUND THE RAILROADS UNABLE TO
REDUCE THEIR LOSSES FROM COMMUTER SERVICES, BUT LOCAL
ADMINISTRATIONS CAME TO THE RESCUE.

After the 1950s most railroads were trying to rid themselves of their increasingly unprofitable commuter services. Cross-subsidizing these trains with income from freight meant that freight tariffs needed to be higher, which was not good at a time when competing truckers were drawing away so much traffic. Here and there, far-sighted state and local authorities began to find ways to make financial contributions, but it was the Staggers Act of 1980 that made it easier for railroads to hive off their commuters to local authorities. The latter typically took over services with organizations created under the auspices of state or city transport departments, while contracting with the original railroad to perform the operations.

The sequence of events leading to state takeover varied between different companies. Thus the Central Railroad of New Jersey, which had very heavy commuter traffic, began to receive state subsidies in 1964 (after some years of operation made more difficult by high taxes levied by the same state). In 1967 it was bankrupt. A decade later, it was part of Conrail and its tracks were progressively abandoned but it was an essential passenger carrier and its busiest lines were taken over by a state organization, NJ Transit. In other cities or states the process was less confused, with both the railroad and the local administration having a clear concept right from the start.

Toward the end of this difficult period, public attitudes toward the automobile began to change. It was realized that the replacement of public transport by acres of tarmac and parking space did nothing to ease congestion, and, in fact, could make the journey to work even more time-consuming and stressful. Taxpayers' money might therefore be better spent on fostering trains and buses. By the end of the century, more and better rail commuter services were being introduced, both conventional and light rail.

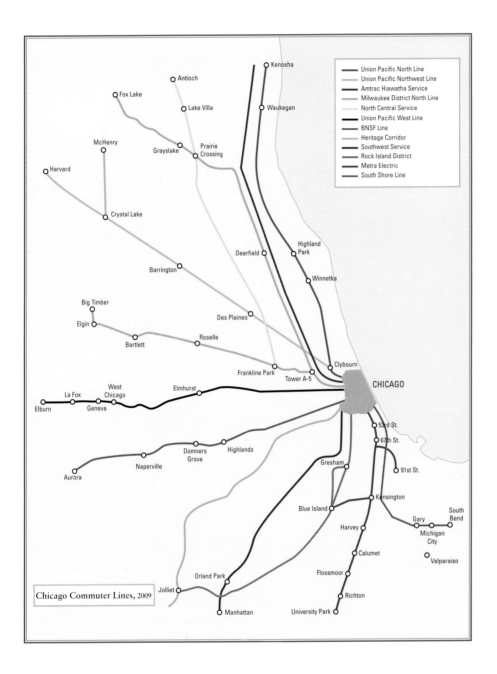

	Union Pacific North Line
	Union Pacific Northwest Line
	Amtrac Hiawatha Service
	Milwaukee District North Line
	North Central Service
	Union Pacific West Line
	BNSF Line
	Heritage Corridor
	Southwest Service
	Rock Island District
	Metra Electric
	South Shore Line

Chicago Commuter Lines, 2009

Chicago's dense suburban lines, as operated by METRA. Metropolitan networks like this provide a good service throughout the day, not just at peak hours.

California and Washington have in recent years been very supportive of their rail passenger services, partly to reduce their expenditure on highways. The lines shown on this map provide comfortable trains that are well patronized.

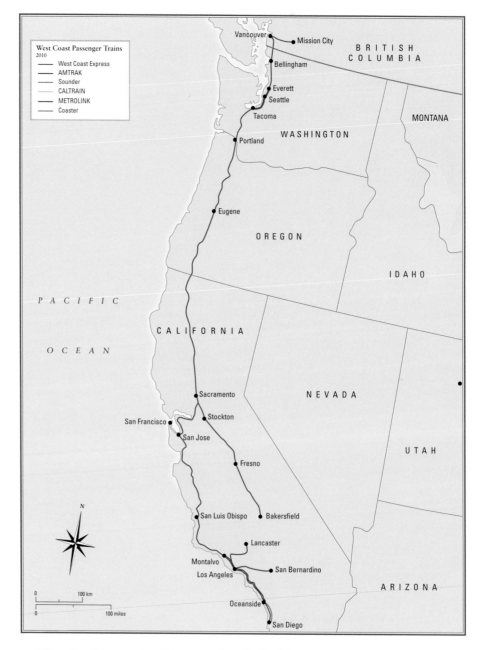

West Coast Passenger Trains
2010
—— West Coast Express
—— AMTRAK
—— Sounder
—— CALTRAIN
—— METROLINK
—— Coaster

Different localities moved at different speeds, and a few did not move at all, but the usual procedure both for conventional and light rail investment was long, drawn-out and highly democratic. Pressure groups would form, proposals made, public debates be held, engineering and commercial studies made, ballots held (typically as part of the electoral voting process), and funding sought. Growing concerns about pollution and energy supply helped the pro-rail argument.

In this way the steadily improving—and already commendable—public transport system of Seattle took almost half a century to offer light rail, for in the 1960s a light rail system was advocated, but the voters did not favor it. In the 1990s three districts in the area agreed to create a single authority to coordinate and develop bus and rail services and thus was born Sound Transit, which has sponsored and supported a coordinated system of buses, regional and commuter trains, and light rail ever since. Being surrounded by water and mountains, and with a population that was not large at first but which over the last three decades has been growing rapidly, Seattle was a special case requiring special treatment. And it did achieve a coordinated network of Cascade regional trains and Sounder commuter trains supported by buses and, increasingly, light rail.

Bigger cities such as Chicago, Los Angeles, and Toronto had extensive commuter railroad systems in need of development. Toronto was quick off the mark with its GO (Government of Ontario) trains. Running mainly over the tracks owned and operated by the Canadian National Railways, the trains were equipped with new bi-level lightweight coaches supplied by Bombardier. Bombardier is a Canadian company, one of whose constituents was the old Montréal Locomotive Works, a subsidiary of American Locomotive Company (ALCO). Bombardier went on to become a global company with enormous railway business. Its bi-level commuter cars, distinguished by their high bow-ended roofs, are used by other American commuter systems, including Metrolink, centered in Los Angeles.

King St Station in downtown Seattle is served by Sounder commuter trains (at left) and the Cascade regional trains (right).

Metrolink, supervised by five Southern California counties, began operations in 1992 and runs over trackage sold by the Southern Pacific, shared with freight railroads, or put together by itself. For most of the time, Amtrak has held its own operating contract, although for five years a private operator, Veolia, was chosen for this task. Starting with just three routes, it has since expanded, and voters evidently supported further extensions, although the economic problems of 2009 postponed these. One of its routes is unusual in that its purpose is to connect two suburbs. In the present century Metrolink suffered three bad accidents, two of which were collisions with freight trains and the other resulted from collision with a vehicle parked on the track. The driver of the vehicle was subsequently sentenced to life imprisonment, the deaths being counted as murders.

The Chicago METRA system, on the other hand, has won several safety awards and most of its accidents have been caused by automobiles held up on grade crossings. It is also unlike Los Angeles in that it does not use Bombardier coaches but conventional bi-levels supplied initially by United States builders and latter by Japanese suppliers. Its standardized diesel locomotive type (the EMD FP40PH) pulls and pushes almost all its trains (some lines use electric multiple units). The system had its beginning in 1974 when the railroad companies evidently were unable to provide badly-needed new equipment; the Regional Transportation Authority (RTA) was founded to take responsibility for public transport. In 1984, it was replaced by METRA, which by 2010 ran trains from five Chicago terminals over about 500 miles (805 km) of route, with further expansions planned.

By 2010, smaller cities across North America were extending, or introducing, their own modern commuter trains, making use of the experience gained by the pioneers. In Minneapolis, for example, much thought and

A METRA commuter train with conventional bi-level coaches passes the Amtrak rolling stock yards in Chicago.

work came to fruition in 2009, when that city's North Star trains came into use. Using Burington Northern Santa Fe (BNSF) trackage, these trains run 40 miles (64 km) to Big Lake, and the system is expected to grow. Local sponsors were sought for the project, and one such sponsor was the Twins baseball team, whose Target Field is served by the trains. Powered by five locomotives built by the lesser-known maker Motive Power Industries of Boise, Idaho, 18 Bombardier cars provide six round-trips on weekdays (five locomotives for just 12 daily short-distance trains exemplifies the difficult economics of commuter lines designed for peak-hour traffic).

A Metrolink train pulls out from Los Angeles. The coach configuration indicates that it is a Bombardier product.

Thanks partly to the rising price of automobile fuel, in 2008 public transport traffic was at its highest since 1956. Railroad commuter ridership rose by almost five percent in that year, and the recession that followed hardly changed the situation. What the recession did mean, however, was that transport authorities lacked the funds to carry out planned projects. Some alleviation was

gained with money from the Federal Recovery and Reinvestment Act (in effect, money already promised but with an earlier payment assured). Most of this was to benefit light rail, but a new line for Metrolink in Southern California and a Long Island Railroad project in New York were among the beneficiaries. A second tunnel under the Hudson River to improve capacity between New Jersey and the Pennsylvania Station in Manhattan was started but then postponed.

Railroad mergers and deregulation, 1960–95

IN THE LAST THREE DECADES OF THE 20TH CENTURY UNITED STATES RAILROADS FOUGHT TO STAY IN BUSINESS WITH THE AID OF MERGERS, DEREGULATION, REVISED LABOR PRACTICES, AND IMPROVED EQUIPMENT.

By 1960, the situation on America's railroads was reaching a crucial point. In 1930, passenger traffic movements on the railroads reached 32 billion, but fell to 19 billion in 1933. They rose to a peak of 71 billion in 1943, then fell to 64 billion in 1946, to 32 billion in 1950, and finally to 21 billion in 1960. Freight, on the other hand, began at 42 billion in 1930, fell to 28 billion in 1933, rose to a peak of 65 billion in 1943, and seesawed mainly between that figure and 58 billion in 1960, with a low of 52 billion in 1949.

The last steam locomotive was retired in 1960, by which time diesel reigned almost supreme (there was still a significant amount of traffic operated by electric traction). Passenger traffic receipts were falling, although the pace of decline had slowed. On the other hand, freight receipts were holding up fairly well. The implications were obvious. As a passenger-carrier, rail seemed to be in terminal decline, but the freight side of the business was in fair shape, with the possibility of even increasing its share of the market. Inevitably, changes would be required if the railroads were to remain viable businesses.

By 1960, diesel-electric locomotives had changed the face of railroad operation—but so, too, had highway vehicles and airplanes. With falling freight and passenger traffic, and decreasing revenue, railroads had to merge to survive. Big was beautiful, or so it seemed to many railroads struggling to compete with other modes of transport, as well as with each other.

The diesel revolution put new life into American railroads. By 1960, 27,000 diesels had replaced some 40,000 steam locomotives in the United States. Canada, too, soon retired its last steam locomotives in 1962. Steam maintenance facilities disappeared fast, steam workshops quickly being converted to diesel repair shops or being shut down entirely. Whole communities were affected. There had been other cost-cutting strategies, too. Centralized Traffic Control (CTC) had been introduced before 1950, making train movement safer and more efficient. By 1965, it was accepted as the safest form of traffic control then available. By clearing signals and operating switches directly from his desk, the dispatcher had complete control of a train's progress. Soon the radio and computer added another dimension to railroad operation. Two-way radio communication between train crews and control towers became normal. Then, new computerized systems for tracking the movement of locomotives and cars appeared, of which Total Operations Processing System (TOPS) was perhaps the most successful.

Probably the most crucial innovation was the hot-box detector. Freight train operation had long been plagued by axleboxes that ran hot. These could cause train fires, or soften and melt the axles, causing a derailment. One of the prime duties of crewmen was to keep axleboxes under observation, but with increasingly long trains they could not always spot the wisps of smoke or flame in time. The new hot-box detectors were trackside heat-sensing devices that could detect trouble on a passing train and not only send a radio warning to the train crew, but also indicate the precise location of the faulty axlebox.

Despite these innovations, the railroads were clearly struggling in the 1970s. Many solutions, even nationalization, were suggested. Such proposals got nowhere, owing to strong conservative opposition and almost every other proposal put to Congress had a feature that some senators or representatives threw out. Clearly, however, planning and action at a national level were needed. Railroads had been hamstrung by regulating legislation since the 1880s. In the late 1970s, President Jimmy Carter had partly deregulated trucking and the airlines. This put additional pressure on the freight railroads, and they demanded parity of treatment. In 1980, at last this was granted by the passing of what came to be known as the Staggers Act—Rep. Harley Staggers (Democrat, West Virginia) chairman of the House Commerce Committee at that time.

The Staggers Act significantly altered the terms under which railroads and shippers could agree freight charges. Henceforth, railroads could offer volume discounts and other tariff incentives, which

Deregulation in 1980 with the passing of the Staggers Act helped the US railroads to both expand the carriage of general merchandise and develop their strengths in the movement of bulk commodities in hopper and tank cars.

By 1963, the total route length for United States railroads was down to 214, 387 miles (345,013 km). The network matched the population and industry spread of the country, the Northeast remaining the best served area.

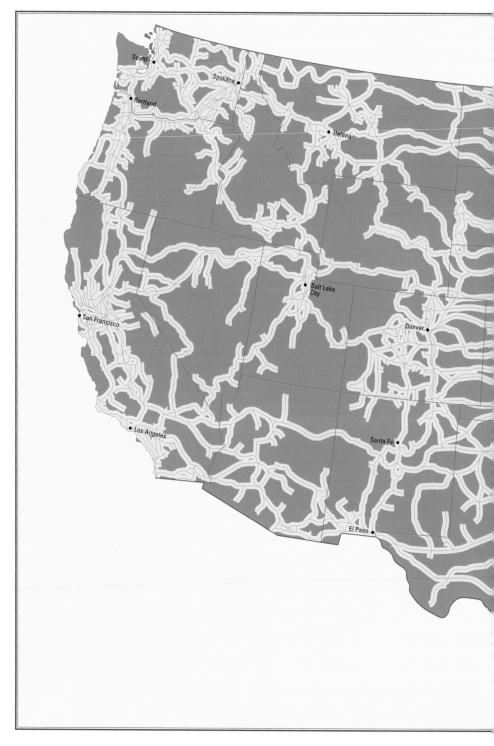

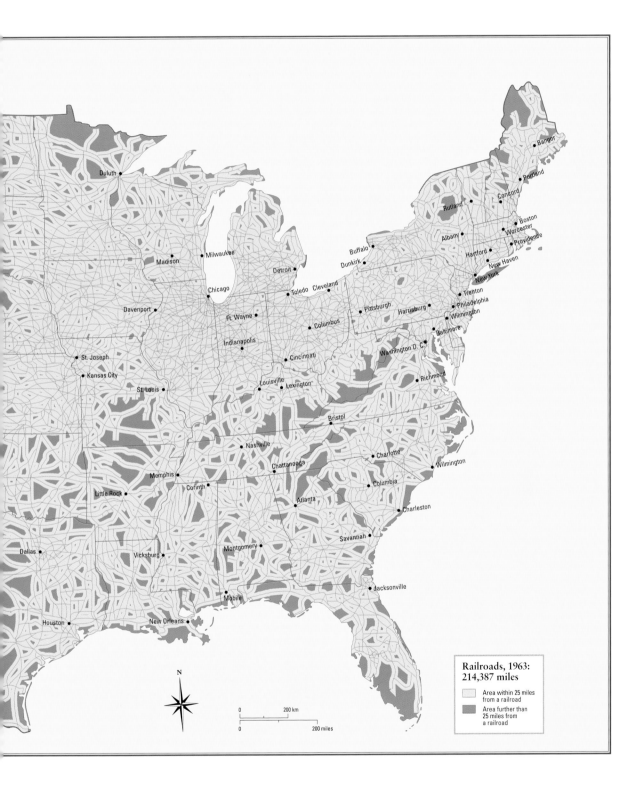

Railroads, 1963:
214,387 miles

☐ Area within 25 miles
from a railroad

■ Area further than
25 miles from
a railroad

A new sight on United States railroads from April 1, 1976 was the new livery and logo of Conrail. The Consolidated Rail Corporation was a federally-funded takeover of the major railroad companies in the Northeast, which were in financial dire straits.

had formerly been prohibited. The ICC. would supervise only those tariffs where there was a real transportation monopoly, which was considerably less than 20 percent of the total. Railroads and shippers could negotiate their own contracts privately, thus withdrawal of services and closure of loss-making lines became easier.

The 1980 deregulation enabled the railroads to expand their carriage of coal and grain, automobiles, and intermodal containers, among other forms of traffic. Railroad investment, which had been meager for too long, increased. The Act also encouraged the development of that specialized class of railroad, the regional line. Such companies could take on lines with low flow densities and operate them profitably. Some of them were quite long. The Wisconsin Central, for example, operated over 2,000 miles (3,200 km) of route, and had 115 locomotives and 5,135 cars. Formed in 1987 by the purchase of the former Lakes States division of the Soo Line, its main line linked Chicago with Minneapolis and extended into Ontario. Another regional was the Iowa Interstate, which took over the Soo Line's main line between Council Bluffs in Iowa and Bureau in Illinois. Like the Wisconsin Central, the Iowa Interstate also acquired failing railroads in other parts, with the aim of revitalizing them.

The post-war merger era had really started earlier than 1980, some say in the late 1940s, when six roads merged to form three. These were the Gulf, Mobile & Ohio with the Alton (the new Gulf, Mobile & Ohio subsequently was merged into its near-parallel competitor, the Illinois Central), the Denver & Rio Grande Western with the Denver & Salt Lake, and the Chesapeake & Ohio with the Pere Marquette (a small road that operated mainly in Michigan). There was also the merger in 1957 of the Louisville & Nashville Railroad with the Nashville, Chattanooga & St. Louis.

At first, only the smaller roads began to disappear; then in 1963 the Chesapeake & Ohio acquired the celebrated old Baltimore & Ohio and, in 1973, the latter together with the Western Maryland became a subsidiary of the Chessie System, as did the Chesapeake & Ohio itself. In 1964, the Norfolk & Western acquired two smaller roads and leased two others. The big news of that year, however, was the announcement that arch-rival Pennsylvania and New York Central were to merge to form the Penn Central. Completed in 1968, the ICC. stipulated that the New Haven Railroad should also be included.

At the time of merger, both the New York City and Pennsylvania Railroad were in the black, but the new company immediately ran into heavy deficits. None of the merging railroads had really prepared in practical terms for the change, and the managements of the two companies, having long regarded each other as opponents, failed to mesh. Working systems and practices were not integrated and each "team" sought to impose its own methods on the whole system. This was accompanied by a failure to combine the physical assets promptly, which was what the merger had promised. Former competing lines continued, in effect, to compete. Meanwhile, the deindustrialization of the region that the Penn Central served removed traditional sources of traffic so that the four-track main lines, about which both companies had boasted in the past, became burdens, still attracting taxes and maintenance costs, but without the traffic to justify them. The Penn Central traded for only two years before becoming the biggest single

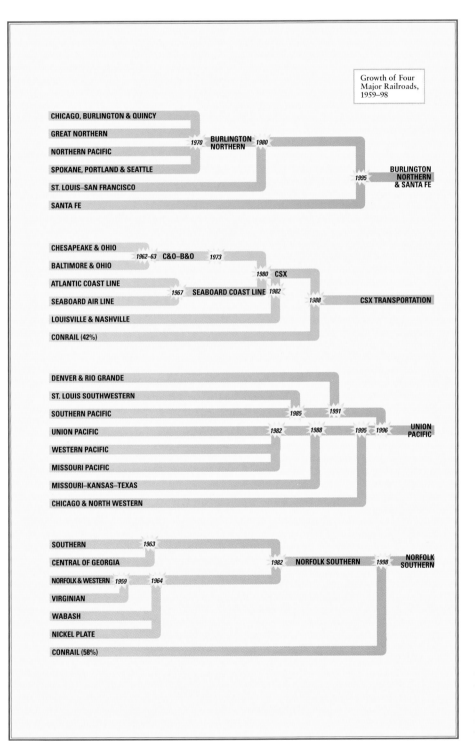

Growth of Four
Major Railroads,
1959–98

CHICAGO, BURLINGTON & QUINCY

GREAT NORTHERN

NORTHERN PACIFIC   1970 BURLINGTON 1980
                                      NORTHERN

SPOKANE, PORTLAND & SEATTLE   BURLINGTON
                                                  1995 NORTHERN
ST. LOUIS–SAN FRANCISCO   & SANTA FE

SANTA FE

CHESAPEAKE & OHIO   1962–63 C&O–B&O 1973

BALTIMORE & OHIO
                                      1980 CSX
ATLANTIC COAST LINE   1967 SEABOARD COAST LINE 1982

SEABOARD AIR LINE   1988 CSX TRANSPORTATION

LOUISVILLE & NASHVILLE

CONRAIL (42%)

DENVER & RIO GRANDE

ST. LOUIS SOUTHWESTERN

SOUTHERN PACIFIC   1985   1991

UNION PACIFIC   1982   1988   1995 1996 UNION
                                                              PACIFIC
WESTERN PACIFIC

MISSOURI PACIFIC

MISSOURI–KANSAS–TEXAS

CHICAGO & NORTH WESTERN

SOUTHERN   1963

CENTRAL OF GEORGIA   1982 NORFOLK SOUTHERN 1998 NORFOLK
                                                            SOUTHERN
NORFOLK & WESTERN 1959   1964

VIRGINIAN

WABASH

NICKEL PLATE

CONRAIL (58%)

Over the years, the survival
of many railroads depended
on mergers or takeovers. This
illustration shows the genesis
of four major roads over four
decades in the second half of
the 20th century.

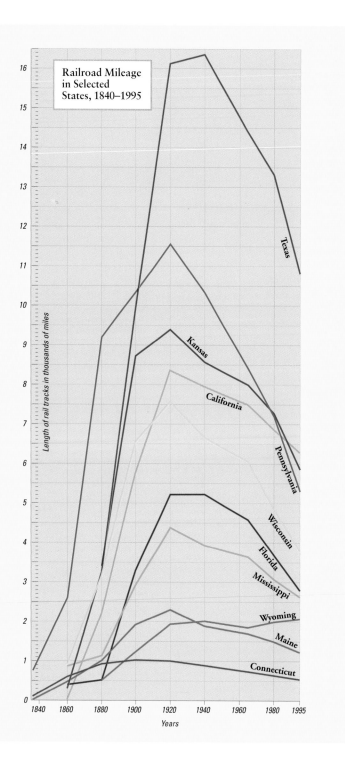

Railroad Mileage in Selected States, 1840–1995

Length of rail tracks in thousands of miles

Years

Texas

Kansas

California

Pennsylvania

Wisconsin

Florida

Mississippi

Wyoming

Maine

Connecticut

bankruptcy in American history. The cataclysm of this failure, and the parlous state of the "anthracite roads" in the same region, created a situation with which the free market economy was unable to cope effectively, so the federal government felt obliged to step in. After long proceedings, Consolidated Rail Corporation (Conrail) was inaugurated on April 1, 1976 to take over the failed and failing lines.

Conrail, a government-owned Class I railroad, was feared by some influential Americans as a fateful step toward dreaded railroad nationalization, a concern already aroused by the establishment in 1971 of Amtrak, the government financed passenger-train operator. Conrail would do well, however, and eventually return to the private sector. Apart from the Penn Central, it incorporated the Erie Lackawanna, Lehigh Valley, Lehigh & Hudson River, Reading, and Central of New Jersey railroads, together with the jointly owned Pennsylvania-Reading Seashore Lines. One of its early moves was to sell the Northeast Corridor lines (Washington–New York–Boston, as well as Philadelphia–Harrisburg) to Amtrak, while retaining trackage rights. It shed the burden of about 6,000 miles (9,656 km) of low-traffic route by selling to short lines or agreeing to operate with subsidy. Its commuter services were steadily sold off to other operators.

Conrail was the largest freight carrier in the East, operating in 12 states plus the District of Columbia, as well as in the Canadian province of Québec. After many trials and tribulations, the new railroad, managed by L. Stanley

Crane, the recently retired president of the Southern Railway, was able to adopt a new approach to railroading. Crane tackled the train-crew problem by avoiding the traditional management posture of confrontation. The unions cooperated, and by adroit negotiation and bargaining, a new labor structure was worked out. Another of Crane's initiatives was to encourage new marketing techniques that focused on the most important commodities: grain, coal, automobiles, intermodal, etc. Trains ran on time more frequently, and operation became more reliable. In a relatively short time, Conrail began running at a profit, and Congress was persuaded to authorize the sale of its stock to the public. Conrail had shown that railroads could be a profitable, successful, and even exciting business.

Elsewhere in the United States, hard-pressed railroads were seeking refuge in mergers. The closure of loss-making lines entailed a protracted and bureaucratic negotiation with the ICC, and, despite the Staggers deregulation, was not always successful. The ICC. also approved or disapproved mergers, another

The railroads branched out into the transportation of newly completed automobiles from manufacturers on specialized double- and sometimes triple-deck railcars called autoracks.

Opposite page: This graph indicates the growth and decline of track mileage in 10 selected states. Notice the steep rise during the second half of the 19th century. In most cases, there was a peak around 1920, after which a steady reduction occurred for the remainder of the 20th century.

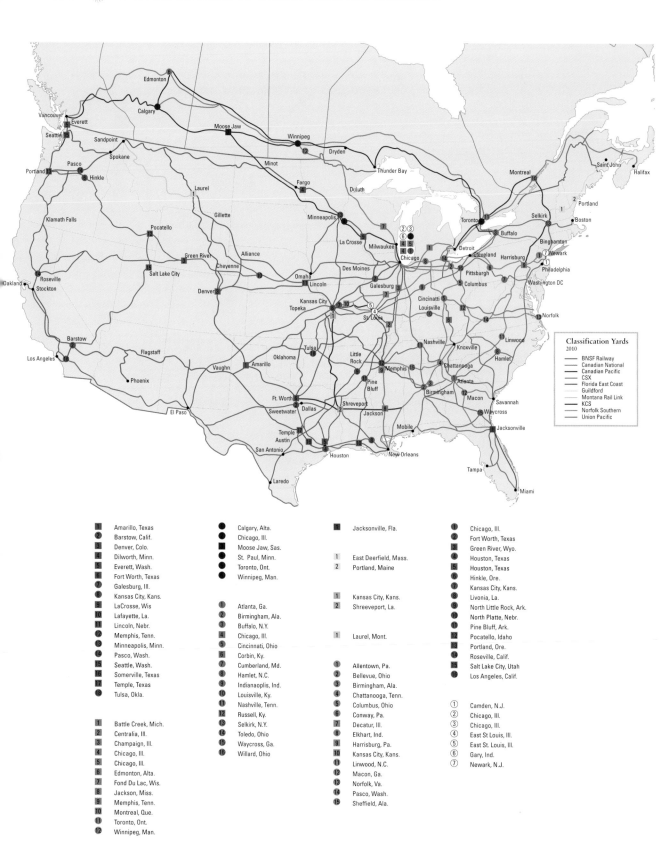

Classification Yards
2010

— BNSF Railway
— Canadian National
— Canadian Pacific
— CSX
— Florida East Coast
— Guildford
— Montana Rail Link
— KCS
— Norfolk Southern
— Union Pacific

■		
1	Amarillo, Texas	
2	Barstow, Calif.	
3	Denver, Colo.	
4	Dilworth, Minn.	
5	Everett, Wash.	
6	Fort Worth, Texas	
7	Galesburg, Ill.	
8	Kansas City, Kans.	
9	LaCrosse, Wis	
10	Lafayette, La.	
11	Lincoln, Nebr.	
12	Memphis, Tenn.	
13	Minneapolis, Minn.	
14	Pasco, Wash.	
15	Seattle, Wash.	
16	Somerville, Texas	
17	Temple, Texas	
18	Tulsa, Okla.	

■		
1	Battle Creek, Mich.	
2	Centralia, Ill.	
3	Champaign, Ill.	
4	Chicago, Ill.	
5	Chicago, Ill.	
6	Edmonton, Alta.	
7	Fond Du Lac, Wis.	
8	Jackson, Miss.	
9	Memphis, Tenn.	
10	Montreal, Que.	
11	Toronto, Ont.	
12	Winnipeg, Man.	

● Calgary, Alta.
● Chicago, Ill.
■ Moose Jaw, Sas.
● St. Paul, Minn.
● Toronto, Ont.
● Winnipeg, Man.

⬤		
1	Atlanta, Ga.	
2	Birmingham, Ala.	
3	Buffalo, N.Y.	
4	Chicago, Ill.	
5	Cincinnati, Ohio	
6	Corbin, Ky.	
7	Cumberland, Md.	
8	Hamlet, N.C.	
9	Indianaoplis, Ind.	
10	Louisville, Ky.	
11	Nashville, Tenn.	
12	Russell, Ky.	
13	Selkirk, N.Y.	
14	Toledo, Ohio	
15	Waycross, Ga.	
16	Willard, Ohio	

■ Jacksonville, Fla.

1	East Deerfield, Mass.
2	Portland, Maine

1	Kansas City, Kans.
2	Shreeveport, La.

1	Laurel, Mont.

⬤		
1	Allentown, Pa.	
2	Bellevue, Ohio	
3	Birmingham, Ala.	
4	Chattanooga, Tenn.	
5	Columbus, Ohio	
6	Conway, Pa.	
7	Decatur, Ill.	
8	Elkhart, Ind.	
9	Harrisburg, Pa.	
10	Kansas City, Kans.	
11	Linwood, N.C.	
12	Macon, Ga.	
13	Norfolk, Va.	
14	Pasco, Wash.	
15	Sheffield, Ala.	

⬤		
1	Chicago, Ill.	
2	Fort Worth, Texas	
3	Green River, Wyo.	
4	Houston, Texas	
5	Houston, Texas	
6	Hinkle, Ore.	
7	Kansas City, Kans.	
8	Livonia, La.	
9	North Little Rock, Ark.	
10	North Platte, Nebr.	
11	Pine Bluff, Ark.	
12	Pocatello, Idaho	
13	Portland, Ore.	
14	Roseville, Calif.	
15	Salt Lake City, Utah	
16	Los Angeles, Calif.	

①	Camden, N.J.
②	Chicago, Ill.
③	Chicago, Ill.
④	East St Louis, Ill.
⑤	East St. Louis, Ill.
⑥	Gary, Ind.
⑦	Newark, N.J.

slow (but careful) process. The fate of the Chicago, Rock Island & Pacific illustrates the complexities. In 1964, the chairman of the Chicago & North Western, Ben Heineman, proposed a merger with the Rock Island (1964 was Rock Island's last year of profitability) and the Milwaukee Road into an Upper Midwest system, selling the lines south of Kansas City to the Santa Fe. The Union Pacific made a counterproposal that would have given it access to Chicago.

The proposal began the longest, most complicated merger so far handled by the ICC. Roads west of Chicago protested;, some petitioned for inclusion, while others asked for a piece of the Rock Island. In 1973, the ICC proposed a restructuring of the railroad systems of the West around the Union Pacific, Southern Pacific, Burlington Northern, and Santa Fe. The railroads involved in the merger, other than the two principals, the Union Pacific and Rock Island, petitioned to dismiss the case and begin again.

In November 1974 the ICC approved the merger, but several conditions were attached. The Union Pacific said that the merger now needed re-evaluation, since the Rock Island of 1974 was not the Rock Island of 10 years before. The Rock Island filed for bankruptcy on March 17, 1975, and on August 4, 1975, the Union Pacific withdrew its offer. The ICC dismissed the case on July 10, 1976, and that was the beginning of the end of the Rock Island, which ceased operation on March 31, 1980. This was the first time the railroad industry had seen an abandonment of such magnitude. (The abandonment of the Milwaukee Railroad's transcontinental line in 1977 was not considered as drastic, because a rump of the Milwaukee survived; nor was the liquidation of the New York, Ontario & Western in 1957 seen as serious, since that railroad had been redundant from the year it was built.) In 1978, the Rock Island had operated more than 7,000 miles (11,000 km) of lines.

The coal-hauling Norfolk & Western Railroad was remarkable for its long adherence to steam traction, and it was not until the late 1950s that it wholeheartedly accepted diesels, thus skipping the first generation of diesel locomotives. This economy of capital expenditure may have been a factor in the Norfolk & Western's solid financial position. It was able to merge with its competitor, the Virginian Railroad, and in 1982 the ICC approved its merger with the Southern Railway, to form the Norfolk Southern, which remains one of the major United States railroads.

In 1967, the ICC approved the merger of two rivals, the Atlantic Coast Railroad and the Seaboard Air Line. The latter, despite its title, was a railroad, competing with Atlantic Coast Railroad for the Florida traffic as well as for freight over much of the South. The merged companies adopted the tautological name of Seaboard Coast Lines. This merger also involved the Louisville & Nashville Railroad, which was controlled by the Atlantic Coast Line. Then, in 1980, the Seaboard Coast Lines merged with the Chessie System to form the second of the big eastern railroads, the CSX.

In the West, the old competitors Great Northern and Northern Pacific amalgamated in 1970, together with the Chicago, Burlington & Quincy, to form the Burlington Northern. The deal also included the Spokane, Portland & Seattle and two lesser lines, the Colorado & Southern Railroad and the Fort Worth & Denver. Ten years later, the Burlington Northern bought the substantial Frisco (St. Louis-San Francisco Railway), gaining penetration into Texas and Alabama. This made the Burlington Northern the dominant western railroad, although it was run a close second by the Union Pacific, which acquired the Missouri Pacific, Western Pacific, and Missouri-Kansas-Texas railroads in the 1980s.

Opposite page: Despite the upsurge of block trains, in the 21st century few long-distance freight trains need classification yards where trains can be re-marshaled and cars exchanged. In this map, yards offering hump switching with car retarders are marked as circles, while those still reliant on flat switching are shown as squares.

By the end of the 1980s, there were just 15 Class I railroads (then defined as those with gross revenues of $50 million or more). These were the Burlington Northern, Union Pacific, Conrail, CSX, Norfolk Southern, Santa Fe, Illinois Central, Southern Pacific, Kansas City Southern, Chicago & North Western, Soo Line, Florida East Coast, Denver and Rio Grande Western, Grand Trunk (the Canadian National's United States lines), and Guilford Industries. The last of these was a type of corporation that was growing in importance, a company that acquired and held small- or medium-sized railroads that might well be physically separated. Another was RailTex, which was founded in 1984 and, within a decade, held and operated a score of lines totaling several thousand miles. Guilford Industries' main acquisitions were the substantial Boston & Maine and Maine Central railroads.

In addition to the Class Is, there were almost 500 Class II and III railroads. These included some big regional corporations as well as a multitude of short lines, mainly occupied in interchanging local traffic with the main-line companies.

Short lines could make low-traffic railroads profitable, largely because they were normally excluded from the pay-and-conditions settlements reached by the unions with the major companies. In this period, those bigger companies were under strong pressure from the brotherhoods, partly because there were too many of the latter, each striving to outdo the other. General railroad strike situations could occur, but could be brought to some kind of conclusion by actual or threatened federal intervention. The issue of retaining firemen on diesel locomotives was a long-fought battle, which took several decades to settle in a rational fashion. The longest strike was that experienced by the Florida East Coast Railroad, which lasted for years. In 1963, the Florida East Coast Railroad had refused to abide by a nationwide agreement on pay increases and the resultant strike included interpersonal violence and stoning of trains, as well as bombs

With cars designed by the Budd Company, the Metroliner was an electric express train service run by the Pennsylvania Railroad, Penn Central, and Amtrak, between Washington, D.C. and New York City from 1968 to 2006. The first-generation, self-powered cars were replaced by similar looking locomotive-powered sets in the early 1980s. The trip between Pennsylvania Station, New York, and Union Station, Washington, D.C. took 3 hours, and the train offered reserved business class and first class seating.

on the track. Non-unionized staff, largely from management, became operating workers. Passenger-train conductors not only checked tickets, but also listed the names of passengers, to help in notifying next-of-kin if anything happened. The strike was not settled until 1973, but by that time the Florida East Coast Railroad had been able to impose all kinds of innovations that the railroad industry obviously needed, and eventually was able to imitate. These included the abolition of the caboose and the running of freight trains over the length of the railroad with just a two-man crew, instead of the three successive five-man crews that national railroad labor agreements had made obligatory (at this time, railroad labor was regarded by the public, quite rightly, as featherbedded).

In 1992, the ICC revised its classification of railroads. Henceforth, Class I railroads were those having income in excess of $250 million per year, Class II had operating revenues of between $20 million and $250 million, and Class III were those with less than $20 million. The only big demotion resulting from this change was that the Florida East Coast Railroad became a Class II, which reflected its regional significance. At that time, there were 15 companies that could be regarded as significant regional railroads.

By the late 1960s, with the general demise of long-distance passenger travel and the loss of the mail contracts, which had provided a steady addition to passenger-train revenue, it was obvious that a radical change in the way railroads dealt with passenger traffic was needed. In its short life, the Penn Central had made some effort to reform services along its Washington–New York–Boston axis. Encouraged by the Department of Transportation, it tried a United States-built turbotrain between Boston and New York, and inaugurated a rapid inter-city service between Washington and New York, using the fast electric trains (Metroliners) that had been ordered by the Pennsylvania Railroad. Running fast trains over poor-quality track, plus managerial torpor (would-be passengers found it near-impossible to obtain timetables), meant that both experiments failed. The Metroliners were put into store, to be resurrected later and operated at slower speeds.

It was clear that to compel railroads to continue passenger services could only result in bankruptcies. In 1970, therefore, the federal government stepped in to form an organization to cater for inter-city passengers. Amtrak was set up by an Act of Congress that year as a government-funded, private corporation to operate inter-city passenger trains. Twenty individual railroads elected to join Amtrak, four of them holding common stock. All preferred stock was held by the United States Department of Transportation.

The railroads were glad to shed their responsibility for passenger services; no longer would they be compelled to cross-subsidize passengers from freight revenue. Out of pride, only the Southern Railway continued to run its own passenger service, but within a few years it had fallen into line. By 2000, Amtrak operated trains over 21,870 miles (35,200 km) of route, and owned 780 miles (1,266 km) of those routes, the Northeast Corridor and Philadelphia–Harrisburg. By virtue of these self-owned routes, it was the only substantial electrified railroad in North America. Amtrak also managed commuter trains under contract in Boston, the Baltimore-Washington area, Connecticut, Virginia, California, and elsewhere for various authorities and state agencies.

By 1983, Amtrak was carrying on its own services (that is, excluding its contract operations) almost 19 million revenue passengers annually, each traveling an average distance of 223 miles (359 km). By the

President Ronald Reagan's budget of 1987 targeted Amtrak, the railroad that carried 21 million passengers a year, including 11.3 million in the Northeast Corridor, proposing to eliminate its Federal subsidy. The budget stated that "as a result, Amtrak would likely enter bankruptcy." Congress had rejected a similar proposal the previous year, but did reduce Federal support of Amtrak by $68 million, to $616 million the next year.

end of the century, passenger numbers exceeded 21 million, with an average trip of 280 miles (450 km), although in the early 1990s, 22 million had been recorded. This fluctuation in passenger traffic reflected the varying fortunes of Amtrak, being subject not only to the trends of economic life, but also to the varying outlooks of successive governments. Overall, Amtrak fared better under Democratic regimes than under Republican, as might be expected from the political philosophies of the two parties. Both Democratic and Republican politicians were eager to cut Amtrak's expenses, however, provided those cuts occurred outside their own constituencies.

In the 1970s, a rolling Northeast Corridor Improvement Project was funded to rebuild the former Pennsylvania Railroad line to its proper standard. Amtrak received financial support for the purchase of new electric locomotives. Then came the new administration of President Ronald Reagan, however, which began a concerted effort to end Amtrak's funding. Amtrak fought back.

Originally, Congress had specified that Amtrak must cover at least 50 percent of its total operating expenses from fares, and Amtrak did reach this goal. In 1983, operating costs were $1,303 million against revenues of $605 million, but in 1987, revenues attained 58 percent of expenses. After that, there were falls and rises and by the end of the century it was recognized that Amtrak could be relied on to maintain at least a 50-percent level. Nothing seemed good enough for the Reagan administration, however, which liked to portray Amtrak as an example of "government waste." Amtrak's president made a vigorous defense of the federal investment in the rail passenger business before Congress, overhauled the management, improved services, and increased the revenue/cost ratio. In the following decades, Amtrak went through other periods when its funding came under fire. In the struggle to maintain its cost/revenue ratio, train services were modified on many occasions and from time to time sizable cities found themselves deprived of a rail passenger service.

"Genesis" locomotives by General Electric were introduced in the 1990s to provide motive power for passenger trains, such as the California Zephyr. The largest customer was Amtrak, which operated more than 200 on its routes. VIA Rail in Canada was also a major customer.

In the 1990s, only Amtrak's New York–Washington service was profitable. The really long-distance services, radiating from Chicago to the West Coast and Gulf, and from New York to Florida, were very popular with the public, but were serious loss-makers. Severe cuts were necessary to meet government pressure in 1995, but this also encouraged the so-called Section 403(b) arrangements, whereby individual states could subsidize their own Amtrak services. This allowed several services to be maintained or even introduced, although sometimes it was difficult to negotiate services covering more than one state. For example, a Portland–Boston service was subsidized by Massachusetts and Maine, but the intermediate state of New Hampshire, which the train also served, made no contribution, which would lead to serious difficulties in 2005.

Amtrak's state partnerships were especially rewarding in the West. The Pacific North West Rail Corridor scheme resulted in the introduction of the popular Cascades service between Vancouver British Columbia, Seattle, Portland, and Eugene, operated by Talgo tilting trains. With popular support, the State of California provided much investment to make possible the services of Amtrak California. The latter ran the San Joaquin Service (Sacramento–Oakland), Capital Corridor (San Jose–Sacramento), and Pacific Surfliner (San Luis Obispo–San Diego).

In the 1990s, Amtrak trains began to include cars for freight service. At a time when line capacity was increasingly scarce, it seemed sensible and profitable to use the Amtrak trains to carry high-value shipments as well as mail. Despite the extra station time needed to pick up and drop vehicles, this idea appeared to work quite well, although it was abandoned when Amtrak came under pressure in the new century. Mail service, which was beginning to make use of "Roadrailer" intermodal vehicles, was also abandoned.

The post-war decline in passenger traffic had put a severe brake on further improvements to passenger cars after the new, all-steel products of Budd and American Car & Foundry manufacture entered service.

The METRA Line was originally built and operated by the Illinois Central Railroad, but was purchased in 1987 by METRA (the Northeast Illinois Regional Commuter Railroad Corporation),to provide a commuter service for Chicago, Illinois, and surrounding suburbs.

Moreover, when Amtrak took over passenger services, there were still many of the older, heavyweight cars around. Car builders either stopped making passenger cars or went out of business. American Car & Foundry left the business for good in 1961. Pullman and Budd held on for a little longer, mainly building for a limited rapid-transit car market. The Pullman Company's sleeping-car operation, controlled by a group of railroads, finally ended in 1968.

Amtrak began by purchasing the cars originally used by the railroads, but it got rid of these as soon as possible, however, and achieved a changeover from steam heating to electric heating powered from the locomotive, the current also provided for lighting and air conditioning in place of under-car batteries. In 1973, federal funds were provided so that Amtrak could buy new cars. These were of stainless steel, arranged as coaches and coach-cafes, and ran on excellent, lightweight trucks of a 1956 design. More new cars were built by Pullman in 1975–76. They were hi-level cars with rather more luxurious fittings, and they filled Amtrak's desperate need for new sleepers and diners.

At the beginning, Amtrak placed a large-scale order for new diesel locomotives from General Motors. These proved to have some defects, which was not a good start, but it soldiered on with these units. In the 1980s, it bought new electric locomotives of General Motors manufacture, but Swedish origin. These were used mainly with the new cars to reintroduce a Metroliner service between Washington and New York. In the 1990s, it received new-generation passenger locomotives from General Motors (F59PH type) and General Electric ("Genesis" type).

In the meantime, gas-turbine trains of both French and United States manufacture were introduced, and used mainly for regional services in New York; they were well liked, but the rise in oil prices in the 1970s made them too costly to operate. Amtrak had imported foreign trains for trials, and one of these, the Spanish Talgo tilting train, gave rise to orders for Amtrak Northwest services around Seattle. On the basis of other trials, the French Alstom company was chosen to provide new, high-speed, tilting trains for the Northeast Corridor. These were assembled in the United States. The service began in December 2000 with a single Boston–Washington round-trip, after which it was steadily extended. Various teething troubles were encountered, and for other reasons, the high speeds for which these trains had been built were not fully exploited. Nevertheless, they were a great step forward and resulted in significant gains in traffic.

In the 1980s, there were signs of improved prospects for the freight railroads, which would encourage a fresh wave of mergers in the 1990s. Partly thanks to new investment, partly to a more efficient deployment of workers, and partly to the sale of underused routes to regional and short railroads, the Class I railroads reduced their labor force from 458,000 in 1980 to just 182,000 in 1996. (In 1917, some 1.4 million people had been employed by railroads, a figure that had been cut by half in 1962.)

In the same 15-year period, the number of freight cars in use was halved, numbers of locomotive units were reduced by almost two-thirds, and track ownership by one-third. At the same time, traffic revenue ton/miles increased by no less than 270 percent. Such a simultaneous reduction of costs and growth of revenue transformed the commercial situation of the big lines.

The merger of the Atchison, Topeka & Santa Fe (to give its full title) with the Burlington Northern was agreed in 1994, and received final approval from the ICC on July 20, 1995. The Santa Fe was one of the original railroads of the Southwest, serving many of the principal cities from Chicago, south to the Gulf

BNSF was formed by the 1995 merger of the Burlington Northern and the Atchison, Topeka & Santa Fe railroads. It was one of the largest networks in North America, second only to Union Pacific and moved more grain than any other US railroad. In this picture the lead locomotive is in the livery of the newly-merged company while the second unit remains in the old Burlington Northern colors.

of Mexico, and west to the Pacific at Los Angeles, Oakland, and San Francisco. It was one of several rail routes to the Pacific that had been completed in the 1880s. The Burlington Northern had more northerly routes from Chicago to the West Coast, so that the combined routes virtually blanketed the western half of the United States. The new railroad was known as the Burlington Northern Santa Fe Corporation (BNSF). It owned 4,400 locomotives and 92,000 freight cars, and had a combined workforce of almost 41,000 operating 31,000 miles (49,888 km) of track. However, the agreement was not reached without a struggle. Many shippers lost the chance of playing one railroad off against another, while other railroads argued that the new combination could give rise to unfair competition. In the final settlement, the Union Pacific was placated by being given trackage rights over a few key sectors of the new combination.

The Union Pacific itself was about to expand. Its chief executive officer together with its proactive board member (and head of its audit committee), Richard Cheney (future United States Vice-President), were introducing severe cost reductions while simultaneously looking for ways to expand. In April 1995, the Union Pacific acquired its one-time partner Chicago & North Western, which gave it access to Chicago over its own tracks. This merger was followed by some severe traffic disruptions because the two lines took a long time to merge on a practical basis, while, thanks to its cuts, the Union Pacific was not ready for extra business. Yet, before properly digesting Chicago & North Western, in August 1995 the Union Pacific announced its intention to buy the Southern Pacific (which earlier had merged with the Denver & Rio Grande Western) in a $3.9-billion cash-stock deal. This merger took place in 1996, and by some measures, it made the Union Pacific the biggest of the United States railroads, but it was not the most popular, however, for it resulted in

The Florida East Coast Railway (FEC) was formed in 1867 by tycoon Henry Morrison Flagler. Today the company only provides freight service, since passenger service was discontinued in 1968 after labor unrest that resulted in violence. Although in the past it has been a Class I railroad, it is now Class II, operating in the state of Florida on lines originally developed by Flagler. The FEC built the first railroad bridges to Key West, which have since been rebuilt into road bridges for vehicle traffic, and known as the Overseas Highway.

crisis. Its already deteriorating safety and reliability performances meant that it was unable to cope with this enlargement. Cheney and his CEO had succeeded in their campaign to capture and control the Southern Pacific, but it appeared that they had given little thought to what would happen afterward.

Severe congestion began to occur, especially in Louisiana and Texas when trains were blocked, sometimes for days, and traffic embargoes imposed. A state of near revolt grew among shippers left without transportation. The Union Pacific proved unable to shift the grain harvest, and grain piled up not only in silos, but also in parking lots and even local stadiums. The cost of all this to the United States economy was reckoned to approach $4 billion and for the Union Pacific, it was reflected in operating losses that approached $1 billion. The only solution was to reverse the disastrous cost-cutting program, invest hurriedly in new locomotives and cars, transfer more power to local managements, construct additional tracks at bottlenecks, and relieve the previously stressed and overworked staff. Even so, the Union Pacific's recovery took several years.

In 1998, the Illinois Central merged into the Canadian National. Subsequently, the latter acquired the Wisconsin Central (and by virtue of a previous Wisconsin Central investment, thereby unenthusiastically obtained ownership of English, Welsh & Scottish, Britain's principal freight company). The Canadian Northern expansion went smoothly and converted the railroad into a major United States carrier. Then the Canadian Northern and Burlington Northern, and Santa Fe negotiated for a merger that would have created something of an American super-railroad, but disillusionment resulting from the Union Pacific/ Southern Pacific chaos, among other things, meant that further mergers came under suspicion, and the Surface Transportation Board would not allow it.

Meanwhile, the Conrail problem was being solved. Beginning as a poor orphan under federal supervision, Conrail had turned its fortunes around and proved strong enough to succeed as a private company. Three railroads, the Norfolk Southern, CSX, and Conrail, competed for the eastern-states traffic, and Conrail was seeking a merger. There was a period of several years of secret negotiations, secret deals, and even secret denials, while in public there was a debate about what to do with Conrail. Both CSX and Norfolk Southern wanted to merge with it because whichever company won the deal would dominate the eastern market. Recommendations that Conrail should join with a western railroad and thereby create what the United States had never had, a coast-to-coast railroad, were hardly noticed. In the end, the realization dawned that neither CSX nor Norfolk Southern could be allowed to swallow Conrail, and the two companies finally agreed to split it in 1997, the takeover being completed in 1999. For several years, there was speculation about which company would swallow up the Kansas City Southern, the smallest of the Class I railroads. But the Kansas City Southern was content to move in its own way, and its acquisition of Mexican lines, together with a traffic agreement with the Canadian National, seemed to assure its independence.

By 2000, therefore, there were five major railroads in the United States, together with the two major Canadian companies, the Canadian National and Canadian Pacific. In that same year, the Union Pacific was the biggest of the United States freight haulers (8.9 million carloads), closely followed by the Burlington Northern Santa Fe (8.2 million carloads). The two competing eastern roads, the CSX and Norfolk Southern, carried, respectively, 7.3 and 6.8 million carloads, while the Kansas City Southern trailed with just 0.93 million.

RENAISSANCE OF THE NORTH AMERICAN RAILROADS

CONTINUAL IMPROVEMENTS MADE TO THE ROLLING STOCK OF UNITED STATES RAILROADS BROUGHT ABOUT NUMEROUS CHANGES IN LOCOMOTIVE AND CAR DESIGN, AND INNOVATIVE MEANS OF PROPULSION WERE EXPLORED. AFTER YEARS OF DIFFICULTY, THE REVIVAL OF THE RAILROADS WAS UNDERWAY.

An intermodal train carrying shipping containers and highway semi-trailers in "piggyback" service, on flatcars, passes through Cajon Pass, between the San Bernardino and San Gabriel Mountains, Southern California, in February 1995.

Although in the earlier part of the 20th century some stretches of main line had been electrified, it proved advantageous to replace electric traction with diesel engines. Diesel-electric locomotives gave railroad operators a great deal of flexibility, plus a haulage capacity that at least equalled that of the ageing electric locomotives, many of which were overdue for replacement. Diesel-electric working over electrified routes meant that locomotives no longer had to be changed at the beginning and end of an electrified section. Before electrification was abandoned, however, sometimes special arrangements had to be made for tunnel ventilation.

In most cases, electrification had been adopted to meet a specific need such as improving the haulage of heavy trains on long, steep grades, or to work long tunnels with smoke problems, and so on. Exceptions were the electrification of the Pennsylvania Railroad in the 1920s and 1930s (from New York City to Washington, and Philadelphia to Harrisburg), and of the New York, New Haven & Hartford Railroad. On these lines, traffic densities were comparable to some of the busiest European routes, and electrification was seen as an investment of faith toward a better service.

In Europe, the usual justification for electrification had been as a response to an increase in traffic intensity rather than as an attempt to increase tractive capacity. In the United States, the capital for electrification could not be recouped easily, so there was little urge for further electrification. One by one, the electrified sections disappeared, with the only significant exception being the Northeast Corridor with its high speeds and relatively high traffic density. The long freight hauls typical of other American roads, although technically suitable for electric haulage, did not usually result in the high traffic intensity that justified the cost of maintaining the electric supply and distribution system. Electrified sections of the Virginian Railroad were switched off in 1962, of the Milwaukee Road in 1972 and 1974, of the Norfolk & Western in 1950, of the Great Northern in 1956, and of the Northern Pacific in 1967.

An early electrification was the Butte, Anaconda & Pacific Railroad. Despite its grand title, it consisted of only 69 miles (110 km) of line connecting copper mines at Butte in Montana with a smelter at Anaconda. Electrified in 1913, the electric operation continued until 1967, by which time all but two of its 30 locomotives were 54 years old. In its last years, its locomotives worked also from Butte to Durant, using trackage rights over the Northern Pacific.

A few other lines remained electrified. Two of these were quite recent additions. The Black Mesa & Lake Powell Railroad in northern Arizona had a single route, 78 miles (125 km) long, opened in the early 1970s for hauling coal. It was electrified on the alternating current, single-phase system at 50 kilovolts, its high tension justified economically because it required only one substation. The Muskingham Electric Railroad of the Central Coal Company in Lancaster, Ohio had a line only 20 miles (32 km) long, which was electrified at 25 kilovolts, 60 Hz. Coal was transported from mine to power station; again, there was only one substation. This operation was semi-automatic as the two electric locomotives were operated by remote control and not normally manned.

Freight cars were improved continuously through the last half of the 20th century, but many still had outdated features. One factor limiting the length or weight of freight trains had been the strength of the drawgear; another was the continued use of lumber in underframe construction. With the major purchases of freight cars in the late 1970s, however, these older cars tended to be used less. In the 1980s, one paradoxical result of the Staggers Act was a reduction in freight car orders from the railroads. Able now to reduce tariffs, they found that with reduced revenue per car-mile, capital investment in cars was less viable. Instead, they turned to leasing, and especially to the leasing company TTX (which was jointly owned by the railroads themselves). By 1987, two-fifths of freight traffic was handled by leased cars, and this percentage would rise still further later. Car orders would grow in the later 1990s, being largely for hoppers and gondolas for the unit coal trains, and flatcars for intermodal service. Orders for specialized covered cars for such commodities as grain, cement, and other bulk freight were also rising. Extra-large hoppers appeared for carrying low-weight materials like plastics. There was an increasing need for tankcars, especially for carrying ethanol. However, a number of messy accidents had prompted a demand for such chemical and other liquid cars to be unlikely to leak in the event of an accident, while chlorine producers were planning to replace their fleets with safer vehicles.

Because of the growing preference for specialized cars, fewer boxcars were ordered. For years, there had been talk of the imminent demise of the traditional boxcar, but it had survived because it could carry so many different kinds of load (and as a result was likely to obtain a return load,

A Pacer Stacktrain is a five-unit intermodal container car, using a specialized type of gondola to hold double-stacked containers. The train is shown here passing through Rochelle Railroad Park, Rochelle, Illinois, in 2005.

something that specialized cars were rarely able to achieve). By the 1990s, however, the boxcar was virtually dependent on a handful of commodities, most notably paper products such as newsprint. Shipments of these were in decline, and it was increasingly difficult for a boxcar to make sufficient revenue runs in the year to pay back its capital cost. By 2006, the annual boxcar order was down to about 2,000 units, and was expected to shrink further, probably to zero, within a few more years.

What became known as intermodal traffic became widespread in the 1950s, initially with the carriage of road semi-trailers on flatcars, although the New York Central favored its own "Flexivan" container-on-flatcar system. The ICC's agreement that railroads carrying their own containers did not need to obtain truck-route certificates eased this process, as did the design of flatcars that could carry two trailers. Intermodal gave the railroads the opportunity of competing with the truckers' door-to-door capacity without the expense and delays of cargo transhipment en route. With the generous clearances of most United States railroads, it was possible to double-stack containers. An innovation of the 1980s pioneered by the Southern Pacific, double-stacking is now the standard method of shipping manufactured goods over long distances, having steadily superseded the carriage of road trailers on flatcars (TOFC, or "piggyback"). The weakness of TOFC, apart from its unsuitability for double-stacking, was that it entailed the haulage of the heavy sets of wheels needed by the semi-trailers for the highway sectors of their run. On the other hand, it did not need terminals equipped with hoists, as did containers. A close relative of "piggyback" was the freight car equipped with a set of tired wheels that could be raised or lowered, enabling it to run over both rail and highway. This was not widely used, although the "RoadRailer" version was successfully exploited by the Norfolk Southern and a handful of other operators.

A familiar vehicle to disappear in the 1980s was the caboose (or waycar), which originally carried the statutory three or four men of the train crew at the rear of the train. The Florida East Coast had shown it could be done, and the other railroads followed suit. The brotherhoods finally accepted that freight trains could run with two- or three-person crews, carried in reasonable comfort on the locomotives. To ensure that the last car of a train really was the last car, an End of Train Device (ETD) was attached to the rear car, usually on the rear coupler. The ETD incorporated a flashing red strobe light, a motion detector, and an air-brake-line monitor. Information on air-brake pressure and motion was transmitted automatically to a receiver in the locomotive cab, helping the engineer to handle trains 1 mile (1.6 km) or more long with greater smoothness and safety than ever before.

An important facility to aid development was the Transportation Test Center near Pueblo, Colorado, which was set up by the Department of Transportation and operated under contract by the Association of American Railroads. Created to develop high-speed, surface-transport vehicles, the center had specialized test facilities. There was a rail dynamics laboratory, a 15-mile (24-km) AC-electrified test track for main-line use, and a 10-mile (16-km) track equipped with third-rail direct current (DC) and light-rail-type catenary for urban applications. In the early 1980s, a great deal of work was done at the center on magnetically-levitated applications.

Released from wartime restrictions, diesel locomotive development was rapid in the last half of the 20th century. The first big freight diesel had developed 5,400 hp in its units and soon, it became possible to have as much as 25,000 hp at the head of a train. Where necessary, as on long, steep grades with heavy trains, another 10,000–15,000 hp could be cut in anywhere from 50 to 100 cars back and operated from the manned unit by remote control. Dynamic braking was introduced, the traction motors being used as generators, which were driven via the wheels from the momentum of the train, producing current to be absorbed in resistances and dissipated as heat. On locomotives equipped with this system, there could be enormous savings of brake-block and tire wear.

From the start, diesel engine manufacturers sought to develop and improve their engines. From 1950, four-stroke engines with individual outputs for traction of 2,000 hp from 16 cylinders were available and by 1960 this had reached 2,400 hp. The 16-cylinder, Electro-Motive Diesel 567 two-stroke engine had reached 2,000 hp by 1959 in its turbocharged form, and 2,500 hp by 1963. Fairbanks-Morse (FM) also had a 2,400 hp, two-stroke, opposed-piston engine.

The Fairbanks- Morse entry and departure from the locomotive industry was subsequently cited as an example of how promising undertakings can fail. In fact FM was much more than a locomotive builder, its main business being in transport machinery, including maritime applications. It was an exponent of the opposed-piston type of diesel engine and supplied these to the navy (some of them found their way to the USSR during World War II, were copied, and used in thousands of Soviet Railways diesel locomotives). Before the war FM had built a few railcars, purchased by a handful of railroads. Progress was then held back by the wartime restriction on diesel locomotive building, which helped some producers like General Motors (GM) but held back others. But in 1944 FM built a switcher and in 1945 introduced a 2,000 hp cab locomotive, whose construction was sub-contracted to General Electric, FM lacking the space for assembly. Then in 1950 FM introduced its C-Liners, cab units in direct competition with GM's Electro Motive Division (EMD) and ALCO (American Locomotive Company). These were quite popular, being built for many railroads including Canadian National and Canadian Pacific (an FM plant soon appeared in Canada). At that time, as the steam locomotive was being phased out, there was a huge demand for diesels, but soon competition became more intense and FM lost out. Allegedly a dispute in its owning family did not help at this juncture. EMD and ALCO probably had superior selling tactics but there was talk of maintenance problems with the Westinghouse-built generators and a somewhat short piston life (possibly linked to the opposed-piston concept). Westinghouse had decided to quit the locomotive side of its business, making impractical further production of the C-Liners. FM's subsequent Train Master road-switcher had moderate success but this was not enough to save the locomotive side of the Company, which closed in 1958 (and a few years later in Canada too).

The caboose, which carried the train crew at the rear of the train, was phased out of service in the 1980s, and from then on the crew traveled in the locomotives. Also largely redundant because of the widespread use of intermodal and specialized cars, the traditional boxcar began to disappear from United States railroads.

Traditionally, switchers had been built as "hood" units, with a single cab at one end, while road passenger and freight locomotives were of the carbody type, whether driving (A-type) or booster (B-type), until about 1949. The majority, whether with four or six axles, had four traction motors.

In the late 1940s, the first example of what were termed general-purpose locomotives was introduced into road service. Based on the traditional switcher format, but with the cab located between a short nose and the main hood, these were dubbed road switchers. First in the field was ALCO, with its famous RS-2 of 1,500 hp and later 1,600 hp. The ALCO RS-2 road-switcher became something of a classic among locomotive enthusiasts in later years. It was introduced in 1946 and was soon in direct competition with GM's EMD, FM and Baldwin; 374 units were built, plus nine built by ALCO's subsidiary the Montréal Locomotive Works (MLW). In 1950s the similar 1,600 hp RS-3 replaced it on the production line and about 1,300 units were built for United States railroads and almost 100 for Canada. During this period FM built over 300 of its competing Train Masters, while Baldwin lagged behind with about 160 of its competing design. However, it was EMD's GP-7 which did best, with over 2,700 units built of that design. Baldwin and FM would soon drop out of the locomotive industry, but would be replaced by a really strong newcomer, General Electric, which had gained experience in this field as supplier of the electric traction equipment used by ALCO.

The hood style of casing suited the visibility requirements of yard and road operation. It also provided easy accessibility to the propulsion-system

components. Given the relatively low speeds of freight trains in the United States, the absence of the streamlined nose and full-width carbody made little difference to aerodynamic drag. The road switcher form became the accepted second-generation standard for freight operation and, with minor changes, remains so to this day.

General Electric entered the road switcher market only in 1959, but when it did, it was with single-engine locomotives of 2,500 hp against the 1,800 hp then available from the designs. ALCO had

The extension of container services to more and more locations has entailed the provision of intermodal yards equipped with specialized equipment for transferring containers between highway and railway.

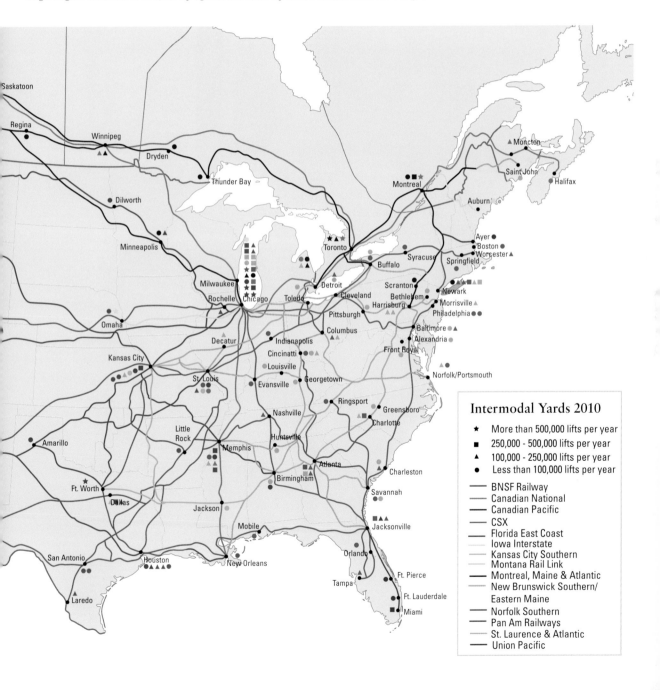

Intermodal Yards 2010

★   More than 500,000 lifts per year
■   250,000 - 500,000 lifts per year
▲   100,000 - 250,000 lifts per year
●   Less than 100,000 lifts per year

─── BNSF Railway
─── Canadian National
─── Canadian Pacific
─── CSX
─── Florida East Coast
─── Iowa Interstate
─── Kansas City Southern
─── Montana Rail Link
─── Montreal, Maine & Atlantic
─── New Brunswick Southern/
      Eastern Maine
─── Norfolk Southern
─── Pan Am Railways
─── St. Laurence & Atlantic
─── Union Pacific

The Union Pacific's first gas turbine-electric locomotive, or GTEL, used a gas turbine to drive an electric generator or alternator. The electric current produced then powered the traction motors. The units exceled when exerting full power to haul heavy loads over long distances, but the system reached its peak between the 1950s and 1960s.

entered the field in 1946 with a design of similar power to that of the Electro-Motive Diesel, using electrical gear supplied by General Electric. The popularity of the road switcher grew rapidly, and the carbody locomotive dropped out of production with the last E9A/B in 1963. Around the same time, certain railroads had become disenchanted with what they regarded as the manufacturers' fixation with electric transmission. In Europe, there were a few examples of locomotives in the 3,500–4,000 hp range with high-speed engines and hydraulic transmissions. Between 1961 and 1963, Krauss-Maffei of Munich, Germany, exported 21 high-power diesel-hydraulic locomotives, each with two 2,000 hp engines and hydraulic transmissions. Three of these went to the Rio Grande, and 17 to the Southern Pacific. However, American conditions uncovered a number of problems with these German locomotives and they were soon retired. There were other attempts by European manufacturers to break into the American market. One of these was by Sulzer Brothers of Winterthur, Switzerland, who sold a few 12- and 16-cylinder engines of 3,000 and 4,000 hp (traction) to three United States railroads through Morrison-Knudsen of Boise, Idaho in 1979–80. These went to the Southern Pacific, Burlington Northern, and Union Pacific and while their operation was reasonably successful, the proposed licensee in the United States did not take up the option.

Another innovation, this time purely American, was the introduction of the gas-turbine locomotive. Gas turbines require less maintenance than diesel engines, and as long as they are exerting full power, they make good use of their fuel; at low power however, their fuel requirement becomes inefficient. In those circumstances, only railroads hauling heavy loads over long distances could find the gas turbine of much use. One such railroad was the Union Pacific, which hauled heavy trains over the long line that climbs up to the Rockies between Cheyenne, Wyoming and Ogden, Utah. After a production batch of 10 gas turbines, the Union Pacific ordered an improved batch of 15 4,500 hp units from General Electric in the early 1950s. On the downhill trip, the turbine was cut out, there being a low-power supplementary diesel engine to provide what little power was needed. These locomotives worked well, but rising oil prices and the small difference between their performance and that of conventional diesel locomotives meant that the concept was not pursued.

One limitation on increased engine power, apart from suitable engines, was the direct-current generator, which had seemed to reach its limit at an input of about 2,800 hp. In the early 1960s, silicon rectifiers had been introduced into railway traction and development was fast, so that by the mid-1960s, devices were small and reliable enough to enable three-phase alternators to be substituted.

This removed the restriction on input power, paving the way for more powerful prime movers and, hence, single-unit locomotives.

In May 1966, General Electric handed over two alternating-current U28Bs to the railroads for trials. Electro-Motive Diesel followed suit with 2,000 hp GP38s and S38s in 1971, offering alternators as an option to DC generators. From January 1972, Electro-Motive Diesel began production of its Dash-2 range, all of which had alternators as well as other high-reliability innovations.

The pattern for the future had emerged with both four- and six-motor designs. Single-engine locomotives of up to 3,600 hp were available by the late 1960s. Theoretically, fewer units per train were needed, but with the increased speeds over better tracks, three, four, and even five units could be found on very long and heavy trains.

Because of their steeply graded lines over the Sierra Nevada and the Rockies, the Union Pacific and Southern Pacific railroads persuaded both Electro-Motive Diesel and General Electric to break with tradition and produce some unique locomotives to their specific requirements. Electro-Motive Diesel DD35s were originally to be B-units to work between pairs of GP35s. They were 5,000 hp locomotives riding on two four-axle trucks, each having two 16-cylinder 567D3A engines. Some 30 were produced in 1963–64 and, in 1965, a further 15 with cabs were delivered to the Union Pacific.

The crowning glory was the DDA40X of 6,600 hp, built from 1969 to 1971. A total of 47 were produced for the Union Pacific, known as "Centennials" in honor of the 100th anniversary of the Golden Spike ceremony of 1869. These, too, were carried on four-axle trucks, and had two 16-cylinder 645 E3A engines and "safety cabs."

The General Electric equivalents were of two designs. Between 1963 and 1965, 26 eight-axle locomotives, classified U50D, were built. They rode on four two-axle trucks, the drawgear being mounted on the truck. Each had two 16-cylinder FDL-16 engines, giving a total of 5,000 hp. They had a General Electric version of the full-width safety cab. A second batch was to a six-axle design and weighed 208½ tons (188 tonnes) each (the heaviest six-axle locomotives in the United States) and, also of 5,000 hp, they had two 12-cylinder FDL-12 engines.

The next change to locomotive outline came with the introduction of the so-called cowl design. Cowl units were produced originally for the Santa Fe Railroad to provide a more acceptable appearance than the typical road switcher for locomotives used on premier passenger trains. It was designed to create an airtight carbody that permitted troubleshooting and even maintenance en route, although in the main, that need had disappeared by then. With freight trains beginning to travel at speeds of up to 80 mph (129 km/h), there was renewed interest in reducing air resistance to improve fuel consumption. At the same time, the design permitted the use of a wider safety or "comfort" cab. Unlike the earlier carbody locomotives, cowl units were built on the road switcher principle, with a separate underframe, with the cowl serving merely to create an airtight carbody. Canada was also receptive to the cowl-style cab which, with the disappearance of the old streamlined cabs of the 1950s, was an alternative way of obtaining the comfort and convenience of a full-width cab, especially valued in a cold climate. In Canada, cowl-style units often had a small notch behind the cab to give better visibility to the rear.

The road switcher provides an ideal locomotive for bi-directional working of a single unit. The cowl configuration does not, and it requires turning at each end of a run when used alone. They became common performers on Amtrak passenger trains, and it was not unusual to see two cowl units facing the same way at the head of a train, which was inconvenient when the terminal was reached and one, or both, had to be turned.

The Comfort Cab had been adopted on a large scale in Canada where climate (and a recent fatal head-on collision) provided the incentive. It was often called the Canadian Comfort Cab but its true alternative name was the Safety Cab, and it had made a modest appearance with a small batch of Union Pacific locomotives. It was wide, and gave enhanced protection to the crew. A later EMD variant became known as the Whisper Cab. In this, the cab was separated from the rest of the body by means of a narrow gap, protecting it from the noise and vibration of the engine.

New developments to ensure high reliability and less maintenance were introduced over the years. As power ratings increased, so did the complexity of electrical controls to obtain optimum performance. To offset this, functions were grouped into discrete modules, and systems were devised to incorporate self-checking features to improve reliability. With the rapid development of electronic devices, constant monitoring of performance became possible, and defects could be spotted before they developed fully.

Until the early 1990s, the direct-current traction motor had dominated the field because it was familiar, highly developed, and reliable. However, it had a snag: it needed substantial maintenance, especially of its commutator and brushes. It was also sensitive to overspeeding and required sophisticated anti-spin protection. Electronics changed all that and it became possible to employ AC motors with ideal characteristics that were virtually maintenance-free.

Interest in AC power heightened in the 1980s. Early in the field in the United States was Electro-Motive Diesel with the F69PH-AC, a joint development with Siemens of Germany. Two locomotives based on the well-known F40PH cowl type were delivered to Amtrak in 1989. The main changes were the engine, which was now a 12-710G3 of 3,000 hp (traction), four asynchronous, three-phase traction motors, microprocessors for the control system, and a potential top speed of 110 mph (177 km/h)

Following the success of these prototypes, Electro-Motive Diesel introduced its S70MAC, which was based on the same control system. Hundreds were delivered, first to the Burlington Northern, and later to other railroads. The AC drive and three-phase, asynchronous motors provided much smoother operation, allowing far better control of wheel-slip under high power, and these locomotives could use 45 percent of theoretical adhesion weight, as opposed to the 25 percent possible with conventional models. Although the latter were about a third cheaper, railroads purchased the newer three-phase models for the sake of their enhanced tractive performance. That enhanced tractive effort at low speeds was accompanied by a horsepower disadvantage at higher speeds, however, which was why the manufacturers began to look at the possibility of building such locomotives in a 6,000 hp version.

By the end of the century, the standard freight locomotive, whether from Electro-Motive Diesel or General Electric, was a hood type with a full-width nose and a safety cab designed with special attention to crew safety and comfort. The wide nose became popular from 1990, and thereafter few new road units were delivered with standard cabs.

This, of course, is not the whole story. Apart from diesel locomotives, the 1970s and 1980s saw the return of fixed-formation, self-propelled vehicles in the shape of gas-turbine trains, known as the turbotrains. They enjoyed some initial success, but the French-designed turbotrains did not meet United States standards of crashworthiness, and a later batch (produced by Rohr Industries) were heavier and less economical. Later, Amtrak began to look again at European technology for high-speed trains, considering French, German, and Swedish designs, with both German and Swedish trains being tried on routes in the Northeast Corridor. In 1993, Amtrak borrowed a Swedish X2000 trainset, running it between Washington, New York City, and Boston. With diesel haulage, it was also taken for a nationwide tour. Later, a German ICE trainset was run over the same route and given the same nationwide treatment. The French TGV and Spanish Talgo were also studied, and one of the latter was operated between Seattle and Vancouver as the Mount Baker International.

It became clear that a single, off-the-shelf train would not suit Amtrak. None of the trains they examined was found to meet all of the performance, aesthetic, and safety criteria. Amtrak was seeking a three-hour New York City–Boston running time, and only a train with tilt technology could meet this, but the well-established Swedish X2000 tilt-train, with radial axles, did not have sufficient power for Amtrak's requirements.

Amtrak's turbotrain Cold Spring exits a tunnel near New York in February 1985. The French-built, self-propelled, turbine-powered trainsets were first introduced to United States railroads in the 1970s.

Moreover, many people demanded an all-American approach, and Amtrak was seeking to establish its own identity with such a project. Its designers were already collaborating with the Henry Dreyfuss design company to produce models of what they would like the high-speed passenger train to be. It was hoped that a contract based on the approved model would be awarded before the end of 1995 to one of three manufacturing consortiums. They would be commissioned to build 24 electric trainsets and two fossil-fueled versions for use elsewhere. In the end, the Talgo concept was accepted for Amtrak Northwest services. The low-slung Talgo cars were hauled by a full-height United States locomotive, the aesthetic mismatch obscured by some fancy screens masquerading as streamlining. These trains proved very successful, both technically and with the public. For the main requirement, high-speed tilting trains for the electrified Northeast Corridor, Alstom's French technology and the Canadian Bombardier company's manufacturing facilities were chosen for the production of 20 high-speed, tilting trainsets. At the same time (late 1990s), 15 locomotives that were similar to the power cars of the new sets were ordered for other services. The new trains were marketed as the Acela service and, despite some teething troubles, proved very successful. Each trainset consisted of a power car at each end, one first-class car, three standard cars, and a bistro car.

Meanwhile, in the 1990s, there was frequent talk of High Speed Rail (HSR) projects for passenger services. Studies were completed in 17 states, and the Clinton administration encouraged planning, provided the necessary funds were also committed by the relevant states. Texas had its own High Speed Rail Authority, established in 1989 under the Texas High Speed Rail Act. In 1992, the Authority awarded the Texas TGV Corporation a franchise to build a 590-mile (949-km) network of high-speed lines linking Dallas, Fort Worth, Houston, Austin, and San Antonio, which would have exploited the technology of the celebrated 186 mph (299 km/h) French TGV. The franchise was cancelled in 1994, however, owing to difficulties in securing the necessary track rights-of-way and the failure to raise sufficient non-government funds.

There were other schemes, too, one of which looked at the possibility of using an unconventional form of land transport. A bi-state governmental commission of California and Nevada examined the feasibility of a high-speed link between Los Angeles and Las Vegas. The proposed system was Maglev (magnetic levitation), which by the 1980s had aroused a great deal of enthusiasm. Maglev was promoted very actively in the 1970s and 1980s as a means of traveling over land at speeds as high as 300 mph (483 km/h). This system employs a guideway (usually of concrete) rather than rails, with

the train floating with a clearance of up to 1 in (2.54 cm) on a magnetic field requiring no power expenditure, with no noise and no need for maintenance. Frictionless forward motion is provided by a linear motor, using the track's permanent field for its excitation. Major experiments in this technology had been carried out for more than a decade in Germany and Japan, using various forms of Maglev, and some very high speeds had been attained. However, there was not yet general acceptance of either the German or Japanese system as a practical or commercially viable, high-speed, high-density people-mover. At the time of writing the only commercial high-speed Maglev line is at Shanghai airport in China.

Concepts such as these, even though their achievement might have been slow in coming, helped to persuade Americans that the railroads were not merely a relic of the past. In any case, without the railroads, the flow of heavy goods and materials would have been exceedingly difficult to achieve. While pipelines could take bulk liquids, and rivers, canals, and coastal shipping could carry other bulk loads, they were slow. The modernized American railroad system was able to move vast quantities of a range of commodities speedily and efficiently. Moreover, it was considerably more fuel efficient than most other modes of transport, and created relatively little pollution. With high traffic densities, far less labor was employed, so that trains had become more responsive to modern needs.

American railroads, it seemed, were beginning to enter a new and extremely interesting era.

In April, 1976, the United States Department of Transportation tested new railroad technologies in western Colorado, with this experimental train. An electromagnetic current pulled the Linear Induction Motor Research Vehicle along an aluminum "reaction rail" set within a standard railroad track. Jet engines helped to reach a speed of 255 mph (410 km/h).

The Cascades train operated by Amtrak in partnership with the states of Washington and Oregon in the Pacific Northwest of the United States and Canada ran through a corridor 156 miles (251 km) from Vancouver, British Columbia, south to Seattle, Washington, continuing 310 miles (499 km) south via Portland, Oregon to Eugene, Oregon. The train was operated in a push-pull configuration with an Electro-Motive Diesel F59PHI locomotive at one end, and a de-motored Electro-Motive Diesel F40PH locomotive called a Non-Powered Control Unit (NPCU) at the other end. The latter were often called "cabbage cars" because they serve as both cab control car and baggage car. The cars, built by the Spanish company Talgo, are designed to passively tilt into curves, allowing the train to pass at higher speeds. Here, Amtrak No. 90253 heads a train at Everett, Washington in 2002.

TROLLEYS AND LIGHT RAIL IN THE 21ST CENTURY

THE DESIRE TO CUT TRAFFIC CONGESTION AND, MORE RECENTLY, TO REDUCE POLLUTION FROM ROAD VEHICLES HAS LED TO THE CONSTRUCTION OF TROLLEY AND LIGHT RAIL SYSTEMS IN MANY UNITED STATES CITIES. RESTORED VINTAGE SYSTEMS, MOREOVER, ARE SEEN AS POSITIVE TOURIST ATTRACTIONS.

The LYNX light rail, rapid transit service in Charlotte, North Carolina, ran state-of-the-art Siemens-built Avanto cars such as this, from 2007.

The surge of interest in light rail that occurred in the United States and Canada in the 1980s produced a number of useful systems, despite the fact that there were setbacks when proposals were vetoed by local authorities or popular votes. The main purpose of light rail transportation (LRT), which was to reduce the excessive use of automobiles, thereby easing congestion and cutting the expense of new highways, had usually achieved. However, by 2000, the accent was broadened somewhat as, increasingly, LRT was seen as a measure against pollution. It was partly because of this that it was regarded as a positive aesthetic factor that could enhance the appeal of those cities that had such systems.

Technical developments began to make their appearance. One was the low-floor vehicle, which not only gave passengers access without a step, but also speeded up loading and unloading, increasing the productivity of vehicles. Traction control based on AC current had a similar impact as on mainline railroads and improved, among other things, the smoothness of the ride. Modular design and the

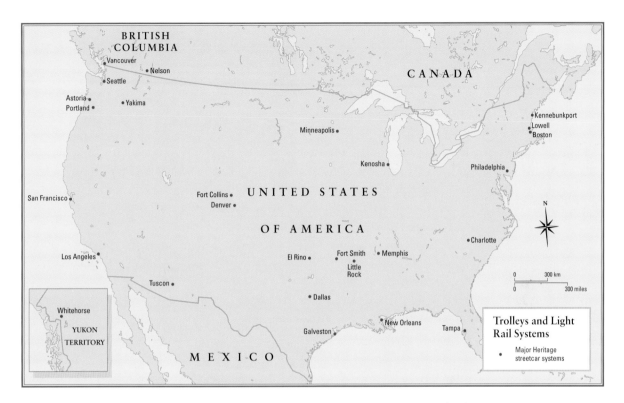

greater use of composite materials simplified maintenance. By 2000, some companies were already experimenting with energy-saving ideas including regenerative braking, where the vehicle's momentum is converted to electricity that is fed back into the system.

Many of these improvements originated in Europe, where manufacturers supplied the American market, either directly or indirectly (assembly was usually required in the United States). The German Siemens company assembled light rail vehicles in Sacramento, California, and in 2006 was supplying Denver, Colorado; Charlotte, North Carolina; and Edmonton and Calgary in Canada. In the 1980s, the Canadian Bombardier company, which had acquired European train builders, had been responsible for a high proportion of the new cars delivered to the United States, and was continuing to supply the market. Japanese companies also participated, when Kinki Sharyo secured orders for, among others, the new systems in Phoenix, Arizona San Jose, California and the Central Link system in Seattle, Washington.

Although some systems used conventional cars, which were clearly developments of the trolleys of previous generations, others were different. For example, when disused railroad lines were made part of the new system, the lines bore some of the characteristics of heavy rail systems. The Los Angeles Sprinter Line, contracts for which were approved in 2004, was one of these and was planned to use two-car diesel formations, rather than the trolley-style concept with its overhead current collection. Siemens, which had supplied conventional LRT vehicles for Los Angeles' other lines, was the supplier, and trains similar to those used by German Railways heavy rail services were chosen.

Several cities in North America have retained their old streetcar systems. Today, however, they tend to act as tourist attractions rather than public transport.

There were still a handful of locations where the old, conventional trolleys could be seen, but these were more in the nature of vintage exhibits with a tourist allure. San Francisco had kept its celebrated cable cars, and had a trolley line using vehicles that were painted in the liveries of defunct United States city trolley lines. New Orleans was equally well known among trolley enthusiasts, since its St. Charles line was served by vintage Perley Thomas cars. Those cars survived the 2005 hurricane and in its aftermath, they also ran on the Canal and Riverfront lines, where the modern cars had been put out of action.

Light rail was considered ideal for routes that carried 3,000–8,000 passengers per hour in each direction and, for most United States cities, it was the peak flow that counted. Below this figure, buses were probably cheaper, while higher traffic might justify a subway or heavy rail line. LRT, where it was not on city streets, could offer commercial speeds of around 12–18 mph (20–30 km/h), with the actual figure depending on the number and duration of stops.

The Hiawatha Line offered a fast, quiet light-rail service to 17 stations between downtown Minneapolis, and Mall of America, Bloomington, Minnesota. Bus routes were timed to connect with trains at Hiawatha Line stations, making it convenient for passengers to get to work, to shopping, or wherever they wanted to go by simply hopping on and off.

In 2004, a dozen cities had new lines under construction that were either completely new systems or additions to existing systems. These were Denver, Colorado; Little Rock, Arkansas; Minneapolis, Minnesota; New Orleans, Louisiana; Phoenix, Arizona; Portland, Oregon; Sacramento San Diego, San Francisco, and San Jose, California; Seattle, Washington; and St. Louis, Missouri. Others were digesting newly built lines or refurbishing older ones.

Funding through the Federal Transit Administration (FTA) helped the construction of new lines. Thus, of the original $1.4 billion estimated cost of the first 20-mile (33-km) line in Phoenix, the FTA granted

The TECO Line Streetcar System in Tampa, Florida was opened in 2002 by the Hillsborough Area Regional Transportation Authority, and managed by Tampa Historic Streetcar, Inc. It was designed to connect downtown to the historic Ybor City district, and as of 2006, comprised 2.3 miles (3.7 km) of single track, several passing sidings, and 12 stations.

almost $6 million. Typically, projects were brought into being by a selected construction company on a design-and-build contract. Once built and accepted, another company would be selected to operate the line. In the case of Phoenix, for example, the five-year operating agreement was won by Alternate Concepts Inc., which already operated the Houston system.

One of the most ambitious light rail developments was in Denver, Colorado, a fast-growing city that was facing severe highway congestion, with each household owning an average of 2.3 automobiles. Successive light rail projects were worked out as parts of an integrated scheme involving other forms of transport, notably buses and heavy rail. There was an exchange of information with private developers as well, so that, for example, housing, retail, and other developments could be coordinated with the opening of new stations. Where possible, such private developments would also include parking spaces for LRT passengers (park-and-ride shuttles based on those stations were also used so that passengers could be drawn from more distant locations). By 2004, the so-called T-Rex (Transportation Expansion Project) lines were coming into service, extending the already existing LRT mileage. The key to the T-Rex plan was the reconstruction of two existing state highways that entered the city, while at the same time building light rail lines parallel with them. This involved some expensive and complex engineering when the junction of the two highways was reconstructed and the LRT route threaded through.

After the T-Rex plan, another called FasTracks had been proposed, which is basically a commuter rail service radiating from Union Station, where LRT already had a terminal and where a bus station would also be built. The FasTracks scheme was approved by Denver voters, but turned down by the state governor and the state's transportation department—a measure, perhaps, of the public support for rail transportation that the LRT lines had generated. Increased sales taxes to finance the new lines seemed to arouse hardly a murmur.

NORTH AMERICAN RAILROADS IN THE 21ST CENTURY

THE EARLY PART OF THE 21ST CENTURY WAS GOOD FOR THE RAILROADS BUT THEN, IN 2008, CAME ECONOMIC RECESSION.

In the first years of the 21st century, the railroads continued to prosper. Wall Street, which until the 1990s had regarded railroad stocks with suspicion, was recommending them as part of a balanced holding. *Fortune* magazine noted that in 2005, the railroads had the second highest growth rate of all industries, behind internet companies. Economic globalization, while it may have reduced traffic originating from some of the traditional United States industries, gave a chance for the railroads to grasp new traffic of the type they most desired—that is, high flows over long distances. In the first five years of the new century, freight ton-miles rose by 18 percent. New technologies, like double-stack container trains and high-capacity autorack cars, were already in place to exploit the new opportunities, and new computerized management procedures speeded processes and reduced costs. Whereas the main concern of the railroads in recent decades had been gaining and keeping enough traffic to preserve them from decline and possible bankruptcy, by the turn of the century, their main anxiety was capacity bottlenecks. Hence there was growing investment in capital projects, including massive programs of double-tracking.

As might be expected, the recession that began in 2008 resulted in reduced freight traffic and hence reduced revenue. This, among other things, meant that some capital projects were slowed down as had, for example, the Union Pacific's double-tracking of the "Sunset Route," which had been a priority to ease congestion. The railroads seemed to recover well, however, and this was partly because competing truckers were also feeling the pinch (there were fewer new or repaired highways, expensive fuel, and new emission regulations). By his acquisition of the Burlington Northern Santa Fe Railroad through his Berkshire corporation, Warren Buffet, the highly respected financier, astonished the public but showed a long-term faith in railroads. By 2010, the tide seemed to be turning. On the Union Pacific, whose best weeks in 2007 had seen 200,000 carloadings, there was a decline to a trough of 133,000 in 2009, but a bounceback to 178,000 by the summer of 2010. Railroads were investing money again, often to upgrade

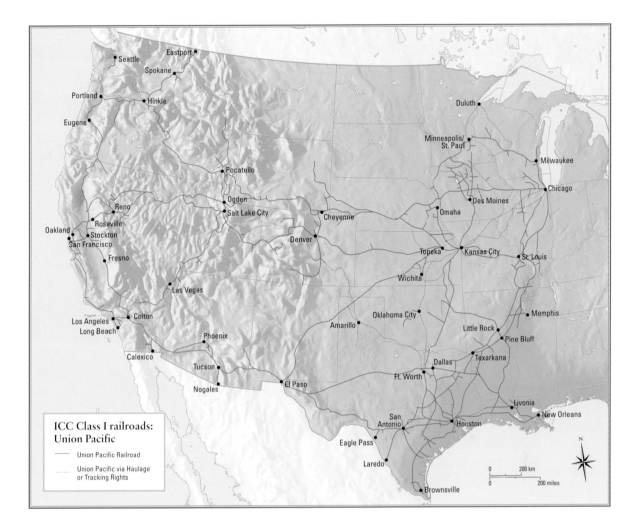

ICC Class I railroads:
Union Pacific

—— Union Pacific Railroad

········ Union Pacific via Haulage
or Tracking Rights

vital routes so as to shorten transits or permit the passage of double-stack container trains, and were taking locomotives out of storage and beginning to order new ones. Interest in low-pollution locomotives continued, and in California the Burlington Northern Santa Fe Railroad was experimenting with a hydrogen fuel-cell switching locomotive.

Over the years, increased demand for railroad transportation strengthened the industry's bargaining position. In the wake of the 1980 Staggers Act, to take advantage of the new freedom to fix rates, the railroads had concluded innumerable long- and medium-term contracts with shippers based on cut-price tariffs. In the new conditions, the railroads had little need to provide such inducements, so there was a steady rise of revenue as new higher tariffs replaced the old. Capacity limitations could mean that a railroad would not take on a new traffic flow unless it brought in as much revenue as the least profitable of the existing traffics. Shippers began to complain about—and even began to suggest a revision of—the Staggers Act, complaining even more when the railroads felt strong enough to imitate the airlines by imposing fuel surcharges.

The historic Union Pacific Railroad operates west and southwest from Chicago. Its network includes the original transcontinental route from Omaha to San Francisco.

The wreckage of two freight trains which collided head-on near Gunter, Texas, in May 2004. The trains collided just outside the small north Texas town, killing an engineer and injuring four other people. An increasing number of accidents on busy railroads prompted new legislation in 2007 to address the issue of rail safety in the 21st century.

For a time, the Surface Transportation Board resisted this, but from about 2000 some railroads were imposing surchages on traffic.

Although the federal government long sought to obscure the threat of global warming, there was growing concern among the states and among the public. The railroads' comparatively small carbon footprint became an additional incentive to favor rail transport. That same public, however, was alarmed by the increasing number of railroad accidents as increased traffic and the railroads' difficulties in hiring long-term staff meant a diminution of highly experienced workers. Derailments of freight trains carrying noxious substances, especially liquids, could cause severe local damage. Following a series of accidents on one eastern railroad, the Federal Railroad Administration in 2007 launched a mass offensive by safety inspectors, who reported over 3,000 safety violations on the railroad concerned over a period of three days. New legislation was discussed to enhance crew rest hours and to impose the latest train control system on all main lines.

The Burlington Northern Santa Fe Railroad was the busiest railroad, shifting over 10 million carloads in 2006. About half of those loads were intermodal, a proportion greater than other railroads (although the Canadian Pacific was reporting over 40 percent intermodal). The next busiest (and probably the most overloaded) was the Union Pacific, with almost 10 million carloads. Next came the CSX Corporation and Norfolk Southern, each with more than 7 million, followed by the two Canadian companies, Canadian National and Canadian Pacific, with the smallest of the Class I railroads, the Kansas City Southern, reporting almost 2 million.

While the rise of intermodal traffic (in which containers had long exceeded trailer-on-flatcar traffic) was the most noticeable trend, there were other changes that, on the whole, worked in the railroads' favor. One of these was the domestic demand for coal from the developing Powder River Basin in Wyoming. This coal was moved over long distances to a variety of destinations, and benefited particularly, but not exclusively, the Burlington Northern Santa Fe Railroad. Capacity problems arose here, not greatly helped by the practice of overloading the coal hoppers, which, after a few years, resulted in an undesirable layer of coal dust over long stretches of main line. In 2006, the construction of a new line in Wyoming by the Dakota, Minnesota & Eastern Railroad to relieve the pressure was under discussion (the Dakota, Minnesota & Eastern Railroad was one of the USA's several regional railroads, and this expansion would elevate it to a Class I railroad). Petroleum products also became a strong source of revenue.

For small and even medium shipments, rail could often outperform pipeline. When ethanol became increasingly fashionable as a petroleum substitute, the railroads were ready to carry it.

The railroads' success in capturing much of the automobile industry's car distribution traffic in the late 20th century led to some disappointment in the early 21st, when car output fell. However, since this drop was due to overseas competition, there was compensation from the increased inflow of Japanese cars. A similar picture was seen in the steel industry, where declining United States output was partly replaced by an import traffic of steel slabs.

Carload traffic, once seen as unprofitable and with a doubtful future, has also rebounded. New IT programs make it easier to incorporate single or short trains into the long-distance block trains that reduce costs and speed services. Short lines and regional railroads, helped by federal tax credits, have responded with capital investment and, in particular, some have strengthened their tracks to take the new bigger freight cars. About a quarter of United States rail shipments are still handled by a short or regional line at some point in their movement. Another way of concentrating the smaller shipments is by the establishment of logistic centers outside main cities. Here small industries, warehouses, and short-distance highway services can be located, with the sponsoring railroad providing a rail link to the main line. Meanwhile, the Norfolk Southern's "RoadRailer" service was also showing the way to hold and gain smaller shipments of high-class merchandise with its services being extended to Canada and elsewhere. The Burlington Northern Santa Fe Railroad also used this handy intermodal vehicle, as did Amtrak until it abandoned its mail service.

The ICC Class I Union Pacific railroad's network covers vast tracts of the United States. Here, locomotives headed by No. 3075 haul a train of Swift Roadrailer units through a tunnel at West Marcel, California in 2000.

Four railroads serve the booming Pacific-coast ports, the Union Pacific and Burlington Northern Santa Fe Railroad in the USA, while the Canadian National and Canadian Pacific handle the Vancouver traffic. However, the eastern railroads also benefit from traffic interchanged from those four. In addition, the CSX holding company also owns Sea Land, a major container shipping line. Despite an imbalance, with empty containers moving back to the ports, the traffic is highly remunerative, in contrast to previous decades when container traffic was only narrowly profitable. The export grain and mineral traffic to the ports is also unbalanced, with empty freight cars moving east, but here again it is still profitable business.

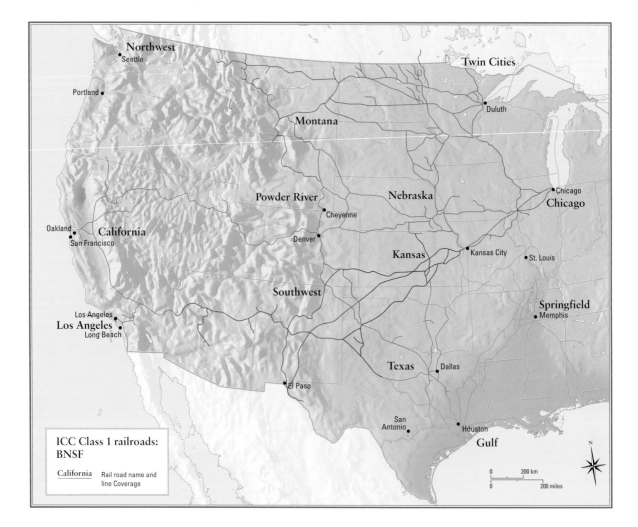

ICC Class 1 railroads:
BNSF

California   Rail road name and
line Coverage

In 2006, the Burlington, Northern & Santa Fe was the busiest of the Class I railroads. Like the Union Pacific, its network covers a large area of the country to the west and southwest of Chicago, with three routes to the Pacific coast.

The twin ports of Los Angeles and Long Beach are the biggest source of international container traffic, followed by Oakland and Tacoma/Seattle. By 2000, there was serious congestion at these ports and considerable investment was needed. Trains to the harbor areas frequently traveled down main streets as well as crossing them at grade. In places this still happens, but at Los Angeles, in particular, the picture has changed. There, trains are handled in the dock areas by Pacific Harbor Line, which exchanges trains with the Union Pacific and Burlington Northern Santa Fe Railroad outside the dock areas. The construction of the grade separated Alameda Corridor has enabled the completed trains to join the main lines without conflicts with highway traffic. The Corridor consists mainly of a concrete cutting and in 2007, it was being extended to Pomona, making a total length of 35 miles (56 km).

To accommodate growing traffic, the Union Pacific began to double-track several hundred miles of its main line between Los Angeles and El Paso. Meanwhile, the Burlington Northern Santa Fe Railroad was

triple-tracking its line over the Cajon Pass, which it shared with the Union Pacific, as well as doubling most of its Chicago–Los Angeles main line.

In 2007, the ever-resourceful Kansas City Southern (KCS) was planning with Mexican partners to build a line across northern Mexico, from the port of Lazaro Cardenas to an interchange with the KCS at Nuevo Laredo, which would end the virtual monopoly of Asian container traffic by the Union Pacific and Burlington Northern Santa Fe Railroad. A longer-term threat to that monopoly was the proposed widening of the Panama Canal to enable container ships to sail directly to United States east-coast ports.

Continued traffic growth implied a need for more tractive power. In 1992, construction of new diesel locomotives had dropped to less than 400, but in the first five years of the new century, deliveries varied from 675 to nearly 1,200. General Motors had sold off its locomotive interest, the new company becoming Electro-Motive Diesel with the same managers and designers in place, but construction moving to London, Ontario. In the ensuing years, it failed to overtake its competitor, General Electric, but remained

A heavy hauling southbound Burlington Northern Santa Fe Railroad stack train rumbles past the station at Emeryville, California, in 2005. Freight traffic on the ICC Class I railroad became increasingly busy at the beginning of the 21st century.

One of the lengthy freight trains of the CSX Corporation railroad, led by locomotive No. 623, hauls a Southbound service through Folkston, Georgia in 2006.

a substantial producer and innovator. The big railroads continued to favor high-power units. The Union Pacific received 1,000 Electro-Motive Diesel SD70M units in 1999, which was the largest order ever placed by a United States railroad. This model and its General Electric competitor were in the 4,400 hp bracket. Electro-Motive Diesel introduced a 6,000 hp design, but this did not find great favor among the railroads. Most were seeking to replace older units on a "two for three" basis, and the existing 4,400 hp locomotives were enough for that.

Contrary to what had once been thought, AC-motored diesels did not supersede conventional DC locomotives. The bigger railroads found it advantageous to buy both, using the AC types on their heavy bulk trains, and the DC variants for lighter, faster services.

Both builders designed new or improved diesel engines, partly to conform to increasingly tight federal emission standards. Really radical innovation in the field of fuel economy and pollution control was achieved by smaller niche companies such as National Railway Equipment in Illinois, and Railpower Technologies. The latter, marketing its units as "Green Goats," was based in Vancouver, British Columbia, but had a production facility at Schenectady, New York, the former home of the old ALCO locomotive company. Some of the designs ("gensets") had three small diesel engines, one or two of which cut out automatically when they were not needed. Others, called "hybrids," had small generator sets that trickle-

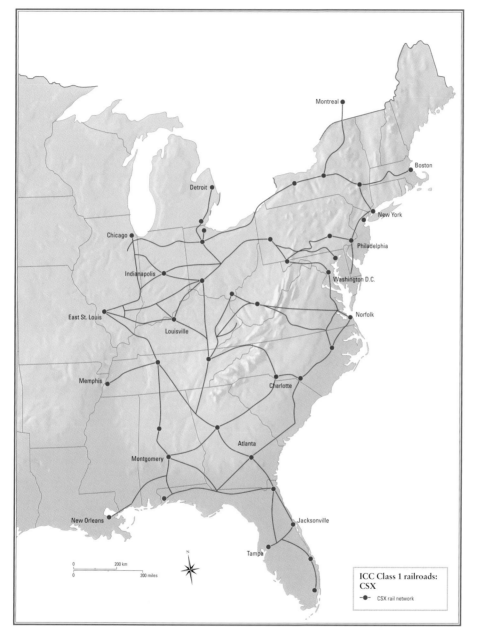

ICC Class 1 railroads:
CSX
- CSX rail network

charged batteries, from which power was drawn as necessary. All these designs achieved substantial fuel savings as well as pollution limitation. Initially, they were offered in the low-power range, mainly for switching or local freights. The Union Pacific ordered a substantial number of them for its lines in Texas and California, where state emission regulations were tightening, and also began experiments with a conventional unit fitted with a catalytic converter.

The CSX Corporation is an eastern railroad, with routes spreading from Boston and Detroit in the North all the way down to New Orleans and Miami in the South. Its network reaches westward from New York, Philadelphia, and Washington, D.C., to Chicago, East St. Louis, and Memphis.

Above: Union Pacific's switching locomotive, No. Y2315, is one of the ultra low emission diesel hybrid, or "genset" types operating out of Mira Loma, California.

The New Mexico Rail Runner Express was a commuter rail system serving metropolitan Albuquerque, New Mexico on a Burlington Northern Santa Fe Railroad. The Rail Runner's locomotives are diesel-electric MP36PH-3Cs built by Motive Power Inc. in Boise, Idaho, capable of running speeds in excess of 100 mph (160.9 km/h).

Another niche producer was Motive Power Industries (MPI), which had formerly specialized in the remanufacture of diesel locomotives. Its passenger diesel locomotive, the MP36, attracted orders in the new century because new federal safety regulations required so many changes to the existing General Electric "Genesis" and Electro-Motive Diesel F59PH that neither company thought further production worth the trouble, given that the passenger market was not large. This provided the opportunity for a small company like MPI to enter the field, and its first order was for Chicago's METRA lines.

The long-distance passenger operator, Amtrak, lacked a clear idea of its future as it faced increasingly onerous budget cuts year by year. It had started the century with the assurance, and possibly belief, that it was moving to a situation in which its revenues would cover operating expenses. Despite cost cutting and useful traffic increases, this began to be seen as unlikely, and its president was replaced. The new incumbent seemed to know his business, which may have been his downfall. He was removed in 2005 by the Amtrak board, which consisted of government appointees. At that time, the federal government was proposing to eliminate federal funding, as part of its policy of breaking up Amtrak, with regional and state governments and maybe private investors taking over specific sectors. Amtrak's president had formulated a different long-term plan, looking to maintain Amtrak's integrity while remedying some of its problems.

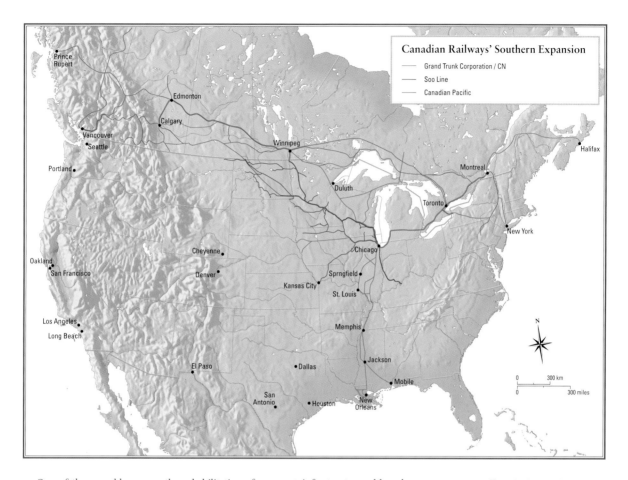

Canadian Railways' Southern Expansion

— Grand Trunk Corporation / CN
— Soo Line
— Canadian Pacific

One of those problems was the rehabilitation of worn-out infrastructure, although some progress had been made, with federal or state assistance. The electrification of the northern part of the New York–Boston line in preparation for the Acela service had been a substantial work. The Pennsylvania government participated in the rehabilitation of the Philadelphia–Harrisburg line with a view to enhanced train service. Another problem was timekeeping as, by this time, nobody outside the Northeast Corridor expected Amtrak to run on time, for despite its incentive payments to the freight railroads over which it ran, the latter seemed unable to give Amtrak trains a clear run. Line congestion was the main cause, but some freight railroads seemed to give Amtrak trains a very low priority. At Chicago, the hub of Amtrak's long-distance operations, trains would arrive many hours late on a regular basis, and hundreds of thousands of dollars were spent on hotel accommodation for passengers who had missed their connections. Amtrak's decision no longer to attach freight cars to its trains for high-value merchandise, an idea that at the time had seemed a good way to increase revenue, had no effect on punctuality.

On the bright side, the services provided in cooperation with the California and Washington State governments were popular, as was the new service of Acela tilting trains for the Northeast Corridor, despite a hiatus in 2005, when the Acela trains had to be withdrawn temporarily for precautionary

Through takeovers, the two major Canadian railroads, Canadian National and Canadian Pacific, have entered the United States railroad scene. Both operate routes to the Pacific coast in Canada. In the United States, the Canadian National's activities are under the Grand Trunk name, while the Canadian Pacific has its own routes and those of the Soo Line.

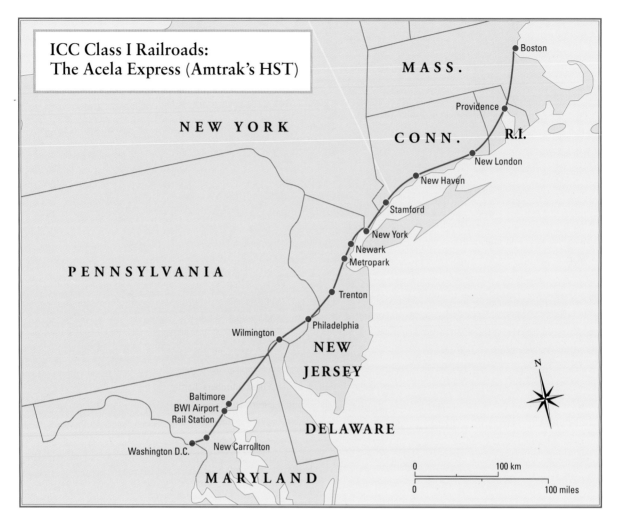

ICC Class I Railroads:
The Acela Express (Amtrak's HST)

Amtrak's Acela Express service relies on electric traction and tilting trains to provide a high-speed service through the Northeast Corridor.

replacements of brake discs. By 2005, Amtrak had won 50 percent of the Washington–New York passenger market. The classic Keynesian remedy for economic recession is capital investment, and this was the rationale of the US administration's decision in 2009 to release federal funds for investment in transportation infrastructure. Wisely, the separate states were handed the initiative in working up projects that would compete for the sums available; this implied that the states would be expected to make a financial contribution. In particular, state subsidies might well be needed to help with future operating costs of the new projects.

The public was beginning to become interested in inter-city passenger trains because airlines were suffering from higher fuel costs, and air passengers did not like higher fares added to the delays of airport security.

As President Obama said in 2010, when he named the 13 rail corridor projects that had been selected, trains are smooth and fast "...and you don't have to take off your shoes."

California, which was already a strong supporter of rail passenger trains, received the most money at this time, which was directed toward a new high-speed line from San Francisco through Los Angeles to San Diego. It also received funds for upgrading some of its conventional services. Florida was next. Here the state government had strongly supported the laying of new high-speed railroads and funds were granted for the first step, an 84-mile (135-km) Orlando to

The Tri-Rail commuter line extended 72 miles (115.9 km) from Miami to Mangonia Park, north of West Palm Beach, Florida. The name referred to the three counties through which the line passed. The line was operated by South Florida Regional Transportation Authority from 1989, using CSX tracks. Passenger cars were distinctive, double-deck units built by Bombardier.

Tampa route, via Disneyland. It was anticipated that initially 16 return trains would cover the trip in about an hour. The Florida scheme, which it was hoped would eventually be extended to Miami, Tallahassee and elsewhere, was expected to become the first new High Speed Train (HST) line to come into service because the state had already found money for its share of the financing. The Florida government's enthusiasm was in contrast to that of Texas, which lost out even though there was a good case for a high-speed connection between Dallas and Houston. Another high-speed project involves the upgrading of the existing Washington–New York–Boston line, currently handled by Acela trains, so as to maintain true High Speed Train (HST) speeds (125 mph/200 kph and faster). Other lines to be upgraded for 90–110 mph (145–177 kph) running were St. Louis–Chicago–Madison in the Midwest and Raleigh-Charlotte in the South.

All this was going to benefit Amtrak even though that corporation had already been improving its act, and the recession had on the whole probably benefited it. Passenger numbers hardly fell when difficult times struck, and in 2009 it actually achieved its second-highest total. It was no longer devoted to cost-cutting, but was extending and improving services, with its Chicago–Milwaukee route a notable beneficiary of this. By 2010 Amtrak was planning the acquisition of new rolling stock, as there had been times in 2009 and 2010 when it simply did not have enough vehicles to carry the traffic that was on offer.

Although the states were free to choose any operator for the new services they were sponsoring, only Amtrak had the right to run trains over the existing freight railroads and non-Amtrak operators would therefore be restricted to entirely new, self-contained lines. However, it could be argued

(and was) that European-style HST services were not suitable for the United States where populations were less concentrated because the ideal territory for HST is where there are big cities about 100–400 miles (160–640 km) apart. Furthermore, the freight railroads were not always keen to carry more Amtrak trains over their tracks.

Amtrak's Acela Express was the United States' only true high-speed tilting train when introduced in December, 2000. Operating at speeds between 75 mph (120 km/h) and 150 mph (241 km/h) on the sharply curved track of the Northeast Corridor, the tilting facility meant that passengers were still assured a comfortable ride.

Primary Canadian Railroads

FREIGHT IS THE ONLY SOURCE OF PROFIT FOR THE MAJOR CANADIAN RAILROADS, AND LOSS-MAKING PASSENGER SERVICES HAVE BEEN TAKEN ON BY A GOVERNMENT-SUBSIDIZED OPERATOR. HOWEVER, INCREASED TRAFFIC WITH THE UNITED STATES AND ABSORPTION OF UNITED STATES LINES PAINT A ROSY FUTURE.

By the 1950s, the Canadian National and Canadian Pacific railroads were well into a program of switching to diesels, although they were a little behind the United States railroads. The Canadian Pacific's Montréal commuter service was long in the hands of immaculate maroon, gray, and gold steam locomotives, however, and it was not until the early 1960s that the two companies were totally equipped with diesels.

Over most of their trunk routes, the Canadian Pacific and Canadian National were in competition, although passenger services were pooled in the Montréal/Ottawa–Toronto service. They united in the 1950s to oppose the construction of the St. Lawrence Seaway, which seemed likely to rob them of their heavy traffic to the Atlantic ports. In this they were unsuccessful, but the Seaway was never the great success its proponents had forecast. Moreover, it had the effect of causing the railways to improve their services, which stood them in good stead in the continuing struggle against highway operators.

The Canadian National was the bigger railroad of the two, although the Canadian Pacific, with its hotels, airline, ocean liners, and hyperactive public relations, was the better known. The Canadian Northern management included men of ideas, but innovation tended to be stifled by its status as a crown corporation. It required government permission for any big changes, and it was subjected to more political pressure than the Canadian Pacific. Moreover, being an example of government participation in business, it was ideologically suspect in many quarters. Although its legislated goal was service rather

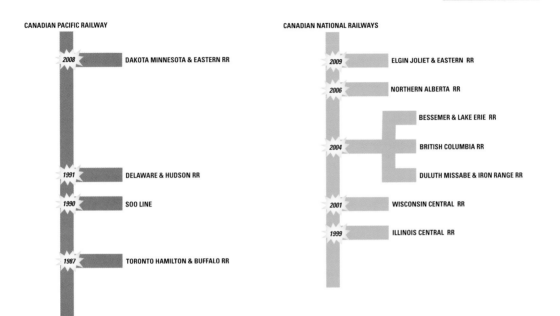

CANADIAN PACIFIC RAILWAY

- 2008 — DAKOTA MINNESOTA & EASTERN RR
- 1991 — DELAWARE & HUDSON RR
- 1990 — SOO LINE
- 1987 — TORONTO HAMILTON & BUFFALO RR

CANADIAN NATIONAL RAILWAYS

- 2009 — ELGIN JOLIET & EASTERN RR
- 2006 — NORTHERN ALBERTA RR
- — BESSEMER & LAKE ERIE RR
- 2004 — BRITISH COLUMBIA RR
- — DULUTH MISSABE & IRON RANGE RR
- 2001 — WISCONSIN CENTRAL RR
- 1999 — ILLINOIS CENTRAL RR

than profit, governments and taxpayers resented deficits. From the 1950s, there were heavy losses of high-value freight as the truckers benefited from highway improvements. Road transport had an undoubted advantage at the collection and delivery ends of a movement, whereas rail transportation was superior over the long haul. Both the Canadian Pacific and Canadian Northern introduced trailer-on-flatcar services to meet this competition while containers, made their appearance later on.

After secret negotiations in the 1950s, the Canadian Pacific succeeded in purchasing Smith Transport, Canada's biggest highway operator. This gave it an enormous competitive advantage. The Canadian Northern quietly began to woo another big trucking outfit, but despite a very persuasive letter to the minister in charge of transportation, the government refused to allow this purchase to proceed.

Nonetheless, from time to time, the Canadian Northern did innovate. In the 1930s, it had been a pioneer in diesel traction and, for better or worse, it had introduced streamlined steam locomotives to Canada. In the 1960s, it pioneered differential pricing with its "Red, White, and Blue" scheme. In this, the days of the year were subdivided by color, the red days being those of high passenger traffic, and the other colors signifying lower levels so that passenger tickets were priced high on the red days and lower on the others. The scheme worked insofar as it smoothed the peaks to the railroad's and passengers' benefit, but it did not end the losses incurred by passenger services. Both railroads, and the Canadian Northern in particular, were obliged to provide loss-making passenger services. The introduction of Budd diesel railcars on the shorter runs reduced losses, but only marginally. The highly publicized Canadian

Both the big Canadian railways have recently expanded by mergers, especially with US railroads. The Canadian National now extends from Hudson's Bay down to the Gulf of Mexico.

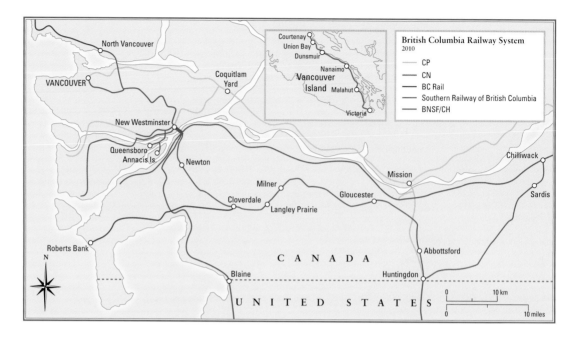

The Vancouver region has developed fast, aided by a quite dense and variegated railroad network.

Pacific and Canadian Northern Super Continental transcontinental services to Vancouver were trains of prestige rather than profit. Only the Montréal–Toronto service and its connections seemed to promise a profit. Cross-subsidizing passenger losses from freight revenues hampered the railways in their struggle to compete with highway operators.

In 1977, the two railroads were relieved of their passenger problems when the government established VIA Rail, a crown corporation entrusted with all the passenger services (except commuter) formerly operated by the railroad companies. It had close parallels with Amtrak in the United States, but had fewer rights in relation to the passage of its trains over the railroad companies' routes and, moreover, was more subject to political pressures (its future was always subject to a government order-in-council, rather than an Act of Parliament). Hence, in most years, its management was preoccupied with resisting, or coping with, reductions in the government's financial support. As a result, by 2010 it was operating considerably fewer trains than it did at the start.

VIA Rail took over the revolutionary Bombardier-built LRC (Light, Rapid, Comfortable) trains that had been on order. These were fast tilting trains intended primarily for the important Montréal–Toronto service. Unfortunately, they proved defective in many ways and spent much of their earlier years in the workshops. This was not a good start for VIA Rail, but on the whole, it did settle down and achieve what was intended—continuance of Canadian railway passenger service where it was socially crucial or otherwise desirable. By 2002, its revenues were almost two-thirds of costs, which in the circumstances was a good performance. Four-fifths of the passengers were accounted for by the Montréal–Toronto trunk route with its extensions to Québec City and London, Ontario. The Toronto–Vancouver service was thrice weekly and tourist oriented. There were still classic long-distance trains from Montréal to the Maritime Provinces, and a large number of services in remote northern regions, often on a once-weekly basis.

In 2000, VIA Rail took the opportunity to purchase 139 European passenger cars built for overnight services through the Channel Tunnel that were never instituted. These were restyled as "Renaissance" cars, but their refurbishment for Canadian conditions, including the Canadian winter, proved expensive, and their integration was further held back when a court ruling obtained by a pressure group obliged VIA Rail to vastly increase its provision of handicapped-accessible accommodation on the new trains. Elsewhere, the longstanding passenger service provided to James Bay by the Ontario Northland Railway continues, as does the Vancouver–Prince George service formerly provided by the Pacific Great Eastern, later British Columbia Rail. In southern Ontario, the GO (Government of Ontario) commuter service, founded in 1967, using bi-level cars and operating in cooperation with the Canadian Northern and Canadian Pacific, has been successful and has set an example for other North American cities. Montréal's Metropolitan Transport Agency took over and considerably renovated the electric and diesel commuter services provided by the Canadian Northern and Canadian Pacific. In Vancouver, BC Transit has been established to provide commuter services.

In 1995, the government decided to privatize the Canadian National, with the proviso that no investor could purchase more than 15 percent. About two-thirds of the purchasers were United States institutions, and this accelerated the Canadian Northern's trend toward becoming a North American, rather than simply a Canadian, corporation. Earlier, the Canadian Northern had consolidated its United States assets, with the Grand Trunk Western (Chicago to Detroit and Cincinnati) and the Duluth, Winnipeg & Pacific being fully integrated. Later, the Central Vermont (Montréal–St. Albans) and Grand Trunk (Montréal–Portland) routes were sold to United States companies.

There was an increasing opportunity for United States–Canada traffic development. The Canadian Pacific had acquired the Delaware and Hudson Railroad and part of the Soo Line, integrating them into its own operations, as well as taking full ownership of the Toronto, Hamilton & Buffalo. In 2008, it acquired the Dakota, Minnesota & Eastern, a Class II railroad with potential opportunities in the Powder River coal area. Initially, the Canadian Northern responded by rebuilding its St. Clair Tunnel between Sarnia and Huron so that it could accept double-stack container trains and the high autorack cars. Its next move was the purchase of the Illinois Central, a Class I railway extending from Chicago down to the Gulf of Mexico, with connections to the promising Mexican economy. Then it took over the Wisconsin Central (WC), giving improved connections between central Canada and the United States (previously, the WC had acquired the Algoma Central in Ontario, whose passenger service Canadian Northern continued to operate).

In 2003, the Canadian Northern acquired two more United States lines, the Bessemer & Lake Erie, and the Duluth, Missabe & Iron Range. These railroads had been built for iron-ore traffic in the Great Lakes region, but offered the Canadian Northern improved connections into the United States. The same year, the Canadian Northern bought BC Rail's shares from the British Columbia government. These acquisitions transformed the Canadian Northern, and they were incorporated with little difficulty. The Canadian Northern also acquired the remaining lines of the former Northern Alberta Railway, but up to 2010 had not acquired the Ontario Northland from the Ontario government. Negotiations to merge with the Burlington Northern Santa Fe (BNSF), which would have created by far the biggest North American railroad company, proceeded smoothly, but eventually the United States Government refused consent.

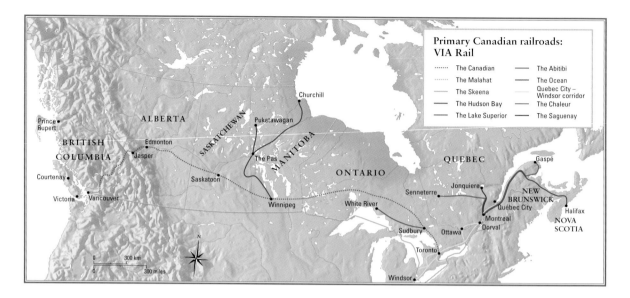

Like Amtrak in the United States, VIA Rail was set up to relieve the Canadian railroads of the burden of operating loss-making passenger services. It runs a number of named trains between major cities.

In 2009 the Canadian Northern succeeded in purchasing the Elgin, Joliet & Eastern, a key link in the Chicago region.

The Canadian Northern continued to be an innovatory railroad, and some of its initiatives were studied by other railroads worldwide. It decided to monitor the progress not only of freight cars or trains, but also shipments. This was an enormous boon for its clients, and led to a move toward instituting fixed and regular schedules for freight operations, that is, to organize all freight strictly to regular timetables, just as once passenger traffic had been regulated. Even support operations like car inspection were timetabled. The Canadian Northern had already lengthened traction sections, obtaining more productivity from locomotives and their crews, and this timetabling regime resulted in further substantial economies as well as more attractive services. In 2006, the Canadian Northern's operating ratio (cost as percentage of revenue) was only 61 percent, considerably better than that of the other big North American railroads.

Apart from services into the United States and to the Atlantic ports, freight in eastern Canada promised little further development, whereas in the West, it was expanding rapidly. Grain and mineral traffic, much of it for export via Vancouver, was very profitable, as were the container trains originating in Vancouver. Both railroads divested themselves of many of their lines in the East. Some of these were sold to private companies and became new railroads, but there was a Canadian innovation in the form of "internal short lines." These were operated in accordance with relaxed operating and labor conditions, just like short-line railroads, but continued to be owned by the Canadian Northern or Canadian Pacific, although with a degree of independence. Meanwhile, the Canadian Pacific emphasized its reorientation by shifting its headquarters from Montréal to Calgary, and hiving off its eastern lines into its St. Lawrence & Hudson Railway, which later became part of the Canadian Pacific's Delaware & Hudson division.

There was increasing cooperation between the Canadian Pacific and Canadian Northern and in the mid-1990s, the former was hoping to sell its eastern lines to Canadian Northern, but the latter's privatization blocked this. There are many locations where the Canadian Pacific and Canadian Northern

Amidst a backdrop of stunning natural beauty, a Canadian National Railway freight train runs along the Athabasca River in Alberta's Jasper National Park.

have parallel, single-track main lines, as in the Fraser Valley of British Columbia, and economies are gained by sending eastbound trains of both companies over one track, and westbound over the other.

Primary Mexican Railroads

Increased trade with the United States and Canada, the privatization of the state railroad, and substantial foreign capital investment put Mexican railroads on a firm footing at the beginning of the 21st century.

For most of the second half of the 20th century, Mexico's dominant railroad was the Mexican National Railways (Ferrocarriles Nacionales de Mexico, or N de M). This had its antecedents in a network of United States-style lines of 3-ft (914-mm) gauge laid in the 19th century that later, with one local exception, was converted to standard gauge. It was the only railroad that could be said to cover virtually the whole country. Like other Mexican lines, it adhered to the Association of American Railroads technical standards, so there was through running of rolling stock into the United States and Canada without the need for transhipment.

N de M was heavily subsidized by the government so that low-traffic lines were kept in operation, fares and tariffs were low, and labor productivity was abysmal. This last factor owed much to the lack of capital investment and, as a result, the steam locomotive survived longer in Mexico than in the United States. Although General Motors and American Locomotive Company (ALCO) diesels were taking over in the 1960s, it was still possible to see postwar ALCO "Northern"-type steam locomotives hauling freight from Mexico City. While N de M was a clear failure as a business, as a service to the Mexican people, it had its merits. Thanks to its low fares, local passenger trains were heavily used by poorer people, and low tariffs helped farmers and small businesses. Dismissing superfluous workers would only have created further unemployment, with its social and psychological consequences.

Of the other railroads, the Sud Pacifico had a long line up into the northwest, where it linked with its virtual owner, the United States Southern Pacific Railroads, which sold it to Mexico in 1951, after which it was known as the Ferrocarril del Pacifico. Another line in northern Mexico was the Chihuahua Pacifico, which also had links with United States railroads and came into Mexican ownership by stages. A private railroad that competed directly with N de M was the Mexicano, whose heavily-graded main line from

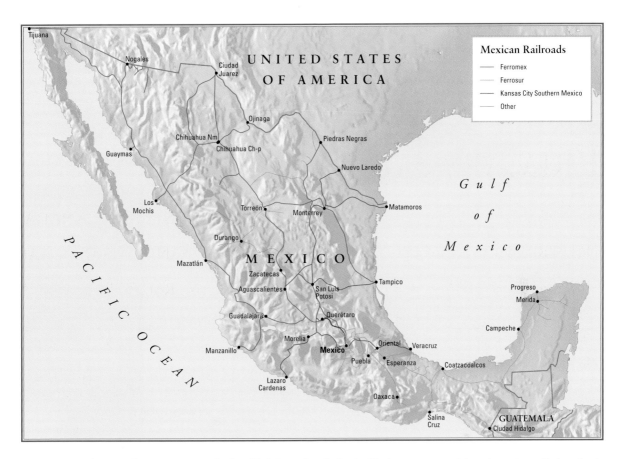

Mexico City to the port of Veracruz was partly electrified. It was bought by the Mexican government in 1946 and within a decade had been integrated into N de M. Its electrification has been abandoned.

In the South, the Yucatan was long isolated from other railroads until the Sureste line was built to the Yucatan capital of Merida. From Merida, the Ferrocarril Unidos de Yucatan operated a number of lines of 3-ft (914-mm) gauge that radiated into the region. In the Yucatan in the 1960s, it was possible to see not only the last operating examples of the traditional American 4-4-0 locomotive, but also the even more ancient crossbar signals.

In the last decades of its life, N de M undertook a degree of modernization. A new line was built from Mexico City to Queretaro and was electrified at 25 kilovolts AC. Locomotives for this line were bought from General Electric in 1982, then stored to await completion of the line. There was a plan to electrify all the core routes, but beyond this initial line, little was achieved and the new private owner of the Queretaro line has not made use of the electrification. The Union Pacific Railroad's Transportation Control System was adopted for the computerized monitoring of N de M operations, but its application was held back by the sudden devaluation of the peso in the mid-1990s. Meanwhile, the signing of the North American Free Trade Agreement in 1992 resulted in increased trade with the United States and Canada, boosting the introduction of regular cross-frontier intermodal freight services.

In recent years, Mexican railroads have benefited from foreign investment, most notably by United States companies. The routes of the main operators are shown here. The largest, Ferromex, has cross-border connections with the BNSF and Union Pacific.

The Al Pacifico train ran from the city of Chihuahua through Copper Canyon to Los Mochis, Mexico. Here it pulls up at the station in the small village of Creel, in about 1990.

In 1995, partly because of new thinking occasioned by the fall of the peso, it was decided to privatize the state railroad. One hoped-for result was the injection of much needed foreign capital into the system. The Mexican government retained ownership of track and structures, and private operators were offered 50-year concessions. The government continued to be responsible for pensions and also for the expected redundancy payments. The accumulated debts were also taken over by the government.

By the end of 1999, N de M (by then, known as FNM) had ceased to be a train operator, the last of its divisions having been sold off. In the late 1990s, almost all passenger services had been discontinued, reducing losses and thereby making the railroads more attractive to purchasers. The new owners did run some socially important passenger trains, but received subsidies for doing so.

The network was divided territorially. United States railroads were keen to buy into the properties, but needed to join with local buyers because foreign investors were not permitted to purchase a controlling interest at that time. Thus the largest of the new companies, Ferromex, with its 5,280 miles (8,500 km) of route, is three-quarters owned by Mexican interests with the Union Pacific Railroad holding 26 percent. Ferromex links Mexico City with the North, and has cross-frontier connections with the Union Pacific and Burlington Northern Santa Fe Railroad railroads. Its main business is long-distance freight, but it operates some state subsidized passenger services as well as a few tourist trains, of which the best known is the "Chepe" over a spectacular section of the old Chihuahua Pacifico line.

The second of the big companies, Transportación Ferroviaria Mexicana (TFM), extends for 2,640 miles (4,250 km) and serves the Northeast, connecting with United States lines at Brownsville and Laredo. Originally, the Kansas City Southern Railroad had a 46 percent interest, but later it contrived to acquire a further 51 percent, making it the virtual owner. The modernization and upgrading of the 785-mile (1,263-km) main line from Mexico City to Nuevo Laredo has been a priority, and by 2005, TFM was claiming to possess the youngest locomotive stock of any North American railroad.

Other regional lines include Ferrosur, which took over the lines of the former Sureste. It connects Mexico City with Veracruz and Puebla, but otherwise lacks solid traffic sources. Ferrosur attempted to merge

with Ferromex in 2002, but the government withheld approval. Another United States company that succeeded in acquiring a controlling interest (in this case total control) is the Genessee & Wyoming, which now operates the Yucatan railroad as FCCM. It provides a link with the rest of Mexico and also continues to operate some of the light-traffic lines from Merida. With subsidies, it maintains passenger services on some lines. The railroad network of Mexico City, including its major marshalling yard, is operated by a terminal railway (TFVM), in which Ferromex, Ferrosur, TFM, and the government each have a one quarter-share. In 2008, Mexico's first commuter service was opened at Mexico City. Minor companies include the Coahuila-Durango and the Istmo de Tehuantepec, which operate small lines that, for local reasons, do not form part of the bigger systems.

Amidst the hustle and bustle, two trains wait at the rural Divisadero Station in Copper Canyon, Mexico.

BRIGHT PROSPECTS FOR LIGHT RAIL

DESPITE THE RECENT RECESSION, LIGHT RAIL HAS CONTINUED ITS LEAP FORWARD.

At the start of the 20th century the trolley was already making, as it were, a second coming, in the form of light rail transport (LRT). In the 1950s and after, the ascendancy of the automobile had resulted in the disappearance of streetcars from most (though not all) cities. But before the end of the century this was increasingly seen as a mistake and some cities were already laying, or relaying, tracks for trolleys. The vehicles running over those tracks were modern versions of streetcars, often designed to run as trains of two or more units.

Some ambitious plans were delayed or scaled down when recession struck in 2008, but this setback was not as dire as anticipated. In 2009, at the depth of the recession, for example, in Texas, the Houston Metropolitan Transport Board decided to go ahead and extend the existing system; Dallas started a Blue Line extension to be added to its existing DART system; Portland, Oregon ordered new streetcars; Cincinnati, Ohio, invited proposals for a city trolley line; Maryland opted for light rail for its projected Carollton-Bethesda line and continued project work on its LRT Red Line in Baltimore; and San Diego, California, ordered nearly 60 new LRT vehicles. That same year the long-debated LRT scheme around Seattle, Washington opened for business. Construction had started in 2000, but had been delayed because of cost overruns. Running through Seattle, this initial line went to Tacoma-Seattle Airport 15 miles (25 km) distant.

There were other projects in progress, and the Federal Recovery and Reinvestment Act offered help to ongoing projects at Denver, Colorado; Portland, Oregon; Dallas, Texas; Salt Lake City, Utah; Seattle,Washington; and Phoenix, Arizona. Phoenix already had a recently opened length of light rail and, like several other cities, soon realized that it was doing so well that extensions were called for. Plans were drawn up, and surveys were made of the public's reaction to the initial services. The Phoenix system was particularly interesting, because it had a low population density and light rail was said to be suitable only for high-density populations. In the event, ridership exceeded expectations as soon as it

One of the Vancouver Sky Trains at work, running over one of the lengthy elevated sections.

opened. Connecting the area downtown to sports arenas, two universities and the airport, among other places, seemed to show that, provided a line served destinations where people wanted to go to and not necessarily where they lived, traffic would be forthcoming.

Interestingly, the presence of two universities probably explained why many passengers reached their departure station on skates; almost half the passengers came to the train under their own power, the others using a bus or the park-and-ride lots that had been built to serve the stations. Two-thirds of the passengers possessed an automobile that could have been used instead. Air pollution was measurably down, and downtown shops saw a 13 percent increase in business that was balanced, however, by a decline for non-downtown establishments.

The line had been financed, like so many others, by a small increase in sales tax, which voters had approved in 2000. With 50 low-floor Japanese-built cars coupled in pairs, a high-density schedule operates throughout the day and well into the evening. There are no special peak-hour schedules; indeed, with so many people traveling for non-work purposes, this would be inappropriate.

Another distinctive light rail line opened in 2009 was the Canada Line of the Vancouver LRT system, whose construction had been pushed forward so as to be ready for the Winter Olympics of 2010. It linked the airport with existing sections of Vancouver's Sky Train system, although its rolling stock was not interchangeable with those earlier lines. The system had been named Sky Train because most of it was an elevated line (the rest was underground) and it was thought that the considerable extra expense was worth it, for aesthetic reasons. A more cynical view, however, was that by keeping the tracks away from street level, opposition from automobile owners was avoided. Certainly, cost-cutting was not a high priority, and stations and structures had a marked individuality of architecture. The first line was opened in 1985 to cope with severe highway congestion. It, and a second line, are operated by a private company appointed by Trans Link, the local authority transport authority, whereas the Canada Line has a different operator, Protrans BC. This latter line is also interesting in that it was built as a public/ private partnership, with a Canadian engineering company having equal financial partnership with two Canadian pension funds (the British Columbia and Québec funds). Trains run as two-, four-, or six-units and are automatic, not requiring a driver. For emergencies, station staff members have been trained in the manual operation of these vehicles.

Elsewhere in Canada, development continues. In 2009, the Calgary system received funds from the federal and provincial governments and from the city authorities to enable it to carry out improvements that experience had shown to be desirable. One was reinforced signaling arrangements, which give the trains more robust priority over automobiles at intersections, and another was an electronic fare collection system. Other cities were also interested in automatic fares, and/or the provision of platform

One of the present-day Toronto streetcars. With about 250 streetcars in service, and others on order in 2010, the future of these lines seemed secure.

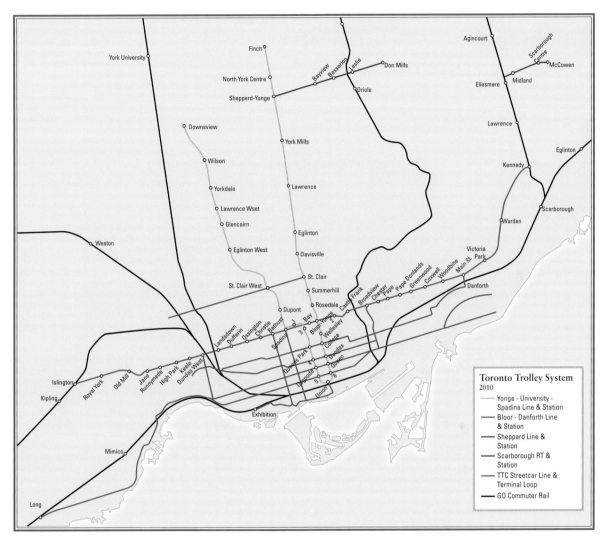

Toronto Trolley System
2010

— Yonge - University - Spadina Line & Station
— Bloor - Danforth Line & Station
— Sheppard Line & Station
— Scarborough RT & Station
— TTC Streetcar Line & Terminal Loop
— GO Commuter Rail

gates, as measures to combat fare evasion, which is reckoned to cost these systems about five percent of their revenues. At Edmonton, extensions were in progress. The long-standing Toronto tramway system was to receive more than 200 new streetcars, made by Bombardier, while at Montréal, which abandoned its last streetcars in 1959, a plan to build a new streetcar line downtown received the approval of the mayor. It had taken Montréalers a half-century to accept that the abolition of trolleys might have been a mistake.

Toronto's trolley system. There is a close integration between the GO (Government of Ontario) conventional rail system and the trolleys.

INDEX

Figures shown in **bold** type signify maps.
Figures in *italics* refer to photographs or
illustrations.

ACKNOWLEDGMENTS

Jeremy Atherton: 352

California State Railroad Museum, Sacramento: 213

Canadian Railway Musuem: 48

Corbis: 8 (George H.H. Huey); 11 (David Muench); 25, 53, 111, 147, 153, 240, 289 (Bettmann); 43 (P.F. Goist); 122-123 (Dave G. Houser); 91; 109; 115 and main cover image (Wolfgang Kaehler); 116–117 (Scott T. Smith); 188 (map source)(Minnesota Historical Society); 217 (Walter Bibikow/JAI); 251; 275, 277 (Underwood & Underwood); 286 (The Mariners' Museum); 329, 350 (Vince Streano); 335 and cover (middle box) (P. Magielsen/zefa); 356-357 (Jim Sugar); 366 (Randy Eli Grothe/Dallas Morning News); 381 (Ursula Gahwiler/Robert Harding World Imagery); 384 (Buddy Mays); 384–385 (Bob Krist); 362 (Layne Kennedy)

Dan Crow: 120 bottom

Edwards Railcar Company: 273 bottom

Robert A. Estremo: 308

Getty Images: 77, 96, 163, 165, 209, 219, 260

GW Travel Limited: 284-285

Mike Halterman: 362

Alan Harris: 234

Harvey Henkelman: 298 top, 301 center

iStockphoto: 45 top (Randy Mayes); 60 bottom (Robert Young);175 (Norman Reid); 189 (Rafael Ramirez); 201 (Vera Bogaerts); 222 (Matthew Mills)

Evan Jennings: 261 right, 273 top

Bob Krone: 299

Sean Lamb: 4, 118, 210 bottom, 226 top, 229, 237, 276, 298 bottom, 300, 301 top, 304, 332, 348,

Library of Congress, Prints & Photographs Division: 19 top, 20, 22, 23, 58, 59 top, 67, 81, 86, 93 (map source), 94, 95 (map source), 97, 99, 100, 103, 104, 110, 114, 119, 131, 132, 137, 146 top, 149 bottom, 162, 168, 188, 206, 204-205, 211, 213, 216, 245, 247, 266, 260, 262, 264, 270, 269, 279, 280, 288, 290, 291, 292, 293, 339

J.B. Macelwane Archives, St. Louis University: 212

Maidenhead Cartographic Services: 203 (map source)

Mid-Continent Railway Historical Society, Inc: 257 (Bill Buhrmaster); 254 (Paul Swanson)

Milepost 92½: 281, 341, 358–359 (Gavin Morrison); 282-283; 355, 367 (Howard Ande)

National Aeronautics & Space Administration (NASA): 214

Robert T. Nordstrom II: 230-231, 343, 344–345, 369, 370, 375

Photolibrary: 54–55

Pennsylvania Railroad Museum: 26, 244

Dan Redlands: 140

Rochelle Railroad Park: 27 (Ross Frein)

Jon Roma: 303

Ed Sanders: 136

Science & Society Picture Library: 29, 31

Smithsonian Institution Archives: 42

Stamford Historical Society: 255

Jon Stubley: 32

Ron Stuckey Collection of John Fuller: 60 top (George Witt)

Jon Sullivan: 161

L. Thomson: 338

John Westwood: 166-167, 170, 228, 233, 268, 307, 311, 312, 314, 315, 325, 327, 316, 318, 320-321

Toronto Transit Commission: 388

www.trainweb.com: 278, 301 bottom, 340 (Geno Dailey), 346

TransLink, Canada: 387